T0210987

Lecture Notes of the Institute for Computer Sciences, Social Informatics and Telecommunications Engineering 418

Editorial Board Members

Ozgur Akan
Middle East Technical University, Ankara, Turkey

Paolo Bellavista
University of Bologna, Bologna, Italy

Jiannong Cao
Hong Kong Polytechnic University, Hong Kong, China

Geoffrey Coulson
Lancaster University, Lancaster, UK

Falko Dressler
University of Erlangen, Erlangen, Germany

Domenico Ferrari
Università Cattolica Piacenza, Piacenza, Italy

Mario Gerla
UCLA, Los Angeles, USA

Hisashi Kobayashi
Princeton University, Princeton, USA

Sergio Palazzo
University of Catania, Catania, Italy

Sartaj Sahni
University of Florida, Gainesville, USA

Xuemin (Sherman) Shen ⓘD
University of Waterloo, Waterloo, Canada

Mircea Stan
University of Virginia, Charlottesville, USA

Xiaohua Jia
City University of Hong Kong, Kowloon, Hong Kong

Albert Y. Zomaya
University of Sydney, Sydney, Australia

More information about this series at https://link.springer.com/bookseries/8197

Carlos T. Calafate · Xianfu Chen ·
Yuan Wu (Eds.)

Mobile Networks and Management

11th EAI International Conference, MONAMI 2021
Virtual Event, October 27–29, 2021
Proceedings

Springer

Editors
Carlos T. Calafate
Technical University of Valencia
Valencia, Spain

Xianfu Chen
VTT Technical Research Centre of Finland
Oulu, Finland

Yuan Wu
University of Macau
Taipa, China

ISSN 1867-8211   ISSN 1867-822X (electronic)
Lecture Notes of the Institute for Computer Sciences, Social Informatics
and Telecommunications Engineering
ISBN 978-3-030-94762-0   ISBN 978-3-030-94763-7 (eBook)
https://doi.org/10.1007/978-3-030-94763-7

© ICST Institute for Computer Sciences, Social Informatics and Telecommunications Engineering 2022
This work is subject to copyright. All rights are reserved by the Publisher, whether the whole or part of the material is concerned, specifically the rights of translation, reprinting, reuse of illustrations, recitation, broadcasting, reproduction on microfilms or in any other physical way, and transmission or information storage and retrieval, electronic adaptation, computer software, or by similar or dissimilar methodology now known or hereafter developed.
The use of general descriptive names, registered names, trademarks, service marks, etc. in this publication does not imply, even in the absence of a specific statement, that such names are exempt from the relevant protective laws and regulations and therefore free for general use.
The publisher, the authors and the editors are safe to assume that the advice and information in this book are believed to be true and accurate at the date of publication. Neither the publisher nor the authors or the editors give a warranty, expressed or implied, with respect to the material contained herein or for any errors or omissions that may have been made. The publisher remains neutral with regard to jurisdictional claims in published maps and institutional affiliations.

This Springer imprint is published by the registered company Springer Nature Switzerland AG
The registered company address is: Gewerbestrasse 11, 6330 Cham, Switzerland

Preface

We are delighted to introduce the proceedings of the 2021 European Alliance for Innovation (EAI) International Conference on Mobile Networks and Management (MONAMI). This conference brought together researchers, developers, and practitioners around the world and aimed to provide an interdisciplinary platform for sharing recent results on mobile networks and management technologies. In particular, MONAMI 2021 put a special focus on IoT and mobile edge computing (MEC), which is an essential component of the upcoming 5G architecture and of fundamental importance to the future mobile computing systems.

The technical program of MONAMI 2021 consisted of 26 papers in oral presentation sessions at the main conference tracks and one workshop. The conference tracks were as follows: Track 1 - The application of artificial intelligence for smart city; Track 2 - Advanced technology in edge and fog computing; Track 3 - Emerging technologies and applications in mobile networks and management; and Track 4 - Recent advances in communications and computing. Aside from the high-quality technical paper presentations, the technical program also featured three keynote speeches given by Zhisheng Niu from Tsinghua University, China, Yan Zhang from the University of Oslo, Norway, and F. Richard Yu from Carleton University, Canada.

Coordination with the General Co-chairs Celimuge Wu, Shiwen Mao, and Xun Shao, was essential for the success of the conference. We sincerely appreciate their constant support and guidance. It was also a great pleasure to work with such an excellent organizing committee team for their hard work in organizing and supporting the conference. In particular, we are grateful to the Technical Program Committee who completed the peer-review process for technical papers and helped to put together a high-quality technical program. We are also grateful to the Conference Managers for their support and all the authors who submitted their papers to the MONAMI 2021 conference.

We strongly believe that the MONAMI conference provides a good forum for all researchers, developers, and practitioners to discuss all science and technology aspects that are relevant to mobile networks and management technologies. We also expect that the future MONAMI conferences will be as successful and stimulating as this year's, as indicated by the contributions presented in this volume.

November 2021

Carlos T. Calafate
Xianfu Chen
Yuan Wu

Organization

Steering Committee Chair

Imrich Chlamtac   University of Trento, Italy

Steering Committee

Jiankun Hu   UNSW Canberra, Australia
Xun Shao   Kitami Institute of Technology, Japan

Organizing Committee

General Co-chairs

Celimuge Wu   The University of Electro-Communications, Japan
Shiwen Mao   Auburn University, USA
Xun Shao   Kitami Institute of Technology, Japan

Technical Program Committee Co-chairs

Carlos T. Calafate   Technical University of Valencia, Spain
Xianfu Chen   VTT Technical Research Center of Finland,
                                   Finland
Yuan Wu   University of Macau, China

Sponsorship and Exhibit Chair

Lexi Xu   China Unicom, China

Local Chairs

Peng Li   University of Aizu, Japan
Cheng Zhang   Ibaraki University, Japan

Workshops Chairs

Liang Zhao   Shenyang Aerospace University, China
Xiaoyan Wang   Ibaraki University, Japan
Biao Han   National University of Defense Technology,
                                   China

Publicity and Social Media Chairs

Chase Wu	Jersey Institute of Technology, USA
Kok Lim Yau	Sunway University, Malaysia
Francisco J. Martinez	University of Zaragoza, Spain
Soufiene Djahel	Manchester Metropolitan University, UK
Yingjie Zhou	Sichuan University, China

Publications Chairs

Di Zhang	Zhengzhou University, China
Keping Yu	Waseda University, Japan

Web Chair

Rui Yin	Zhejiang University City College, China

Technical Program Committee

Junbo Wang	Sun Yat-sen University, China
Bo Gu	Sun Yat-sen University, China
Wei Zhao	Anhui University of Technology, China
Yu Gu	Hefei University of Technology, China
Xiujun Wang	Anhui University of Technology, China
Mohammad Khan	East Tennessee State University, USA
Tianheng Xu	Chinese Academy of Sciences, China
Rongpeng Li	Zhejiang University, China
Changqing Luo	Virginia Commonwealth University, USA
Stephan Sigg	Aalto University, Finland
Ruozhou Yu	North Carolina State University, USA
Bo Ji	Virginia Tech, USA
Zehui Xiong	Singapore University of Technology and Design, Singapore
Qinlin Zhao	Macau University of Science and Technology, Macau SAR, China
Liping Qian	Zhejiang University of Technology, China
Deze Zeng	China University of Geosciences, China
Zheng Chang	University of Jyvaskyla, Finland
Ruidong Li	National Institute of Information and Communications Technology, Japan
Xiaoqi Tan	University of Toronto, Canada
Xumin Huang	Guangdong University of Technology, China
Monica Aguilar	Universitat Politècnica de Catalunya, Spain
Claudio E. Palazzi	University of Padua, Italy

Enrico Natalizio   Loria, Université de Lorraine, France
Jose Cano   University of Glasgow, UK
Pietro Manzoni   Technical University of Valencia, Spain
Johann Marquez-Barja   University of Antwerp, Belgium
Claudia Campolo   Reggio Calabria University, Italy
Valeria Loscri   Inria, France
Francisco Martinez   University of Zaragoza, Spain
Chaker Kerrache   University of Ghardaia, Algeria

Contents

The Application of Artificial Intelligence for Smart City

A Portable Brain-Computer Interface Using Micro-Display for Future
Mobile Communication System 3
  Xi Zhao, Guiying Xu, and Honglin Hu

DASH Live Video Streaming Control Using Actor-Critic Reinforcement
Learning Method 17
  Bo Wei, Hang Song, Quang Ngoc Nguyen, and Jiro Katto

Machine Learning Enhanced CPU-GPU Simulation Platform for 5G
System 25
  Yuling Ouyang, Caiyuan Yin, Ting Zhou, and Yan Jin

Deep Reinforcement Learning-Based Resource Allocation for 5G
Machine-Type Communication in Active Distribution Networks 39
  *Qiyue Li, Hong Cheng, Yangzhao Yang, Haochen Tang, Zhi Liu,
  Yangjie Cao, and Wei Sun*

AppSense: Detecting Smartphone Usage via WiFi Signals 60
  Tao Liu, Peng Li, and Cheng Zhang

A Distributed Computation Offloading Strategy for Edge Computing
Based on Deep Reinforcement Learning 73
  *Hongyang Lai, Zhuocheng Yang, Jinhao Li, Celimuge Wu,
  and Wugedele Bao*

Advanced Technology in Edge and Fog Computing

How to Select SF and BW for 2.4 GHz LoRa Ad-Hoc Communication:
From Energy Consumption Perspective 89
  Haibo Luo, Lianghui Xiao, Lingxin Wu, Zhiqiang Ruan, and Wen Lin

FSE-MV: Compressed Domain Video Information Assisted Hybrid
Real-Time Vehicle Speed Estimation 100
  Yangjie Cao, Qi Wu, Bo Zhang, Zhi Liu, and Junfeng Li

WiMPP: An Indoor Multi-person Positioning Method Based on Wi-Fi
Signal 115
  Pengsong Duan, Biao Ye, Chenfei Jiao, Weixing Zhang, and Chao Wang

Task Scheduling and Resource Management in MEC-Enabled Computing
Networks 127
  Jie Feng, Wenjing Zhang, Lei Liu, Jianbo Du, Ming Xiao, and Qingqi Pei

Unlicensed Assisted Ultra-Reliable and Low-Latency Transmission 138
  Qiqi Xiao, Jiantao Yuan, Rui Yin, Wei Qi, Celimuge Wu, and Xianfu Chen

Relay-Assisted Task Offloading Optimization for MEC-Enabled Internet
of Vehicles 152
  Heli Zhang, Haonan Zhang, Xun Shao, and Yusheng Ji

**Emerging Technologies and Applications in Mobile Networks and
Management**

WiMTAR: A Contactless Multi-target Activity Recognition Model 167
  *Pengsong Duan, Chen Li, Chenfei Jiao, Wenning Zhang,
  and Jinsheng Kong*

WiBFall: A Device-Free Fall Detection Model for Bathroom 182
  Pengsong Duan, Jingxin Li, Chenfei Jiao, Yangjie Cao, and Jinsheng Kong

A Decentralized Scheduling Function for TSCH-Based Wireless Networks 194
  *Wei Yang, Yuanlong Cao, Xun Shao, Hao Wang, Zhiming Zhang,
  and Qinghua Liu*

Feature Detection Based Spectrum Sensing in NOMA System 201
  Jingyi Wu, Tianheng Xu, Ting Zhou, and Kaijie Wang

A Scalable IoT Data Collection Method by Shared-Subscription
with Distributed MQTT Brokers 218
  Ryohei Banno and Toshinori Yoshizawa

A Fog-Based IOV for Distributed Learning in Autonomous Vehicles 227
  Pawan Subedi, Beichen Yang, and Xiaoyan Hong

Recent Advances in Communications and Computing

Time-Based Distributed Collaborative Filtering Recommendation
Algorithm 245
  *Qiao Li, Xiantong Hu, Linfei Zhou, Xiao Zheng, Wei Zhao,
  Yunquan Gao, and Xuangou Wu*

A Novel Visual-Identification Based Forwarding Strategy for Vehicular
Named Data Networking 256
  Minh Ngo, Satoshi Ohzahata, Ryo Yamamoto, and Toshihiko Kato

A Sleep Scheduling Algorithm with Limited Energy Collection in Energy
Harvesting Wireless Sensor Networks 270
    Fei Gao, Wuyungerile Li, Pengyu Li, and Ruihong Wang

NOMA-Based Statistical Signal Transmission for Beyond 5G
Communications 282
    Tianheng Xu, Ning Zhang, Ting Zhou, Honglin Hu, and Xiaoming Tao

Fuzzy MP - A Fuzzy Digital Signature Scheme with Biometrics 299
    Tiong-Sik Ng and Andrew Beng-Jin Teoh

A Fuzzy Logic Controller for Greenhouse Temperature Regulation System
Based on Edge Computing 316
    Yue Ren, Celimuge Wu, Tsutomu Yoshinaga, and Wugedele Bao

Workshop: The New Era of Computer Network by using Machine Learning

Moving Object Recognition for Airport Ground Surveillance Network 335
    Zhizhuo Zhang, Xiang Zhang, Donghang Chen, and Haifei Yu

IOT Based Sensor Monitoring System for Smart Complex and Shopping
Malls 344
    Vipul Narayan and A. K. Daniel

Author Index 355

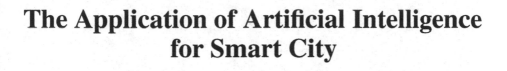

The Application of Artificial Intelligence
for Smart City

A Portable Brain-Computer Interface Using Micro-Display for Future Mobile Communication System

Xi Zhao[1,2], Guiying Xu[1,2], and Honglin Hu[1,2(✉)]

[1] University of Chinese Academy of Sciences, Beijing 100049, China
[2] Shanghai Advanced Research Institute, Chinese Academy of Sciences, Beijing, China
huhl@sari.ac.cn

Abstract. 5G is gradually realizing low latency and high reliable transmission between devices. In the next-generation mobile communication system, in addition to the further evolution for conventional communication technology, a new way of human-machine communication (HMC) represented by brain-computer interfaces (BCIs) will appear to achieve more efficient human-machine communication. BCIs based on steady-state visual evoked potential (SSVEP) are becoming one of the most popular research direction because of its high accuracy and less dependency on data training. However, the implementation of SSVEP-BCIs depends on external visual stimuli which usually use computer monitor to display the external stimuli. Therefore, this kind of BCIs usually has poor portability and wearability. This disadvantage is hindering the combination of BCIs based on SSVEP and specific control scenarios such as aircraft control, which require high wearability of control devices. The current portable schemes usually make use of the binocular effect and AR glasses to improve portability but no BCI system has been designed by making full use of the conclusion that stimulating single eye can also stimulate the brain to produce strong responses. In order to improve the portability of the BCIs based on SSVEP, a monocular-based scheme is proposed in this study. A brain-controlled aircraft system based on SSVEP is designed to verify the feasibility of this wearable scheme.

Keywords: BCI · SSVEP · AR

1 Introduction

According to the current progress of 5G research and application, 5G has been applied to the following three usage scenarios: enhanced mobile broadband (eMBB), massive machine-type communications (mMTC), and ultrareliable low-latency communications (URLLC) [1]. In particular, eMBB successfully realizes the efficient transmission of data between users, mMTC focuses on the highly reliable connection between a large number of machines in the Internet of things

© ICST Institute for Computer Sciences, Social Informatics and Telecommunications Engineering 2022
Published by Springer Nature Switzerland AG 2022. All Rights Reserved
C. T. Calafate et al. (Eds.): MONAMI 2021, LNICST 418, pp. 3–16, 2022.
https://doi.org/10.1007/978-3-030-94763-7_1

(IoT), and URLLC is applied to the real-time scenarios with low-latency and high-reliability represented by vehicle networking. These scenarios are gradually realizing the information communication with high efficient between devices.

Although the mentioned 5G technology has been gradually applied to various industries to improve the quality of our life, the conventional keyboard and mouse communication method is still used in the human-machine communication (HMC) between users and external devices. It can be predicted that exploring more efficient HMC methods will be one of the most important research direction of the next-generation mobile communication. With the exploration of the brain mechanism, brain-computer interface (BCI) is becoming a high-profile research direction of the HMC schemes. At present, BCI technology is considered to have a great prospect in the field of IoT to realize smart healthcare [2], and to replace the conventional HMC tools such as keyboard and mouse to control external devices.

BCIs can help users to interact with the machine directly via using the neural activities [3]. The ultimate goal of BCIs is to achieve more efficient human-machine interface and liberate human hands. At present, BCIs have realized several application scenarios, such as medical auxiliary rehabilitation [4], disease surveillance, auxiliary control external equipment [5], etc. With the further exploring of the paradigm of BCIs in recent decades, the BCIs based on steady-state visual evoked potential (SSVEP) are becoming one of the most famous BCI paradigms because of its high signal-to-noise ratio (SNR) and observable features [6].

The primary visual cortex of brain will produce specific responses which is highly correlated with the stimulus frequency, when the user is gazing at a visual stimulus flashing with a specific frequency. The neural responses can be recorded by the electroencephalogram (EEG, a common non-invasive brain responses acquisition scheme), so that the data processing unit can further process the collected neural data. Then, the collected neural data can be detected after corresponding processing. Finally, the detection results will be mapped to the control commands to control the external device. Compared with other types of BCIs like P300 [7,8], motor imagery [9,10] and slow cortical potential [11], SSVEP-BCIs [12] can stimulate the brain to produce a more stable response, so this kind of BCIs can usually achieve the highest information transfer rate (ITR). At present, the BCIs based on SSVEP have realized several application scenarios such as keyboard typing [13], aircraft control [5], robotic arm control [14], etc.

David and Berndt proposed in [15] that interactive devices which can inspire users to buy and use in the next-generation mobile communication era must be portable. However, as described above, the SSVEP-BCIs usually require additional monitors to display the external stimuli. This disadvantage leads to poor portability and wearability of SSVEP-BCIs. Poor portability is hindering the further application of SSVEP-BCIs in control scenarios that require high device portability, such as aircraft control. Some recent studies have used augmented reality (AR) technology to improve the portability of SSVEP-BCIs. In the paper [16], the authors have successfully verified that the SSVEP stimulation presented by AR smart glasses can be used in the field of BCIs. Furthermore, a robot control system based on SSVEP-BCIs is realized by using AR glasses [17]. The scheme of using AR glasses to display external stimulation in the industrial manufacturing workshop helps the SSVEP-BCIs to control the machine tools [18]. The aboved studies have shown that the combination of AR technology and BCIs can effectively improve the portability and wearability of SSVEP-BCIs.

However, the above-mentioned SSVEP-BCIs are based on binocular vision, there are no monocular vision-based portable BCIs. [19] has been proved that there is no significant difference between monocular and binocular vision under SSVEP stimulation. In order to further improve the portability and wearability of SSVEP-BCI equipments on the basis of the above schemes, a monocular micro-display based on AR technology is used to display the external stimuli in this study. In application such as UAV control, we usually hope that any user can directly control the UAV after wearing the devices. Therefore, data training will reduce the user experience. UAV usually needs to fly in the open air, which means that the light can interfere with visuli stimuli. Thus, the decoding algorithm is required to have nice environmental robustness. In addition, due to the need to process the EEG signal in real time, the algorithm with high complexity is not suitable for such online system. An aircraft control system using SSVEP signal detection method based on canonical correlation analysis (CCA) [20] is designed to verify the feasibility of the proposed stimulation display scheme.

This paper proceeds as the following sections. The Sect. 2 will introduce the hardware platform of the aircraft control system and the features of SSVEP signals. The Sect. 3 will describe the overall architecture of the control system and the neural signal detection algorithm. In the Sect. 4, we will show the performance of the brain-control system under the monocular micro-display scheme. The summary and future vision are presented in the Sect. 5.

2   Hardware Platform

2.1   Aircraft

The DJI MAVIC AIR quadcopter (Fig. 1(a)) is selected as the terminal to present the control instructions of the brain control system. This kind of quadcopter has the advantages of small size, supporting WiFi connection and allowing the secondary development of Android and Windows. Furthermore, the aircraft supports automatic obstacle avoidance, real-time image transmission, low-power automatic return and other safety functions. These safety functions effectively provided a guarantee for the hidden of dangers caused by the unstable factors introduced by the brain control of the BCIs. The Windows SDK provided by DJI is used to realize the mapping of brain control commands to aircraft control operations.

2.2   AR Monocular Micro-Display

A monocular micro-display (Mad gaze-χ5 smart glasses) based on AR technology is used to display the external SSVEP stimuli (Fig. 1(b)). The micro-display

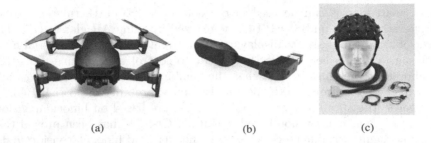

(a)   (b)   (c)

Fig. 1. The equipments that the user needs to wear when controlling the aircraft.

weighs 70 g and has a resolution of 800 × 480 with a refresh rate 60 Hz. The device is usually worn in the right eye (Fig. 2). When the user uses the micro-display to control the aircraft, the SSVEP stimuli will be displayed in the form of video in the above-mentioned micro-display. Table 1 compares the weight, size and wearability of three kinds of SSVEP stimulation display schemes. From the comparison, the proposed scheme has the best portability and wearability.

Table 1. Three stimulation display schemes of SSVEP-BCIs. ✗ indicates that the scheme is not wearable. ✔ indicates that the scheme is wearable.

Display type	Weight	Size	Wearability
LCD display	2700 g	23.8 in	✗
AR smart glasses	129 g	0.8 in × 2	✔
Monocular micro-display	70 g	0.5 in	✔

2.3   Neural Data Acquisition Device

Neural data are collected using a 64-channel Quick-Cap provided by Neuroscan Fig. 1(c). 11 electrodes are selected to record the neural data (one reference electrode, one GND electrode), and these electrodes are placed in the standard electrode position (PZ, POZ, PO3, PO4, PO5, PO6, OZ, O1, O2, GND, REF), as shown in Fig. 3. The sample rate of the sensor is set 1000 Hz. The neural data of all channels need to be processed by a bandpass filter 3 Hz 40 Hz before detection to reduce the linear noise.

2.4   SSVEP Stimulation Design

The joint frequency-phase modulation (JFPM) method [21] is used to present visual flicker stimuli on the micro-display (Fig. 1(b)). The stimuli can be generated by

$$s = \frac{1}{2} + \frac{1}{2} \times \sin\left(2\pi f\left(\frac{t}{\text{Refresh Rate}}\right) + \phi\right), \tag{1}$$

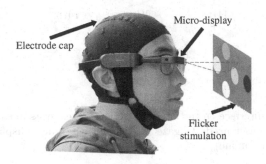

Fig. 2. The equipments that the user needs to wear when controlling the aircraft.

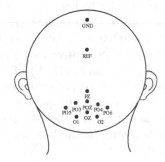

Fig. 3. Electrode map of neural data acquisition equipment.

where f and ϕ are the frequency and phase of the scintillation stimulus, respectively. t indicates the frame index in the stimulus sequence. Five rounded stimuli are used to encode five flight commands of the aircraft. The dynamic range of the stimulation signal is from 0 to 1, where 0 represents complete darkness and 1 represents the highest luminance. The radius of each flicker stimulus is 280 pixels. Figure 4 depicts the corresponding frequencies of the five flicker stimuli, the aircraft control instructions corresponding to each flicker target, and the spatial position on the micro-display. The stimulus program was established under MATLAB (MathWorks, Inc.) using the physics Toolbox Version 3 [22].

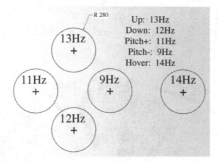

Fig. 4. The control interface on the micro-display. The red cross in each flashing target is the area that the user needs to gaze when using the micro-display to control the aircraft. (Color figure online)

2.5   The Features of SSVEP

When the subjects are gazing at the flicker stimulus at a specific frequency, the external cortex corresponding to the primary visual area of the brain will produce fundamental responses and harmonic waves as the same frequency as the visual stimulus. The features can be more obvious via calculating the amplitude response of the discrete Fourier transform (DFT) of the neural data collected from a certain channel. The amplitude response of the OZ channel is shown in Fig. 5 when the data length is 5 s and the frequency of the stimulus 7 Hz. The fundamental wave with the same frequency as the stimulus is marked by the red circle, and the green circle marks the high-order harmonics with the same frequency doubling as the stimulus.

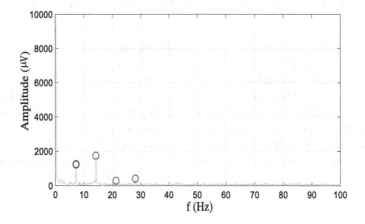

Fig. 5. Amplitude response of OZ channel in cerebral cortex when the stimulus frequency 7 Hz.

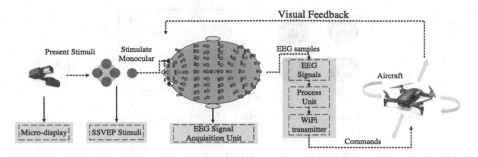

Fig. 6. System architecture of the brain-controlled aircraft based on SSVEP-BCIs.

3   Software Implementation

3.1   System Architecture

The structure of the aircraft control system is shown in Fig. 6. The user wears the micro-display and chooses to gaze at the flicker target in the micro-display according to the specific operation user wants the aircraft to perform. The signals generated induced by the visual stimuli will be recorded by the neural signal recording devices, and these recorded signals will be transmitted to the computer for processing and detection. Finally, the detection results will be transmitted to the aircraft via WiFi, and the aircraft will perform the corresponding commands.

3.2   Detection Algorithm

The aircraft needs to work in a open outdoor environment. Meanwhile, asynchronous control is usually required for this kind of control system. Thus, we use the CCA detection algorithm based on sine and cosine reference signal, which does not need data training and has good environment robustness [20]. In this method, the collected neural data is represented by $s \in R^{N_c \times N_t}$, where N_c is the number of electrode channels and N_t is the length of neural data in each channel. The reference signal can be set as

$$r(t) = \begin{pmatrix} r_1(t) \\ r_2(t) \\ r_3(t) \\ r_4(t) \\ \ldots \\ \ldots \\ r_{2N_h-1}(t) \\ r_{2N_h}(t) \end{pmatrix} = \begin{pmatrix} \sin(2\pi ft) \\ \cos(2\pi ft) \\ \sin(2 \times 2\pi ft) \\ \cos(2 \times 2\pi ft) \\ \ldots \\ \ldots \\ \sin(N_h \times 2\pi ft) \\ \cos(N_h \times 2\pi ft) \end{pmatrix} \tag{2}$$

$$,t = 1/L, 2/L, ..., T/L,$$

where f is the frequency of stimuli, T is the number of sampling points, L is the sampling rate (according to Sect. 2.3, $L = 1000$) and N_h is the number

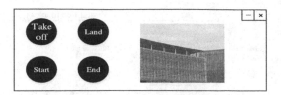

Fig. 7. Control interface of aircraft on PC.

of harmonic waves ($N_h = 5$ in this study). The purpose of the neural signal detection algorithm based on CCA is to find two sets of coefficients $\boldsymbol{w}_s \in \boldsymbol{R}^{N_c}$ and $\boldsymbol{w}_r \in \boldsymbol{R}^{2N_h}$ to satisfy the following:

$$\max \rho = \frac{E(\boldsymbol{w}_s^T \boldsymbol{s} \boldsymbol{w}_r^T \boldsymbol{r})}{\sqrt{E(\boldsymbol{w}_s^T \boldsymbol{s})E(\boldsymbol{w}_r^T \boldsymbol{r})}}, \tag{3}$$

where $\boldsymbol{s}$ is the collected neural signal and $\boldsymbol{r}$ is the reference signal which can be generated from Eq. (2). The final detection results can be calculated as

$$f_s = \max_f \rho(f), \quad f = f_1, f_2, ..., f_5, \tag{4}$$

where $f_1, f_2, ..., f_5$ are the frequencies of the visual stimuli. In the actual aircraft use scenario, it is not necessary to output commands to the aircraft all time. The aircraft needs to keep hovering when the user state is idle. Thus, the control instructions will be mapped to the aircraft only if

$$\rho > \gamma. \tag{5}$$

If Eq. (5) is not satisfied, the aircraft only maintain hovering.

3.3 Operation Instruction

In this study, a desktop application based on C# programming environment is designed to realize the mapping between the detection results of neural signals and the control instructions of aircraft. The interface of the desktop platform is shown in Fig. 7. When users use the BCI system to control the aircraft, they need to go through the following operations:

- The user should wear the micro-display and EEG electrode cap and check if the devices are securely worn.
- The conductive medium needs to be injected into the electrode channels of the electrode cap to establish a stable connection between the electrode cap and scalp.
- The aircraft control platform at PC should be opened, and the deployment of aircraft needs to be completed via click the take-off button.
- The aircraft will enters the brain control mode if the start button is clicked. In this mode, the user can choose to gaze at the corresponding visual stimuli according to their own needs, and the aircraft will execute the corresponding control instructions.

3.4   Emergency Response

In practical application scenarios, aircraft needs to adapt to different work environments. Therefore, the brain-controlled aircraft is set up as follows:

– When the distance between the aircraft and the user exceeds the maximum control distance of the WiFi, the aircraft will automatically return.
– When the power of the aircraft is too low, the aircraft will automatically return to ensure safety.
– All emergency obstacle avoidance functions are activated so that users can safely control aircraft in complex environments.
– When the user exits the brain control mode, the aircraft will automatically return.

4   Results and Analysis

4.1   The Description of Online Experiment

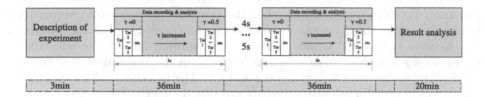

Fig. 8. The flow of online experiment.

An online BCI experiment is designed to verify the feasibility of the micro-display scheme. In order to be consistent with the user's normal use of aircraft, the experiments were carried out outside on a sunny day with normal ligh illumination (400 lux to 1000 lux). Four subjects participated in the online experiment. All subjects were asked to read and sign an informed consent form before the formal experiment, and the corresponding rewards were given to all subjects after experiments. All EEG experiments were approved by the Ethics Committee of ShanghaiTech university.

Before the formal experiment, all subjects were informed of the process of the experiment. The online experiment verifies the feasibility of the micro-display-assisted display scheme when the time window is set as 3 s, 4 s, 5 s, 6 s. The detailed experiment flow is shown in Fig. 8. Under each time window and each threshold value γ, the subjects gazed at each flicker target for 1 min and recorded the flight posture of the aircraft. The one flicker target correspond to one flight command of the aircraft. Thus, other flight attitudes which do not correspond to the flicker target are recorded as the wrong flight commands. When the gaze tasks of all targets are completed under the same time window and the same threshold value γ, the subject remained idle for one minute, at which time any flight attitudes of the aircraft except hovering are recorded as the wrong command. The subject would keep gazing at all targets repeatedly and switching to remain idle until the data collection of all the time window and threshold value γ were completed.

4.2   The Paradigms of Idle State Detection

The accuracy of the detection algorithm for all subjects are shown in Table 2 to Table 5 under different time windows and different idle thresholds γ. The detection accuracy can be calculated as

$$acc = \frac{C_r}{C_r + C_w} \cdot 100 \quad (\%) \tag{6}$$

where C_r and C_w represent the number of correct commands and wrong commands respectively. The detection algorithm could not effectively identify the idle state of all subjects when $\gamma = 0, 0.1, 0.2$. The idle state of all subjects could be identified when the threshold value $\gamma = 0.3$. But the idle state of S2 and S4 could not be effectively recognized when $\gamma = 0.4$. All subjects were unable to output normal operation instructions when the threshold value $\gamma \geq 0.5$. According to the description of the above results, it can be concluded that the correlation between the SSVEP signals generated by the brain excited the monocular micro-display and the reference signals in the CCA detection algorithm based on sine and cosine wave is between 0.2 and 0.5. The threshold value γ and the time window of collected neural signals need to be adjusted according to the EEG signal quality of different users, so as to ensure a better user experience.

4.3   The Detection Performance

As can be seen from Fig. 9, the highest average signal recognition accuracy is achieved when the time window is 6 s and the threshold value $\gamma = 0.3$ (83.15%).

Table 2. The accuracy of subject 1 detected by the algorithm under different time window and threshold values γ. ✓ indicates that the idle state detection of the subject can be realized under this time window and threshold value γ.

S1	3 s	4 s	5 s	6 s
$\gamma = 0$	57.8%	55.9%	71.1%	61.4%
$\gamma = 0.1$	50.7%	54.7%	57.4%	62.7%
$\gamma = 0.2$	55.9%	52%	88.5%	58.5%
$\gamma = 0.3$	65.6% ✓	62.9% ✓	76.6% ✓	100% ✓
$\gamma = 0.4$	84.5% ✓	82.7% ✓	97.8% ✓	92.8% ✓
$\gamma = 0.5$	0	0	0	0

Table 3. The accuracy of subject 2 detected by the algorithm under different time window and threshold values γ. ✓ indicates that the idle state detection of the subject can be realized under this time window and threshold value γ.

S2	3 s	4 s	5 s	6 s
$\gamma = 0$	36.7%	52.4%	57.5%	51.1%
$\gamma = 0.1$	54.7%	41.0%	41.0%	61.0%
$\gamma = 0.2$	41.3%	55.8%	53.7%	53.1%
$\gamma = 0.3$	38.3%	62.2% ✓	62.2% ✓	73.4% ✓
$\gamma = 0.4$	30.8%	0	0	0
$\gamma = 0.5$	0	0	0	0

Table 4. The accuracy of subject 3 detected by the algorithm under different time window and threshold values γ. ✓ indicates that the idle state detection of the subject can be realized under this time window and threshold value γ.

S3	3 s	4 s	5 s	6 s
$\gamma = 0$	56.1%	71.4%	71.1%	78.6%
$\gamma = 0.1$	48.8%	68.4%	68.9%	61.4%
$\gamma = 0.2$	61.9%	61.9%	55.3%	74%
$\gamma = 0.3$	62.5% ✓	67.4% ✓	90.2% ✓	87.2% ✓
$\gamma = 0.4$	71.1% ✓	78.9% ✓	97% ✓	94.1% ✓
$\gamma = 0.5$	0	0	0	0

S1 achieved the best accuracy (100%) when the time window was 6 s and $\gamma = 0.3$, while the recognition accuracy of S3 is 73.4%. The above experimental results show that the subjects can control the aircraft stably in outdoors with complex light interference via using the proposed scheme. This conclusion fully proves that the scheme proposed in this study is feasible.

5   Discussion and Conclusion

In this study, the CCA-based detection algorithm with correlation coefficient threshold can obtain high accuracy (Fig. 9) under aircraft control scenario. Due to the optimization of this algorithm, some poor quality neural signals only correspond to the hovering operation of the aircraft, which corresponds to a more reliable control of the aircraft. According to the oral evaluation of the four subjects, they were more willing to use the micro-display to display the extra stimulation rather than computer display.

Table 5. The accuracy of subject 4 detected by the algorithm under different time window and threshold values γ. ✓ indicates that the idle state detection of the subject can be realized under this time window and threshold value γ.

S4	3 s	4 s	5 s	6 s
$\gamma = 0$	71.4%	59.2%	68.3%	71.8%
$\gamma = 0.1$	69.1%	51.1%	72.1%	70.3%
$\gamma = 0.2$	61.1%	61.1%	65.9%	70.0%
$\gamma = 0.3$	65.9% ✓	63.1% ✓	78.3% ✓	94.4% ✓
$\gamma = 0.4$	81.8% ✓	0%	0%	0%
$\gamma = 0.5$	0	0	0	0

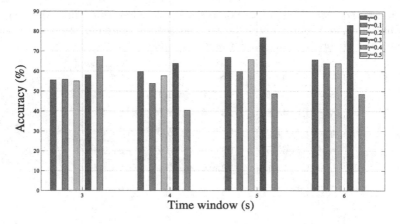

Fig. 9. Average signal classification accuracy of all subjects under different time windows and different threshold value γ.

From the experimental results, it can be seen that in the outdoor environment where the light is complex, three subjects can control the aircraft with a high accuracy (more than 90%) by using the proposed scheme, and the average accuracy of all subjects reaches 83.3%. These conclusions show that the proposed wearable scheme is feasible in complex scenarios.

With the further development of human-machine interface technology and the further improvement of biological signals processing ability, BCIs are gradually coming into the public vision. Its application in the field of human-machine interface and smart healthcare is the inevitable trend of the development of the biological signal processing technology. The improvement of portability and wearbility of BCI equipments can greatly increase the competitiveness of BCI product. Meanwhile, improving the portability and wearability is one of the key technologies to expand the application scenarios of the SSVEP-BCIs. This study combines the respective advantages of SSVEP-BCI and monocular AR micro-display. Through the use of monocular micro-display, the portability and weara-bility of SSVEP-BCIs can be effectively improved. Compared with the previous research schemes of using computer monitors and binocular AR smart glasses, the monocular micro-display proposed in this paper has the best portability and wearability. From the experiment results in Sect. 4, the SSVEP stimuli shown in the micro-display has available signal detection accuracy under the CCA-based method. It can be predicted that more portable solutions and more application scenarios for SSVEP-BCIs based on micro-display will be developed in the future.

Acknowledgments. The authors' work was supported in part by the Science and Technology Commission Foundation of Shanghai (No. 21JM0010200).

References

1. Zhang, L., Liang, Y.C., Niyato, D.: 6G visions: mobile ultra-broadband, super internet-of-things, and artificial intelligence. China Commun. **16**(8), 1–14 (2019). https://doi.org/10.23919/JCC.2019.08.001
2. de Oliveira Júnior, W.G., de Oliveira, J.M., Munoz, R., de Albuquerque, V.H.C.: A proposal for internet of smart home things based on BCI system to aid patients with amyotrophic lateral sclerosis. Neural Comput. Appl. **32**(15), 11007–11017 (2018). https://doi.org/10.1007/s00521-018-3820-7
3. Vidal, J.J.: Toward direct brain-computer communication. Ann. Rev. Biophys. Bioeng. **2**(1), 157–180 (1973). https://doi.org/10.1146/annurev.bb.02.060173.001105
4. Mane, R., Chouhan, T., Guan, C.: BCI for stroke rehabilitation: motor and beyond. J. Neural Eng. **17**(4), 041001 (2020). https://doi.org/10.1088/1741-2552/aba162
5. Yan, N., et al.: Quadcopter control system using a hybrid BCI based on off-line optimization and enhanced human-machine interaction. IEEE Access **8**, 1160–1172 (2020). https://doi.org/10.1109/ACCESS.2019.2961246
6. Hwang, H.J., Lim, J.H., Jung, Y.J., Choi, H., Lee, S.W., Im, C.H.: Development of an SSVEP-based BCI spelling system adopting a qwerty-style led keyboard. J. Neurosci. Methods **208**(1), 59–65 (2012). https://doi.org/10.1016/j.jneumeth.2012.04.011
7. Jin, J., Chen, Z., Xu, R., Miao, Y., Wang, X., Jung, T.P.: Developing a novel tactile p300 brain-computer interface with a cheeks-stim paradigm. IEEE Trans. Biomed. Eng. **67**(9), 2585–2593 (2020). https://doi.org/10.1109/TBME.2020.2965178
8. Tidoni, E., Abu-Alqumsan, M., Leonardis, D., Kapeller, C., Fusco, G., Guger, C., Hintermüller, C., Peer, A., Frisoli, A., Tecchia, F., Bergamasco, M., Aglioti, S.M.: Local and remote cooperation with virtual and robotic agents: a p300 BCI study in healthy and people living with spinal cord injury. IEEE Trans. Neural Syst. Rehab. Eng. **25**(9), 1622–1632 (2017). https://doi.org/10.1109/TNSRE.2016.2626391
9. Sreeja, S., Samanta, D.: Classification of multiclass motor imagery EEG signal using sparsity approach. Neurocomputing **368**, 133–145 (2019). https://doi.org/10.1016/j.neucom.2019.08.037
10. Ang, K.K., Guan, C.: EEG-based strategies to detect motor imagery for control and rehabilitation. IEEE Trans. Neural Syst. Rehab. Eng. **25**(4), 392–401 (2017). https://doi.org/10.1109/TNSRE.2016.2646763
11. Sosnik, R., Zur, O.B.: Reconstruction of hand, elbow and shoulder actual and imagined trajectories in 3D space using EEG slow cortical potentials. J. Neural Eng. **17**(1), 016065 (2020). https://doi.org/10.1088/1741-2552/ab59a7

12. Zhang, M., Wang, Z., Hu, H.: A new SSVEP-based BCI utilizing frequency and space to encode visual targets. Sci. China Inf. Sci. **63**(8), 1–3 (2020). https://doi.org/10.1007/s11432-019-2652-6
13. Nakanishi, M., Wang, Y., Chen, X., Wang, Y.T., Gao, X., Jung, T.P.: Enhancing detection of SSVEPs for a high-speed brain speller using task-related component analysis. IEEE Trans. Biomed. Eng. **65**(1), 104–112 (2018). https://doi.org/10.1109/TBME.2017.2694818
14. Xu, Y., Ding, C., Shu, X., Gui, K., Bezsudnova, Y., Sheng, X., Zhang, D.: Shared control of a robotic arm using non-invasive brain-computer interface and computer vision guidance. Robot. Auton. Syst. **115**, 121–129 (2019). https://doi.org/10.1016/j.robot.2019.02.014
15. David, K., Berndt, H.: 6G vision and requirements: is there any need for beyond 5G? IEEE Veh. Technol. Mag. **13**(3), 72–80 (2018). https://doi.org/10.1109/MVT.2018.2848498
16. Zhao, X., Liu, C., Xu, Z., Zhang, L., Zhang, R.: SSVEP stimulus layout effect on accuracy of brain-computer interfaces in augmented reality glasses. IEEE Access **8**, 5990–5998 (2020). https://doi.org/10.1109/ACCESS.2019.2963442
17. Arpaia, P., Duraccio, L., Moccaldi, N., Rossi, S.: Wearable brain-computer interface instrumentation for robot-based rehabilitation by augmented reality. IEEE Trans. Inst. Measure **69**(9), 6362–6371 (2020). https://doi.org/10.1109/TIM.2020.2970846
18. Angrisani, L., Arpaia, P., Esposito, A., Moccaldi, N.: A wearable brain-computer interface instrument for augmented reality-based inspection in industry 4.0. IEEE Trans. Inst. Meas. **69**(4), 1530–1539 (2020). https://doi.org/10.1109/TIM.2019.2914712
19. Daniela, O.R., Verónica, H.I., John, O.G.: SSVEP study in monocular and binocular vision. In: 2019 XXII Symposium on Image, Signal Processing and Artificial Vision (STSIVA), pp. 1–5 (2019). https://doi.org/10.1109/STSIVA.2019.8730241
20. Lin, Z., Zhang, C., Wu, W., Gao, X.: Frequency recognition based on canonical correlation analysis for SSVEP-based BCIS. IEEE Trans. Biomed. Eng. **54**(6), 1172–1176 (2007). https://doi.org/10.1109/TBME.2006.889197
21. Manyakov, N.V., Chumerin, N., Robben, A., Combaz, A., van Vliet, M., Hulle, M.M.V.: Sampled sinusoidal stimulation profile and multichannel fuzzy logic classification for monitor-based phase-coded SSVEP brain-computer interfacing. J. Neural Eng. **10**(3), 036011 (2013). https://doi.org/10.1088/1741-2560/10/3/036011
22. Brainard, D.H.: The psychophysics toolbox. Spatial Vis. **10**(4), 433–436 (1997). https://doi.org/10.1163/156856897X00357

DASH Live Video Streaming Control Using Actor-Critic Reinforcement Learning Method

Bo Wei[1]([✉]), Hang Song[2], Quang Ngoc Nguyen[1], and Jiro Katto[1]

[1] Department of Computer Science and Communication Engineering, Waseda University, Tokyo, Japan
weibo@aoni.waseda.jp
[2] School of Engineering, The University of Tokyo, Tokyo, Japan

Abstract. With the COVID19 pandemic, video streaming traffic is increasing rapidly. Especially, the live streaming traffic accounts for large amount due to the fact that many events have been switched to the online forms. Therefore, the demand to ensure a high-quality streaming experience is increasing urgently. Since the network condition is expected to fluctuate dynamically, the video streaming needs to be controlled adaptively according to the network condition to provide high quality of experience (QoE) for users. In this paper, a method was proposed to control the live video streaming using the actor-critic reinforcement learning (RL) technique. In this method, the historical video streaming logs such as throughput, buffer size, rebuffering time, latency are taken consideration as the states of RL, then the model is established to map the states to an action such as bitrate decision. In this study, the live streaming simulation is utilized to evaluate the method since the model needs training and the simulation can generate data much faster than real experiment. Experiments were conducted to evaluate the proposed method. Results demonstrate that the total QoE in Bus and Car scenarios show the best performance. The QoE of Tram case shows the lowest due to the low bandwidth.

Keywords: QoE · Dash · Live streaming · Actor-critic

1 Introduction

Recently, the video streaming traffic has been increasing dramatically which account for a large amount of the total internet traffic. Especially, during the pandemic period, the live streaming becomes a major part since educations, works, meetings have been shifted to online forms. How to ensure a high-quality video streaming is essential. Since the network conditions of different users are expected to be changing dynamically, keeping the same video streaming quality may cause impairment to the quality of experience (QoE) of users. If the streaming is kept at a low level, the network may not be fully exploited. While keeping the streaming at a high level, the video may stall due to bad network conditions. Therefore, a common way to control the video streaming is to adaptively choose the streaming quality according to the network condition. This dynamic

© ICST Institute for Computer Sciences, Social Informatics and Telecommunications Engineering 2022
Published by Springer Nature Switzerland AG 2022. All Rights Reserved
C. T. Calafate et al. (Eds.): MONAMI 2021, LNICST 418, pp. 17–24, 2022.
https://doi.org/10.1007/978-3-030-94763-7_2

strategy provides a solution to video streaming in fluctuating networks especially in mobile networks.

Over the past years, adaptive video streaming has been widely studied [1, 2]. And dynamic adaptive streaming over HTTP (DASH) [3] has become the standard for dynamic streaming. In DASH, the videos are encoded into different qualities and the users can request different quality level according to their own network conditions. In DASH mechanism, the key part is the adaptive bitrate (ABR) control technique. The ABR will decide the bitrate level to be requested according to the network conditions. Many video streaming providers, such as YouTube and Netflix have utilized the ABR technology. By using ABR methods, the proper bitrate of video chunk can be selected to realize high QoE video transmission.

ABR methods have been studied for on-demand videos [4], where the contents are created completely before the access from users. While for live streaming, the videos are generated in real time and there are some different factors need to be taken consideration such as the latency [5, 6]. In the live streaming scenarios, the factors which influence the QoE bitrate, quality switch, rebuffering time, latency and etc. In is paper, the ABR method for DASH live streaming is proposed which utilizing actor-critic (AC) reinforcement learning technique. The proposed method is a model which relates the network condition status to the bitrate selection and other decisions. To train the model, data are necessary. However, if the data generated by real experiment, it will be extremely slow since the data will only be generated together with the real live streaming. Here, the live streaming simulator provided in MMGC2019 is employed which can experience the streaming and record the status logs much faster than real experiment [7]. In the experiment, the QoE metric provided in MMGC2019 is also utilized to evaluate the performance of the proposed method.

Experiments are conducted to evaluate the proposal, the QoE of different methods are evaluated and compared in different scenarios. Experiment results indicate that the QoE in Bus and Car scenarios show the best performance. The QoE of Tram case shows the lowest due to the low bandwidth.

2 Related Work

The final goal of ABR method is to control video transmission according to network conditions to ensure a high-quality streaming experience. The selected bitrate is adjusted to maximize the QoE of the video service, by increasing the video quality, and decreasing the rebuffering event and delay.

The existing methods can be classified into three categories. Throughput-based strategy utilize the predicted throughput for the bitrate selection [8–13]. These methods predict future throughput with techniques such as harmonic mean or moving average, and then choose the maximum bitrate which is lower than the predicted value. Buffer-based strategy utilize buffer information to control the video streaming [14, 15]. Buffer-based method only takes the buffer occupancy into account and selects the lower bitrate when the buffer status is low and vice versa. Hybrid strategy takes different information such as throughput prediction, buffer occupancy, rebuffering time and so on into account when select the action to reach the best QoE. Leading hybrid methods include the model predictive control (MPC) approach [16] and machine learning approach Pensieve [17]. In MPC, a principled control-theoretical model is developed and the MPC algorithm is proposed to optimally combine the throughput prediction and buffer occupancy for decision of the future video chunks downloading. In Pensieve, a neural-network model is established and the reinforcement learning model is used for training and generate the selection algorithm of the bitrate based on former collected observations of bandwidth, buffer occupancy and bitrate.

Traditionally, the ABR methods are designed from the view of single users. While in the networks, the global quality of different users is also important which means that whether different users are getting fair video streaming experience. In the former studies, it was found that ABR methods works well for single user consideration may not be effective in multi-user scenarios [18]. Several methods have been proposed to ensure the fair, stable, and efficient video streaming in multiuser networks [19–22].

While for the live streaming, it has some differences compared with on-demand counterpart. The biggest difference is that the latency is an essential factor in QoE. If the latency is too large, the live streaming will be meaningless since the real-time experience is the core. Therefore, when the latency is too large, there will be a skip mechanism to give up some contents to catch up with the newest contents. Since the real experiment will take a long time to develop and evaluate the ABR methods, simulation is considered to be the suitable methodology. MMGC19 has provided a live streaming simulator. In this study, the development and evaluation will be based on the simulator.

3 Simulation Mechanism

The general framework of the live streaming is shown in Fig. 1. The live event is recorded by the video camera and the raw video is transmitted to the transcoding server to generate the video contents at different levels. Then the contents are transmitted to CDN servers to be accessed by the user. On the client side, the streaming application has an ABR engine to control the video streaming, it will generate decisions according to the current network condition.

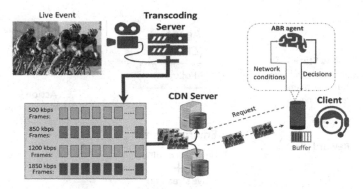

Fig. 1. The framework for the live streaming.

To simulate the live streaming mechanism, the simulator behaves in a frame-level way. In the simulator, the video information and the network trace information are necessary to run the simulation. During the simulation, every frame will be "downloaded" and the time consumption will be calculated numerically using the network bandwidth and the size of the frame. Meanwhile, other logs such as client buffer size, rebuffering time, newest content, latency and others are calculated and updated. The QoE for the frame will be calculated and stored. At the end of the simulation, the QoE will be summed up to assess the streaming. In the simulator, there is a skip-frame mechanism by which the client will give up the downloading of some frames to catch up with the live event, in case of a large latency.

The video content in the simulator is described by frame and the frame rate is 25 fps. It is divided into 2-s segments and each segment is encoded into 4 bitrate level for being requested. The available bitrates are 500 kbps, 850 kbps, 1200 kbps, and 1850 kbps. During the simulation, the bitrate selection will be triggered at the beginning of each segment. There are three parameters to be input, the bitrate, the target buffer and the latency limit. The bitrate is the chosen video quality level. The target buffer is the threshold to resume the streaming after rebuffering. The latency limit is the threshold to trigger skip frame mechanism.

4 Proposed Method

In this paper, reinforcement learning technique is utilized to develop a policy model to control the video streaming as shown in Fig. 2. When the live streaming is on-going, the client will monitor the network conditions by a set of parameters, which are defined as states in the RL model. The states include the throughput, buffer level, latency, skip time, rebuffering etc. During the streaming, the control model will generate an action based on current states. Then, the bitrate, target buffer, latency limit included in the action, will be applied to the next segment downloading. At the end, the total QoE will be utilized. Based on the <state, action, reward> data sets, the parameters of the policy model will be trained using actor-critic policy gradient method. The RL model will be optimized repeatedly to improve the QoE.

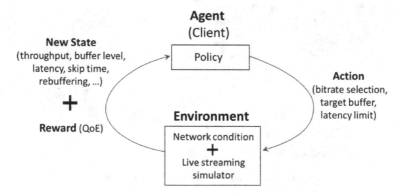

Fig. 2. Reinforcement learning framework for ABR control.

For the policy model, the three actions are independently built. The bitrate selection is modeled as discrete actions where each action represents a bitrate level. Here, 4 bitrate level are set. The target buffer is also modeled as discrete actions which has two choice, 0.5 s or 1 s. The latency limit is modeled as continuous actions. Here, the latency limit can be selected within the range from 0 to 8. The state parameters are connected to the policy layer using linear combination as the following equation:

$$\varphi = \vec{w} \bullet \vec{s} \tag{1}$$

where $\vec{s}$ are the state values of the network condition. $\vec{w}$ are the coefficient for different state parameter. φ is the output of the linear combination. In the ABR policy, the hyperbolic tangent function is utilized to output a value within -1 to 1 as follows:

$$y_{abr} = \frac{e^{2\varphi_{abr}} - 1}{e^{2\varphi_{abr}} + 1} \tag{2}$$

Then, a piecewise function is utilized to decide the bitrate selection as:

$$a_{abr} = \begin{cases} 1, & y_{abr} < -0.5 \\ 2, & -0.5 < y_{abr} < 0 \\ 3, & 0 < y_{abr} < 0.5 \\ 4, & y_{abr} > 0.5 \end{cases} \tag{3}$$

Similar to ABR, in the target buffer policy, the logistic function is used to output the value within 0 to 1. If the value is lower than 0.5, the target buffer will be selected as 0.5 s and vice versa. In latency limit polity, the logistic function is utilized to output a value and multiplied by 8 to decide the latency limit as follows:

$$a_{latency} = 8 * \frac{1}{1 + e^{-\varphi_{latency}}} \tag{4}$$

5 Evaluation

5.1 Metrics

In order to evaluate the performance of the control method, an evaluation standard is necessary. In MMGC2019, a QoE metric is provided which includes different factors. This metric is also adopted as follows:

$$qoe[n] = 0.04 * q[n] - 1.85 * T_{rebuf} - w_1 * T_{latency} - 0.02 * |q[n] - q[n-1]| - 0.5 * T_{skip} \tag{5}$$

This equation stands for the QoE reward of the nth frame. It is calculated every time when one frame is downloaded. At the end of the streaming, all the $qoe[n]$ are summed up to generate a total QoE for the streaming session. In Eq. (5), $q[n]$ is the bitrate, T_{rebuf} is the rebuffering time, T_{delay} is the latency, T_{skip} is the skipped time. w_1 is the penalty coefficient of latency. It has two values. When the latency is larger than 1 s, it is set as 0.01. When it is less than 1 s, it is set as 0.005.

5.2 Experiment Results

The live streaming simulation was carried out using 6 different network traces. The traces include the bandwidth logs at every second. These traces are obtained from an open dataset by Mobile High-Speed Downlink Packet Access (HSDPA) [23]. The 6 network bandwidth logs were measured in the scenarios of Bus, Metro, Tram, Ferry, Car and Train. Three of the traces are shown in Fig. 3 which demonstrate the dynamics of the network conditions. In bus case, it can be observed that the bandwidth is almost under 2 Mbps before 200 s. Between 130 s and 200 s, the bandwidth is low. And after 200 s, the bandwidth increases to about 5 Mbps. In car case, the bandwidth is about 2 Mbps. In tram case, the bandwidth is relatively low compared with the other cases which may only support video streaming with a lower quality.

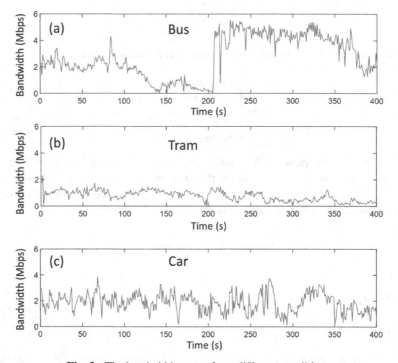

Fig. 3. The bandwidth traces from different conditions.

Figure 4 shows the simulation results in all the scenarios, from which we can obtain the total QoE performance of the live streaming in different conditions. It is found that the QoE in tram case is the lowest. This is because the bandwidth in tram case is the smallest compared with other conditions, thus the video quality selected in tram case is always small. In this case, the total QoE in tram case is the smallest. The total QoE in bus case shows the highest value because the bandwidth of which is the highest after about 200 s, and the bandwidth before 130 s is not low. The total QoE of Car case is also high, as the bandwidth is always not low and fluctuate between the value from 0−4 Mbps. From the experiment results, we can conclude that the bandwidth is fluctuating differently in various communication conditions. The ABR method control scheme plays differently in different network conditions.

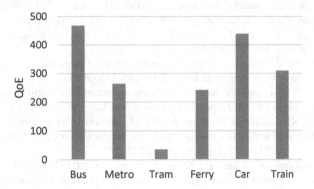

Fig. 4. The experiment results of different scenarios.

6 Conclusion and Future Work

In this paper, ABR method was proposed to control the video streaming using the actor-critic reinforcement learning (RL) technique. In this method, the historical streaming logs such as throughput, buffer size, rebuffering time, latency are taken into consideration. And the live streaming simulation is utilized to evaluate the proposal since the model needs training and the simulation can generate data much faster than real experiment. Experiment results indicate that the QoE in Bus and Car scenarios show the best performance. The QoE of Tram case shows the lowest due to the low bandwidth.

Acknowledgement. This research is supported by JSPS KAKENHI Grant Number 20K14740 and Waseda University Grant for Special Research Projects (Project Number: 2021C-132, 2021E-013).

References

1. Sani, Y., Mauthe, A., Edwards, C.: Adaptive bitrate selection: a survey. IEEE Commun. Surv. Tutor. **19**(4), 2985–3014 (2017)
2. Miller, K., Al-Tamimi, A.K., Wolisz, A.: QoE-based low-delay live streaming using throughput predictions. ACM Trans. Multimed. Comput. Commun. Appl. **13**(1), 4–41 (2016)
3. Sodagar, I.: The MPEG-DASH standard for multimedia streaming over the internet. IEEE Multimedia **18**(4), 62–67 (2011)
4. Kua, J., Armitage, G., Branch, P.: A survey of rate adaptation techniques for dynamic adaptive streaming over HTTP. IEEE Commun. Surv. Tutor. **19**(3), 1842–1866 (2017)
5. Bouzakaria, M., Concolato, C., Feuvre, J.L.: Overhead and performance of low latency live streaming using MPEG-DASH. In: Proceedings of IISA 2014, pp. 92–97. United States (2014)

6. Wang, B., Ren, F., Zhou, C.: Hybrid control-based ABR: towards low-delay live streaming. In: Proceedings of ICME 2019, pp. 754–759. Shanghai, China (2019)
7. https://www.aitrans.online/MMGC/
8. Wei, B., Song, H., Wang, S., Kanai, K., Katto, J.: Evaluation of throughput prediction for adaptive bitrate control using trace-based emulation. IEEE Access **7**, 51346–51356 (2019)
9. Wei, B., Okano, M., Kanai, K., Kawakami, W., Katto, J.: Throughput prediction using recurrent neural network model. In: Proceedings IEEE 7th Global Conference on Consumer Electronics (GCCE), pp. 107–108. Nara, Japan (2018)
10. He, Q., Dovrolis, C., Ammar, M.: On the predictability of large transfer TCP throughput. ACM SIGCOMM Comp. Commun. Rev. **35**(4), 145–156 (2005)
11. Liu, Y., Lee, J.Y.: An empirical study of throughput prediction in mobile data networks. In: Proceedings of IEEE GLOBECOM 2015, pp. 1–6. San Diego, CA, USA (2015)
12. Wei, B., Kanai, K., Kawakami, W., Katto, J.: HOAH: a hybrid TCP throughput prediction with autoregressive model and hidden markov model for mobile networks. In: IEICE Transactions on Communications, E101. B(7), pp. 1612–1624 (2018)
13. Wei, B., Kawakami, W., Kanai, K., Katto, J., Wang, S.: TRUST: a TCP throughput prediction method in mobile networks. In: Proceedings of IEEE Global Commun. Conference (GLOBECOM), pp. 1–6. Abu Dhabi, UAE (2018)
14. Huang, T.Y., Johari, R., McKeown, N., Trunnell, M., Watson, M.: A buffer-based approach to rate adaptation: evidence from a large video streaming service. In: Proceedings of ACM SIGCOMM 2014, pp. 187–198. Chicago, IL, USA (2014)
15. Spiteri, K., Urgaonkar, R., Sitaraman, R.K.: BOLA: near-optimal bitrate adaptation for online videos. In: Proceedings of IEEE INFOCOM 2016, pp. 1–9. San Francisco, CA, USA (2016)
16. Yin, X., Jindal, A., Sekar, V., Sinopoli, B.: A control-theoretic approach for dynamic adaptive video streaming over HTTP. ACM SIGCOMM Comp. Commun. Rev. **45**(4), 325–338 (2015)
17. Mao, H., Netravali, R., Alizadeh, M.: Neural adaptive video streaming with pensieve. In: Proceedings of ACM SIGCOMM 2017, pp. 197–210. Los Angeles, CA, USA (2017)
18. Wei, B., Song, H., Wang, S., Katto, J.: Performance analysis of adaptive bitrate algorithms for multi-user DASH video streaming. In: Proceedings of IEEE WCNC 2021, pp. 1–6. Nanjing, China (2021)
19. Jiang, J., Sekar, V., Zhang, H.: Improving fairness, efficiency, and stability in HTTP-based adaptive video streaming with festive. IEEE/ACM Trans. Netw. **22**(1), 326–340 (2014)
20. Li, Z., et al.: Probe and adapt: Rate adaptation for HTTP video streaming at scale. IEEE J. Sel. Areas Commun. **32**(4), 719–733 (2014)
21. Zhou, C., Lin, C.W., Zhang, X., Guo, Z.: TFDASH: a fairness, stability, and efficiency aware rate control approach for multiple clients over DASH. IEEE Trans. Circuits Syst. Video Technol. **29**(1), 198–211 (2019)
22. Wei, B., Song, H., Katto, J.: FRAB: a flexible relaxation method for fair, stable, efficient multi-user dash video streaming. In: Proceedings of IEEE ICC 2021, pp.1–6. Montreal, Canada (2021)
23. HSDPA Dataset. http://home.ifi.uio.no/paalh/dataset/hsdpa-tcp-logs

Machine Learning Enhanced CPU-GPU Simulation Platform for 5G System

Yuling Ouyang[1,2], Caiyuan Yin[1], Ting Zhou[1,2(✉)], and Yan Jin[3,4]

[1] Shanghai Advanced Research Institute, Chinese Academy of Sciences,
Shanghai, China
{ouyangyuling,yincaiyuan2018,zhouting}@sari.ac.cn
[2] Shanghai Frontier Innovation Research Institute, Shanghai, China
[3] College of Sciences, Shanghai Institute of Technology, Shanghai, China
jinyan@sit.edu.cn
[4] Key Laboratory of Wireless Sensor Network and Communication,
Shanghai Institute of Microsystem and Information Technology,
Chinese Academy of Sciences, Shanghai, China

Abstract. The exponential growth of mobile terminals and the explosion of data volume are promoting the continuous evolution of mobile communication network and also increasing the complexity of the system. Meanwhile, 5G system-level simulation also requires more complex operations and more data processing. Conventional system simulation platform based on CPU can not satisfy the computing power requirement of system-level simulation of 5G. For tremendously shorten the execution time, we proposed to develop the CPU-GPU based parallelization platform, which adopts Logistic Regression algorithm to optimizing the use of computational resources. Numerical results demonstrate the effectiveness in terms of reducing execution time and guaranteeing reliability of system-level simulation result in 5G scenarios.

Keywords: CPU · GPU · System-level simulation · Logistic regression · enhanced Mobile Broadband (eMBB)

1 Introduction

With the popularity of intellectual mobile terminals, the mobile communication services will rise 1000-fold by 2020 [1–3]. To meet application requirements, ITU officially unveiled its vision for 5G, identifying three scenarios for enhanced Mobile Broadband (eMBB), ultra Reliable & Low Latency Communication (uRLLC) and massive Machine Type of Communication (mMTC) [4]. In 5G systems, various techniques are also taken into consideration including mmwave communications, massive multi-input multi-output (MIMO), enhanced device-to-device (D2D) communications, enhanced small cells, non-orthogonal multiple access (NOMA), multi-band carrier aggregation, dual connectivity, and so on [5].

© ICST Institute for Computer Sciences, Social Informatics and Telecommunications Engineering 2022
Published by Springer Nature Switzerland AG 2022. All Rights Reserved
C. T. Calafate et al. (Eds.): MONAMI 2021, LNICST 418, pp. 25–38, 2022.
https://doi.org/10.1007/978-3-030-94763-7_3

In order to study various technologies of 5G, system-level simulation is inevitably used to ensure the realistic feasibility of theoretical results. In the eMBB scenario, the layered heterogeneous network architecture will bring more complex topology structure and more intensive data operation to system simulation [6, 7]. Conventional CPU serial mode applied to 4G system-level simulation has obvious disadvantage of low efficiency, which cannot meet the requirements of 5G system-level simulation.

There are three major approaches to deal with large scale simulation in literature. The first approach proposed CPU-based parallel distributed simulation platforms [8–10], while Multi-core CPUs are expensive and suitable for handling logical rather than massive data operations. The overhead may increase drastically in mobile environment if the network topology and machines mapping is not dynamically managed. The second approach aims to realize the simulation entirely on the GPU [11–13]. However, the GPU is not fully X86 compliant and did not support CPU features, needs a specific software architecture to disclose its power and did not support memory lock mechanism. The third approach aims to increase the efficiency of the simulation locally by offloading the most CPU-intensive part of the simulation from the CPU to a dedicated co-processor [14, 15], such as GPU. In this case, whether the computing resources can be reasonably utilized will be the key factor to determine the simulation efficiency [16].

Motivated to greatly improve the simulation efficiency, we propose a method of introducing machine learning to optimize the allocation of computing resources. In conclusion, our main contributions can be summarized by the following three aspects:

- A parallelization simulation platform with CPU and GPU is proposed. The platform aims to reduce the operation time by allocating resources reasonably to parallelized modules.
- The classification algorithm of parallel modules is designed with the idea of machine learning. According to the Logical operational complexity, Numerical operational complexity and execution times of the parallel module, the appropriate weight coefficients are given by training. Finally, the parallel modules are classified by fitting function [17, 18].
- Experiments on large-scale 5G system-level simulation of eMBB scenario have demonstrated that the proposed CPU-GPU based parallelization simulation platform consistently outperformed standard CPU computational baselines for operation time.

The remainder of this paper is organized as follows. Section 2 describes details of the architecture of CPU+GPU parallel computing platform proposed by us. Section 3 is dedicated to the Logistic Regression algorithms and parallel gain analysis, respectively, utilized for allocation of computing resources and theoretical location of the optimization target. Comprehensive experiments on 5G system-level simulation are carried out in Sect. 4. This work is concluded by summarizing our main contributions in Sect. 5.

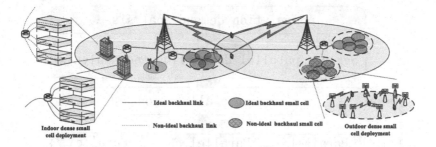

Fig. 1. Typical application scenarios for 5G eMBB.

2   5G System Simulation Parallel Framework

Wireless networks beyond 5G (fifth-generation) and 6G (sixth-generation) are supporting a large scale of novel usage scenarios and applications with high reliability, low latency, and higher frequencies. Accurate scenario characterization and simulation modelling are fundamental to evaluate the designed technologies and system performance [19]. A typical eMBB scenario is shown in Fig. 1. In order to efficiently design and implement 5G simulation system, it is necessary to deeply analyze the characteristics and implementation schemes of various application scenarios and candidate technologies [20, 21].

The design of the whole platform includes two parts: 5G system simulation framework design and resource parallel architecture design. In Fig. 2 shows the parallel simulation analysis process in the form of flow chart. On the design of the 5G system simulation framework, in view of 5G network virtualization, definable network, as well as complex scenarios and business types, we have adopted the dynamic modeling technology, layering and modeling the networking, analyzing the dependencies between the internal modules of the program to decoupling the program. Further to componentization and interface decoupling design for all levels of modular simulation object model, at the same time, the simulation model components and simulation parameters are obtained by mapping based on the simulation scenarios and business model. Then dynamic configuration is carried out according to the simulation parameters, which is combined into a specific simulation process. The coupling between the conceptual model and the implementation model is solved through the design of layering, encapsulation and interface decoupling.

To meet the simulation requirements for large-scale node deployment and mass data processing in 5G system simulation, the platform adopts distributed CPU+GPU heterogeneous parallel architecture to solve intensive computing simulation in the resource parallel architecture design. The CPU has been characterized as strong single-core processing capacity and fast computational speed, it is benefit for complex logical operations. Single-chip GPU usually has thousands of stream processor cores, its single-precision floating-point computing power is 10 times higher than CPU, which is suitable for data parallel processing brought by hundreds or even thousands of nodes accessing in 5G system. Multicore CPU

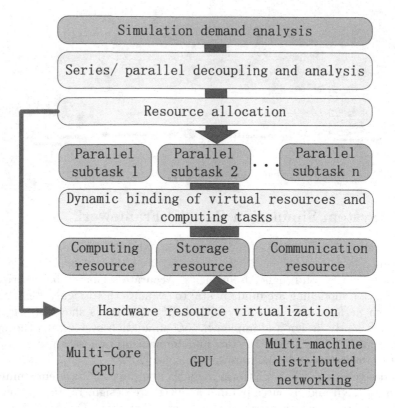

Fig. 2. Framework of the parallel simulation platform.

parallel solution can improve the computational and processing ability of simulation platform to a certain extent, but under limited resources circumstance, how to make full use of the computer capacity to achieve the maximum simulation efficiency is a key issue.

3   Classification Algorithm and Parallel Gain Analysis

3.1   Classification Algorithm

Different from the traditional CPU parallel scheme, our proposed scheme needs to decide whether to allocate CPU resources or GPU resources according to the computing characteristics of each module through machine learning. Since the performance of CPU and GPU is different, logistic regression algorithm in machine learning is considered to classify parallel computing modules. This means that an existing sample space is necessary for us to apply logistic regression algorithm to determine whether a program module should be run on CPU or GPU.

Table 1. Parameters related to execution time.

Parameters	Notations
Numerical operational complexity	x_{no}
Logical operational complexity	x_{lo}
Execution times	x_{et}

Therefore, the first step is to establish a relatively reliable data set by actually running the program, which is a heavy but necessary step. This data set is composed of two parts $\boldsymbol{\Phi} = [\mathbf{x}_1, \mathbf{x}_2, \cdots, \mathbf{x}_j, \cdots, \mathbf{x}_m]$, $\mathbf{Y} = [y_1, y_2, \cdots, y_j, \cdots, y_m]$, $\boldsymbol{\Phi}, \mathbf{Y} \in \mathbb{N}^{1 \times m}$, $\mathbf{x}_j$, y_j respectively represents a program module and its corresponding classification, and m represents the number of elements in data set $\boldsymbol{\Phi}$ and $\mathbf{Y}$. Each element $\mathbf{x}_j$ contains parameters that affect the execution time of the program module, as detailed in Table 1. So $\mathbf{x}_j$ can be represented as $\mathbf{x}_j = [x_{no_j}, x_{lo_j}, x_{et_j}]^\mathrm{T}$, each $\mathbf{x}_j$ corresponds to a element y_j in $\mathbf{Y}$ that is either 0 or 1. When the value is 0, it means that the sample program is suitable for running on the CPU; otherwise, it is suitable for running on the GPU.

We introduce the weight vector $\boldsymbol{\theta} = [\theta_1, \theta_2, \theta_3]^\mathrm{T}$, so the correspondence between $\boldsymbol{\Phi}$ and $\mathbf{Y}$ can be expressed as a fitting function

$$\mathbf{H} = \frac{1}{1 + e^{-\boldsymbol{\theta}^\mathrm{T} \boldsymbol{\Phi}}}, \tag{1}$$

where $\mathbf{H} = [h_1, h_2, \cdots, h_j, \cdots, h_m]$, h_j represents the estimation result of the fitting function for the value of y_j.

To better show the error between y_j and h_j, we define a cost function

$$cost(y_j, h_j) = \begin{cases} -ln(h_j), & y_j = 1 \\ -ln(1 - h_j), & y_j = 0 \end{cases} \tag{2}$$
$$= -y_j ln(h_j) - (1 - y_j) ln(1 - h_j),$$

when y_j is equal to 1, if the prediction of h_j is also 1, then the loss is 0, and the prediction is correct. Conversely, if the prediction is 0, the loss will be infinite. Extended it to m samples to obtain the loss function

$$\boldsymbol{J} = -\frac{1}{m} [\sum_{j=0}^{m} (y_j ln(h_j) + (1 - y_j) ln(1 - h_j))]. \tag{3}$$

the loss function is a convex function, which is convenient to get the parameter $\boldsymbol{\theta}$, so as to minimize the loss function $\boldsymbol{J}$.

We want to solve the problem of minimizing $\boldsymbol{J}$, and we first give an arbitrary initial value of $\boldsymbol{\theta}$, then change the value of $\boldsymbol{\theta}$ to make $\boldsymbol{J}$ smaller, and keep changing the process of making $\boldsymbol{J}$ smaller until $\boldsymbol{J}$ is approximately equal to the minimum.

Algorithm 1. Logistic Agression algorithm steps.

Input: Data set $\boldsymbol{\Phi}$, $\boldsymbol{Y}$, weight vector $\boldsymbol{\theta}$, learning rate α, a set of parallel modules to be classified $\boldsymbol{\Omega}$.

Output: Classification results set $\boldsymbol{\Lambda}$.
1: Initialize the weight vector $\boldsymbol{\theta}$ and learning rate α.
2: Get the estimation result $\mathbf{H}$ of function (1) with $\boldsymbol{\theta}$ and $\boldsymbol{\Phi}$;
3: Use (3), (5), combining (4) to get the iteration function of $\boldsymbol{\theta}$;
4: After sufficient iterations, update weight vector $\boldsymbol{\theta}$;
5: Substitute $\boldsymbol{\Omega}$ for $\boldsymbol{\Phi}$ in the fitting function (1) to classify the parallel modules set $\boldsymbol{\Omega}$ by using updated weight vector $\boldsymbol{\theta}$;
6: **return** the set of the parallel module classification results $\boldsymbol{\Lambda}$.

The iterative formula for $\boldsymbol{\theta}$ is as follows

$$\theta_i := \theta_i - \alpha \frac{\partial \boldsymbol{J}}{\partial \theta_i}, \tag{4}$$

where α in the formula is called the learning rate, which controls the magnitude of change during each iteration in the direction of decreasing $\boldsymbol{J}$. The partial derivative of $\boldsymbol{J}$ with respect to indicates the direction in which $\boldsymbol{J}$ changes the most. Since we are dealing with a minimum, the gradient direction is the opposite direction of the partial derivative. Combining (1) and (3), take the partial derivative of $\boldsymbol{J}$ with respect to θ, written as

$$
\begin{aligned}
\frac{\partial \boldsymbol{J}}{\partial \theta_i} &= -\frac{1}{m} \sum_{j=0}^{m} [(y_j \frac{1}{h_j} - (1 - y_j)\frac{1}{1 - h_j})\frac{\partial h_j}{\partial \theta_i}] \\
&= -\frac{1}{m} \sum_{j=0}^{m} [(y_j \frac{1}{h_j} - (1 - y_j)\frac{1}{1 - h_j})h_j(1 - h_j)\frac{\partial \boldsymbol{\theta}^{\mathrm{T}} \boldsymbol{x}}{\partial \theta_i}] \\
&= -\frac{1}{m} \sum_{j=0}^{m} [y_j(1 - h_j) - (1 - y_j)h_j)x_i] \\
&= -\frac{1}{m} \sum_{j=0}^{m} (y_j - h_j)x_i,
\end{aligned} \tag{5}
$$

where $i = 1, 2, 3$. Combining (4) and (5)

$$\theta_i := \theta_i - \alpha \frac{1}{m} \sum_{j=0}^{m} (h_j - y_j)x_i. \tag{6}$$

After sufficient iterations, $\boldsymbol{\theta}$ is obtained with a minimum value of $\boldsymbol{J}$. Take $\boldsymbol{\theta}$ as the weight value to classify the parallel modules set $\boldsymbol{\Omega} = [\mathbf{m}_1, \mathbf{m}_2, \cdots, \mathbf{m}_k, \cdots, \mathbf{m}_n]$, $\mathbf{m}_k$ can be represented as $\mathbf{m}_k = [x_{no_k}, x_{lo_k}, x_{et_k}]^{\mathrm{T}}$, and parameters in Table 1 can be obtained by checking the design of the program. A predicted classification result set $\boldsymbol{\Lambda} = [l_1, l_2, \cdots, l_k, \cdots, l_n]$ can be obtained through the fitting function (1) by replacing Ω for Φ. If l_k is close to 0, the $\mathbf{m}_k$ module should be run with CPU, otherwise it should be run with GPU. The proposed Logistic Aggression algorithm above is summarized in Algorithm 1.

3.2 Parallel Gain Analysis

The parallel gain can be defined as

$$G = \frac{T_S}{T_P} = \frac{T_S}{T_{pr} + T_c + T_{po}},$$

(7)

where G denotes the parallel gain; T_S denotes the time of serial computing; T_P denotes the time of parallel computing; T_{pr} denotes the preparation time of parallel computing; T_c denotes the execution time of parallel computing; and T_{po} denotes the processing time after parallel computing.

Then T_{pr} can be written as

$$T_{pr} = T_{pms} + T_{ptd},$$

(8)

where T_{pms} denotes the time of parallel management mechanism starting; T_{ptd} denotes the time of parallel task distribution, they are related to context of computing environment and computing tasks. The impact of the computation environment context (CPU frequency, GPU frequency, memory bandwidth, memory delay, transmission bandwidth, transmission delay) is fixed, but the computing tasks are related to computing resources required for parallelizing tasks, allocation scheme of the computing task will affect T_{ptd}

T_c is the maximum execution time for every parallel task, written as

$$T_c = max(T_{pte}(i)), i \in [1, Task_{number}],$$

(9)

where $T_{pte}(i)$ is the execution time of the parallel task i.

T_{po} is the time overhead required by serial computation task to obtain computation results from parallel service process, including data transfer time and memory access time. T_{po} is related to the space occupied by the parallel task results and the context of the computing environment.

By integrating (7), (8) and (9), G can written as

$$G = \frac{T_S}{T_{pms} + T_{ptd} + max(T_{pte}(i)) + T_{po}}$$
$$= \frac{1}{\frac{T_{pms}}{T_S} + \frac{T_{ptd}}{T_S} + \frac{max(T_{pte}(i))}{T_S} + \frac{T_{po}}{T_S}}.$$

(10)

Let $T_{pms}/T_S = k_{pms}$, $T_{ptd}/T_S = k_{ptd}$, $T_{po}/T_S = k_{po}$ and $max(T_{pte}(i))/T_S = k_{pte}$, then G is written as

$$G = \frac{1}{k_{pms} + k_{ptd} + k_{pte} + k_{po}}.$$

(11)

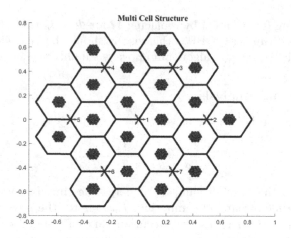

Fig. 3. eMBB simulation scenario diagram.

– *Case1:* When the amount of computation is small, more computational power is used to handle the logical operations between modules. The preparation time and result feedback time will account for a large proportion. Which means $k_{pms} \gg 0$, $k_{ptd} \gg 0$ and $k_{po} \gg 0$. When $(k_{pms} + k_{ptd} + k_{po}) < (1 - k_{pte})$, parallel computation has gains, otherwise the computing efficiency will decrease after the parallelization.

– *Case2:* When the amount of computation is large, the computational power is concentrated on the processing of data. The preparation time and result feedback time will account for a relatively small proportion of the total time. As the amount of computation goes to infinity, $k_{pms} \rightarrow 0$, $k_{ptd} \rightarrow 0$ and $k_{po} \rightarrow 0$. Then there is: $G \approx 1/k_{pte} = T_S/max(T_{pte}(i))$, which is an ideal parallel effect and the upper bound of the parallel acceleration gain.

Our platform is designed for the *Case2*, k_{pte} becomes the main factor that affects parallel gain. Since T_S is a constant, we need to consider minimizing $max(T_{pte}(i))$ for increase the parallel gain. CPU specialize in processing program tasks with complex instruction scheduling, looping, branching, logical judgment, and execution. Its parallel advantage is at the program execution level. GPU specialize in data-intensive computing tasks and illogical parallel computing, such as floating point operations and matrix operations. By designing a reasonable allocation scheme of computing resources and assigning CPUs and GPUs the computing tasks suitable for their characteristics, the maximum execution time T_c for all parallel task will be compressed as much as possible, so as to improve the overall computing efficiency theoretically.

Table 2. Simulation parameters.

Parameters	Macro cell	Small lell
Layout	Cellular grid, 7 macro base stations, 3 sectors per macro base station	Small base stations are evenly distributed in the cellular
Bandwidth	20 MHz	
Carrier frequency	2.0 GHz	3.5 GHz
BS transmitting power	46 dBm	24 dBm
Channel profile	3D-UMx channel	
Pass loss model	$128.1 + 37.6\log(R)$ R in km	$140.7 + 36.7\log(R)$ R in km
Penetration loss	20 dB	
Shadow standard deviation	8 dB	10 dB
Antenna pattern	3D Directional antenna	2D Omni-directional antenna
The antenna pattern	$A_H(\varphi) = -min\left\{ 12(\frac{\varphi}{\varphi_{3dB}})^2, A_m \right\}$ where $A_m = 20, \varphi_{3dB} = 70°$	$A_H(\phi) = 0$
Antenna gain	8 dBi	5 dBi
UE antenna gain	0 dBi	
Antenna configuration	BS: 1Tx, UE: 2Rx	
UE release	The user number of per sector is 20, randomly distributed	
Distance between BSs	200 m	20 m
Traffic model	Full buffer	

4 5G System-Level Simulation and Results Evaluation

In this section, we first introduce the 5G system-level simulation program used to verify CPU-GPU heterogeneous parallel mechanism. Subsequently, the heterogeneous parallel mechanism of CPU-GPU was compared with the traditional serial mechanism from the two dimensions of simulation error and operation efficiency, proving the effectiveness of the heterogeneous parallel mechanism of CPU-GPU.

4.1   5G System-Level Simulation

The simulation scene adopts macro base station and micro base station joint deployment mode, micro base station is uniformly deployed in the coverage area of the macro base station. 5G system-level simulation deployment diagram is shown in Fig. 3. The macro base station and the micro base station are deployed at different frequencies to avoid interference between them. The output of the 5G system-level simulation program is cell edge throughput and average throughput. Major simulation parameters are list in Table 2 [22].

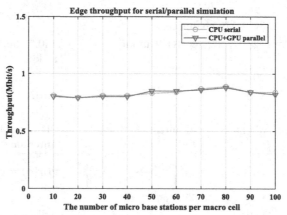

(a) Edge throughput for serial/parallel simulation.

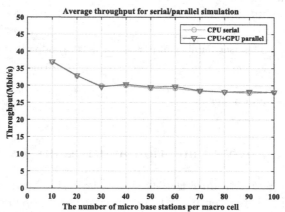

(b) Average throughput for serial/parallel simulation.

Fig. 4. Throughput for serial/parallel simulation.

4.2   Results Evaluation

With the parameters provided in Table 2, simulation is carried out respectively in serial and parallel simulation mode. The serial simulation is calculated using CPU, and the parallel simulation is completed on our proposed CPU-GPU platform. Gradually increasing the number of micro base stations and observe the curve of edge throughput and average throughput. Each time the number of micro base stations was increased, the program was run three times and the average result was taken. Figure 4 shows the throughput of the system in both serial and parallel simulations. Comparing the edge throughput and average throughput of the two simulation modes, edge throughput as shown in Fig. 4(a), and the average throughput as shown in Fig. 4(b). The results of serial simulation tend to be consistent with those of parallel simulation, and the error is mainly

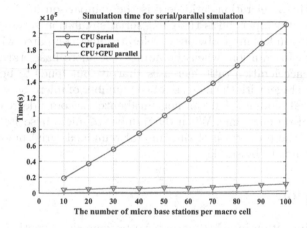

Fig. 5. Simulation time for serial/parallel simulation.

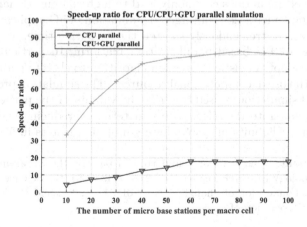

Fig. 6. Speed-up ratio for CPU/CPU+GPU parallel simulation.

related to some random processes in the program, such as noise and other factors. This demonstrates the reliability of our parallel computing platform, which is comparable to traditional simulation platforms in the accuracy of simulation results.

We also recorded the elapsed time under serial simulation and our parallel simulation, and took the average of the results of three times experiments. Meanwhile, the time consumption under the CPU parallel computing scenario is added for comparison. Simulation time is shown in Fig. 5. We can observe that under the three simulation scenarios, the curve of time duration changing with the number of base stations is almost linear. But it is clear that the gradient of the CPU serial scenario is much higher than the gradient of the other two scenarios. Our parallel simulation scenarios consumes the least amount of time.

To better understand the perform difference between our parallel simulation and CPU parallel simulation, we depict the acceleration ratio of the two scenarios in Fig. 6. The acceleration ratio here is the comparison of simulation time, and the object of comparison is the CPU serial simulation scene. Our parallel simulation platform has more obvious accelerate effect compared with CPU parallel simulation. In addition, when the number of micro base stations does not exceed 50, the acceleration ratio increases sharply, but tends to be stable after 60. In the early stage, with the increase of the number of micro base stations, the run time of serial modules that can not parallelized account decreasing proportion in the total running time. When the number of micro base stations reaches a certain scale, the proportion of run time of remained serial modules to total running time tends to be stable.

5   Conclusion

System-level simulation in 5G scenario have become significantly important for the research of new technologies in communication industries. However, large-scale system-level simulations commonly lead to high computational cost, which make efficient implementations of targeted simulation of 5G application scenario challenging tasks. To tremendously shorten the execution time, we proposed to develop the CPU-GPU based parallelization platform. In particular, the proposed platform adopts Logistic Regression algorithm to classify parallel modules for optimizing the use of computational resources. The simulation program under 5G system-level simulation is used to verify the validity of the platform. Numerical results demonstrate the effectiveness in terms of reducing execution time and guaranteeing reliability of system-level simulation results in 5G scenarios.

Acknowledgement. This work was supported in part by the Program of Shanghai Academic/Technology Research Leader (No. 21XD1433700), the Science and Technology Commission Foundation of Shanghai (No. 20DZ1101200), and the Youth Innovation Promotion Association of CAS.

References

1. 3rd Generation Partnership Project (3GPP): NR; NR and NG-RAN Overall Description; Stage-2 (Release 15), 3GPP TS 38.300 V15.12.0 (2021)
2. 3rd Generation Partnership Project (3GPP): Study on New Radio Access Technology; Radio access architecture and interfaces (Release 14), 3GPP TS 38.801 V14.0.0 (2017)
3. 3rd Generation Partnership Project (3GPP): Study on Scenarios and Requirements for Next Generation Access Technologies (Release 14), 3GPP TS 38.913 V14.3.0 (2017)
4. International Telecommunication Union (ITU): Framework and Overall Objectives of the Future Development of IMT for 2020 and Beyond, ITU-R M.2083-0 (2015)
5. Cho, S., Chae, S., Rim, M., Kang, C.G.: System level simulation for 5G cellular communication systems. In: International Conference on Ubiquitous and Future Networks 2017, Milan, Italy, pp. 1–4. IEEE (2017)
6. Hwang, I., Song, B., Soliman, S.S.: A holistic view on hyper-dense heterogeneous and small cell networks. IEEE Commun. Mag. **51**(6), 20–27 (2013)
7. Ge, X., Tu, S., Mao, G., Wang, C., Han, T.: 5G ultra-dense cellular networks. IEEE Wirel. Commun. **23**(1), 72–79 (2016)
8. Dhiyagu, D., Shanmughasundaram, R.: Dependency and utilization aware task allocation for multi-core embedded processors. In: 2019 Innovations in Power and Advanced Computing Technologies, Vellore, India, pp. 1–5. IEEE (2019)
9. Jian-zhen, C., Bin, L., Dan-ping, S.: The multi-core CPU parallel computation for CFD simulation of flowmeter. In: 2008 International Symposium on Information Science and Engineering, Shanghai, China, pp. 367–370. IEEE (2008)
10. Singh, T., Srivastava, D.K., Aggarwal, A.: A novel approach for CPU utilization on a multicore paradigm using parallel quicksort. In: Proceedings of 3rd International Conference on Computational Intelligence & Communication Technology, Ghaziabad, India, pp. 1–6. IEEE (2017)
11. Yao, W., Li, J., Tan, B., Hao, S.: Interference management scheme of ultra dense network based on clustering. In: Proceedings of IEEE 2nd Information Technology, Chengdu, China, pp. 374–377. IEEE (2017)
12. Jin, S., et al.: Understanding GPU-based lossy compression for extreme-scale cosmological simulations. In: 34th IEEE International Parallel and Distributed Processing Symposium, New Orleans, LA, USA, pp. 105–115. IEEE (2020)
13. Huang, Y., Li, Y., Zhang, Z., Liu, R.W.: GPU-accelerated compression and visualization of large-scale vessel trajectories in maritime IoT industries. IEEE Internet Things J. **7**, 10794–10812 (2020)
14. Di, Y., Weiyi, S., Ke, S., Zibo, L.: A high-speed digital signal hierarchical parallel processing architecture based on CPU-GPU platform. In: Proceedings of IEEE 17th International Conference on Communication Technology, Chengdu, China, pp. 355–358. IEEE (2017)
15. Raju, K., Chiplunkar, N.N., Rajanikanth, K.: A CPU-GPU cooperative sorting approach. In: 2019 Innovations in Power and Advanced Computing Technologies, Vellore, India, pp. 1–5. IEEE (2019)
16. Xu, T., Zhou, T., Tian, J., Sang, J., Hu, H.: Intelligent spectrum sensing: when reinforcement learning meets automatic repeat sensing in 5G communications. IEEE Wirel. Commun. **27**(1), 46–53 (2020)
17. Sang, J., Zhou, T., Xu, T., Jin, Y., Zhu, Z.: Deep learning based predictive power allocation for V2X communication. IEEE Access **9**, 72881–72893 (2021)

18. Shang, X., Hu, H., Li, X., Xu, T., Zhou, T.: Dive into deep learning based automatic modulation classification: a disentangled approach. IEEE Access **8**, 113271–113284 (2020)
19. He, D., Ai, B., Guan, K., Wang, L., Zhong, Z., Kürner, T.: The design and applications of high-performance ray-tracing simulation platform for 5G and beyond wireless communications: a tutorial. IEEE Commun. Surv. Tutor. **21**(1), 10–27 (2019)
20. Xu, T., Zhang, M., Zhou, T.: Statistical signal transmission technology: a novel perspective for 5G enabled vehicular networking. IEEE Wirel. Commun. **24**(6), 22–29 (2017)
21. Zhou, T., Xu, B., Xu, T., Hu, H., Lei, X.: User-specific link adaptation scheme for device-to-device network coding multicast. IET Commun. **9**(3), 367–374 (2015)
22. Li, K., Xu, J., Yang, Y.: System simulation modeling and key technology evaluation in 5G. ZTE Technol. J. **22**(3), 41–46 (2016)

Deep Reinforcement Learning-Based Resource Allocation for 5G Machine-Type Communication in Active Distribution Networks

Qiyue Li[1,2], Hong Cheng[1,2], Yangzhao Yang[3], Haochen Tang[1,2], Zhi Liu[4(✉)],
Yangjie Cao[5], and Wei Sun[1,2]

[1] School of Electrical Engineering and Automation, Hefei University of Technology,
Anhui, China
[2] Engineering Technology Research Center of Industrial Automation,
Hefei, Anhui, China
[3] Shenzhen Cyberaray Network Technology Co., Ltd, Shenzhen, China
[4] The University of Electro-Communications, Chofu, Japan
liu@ieee.org
[5] Zhengzhou University, Zhengzhou, China

Abstract. With the development of smart grids and active distribution networks (ADNs), reliable and low-latency communication is the key to advanced applications such as energy management and situation awareness (SA). However, with the increasing amount of data and location information to be collected, ensuring the real-time transmission of sampling data has become a challenge. In addition, the operating environment of ADNs is complex, and external interference will affect the reliability of transmission. In particular, the occurrence of power emergencies is random, and the high reliability of emergency data transmission caused by emergencies has attracted much attention. Although repeated data transmission in 5G machine-type communication (MTC) can improve the reliability, how to dynamically allocate communication resources according to the transmitted data and external interference remains a problem. To this end, we propose a scheme of repeated data transmission to eliminate the influence of external interference on the outage probability of emergency data transmission. Our scheme is modeled as a dynamic programming problem to maximize the energy efficiency. First, external interference is considered in the calculation of the transmission outage probability of smart meters (SMs), and the number of repeated transmissions of emergency data is placed in the position of the index, which is determined by reaching the target outage probability. Then, to allocate

This work is supported in part by grants from the National Natural Science Foundation of China (52077049, 51877060), Anhui Provincial Natural Science Foundation (2008085UD04), Fundamental Research Funds for the Central Universities (PA2020GDJQ0027, JZ2019HGTB0089, PA2019GDQT0006), and the 111 Project (BP0719039).

© ICST Institute for Computer Sciences, Social Informatics and Telecommunications Engineering 2022
Published by Springer Nature Switzerland AG 2022. All Rights Reserved
C. T. Calafate et al. (Eds.): MONAMI 2021, LNICST 418, pp. 39–59, 2022.
https://doi.org/10.1007/978-3-030-94763-7_4

dynamic resource in real time in a changing environment, we propose a deep reinforcement learning method, which has fast computing speed, can more quickly allocate resources and reduce the delay of data transmission. Simulation results have verified the superiority of the proposed scheme.

Keywords: Situation awareness · Reliable and low-delay data communication · Resource allocation · Deep reinforcement learning

1   Introduction

An active distribution network (ADN) can actively use the adjustable resources in the distribution network to achieve active planning, management and control services. Its purpose is to solve the problem of grid compatibility and renewable resource consumption. An ADN has two key components: I) massive information collection and II) effective monitoring and accurate diagnosis [1]. Figure 1 describes a structure of ADN. Advanced metering infrastructure (AMI) is composed of many SMs to collect a tremendous amount of data in real time. Simultaneously, ADNs require rapid detection of system events (including system faults and power quality fluctuations) to achieve comprehensive situation awareness (SA), which can be used to monitor and identify normal and abnormal activities of ADN [2]. With the increasing demand of ADNs for situation awareness (SA), how to effectively transmit monitoring data (especially emergency data generated by emergencies) is a significant research topic [3].

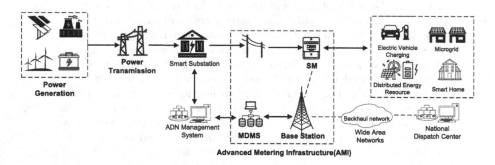

Fig. 1. A typical ADN structure.

Compared with the traditional communication mode, the 5G communication transmission speed is improved, the reliability is more significant, and the energy consumption is reduced. Therefore, we choose to apply 5G communication in AMI for information transmission. However, massive short messages in 5G uplink make it very difficult to schedule and allocate resources (such as time-frequency resources and modulation and coding schemes). In addition, the occurrence of system failures, power quality fluctuations and other emergencies is random. Low delay and high reliability of emergency data transmission are the keys to ensuring the realization of SA in ADNs. On the one hand, using grant-free scheduling can reduce delay instead of scheduling based on the long-term evolution (LTE) grant-based scheduling method because waiting for grants will increase delay [4]. In this type of fast uplink access without grants, there is no need to send scheduling requests or wait for scheduling grants [5]. On the other, repeated transmission of data is the key factor to improve the reliability performance [4], but using the classic hybrid automatic repeat request (HARQ) retransmission process will introduce additional delay [4]. Therefore, to ensure the reliability of transmission, we repeatedly transmit the emergency data to the instrument data management system (MDMS) without waiting for grant or sending repeated requests. In other words, in data transmission, multiple copies of emergency data are simultaneously transmitted to eliminate the impact of interference on the transmission outage probability. Massive data must be transmitted, and emergency data must be repeatedly transmitted, which requires real-time resource allocation. This paper proposes a resource allocation method based on deep reinforcement learning, which combines with a neural network to speed up the calculation speed, more quickly allocate the resource and reduce the transmission delay.

In 5G networks, high reliability and low delay are the most stringent requirements for communication. In the 3rd-Generation Partnership Project (3GPP) standard, a general URLLC requirement is 99.999% target reliability with 1-ms (two-way) user-plane latency [6]. The reliability here is defined as the percentage of packets that are correctly received within the delay budget. Decreasing the transmission time interval (TTI) length is an efficient method to shorten the latency in the system [7,8]. However, there is a contradiction between low latency and ultra-high reliability. This paper proposes a resource-scheduling method for the repeated transmission of emergency data. This method belongs to grand-free scheduling, i.e., it sends multiple copies of the same packet without waiting for acknowledgment (ACK). Waiting for ACK will increase the delay, and the interference in the transmission process will affect the reliability of communication. Therefore, our method reduces the delay by not waiting for ACK and improves the reliability by increasing the number of emergency data repeated transmissions.

For 5G communication, it is difficult to simultaneously satisfy the requirements of maximal reliability and minimal total resource consumption of data transmission. To maximize the reliability of data scheduling, we consider that in the case of external interference, we can reduce the transmission outage probability of SMs by repeatedly transmitting the emergency data. To reduce the total resource consumption, we establish the energy efficiency formula of the transmission process with the parameters of data packet size, repeated transmission times, SM transmission power and selection of MTC. Then, we model the resource allocation as a dynamic programming problem with the objective function of maximizing the energy efficiency. The Lagrange multiplier method can be used to solve the problem [9]. However, the parameters of data packet size and repeated transmission times are also time-varying. How to adaptively allocate resources according to the dynamic changes of parameters is also a difficult problem. Therefore, we attempt to use deep reinforcement learning to solve the resource allocation problem of 5G networks. The trained deep reinforcement learning model can quickly solve the problem of resource allocation to achieve resource allocation and scheduling under time-varying conditions. The results show that our method is superior in reliability and calculation speed.

Our contributions are as follows:

1) For emergency data, we propose an algorithm to calculate the number of data repeated transmissions. The algorithm considers noise interference, path loss, and the outage probability of SMs to minimize the number of data transmission repeats while satisfying the target reliability.
2) Aiming at the resource allocation and scheduling problem of a 5G communication network, a deep reinforcement learning method is proposed. This method can allocate and schedule resources in real time according to the network time variance and reduce the total resource consumption to the greatest extent.
3) Extensive simulations are conducted. The simulation results prove the superiority of the designed system and method and provide a new method for 5G communication network resource allocation and scheduling.

The remainder of this paper is organized as follows. Section 2 summarizes the related literature on wireless resource allocation and event detection. Section 3 introduces the system model. Section 4 models the problem. Section 5 uses reinforcement learning to allocate and schedule resources. In Sect. 6, we perform simulations and experiments to verify the effectiveness of our proposed framework. Finally, we summarize the entire paper in Sect. 7.

2   Related Work

A 5G communication network has the characteristics of a large structure and complex interference, which introduces higher requirements for the reliability and low delay of wireless transmission. To satisfy the requirements of low delay and high reliability of wireless communication, we must make full use of scarce bandwidth resources through an appropriate resource allocation algorithm, which can also reduce the energy consumption.

The resource allocation in MTCs is mainly to optimize the allocation of wireless resources in terms of transmission power, time slot, and spectrum. Researchers have proposed many methods for this work. According to the users are mobile and the SMs are static, a two-stage wireless resource allocation method is proposed to maximize the total rate of cellular users while obtaining the minimum transmission power [10]. The method uses machine-to-machine (M2M) communication between the SMs. In [11], a cloud-fog-based model was proposed. This model attempts to summarize the general algorithm for different types of computing services for resource management to achieve load balancing between requests and services. A spectrum allocation technique is designed to set the minimum BER threshold and evaluate the availability of white holes in unlicensed bands [12]. A wireless resource management technology based on an LTE-A network was proposed [13] to realize automatic meter reading and prevent overload of cellular base stations. However, these resource allocation methods do not consider MCS assignment or the emergency transmission problem in the case of interference.

Reasonable resource allocation is very important to improve the system performance. For example, a 5G-based framework is proposed to reasonably reserve RBS for emergency data and realize the energy-saving resource optimal allocation method [9]. In this method, the resource allocation problem is transformed into a univariate integer programming problem; then, the dual problem is constructed by using Lagrange duality theory. The results show that compared with the traditional greedy algorithm, this algorithm better maximizes the energy efficiency. Although MCS assignment and emergency data transmission are considered in the above method, the reliability of emergency data transmission and dynamic real-time resource allocation are not considered.

To solve the real-time problem of resource allocation, some studies adopt deep reinforcement learning methods. In [14], a real-time adaptive computing resource allocation strategy was designed. In [15], resource allocation methods based on Q-learning and deep reinforcement learning were proposed, but these methods only analyze the real-time performance of resource allocation and do not consider the reliability of resource allocation, i.e., the emergency transmission problem caused by emergencies. Moreover, the Q-learning algorithm will produce a large state space and action space, which greatly increases the computational complexity of the problem.

Because these methods cannot simultaneously satisfy the requirements of high-reliability and low-delay communication, we propose a data scheduling and resource allocation solution for 5G MTC based on deep reinforcement learning. We can improve the reliability of transmission through repeated transmission of emergency data. In addition, we use deep reinforcement learning to achieve dynamic real-time resource allocation and reduce the total resource consumption to maximize the energy efficiency.

3   System Model

AMI is an important component of ADN. To realize the SA of an ADN, we accessed the 5G network to a single-cell uplink channel in AMI. The network structure is shown in Fig. 2. In AMI applications, we assume that all spectrum resources can be allocated to the SMs for 5G uplink data transmission, and the data collected by each sensor in the sampling period can only be sent in a single slot. In addition, because the sampling time of each sensor is much smaller than the 5G time slot, it can be ignored. Simultaneously, we assume that when the sensor detects an emergency, the additional packets containing the emergency event occurrence flag must be immediately sent by SMs.

As shown in Fig. 3, the resource allocation of the 5G network is in the time and frequency domains [16]. In the time domain, the time slot is the

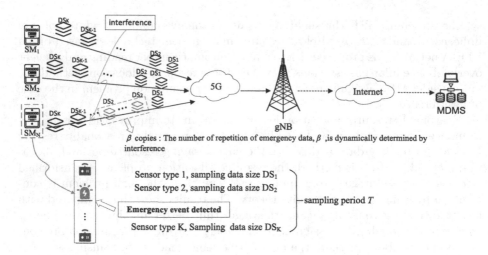

Fig. 2. Network structure (β is the number of repeat transmission times of emergency data).

smallest unit, which contains 14 OFDM symbols. In the frequency domain, the system bandwidth consists of several subchannels, and each subchannel includes 12 consecutive subcarriers. Each resource block (RB) occupies a time slot and a subchannel as the basic unit of data transmission. In addition, 5G NR supports multiple subcarrier spacings and diverse transmission bandwidths. Table 1 shows different transmission bandwidths and corresponding slot durations [17].

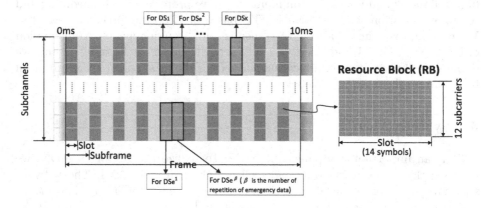

Fig. 3. 5G-based resource block structure in our framework.

According to [18], the next generation of SMs is equipped with voltage sensors, current sensors, and temperature and humidity sensors, which can be used to monitor different types of emergencies. We collect the data sent by SMs in a gNB, including the data generated by normal power activities and emergency data generated by emergencies. When an emergency occurs, in the data repeated transmission scheme, the number of emergency data repeats is determined according to the average signal-to-noise ratio and the outage probability of SMs; appropriate resource blocks are allocated for normal data packets and emergency data packets that must be repeated in 5G wireless resources. The optimal allocation decision can usually be obtained by solving an optimization problem. However, due to the huge search space and long solving time of this type of resource allocation and scheduling problem, it cannot keep up with the rapid change of sampling data. Therefore, we use the DRL agent to make real-time allocation decisions by collecting the sensor location and packet length information.

4   Problem Formulation

4.1   Repeated Data Transmission Analysis

In this section, we discuss how to reduce the outage probability of SMs [19] by increasing the time of emergency data repeat transmission β in the case of interference. As shown in (1), with the increase in β, the outage probability of SMs will gradually decrease.

$$P_a = [0.05(1 + erf(0.1 * (\frac{\gamma - \overline{\gamma}}{\sigma\sqrt{2}})))]^{\beta} < a \tag{1}$$

$$\beta = \lceil \frac{\log a}{\log [0.05(1 + erf(0.1 * (\frac{\gamma - \overline{\gamma}}{\sigma\sqrt{2}})))]} \rceil \tag{2}$$

In Eqs. (1) and (2), σ and a are fixed parameters, γ is the signal-to-noise ratio threshold, $erf(\cdot)$ is the error function, and $\overline{\gamma}$ is the average signal-to-noise ratio of the sensor. Additionally:

$$\overline{\gamma} = \frac{P_r}{N} = \frac{P_t(n) \cdot}{N}(\frac{d_0}{d})^{\lambda} \tag{3}$$

In Eq. (3), $P_t(n)$ is the transmit power of the nth sensor, λ is the path loss exponent, d_0 is the reference distance from the system to the base station, and d is the actual distance from the system to the base station. N is the interference variance, which includes thermal noise N_0 and other interference N_1. In other words, the change in interference will affect the number of repetitions.

4.2   Problem Formulation

In an AMI application system of ADN, it is assumed that there are N SMs, each SM has K sensors, and the emergency packets must be repeatedly transmitted; i.e., there are $L(L = N \times K)$ packets to allocate resources, including a_e emergency packets that need to repeatedly transmit. To maximize the energy efficiency and optimize the resource allocation, we take the maximal ratio of the size of all transmitted data (bytes) to the energy consumed by all RBs (joules) as the objective function to form problem P0:

$$maxE =$$

$$[\sum_{l=1}^{L-a_e} \sum_{m=1}^{M} \sum_{t=1}^{T} (x_{l,m,t} \times DS_{l,m,t})$$

$$+ \sum_{1}^{\beta} \sum_{1}^{a_e} \sum_{m=1}^{M} \sum_{t=1}^{T} (x_{\beta,a_e,m,t} \times DS_{\beta,a_e,m,t})]$$

$$\div [\sum_{l=1}^{L-a_e} \sum_{m=1}^{M} \sum_{t=1}^{T} (x_{l,m,t} \times \lceil \frac{DS_{l,m,t}}{R_l} \rceil \times P_{l,m,t})$$

$$+ \sum_{1}^{\beta} \sum_{1}^{a_e} \sum_{m=1}^{M} \sum_{t=1}^{T} (x_{\beta,a_e,m,t} \times \lceil \frac{DS_{\beta,a_e,m,t}}{R_{\beta,a_e,m,t}} \rceil \times P_{\beta,a_e}, m, t)]$$

$$\beta \geq 1, a_e \geq 1$$

(4)

where $x_{l,m,t}$ is a binary variable. When data DS_l are transmitted at time slot t with MCS selection m, $x_{l,m,t} = 1$; otherwise, $x_{l,m,t} = 0$. $P_{l,m,t}$ is the transmission power when transmitting normal data DS_l at time slot t with MCS selection m. $R_{l,m,t}$ is the transport block size (TBS) at time slot t with MCS selection m. β is the number of data repeated transmission. Additionally, when the emergency data $DS_{\beta,a_e,m,t}$ are transmitted at time slot t with MCS selection m, $x_{\beta,a_e,m,t} = 1$; otherwise, $x_{\beta,a_e,m,t} = 0$. $P_{\beta,a_e,m,t}$ is the transmission power when transmitting emergency data $DS_{\beta,a_e,m,t}$ at time slot t with MCS selection m. $R_{\beta,a_e,m,t}$ is the TBS at time slot t with MCS selection m.

The constraints are as follows:

$$P + 10 \times \lg \lceil \frac{DS}{R} \rceil + (\alpha - 1) \times PL_n - IoT \geq SINR \tag{5}$$

$$P \times \lceil \frac{DS}{R} \rceil \leq P_{max} \tag{6}$$

$$\sum_{l=1}^{L-a_e} \sum_{m=1}^{M} (x_{l,m,t} \times \lceil \frac{DS_{l,m,t}}{R_{l,m,t}} \rceil)$$

$$+ \sum_{1}^{\beta} \sum_{1}^{a_e} \sum_{m=1}^{M} (x_{\beta,a_e,m,t} \times \lceil \frac{DS_{\beta,a_e,m,t}}{R_{\beta,a_e,m,t}} \rceil) \leq Y \tag{7}$$

$$\forall t \in [1, T]$$

$$\sum_{m=1}^{M} \sum_{t=1}^{T} x \leq 1, \forall n \in [1, N] \tag{8}$$

$$x \in \{0, 1\} \tag{9}$$

Constraint (5) is the power control model of the cellular network uplink channel [20], where α is the path-loss compensation factor that can be set from 0.0 to 1.0 in steps of 0.1. PL_n is the downlink path loss measured by the base station, and it can be considered a constant value for fixed SMs; IoT is interference over thermal, which can be ignored in our system. $SINR$ is the signal-to-noise ratio (SINR) requirement of MCS selection m.

Constraint (6) indicates that the total power consumed by each packet is less than the maximum transmission power of each SM.

Constraint (7) indicates that the number of RBs in each time slot must be less than Y.

Constraint (8) indicates that each data packet can only have one MCS selection and transmission in a single slot.

Constraint (9) indicates that x is a binary variable.

Clearly, P0 is a complex mixed integer programming problem, which takes a long time to solve. In addition, to solve P0, we must calculate the parameter of data repetition times, so we cannot obtain the solution in a short time. Therefore, we use the deep reinforcement learning method based on the actor-critic (AC) algorithm to build a real-time scheduling and resource allocation framework. First, the data sent by SMs are classified; then, parameters such as the distance from SM to gNB and the number of emergency data repeats are collected. Finally, the data packet and its related parameters are input into the neural network to output the decision results.

5   Deep Reinforcement Learning Assisted Scheduling and Resource Allocation

In this section, we will introduce the structure of our proposed deep reinforcement learning method for scheduling and resource allocation based on a pointer network. This method is a low-complexity approximation method and can be used to solve our problems.

5.1   Pointer Network

To solve our problem, this paper proposes a scheduling resource allocation algorithm based on a pointer network. The basis of the pointer network is the seq2seq framework [21, 22]. Seq2seq is an encoder-decoder structure network, and both its input and output are a sequence. The encoder transforms a variable-length signal sequence into a fixed-length vector expression, the decoder transforms the fixed-length vector into a variable-length target signal sequence, and the conditional probability $p(Y|X, \pi)$ solves the output sequence. Here, $X = x_1, x_2, \cdots , x_n$ is the input sequence, $Y = y_1, y_2, \cdots , y_m$ is the output sequence, and the conditional probability conforms to the probability chain rule, which can be expressed as:

$$p(Y|X; \pi) = \prod_{i=1}^{I} p(y_i|y_1, ..., y_{i-1}, X) \tag{10}$$

The resource allocation problem of the 5G single-cell uplink channel in this paper is also a mapping problem and requires that the input sequence and output sequence of the pointer network are exactly identical, but the sequence order changes. Therefore, we add an attention mechanism [23] to seq2seq to form a new pointer network structure (see Fig. 4).

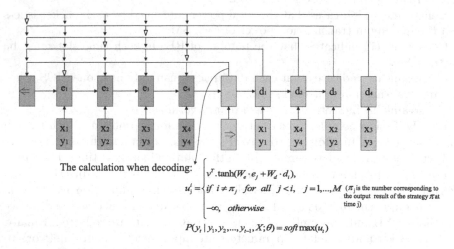

The calculation when decoding:
$$u_j^i = \begin{cases} v^T . tanh(W_e \cdot e_j + W_d \cdot d_i), \\ if \ i \neq \pi_j \ \ for \ all \ \ j < i, \ \ \ j = 1,...,M \ \ (\pi_j \text{ is the number corresponding to} \\ \qquad\qquad\qquad\qquad\qquad\qquad\qquad\qquad\text{the output result of the strategy } \pi \text{ at} \\ -\infty, \ \ otherwise \qquad\qquad\qquad\qquad\qquad\quad \text{time } j) \end{cases}$$

$$P(y_t | y_1, y_2,..., y_{t-1}, X; \theta) = soft \max(u_t)$$

The pointer network stops when the RBs of 5G module in one sampling period T are used up

Fig. 4. Pointer network architecture.

The conditional probability model of the attention mechanism is established as follows:

$$u_j^i = \begin{cases} v^T \cdot tanh(W_e \cdot e_j + W_d \cdot d_i), \\ if \ \ i \neq \pi_j \ \ for \ \ all \ \ \ j < i \qquad for \ \ j = 1,...,M \\ -\infty, otherwise \end{cases} \tag{11}$$

$$p(y_i | y_1,..., y_{i-1}, X) = softmax(u^i) \tag{12}$$

where e_j and d_i are the jth and ith hidden layer outputs of the time sequence, respectively; v^T, W_e and W_d are parameters of the neural network that can be trained; π_j is the number that corresponds to the output result of strategy π at time j. The result of the softmax function is a probability distribution, i.e., the weight assigned to the input sequence. The probability distribution can be used as a pointer to the input sequence so that when predicting the elements, we can find the element with the largest weight in the input sequence. According to 11, to ensure that our model only points to the unselected packets, we set the logits of selected package to $-\infty$. During decoding, the pointer network points to the packet in the input packet and stops when the 5G-based resources are exhausted.

5.2   Beam Search

In the decoding process, for reducing the time complexity of the decoding truncation and improving the accuracy, we use the beam search method to decode; i.e., in each step of the decoding stage, according to the probability distribution calculated by softmax, we reserve the top h optimal sequences. A larger h corresponds to a higher calculation cost, but the relative accuracy also improves. The decoding process is described in Algorithm 1.

5.3   Problem Redefinition

Considering the proposed dynamic programming problem of resource allocation in this paper, we combine reinforcement learning with a deep neural network and propose a neural combination optimization model. The model builds a policy network based on the pointer network to output the policy of the problem. To estimate the expected value of the objective function and reduce the gradient variance, an estimation network is constructed. A reinforcement learning framework actor-critic network based on a strategy gradient is used to train model parameters instead of a supervised manner.

For problem P0, we assume that the sensor captures $L(L = N \times K)$ packets. The 3D parameter sequence of L data packets $x = \{(DS_i, \beta_i, d_i)\}_{i=1}^{L}$ in one sampling period T is given. If the data is generated by emergencies, β_i is calculated by the formula in Sect. 4.1. Otherwise, $\beta_i = 1$. The optimization objective of the model is to learn random strategy $p(\pi|x)$ to output the 5G uplink channel resource allocation result with higher energy efficiency under the condition of a given three-dimensional parameter sequence of M data packets $\pi = (s_1, a_1, s_2, a_2, ..., s_T, a_T)$. a_j represents the data packet that is output by the pointer network selecting the MTC and time slot at time j. $a_j = \{R_j, P_j\}$, R_i and P_j are the transport block size (TBS) and transmission power at a certain time slot with MCS selection. s_j depends on the state of the previous time s_{j-1}, MTC and time slot selected by the data packet, which is output by pointer network a_j at time j. The following reward is defined to evaluate the action under a state: We express the energy efficiency formula as the value function $r(\pi)$ of the model.

$$r(\pi) = \sum_{i=1}^{D}[DS_i \times P_i] \div \sum_{i=1}^{D}[(DS_i \div R_i) \times P_i] \tag{13}$$

Among them, D is the number of selected output packets of the pointer network among M data packets, DS_i is the data packet size, P_i is the transmission power, and R_i is the transport block size in one MCS and a specific time slot. We sample the data transmitted through SMs for a sampling period to fit the parameters.

Algorithm 1:Beam Search

Procedure decoding(Number of steps $g = 0$,hash_table = start,BEAM = start)
1.   **While** $BEAM \neq \phi$ **do**
2.   SET=ϕ
3.   **For** each state in $BEAM$ **do**
4.   **For** each successor of $state$ **do**
5.   if successor == goal **Return** g + 1
6.   SET = SET $\cup \{successor\}$
7.   **end for**
8.   **end for**
9.   **end**
10.   BEAM$\neq \phi$
11.   g = g + 1
12.   **While**(BEAM$\neq \phi$) and (B >| BEAM|) **do**
13.   state = successor in SET with smallest h value
14.   SET = SET $\setminus \{state\}$
15.   if state $\notin$ hash_table
16.   if hash_table is full **Return** ∞
17.   hash_table = hash_table $\cup \{state\}$
18.   hash_table = hash_table $\cup \{state\}$
19.   **end**
20.   **Return** ∞
21.**end Procedure**

5.4   Optimize Using the Strategy Gradient

The iterative process of traditional reinforcement learning methods must collect a large amount of data to update the strategy gradient. However, in many complex real scenes, it is difficult to obtain massive training data, so local optimal solutions emerge. This problem can be solved by using the strategy gradient method based on the AC framework to optimize the parameters of the pointer network. The AC-based strategy gradient algorithm is divided into two parts: the actor network selects a behavior based on probability, the critic network determines the score of behavior based on the actor's behavior, and the actor modifies the probability of selecting behavior according to the critic's score. The policy gradient network can only be updated at the end of the round. Each step of the selection affects the network, so an array is required to store the state, probability distribution of the next selection action, and reward of the selection action. At the end of the round, parameters θ update to θ_{t+1}.

First, the actor network is introduced. Because the parameters and repeated transmission times of the packets are different, the order of RBs allocated to the packets by agents is not necessarily identical. We assume that strategy π will lead the agent along path $\pi = (s_1, a_1, s_2, a_2, ..., s_T, a_T)$.

$$p_\theta(\pi) = p(s_1) \prod_{t=1}^{T} p_\theta(a_t|s_t)p(s_{t+1}|s_t, a_t) \tag{14}$$

$r(\pi)$ is the value function, which is a random variable. If the expectation of the reward is obtained, then (15):

$$L(\theta) = E_{\pi \sim p_\theta(\pi)} r(\pi) = \sum_\pi r(\pi) p_\theta(\pi) \tag{15}$$

To find the optimal parameters θ, let (16):

$$\max L(\theta) = max \sum_\pi r(\pi) p_\theta(\pi) \tag{16}$$

Calculate the gradient of the objective function as shown in (17):

$$
\begin{aligned}
\nabla L(\theta) &= \sum_\pi r(\pi) \nabla p_\theta(\pi) \\
&= \sum_\pi r(\pi) p_\theta(\pi) \frac{\nabla p_\theta(\pi)}{p_\theta(\pi)} \\
&= \sum_\pi r(\pi) p_\theta(\pi) \nabla log p_\theta(\pi)
\end{aligned} \tag{17}
$$

The calculation of the gradient is converted to solving for the expectation of $r(\pi) P_\theta(\pi) \nabla log p_\theta(\pi)$. Then, the Monte Carlo method can be used for approximate estimation to obtain the B sampling results of the current strategy π, and we have (18):

$$
\begin{aligned}
\nabla J(\theta) &= E_{\pi \sim p_\theta(\pi)} [r(\pi) P_\theta(\pi) \nabla log p_\theta(\pi)] \\
&\approx \frac{1}{B} \sum_{i=1}^{B} r(\pi^i) P_\theta(\pi^i) \nabla log p_\theta(\pi^i) \\
&= \frac{1}{B} \sum_{i=1}^{B} \sum_{t=1}^{T_i} (r(\pi^i) P_\theta(\pi^i) \nabla log p_\theta(a_t^i | s_t^i)
\end{aligned} \tag{18}
$$

Since the sum of the actions taken and the probability is 1, there may be a situation in which the probability value of a good action decreases, and the probability of a bad action increases after normalization. Therefore, it is necessary to introduce a baseline b to make $\nabla L(\theta)$ positive and negative and rewrite it as shown in (19):

$$\nabla J(\theta) = \frac{1}{B} \sum_{i=1}^{B} \sum_{t=1}^{T_i} (r(\pi^i) - b_i) \nabla log p_\theta(a_t^i | s_t^i) \tag{19}$$

Then, the parameters are optimized by using the strategy gradient method and stochastic gradient ascending method. The gradient of (19) is confirmed using the well-known REINFORCE algorithm [24]:

A common baseline choice is the exponential moving average of network rewards over time. Using parameter benchmarks to estimate the expected resource size $E_{\pi \sim p_\theta(\pi)} r(\pi)$ can usually improve learning. Therefore, an auxiliary network was introduced, which is called the critic network, whose parameters are θ_ν. The critical network uses the mean square error of objective predictions $E_{\pi \sim p_\theta(\pi)} r(\pi)$ and actual resource $D(\theta_\nu)$ to train with stochastic gradient ascent, as shown in (20):

$$D(\theta_\nu) = \frac{1}{B} \sum_{i=1}^{B} \parallel b_{\theta_\nu} - E_{\pi \sim p_\theta(\pi)} r(\pi) \parallel_2^2 \qquad (20)$$

Critical network structure for resource allocation: First, we map the input sequence to baseline prediction b_{θ_c}. The critic network consists of three network modules: (1) an LSTM encoder, (2) an LSTM process block, and (3) a neural network decoder. The encoder of this network has an exactly identical structure to the pointer network encoder, and it encodes the input sequence into a sequence of latent storage states and hidden states. A process block of a critic network, such as [21], is essentially an attention mechanism. At the end of the process block, the hidden state obtained by the neural network decoder is decoded into the baseline prediction. Our training algorithm is described in Algorithm 2:

5.5   Resource Scheduling Framework

This paper proposes a resource allocation algorithm based on reinforcement learning. The algorithm framework is shown in Fig. 5. First, sample data containing interference signals are sampled at time t, and these data are sent to the 5G network by SMs. The 5G network will classify normal data and emergency data according to the additional data packet with emergency data flags.

Algorithm 2: Actor-Critic

Procedure Train(number of training steps T, batch size B, training set S)
Input actor network $p_{\theta_p}(\pi|s)$ and critical network $V_{\theta_\nu}(s)$
1. Initialize actor network and critical network parameters θ_p, θ_ν
2. **For** $i \in [1, T]$ **do**
3. $s_1, s_2, ..., s_B \sim \text{SampleInput}(S)$
4. $\pi_1, \pi_2, ..., \pi_B \sim \text{SampleSolution}((p_{\theta_p}(.|s)))$
5. $b_1, b_2, ..., b_B \sim (V_{\theta_\nu}(s))$
6.   Update actor network parameters θ_p:
         $\nabla_{\theta_p} J \leftarrow \frac{1}{B} \sum_{i=1}^{B} (L(\pi_i|s_i) - b_{\theta_\nu}(s_i)) \nabla_{\theta_p} log p_{\theta_p}(\pi_i|s_i)$
         $\theta_p \leftarrow Adam(\theta_p, \nabla_{\theta_p} J)$
7.   Calculate the objective function value of the critical network:
         $L(\theta_\nu) \leftarrow \frac{1}{B} \sum_{i=1}^{B} ||b_{\theta_\nu}(s_i) - L(\pi_i|s_i)||_2^2$
8.   Update critical network parameters θ_ν:
9. $\theta_\nu \leftarrow Adam(\theta_\nu, \nabla_{\theta_\nu} L)$
10. **End for**
11. **Return** θ_p, θ_ν

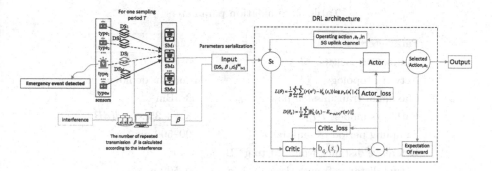

Fig. 5. Algorithm framework-based deep reinforcement learning.

In the case of interference, the number of repeated transmissions of emergency data β is determined by Formulas 1, 2 and 3 in Sect. 4.1. Finally, the number of repeated transmissions β, packet size DS, and distance between SM and gNB d are taken as the input of the pointer network in deep reinforcement learning, and the maximum energy efficiency is the objective function. Through the training of samples, the output of the pointer network is the result of resource allocation.

6 Simulation

6.1 Setup

In this section, we will evaluate the performance of the scheduling algorithm. An AMI application consists of massive SMs, a 5G communication network for information interaction with gNB, and an MDMS. Table 1 lists different configurations of the 5G network system bandwidth and subcarrier interval [17]. We set the system bandwidth and subcarrier interval to 20 MHz and 15 kHz, respectively. Accordingly, the number of subchannels Y is 106, and the duration of each time slot is 1 ms. Detailed parameters for simulation are listed in Table 2. In addition, there are 16 MCS options in the channel, and each MCS corresponds to different TBS and SINR ranges [25], as shown in Table 3.

Table 1. Transmission bandwidth configuration and time slot duration

Time slot duration	SCS (kHz)	10 MHz	15 MHz	20 MHz	...	100 MHz
		NRB	NRB	NRB	...	NRB
1 ms	15	52	79	106	...	N/A
0.5 ms	30	24	38	51	...	273
0.25 ms	60	11	18	24	...	135

Table 2. Simulation parameters

Parameters	Values
Number of packets, M	50–500
Network topology	Random deployment
Maximum transmission power, P_{max}	23 dBm
Path loss model, PL_N	$13.6 + 35 \times \lg d(dB)$
Sampling period of sensors, T_k	100–500 ms
Reference distance from SM to gNB, d_0	50 m
Actual distance from SM to gNB, d	50–500 m
Sampling data size, DK	300–500 bytes
Observation period, T	500 ms
SNR threshold	40 dB
σ	2
Outage probability threshold, a	0.01
Path loss exponent, λ	2
Thermal noise variance, N_0	1 dB

We assume that all SMs can detect emergency events in ADNs, and the events detected depend on the type of sensor installed, such as the voltage sag that can be detected by the voltage sensor. Combined with the collected data samples, the method in [9] is used to calculate the number of emergency data in a unit time slot. Then, we reduce the outage probability of SMs by increasing the number of repeat transfers of emergency data; i.e., we determine the number of repeat transfers according to the threshold of outage probability.

In the experiment, we set the relevant parameters of the deep reinforcement learning model, and the batch size is 128; i.e., we use a small batch of 128 sequences, including 128 hidden LSTM units, and embed J parameters of each packet into 128 dimensional space. The initial learning rate is 10^{-4}, and the optimization reduction coefficient is 0.96 per 5000 steps. We use Adam optimizer to train the model.

6.2   Experiment Result

To evaluate our proposed algorithm, we compare the deep reinforcement learning algorithm with the optimal Lagrangian algorithm and greedy algorithm. The optimal Lagrange algorithm transforms the problem into the optimal programming problem in the mathematical model to obtain the global optimal solution. In theory, the greedy algorithm does not consider global optimization and only considers the local optimal selection. The results show that the calculation result of this method is close to the optimal value, which verifies the correctness of the algorithm and is obviously better than that of the greedy algorithm. We provide

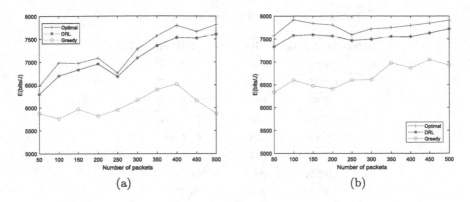

Fig. 6. Energy efficiency comparison of three algorithms. (a) N = 4; (b) N = 8.

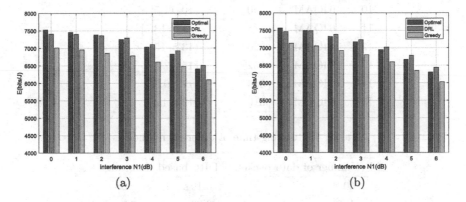

Fig. 7. Energy efficiency under interference. (a) N = 4, L = 300; (b) N = 8, L = 300.

the simulation results in terms of energy efficiency, scheduling time, and resource allocation ratio.

Table 4 compares the operation time between deep reinforcement learning and the traditional Lagrange multiplier method for the same scale problem. The method based on deep reinforcement learning has a much shorter running time than the optimal Lagrange multiplier method, which can be applied to real-time scenes.

Figure 6, we compare the experimental results of our proposed method and two other methods: the optimal Lagrange multiplier method and the greedy algorithm. The results show that the computational results of this method are close to optimal, which verifies the correctness of the algorithm and is obviously better than that of the greedy algorithm. In addition, with the increase in number of packets, the calculation results of the greedy algorithm significantly decrease, while the calculation results of the other two algorithms fluctuate; thus, the greedy algorithm has a worse effect than other algorithms. However, our deep reinforcement learning algorithm performs well at different scales.

Table 3. TBS and SINR range of each MCS

Index	Modulation	TBS (bits)	SINR range (dB)
0	QPSK	56	$(-9, -7]$
1	QPSK	72	$(-7, -5]$
2	QPSK	104	$(-5, -3]$
3	QPSK	120	$(-3, -1]$
4	QPSK	136	$(-1, 1]$
5	QPSK	144	$(1, 3]$
6	QPSK	208	$(3, 5]$
7	16QAM	280	$(5, 7]$
8	16QAM	336	$(7, 8.5]$
9	16QAM	408	$(8.5, 10]$
10	64QAM	440	$(10, 11.5]$
11	64QAM	488	$(11.5, 13.5]$
12	64QAM	520	$(13.5, 15]$
13	64QAM	552	$(15, 17]$
14	64QAM	584	$(17, 19.5]$
15	64QAM	616	$(19.5, \inf]$

Table 4. Running time of different methods

M (Number of data packets)	DRL based	Lagrange
M = 50	0.19 s	15.08 s
M = 100	0.82 s	27.89 s
M = 200	2.03 s	182.64 s
M = 300	10.83 s	901.07 s

Figure 7 compares the energy efficiency of the optimal Lagrange multiplier method, deep reinforcement learning algorithm and greedy algorithm when the number of SMS is different and the number of packets is fixed. The results show that with the increase of interference, the energy efficiency of the three algorithms shows a downward trend, but the decline speed of deep reinforcement learning is lower than that of the other two algorithms. When the external interference $N1 > 3$, the energy efficiency of deep reinforcement learning algorithm is greater than that of the best Lagrangian algorithm, which shows that the deep reinforcement learning algorithm in this paper has strong anti-interference ability.

Figure 8 shows the target value changes of multi-round training for the same datasets under different batch training sizes. The results show that for a larger batch training size, the convergence of the pointer network is better, the training time is shorter, and the optimal value can be more quickly calculated.

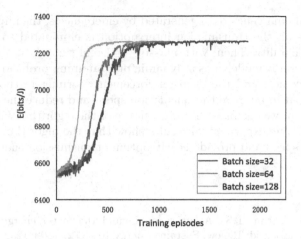

Fig. 8. Energy efficiency with different batch sizes.

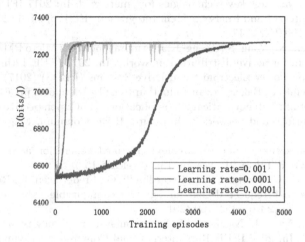

Fig. 9. Energy efficiency with different learning rates.

Figure 9 shows the change in training target values of the same data set under different learning rates. The results show that at a higher learning rate, the convergence is better, but the computational stability is worse. A smaller learning rate corresponds to better computational stability but a slower convergence rate.

7   Conclusion

This paper proposes a data repeat transmission scheme and uses a deep reinforcement learning method for resource allocation. To realize the SA of ADNs, data transmission must satisfy the requirements of low latency and high reliability. A framework based on 5G is proposed. First, by increasing the number of repeated transmissions of emergency data generated by emergencies, the impact of external interference on the transmission interruption is eliminated to improve the transmission reliability. Then, with massive and real-time data, the 5G uplink resource allocation is modeled as a dynamic programming problem to maximize the energy efficiency, and the deep reinforcement learning method is used to solve the problem to improve the calculation speed and reduce the transmission delay. In addition, we compare the performance of the algorithm with other typical algorithms. The experimental results show that the algorithm can improve the calculation speed and provide nearly optimal transmission energy efficiency.

References

1. Bayram, I.S., Ustun, T.S.: A survey on behind the meter energy management systems in smart grid. Renew. Sustain. Energy Rev. **72**, 1208–1232 (2016)
2. Dong, Z., Xu, T., Li, Y., Feng, P., Gao, X., Zhang, X.: Review and application of situation awareness key technologies for smart grid. In: 2017 IEEE Conference on Energy Internet and Energy System Integration (EI2), pp. 1–6 (2017). https://doi.org/10.1109/EI2.2017.8245450
3. Sun, Y., Chen, X., Yang, S., Tseng, K.J., Amaratunga, G.: Micro PMU based monitoring system for active distribution networks. In: 2017 IEEE 12th International Conference on Power Electronics and Drive Systems (PEDS) (2017)
4. Sesia, S., Toufik, I., Baker, M.: Introduction to LTE-Advanced, pp. 613–622 (2011)
5. Schulz, P., et al.: Latency critical IoT applications in 5G: perspective on the design of radio interface and network architecture. IEEE Commun. Mag. **55**(2), 70–78 (2017)
6. 5G; study on scenarios and requirements for next generation access technologies (V15.0.0); 3GPP TR 38.913 version 15.0.0 release 15
7. Pedersen, K.I., Khosravirad, S.R., Berardinelli, G., Frederiksen, F.: Rethink hybrid automatic repeat request design for 5g: five configurable enhancements. IEEE Wirel. Commun. **24**(6), 154–160 (2017)
8. Xiaotong, S., Nan, H., Naizheng, Z.: Study on system latency reduction based on shorten TTI. In: 2016 IEEE 13th International Conference on Signal Processing, ICSP (2016)
9. Li, Q., Tang, H., Sun, W., Li, W., Xu, X.: An optimal wireless resource allocation of machine-type communications in the 5g network for situation awareness of active distribution network. In: 2020 IEEE International Conference on Communications, Control, and Computing Technologies for Smart Grids (SmartGridComm) (2020)
10. Kong, P.Y., Song, Y.: Joint consideration of communication network and power grid topology for communications in community smart grid. IEEE Trans. Industr. Inf. **16**(5), 2895–2905 (2020)
11. Zahoor, S., et al.: Cloud-fog-based smart grid model for efficient resource management. Sustainability **10**, 2079 (2018)
12. Al-Rubaye, S., Al-Dulaimi, A., Cosmas, J.: Spectrum allocation techniques for industrial smart grid infrastructure. In: IEEE International Conference on Industrial Informatics (2017)
13. Yaacoub, E., Kadri, A.: LTE radio resource management for real-time smart meter reading in the smart grid. In: IEEE International Conference on Communication Workshop, pp. 2000–2005 (2015)

14. Yang, T., Hu, Y., Gursoy, M.C., Schmeink, A., Mathar, R.: Deep reinforcement learning based resource allocation in low latency edge computing networks, pp. 1–5 (2018)
15. Ji, L., Hui, G., Lv, T., Lu, Y.: Deep reinforcement learning based computation offloading and resource allocation for MEC. In: 2018 IEEE Wireless Communications and Networking Conference (WCNC) (2018)
16. 5G; NR; physical channels and modulation (V16.1.0); 3GPP TS 38.211 version 16.1.0 release 16
17. 5G; NR; base station (BS) radio transmission and reception (V1.0.0); 3GPP TS 38.104 version 1.0.0 release 15
18. Albu, M., Sanduleac, M., Stanescu, C.: Syncretic use of smart meters for power quality monitoring in emerging networks. IEEE Trans. Smart Grid **8**, 485–492 (2016)
19. Park, J., Hwang, J.-N., Li, Q., Yiling, X., Huang, W.: Optimal dash-multicasting over LTE. IEEE Trans. Veh. Technol. **67**(5), 4487–4500 (2018)
20. Castellanos, CÚ., Villa, D.L., Rosa, C., Pedersen, K.I., Michel, J.: Performance of uplink fractional power control in UTRAN LTE. In: Vehicular Technology Conference (2008)
21. Vinyals, O., Fortunato, M., Jaitly, N.: Pointer networks. Computer Science, **28** (2015)
22. Sutskever, I., Vinyals, O., Le, Q.V.: Sequence to sequence learning with neural networks. In: NIPS (2014)
23. Bahdanau, D., Cho, K., Bengio, Y.: Neural machine translation by jointly learning to align and translate. Computer Science (2014)
24. Williams, R.J.: Simple statistical gradient-following algorithms for connectionist reinforcement learning. Mach. Learn. **8**, 229–256 (1992)
25. 3GPP: physical layer procedures for data (release 16) (V16.1.0); 3GPP TS 38.214 version 16.1.0 release 16

AppSense: Detecting Smartphone Usage via WiFi Signals

Tao Liu[1], Peng Li[1(⊠)], and Cheng Zhang[2]

[1] The University of Aizu, Aizuwakamatsu, Japan
{d8212107,pengli}@u-aizu.ac.jp
[2] Ibaraki University, Mito, Japan
cheng.zhang.abbott@vc.ibaraki.ac.jp

Abstract. Mobile usage reveals some of the user's daily behavior habits and is essential. Efforts in this field of research have never stopped and have achieved a series of results. However, some active inspections often encounter difficulties in not getting specific data due to the obturated nature of the operating system. Universal passive detection often needs to compromise smartphone software which will face serious privacy breaches. In this paper, we propose AppSense, a non-invasive system that can detect smartphone usage via off-the-shelf WiFi devices by identifying various operations. The machine learning technique is utilized to divide smartphone operation actions into seven categories. These actions represents the usages of the device. A prototype was developed to evaluate the performance of AppSense and experimental results show that the average accuracy of seven operations recognition is 86.43%.

Keywords: CSI · Smartphone · Wi-Fi

1 Introduction

The advent of the mobile Internet and internet of things era has accelerated the development of the smartphone industry. According to the data from polling institutions Pew Research Center [22], the average global popularity of smartphones has reached 59%, and the highest country has even reached 94%. In view of the frequency with which we carry and use our smartphone, detection of smartphone usage scenarios becomes important.

Some smartphones now have built-in application monitoring programs to show the use duration of each application, such as the "Screen Usage Time" features in iPhone [21]. However, this kind of active inside programs will occupy the system resources and only provide a single result but not the specific raw data. As a comparison, some passive ways use the "side-channel" based scheme to collect private intelligence on mobile devices. For example, Shukia et al. [9] try to extract the passwords from the perspective of the screen display, which means they need

Supported by organization x.

© ICST Institute for Computer Sciences, Social Informatics and Telecommunications Engineering 2022
Published by Springer Nature Switzerland AG 2022. All Rights Reserved
C. T. Calafate et al. (Eds.): MONAMI 2021, LNICST 418, pp. 60–72, 2022.
https://doi.org/10.1007/978-3-030-94763-7_5

a reflection of the screen or a low-resolution video of the content typed on the screen. Similarly, Liu et al. [6,27] use the microphones' acoustic information as the "side-channel", the motion sensors inside the phone were also proposed to relate to the operator movements [7]. Even so, all the above methods need to put detection devices very close to the target or to compromise smartphone software, which is difficult in practice. A more transparent and cheap scheme would be a better choice.

We consider Wi-Fi signal as perceptual tools whiches fluctuation can be associated with movement interference. Comparing with other perception methods, the advantages of the wireless signal are as obvious. First, it's a device-free way, we don not need any special equipment because Wi-Fi signals almost exist everywhere whether in public or private spaces. Second, it has a wide range of dissemination, we can know from the fundamentals of wireless communication [16] that even one common commercial routers could have a transmission distance of dozens of meters, in LoS (line-of-sight) or NLoS condition. There are some existing works realize motion and behavior recognition using WiFi signals [4,13,25], but they only focus on large-size movement. WindTalker [5] and Wipass [26] used WiFi signals to identify the operation of the phones to unlock. However, their work are restricted that the mobile phones must be the signal transmitter. WindTalker even must use directive antennas and both of them need numerous attempts before unlocking the smartphone.

In this paper, we propose AppSense, a system that can get smartphone usage information by detecting the WiFi signals. Specifically, AppSense uses the ubiquitous signals changes, which caused by physical operations of smartphones, as the motion sensors to identify smartphone operation actions including click, long-press, cross-slip, longitudinal-slip, double-click, power-button and static.

To obtain a satisfying effect, AppSense needs to deal with the corresponding challenges. The first is adaptability to different perceived environments. Unlike wearable devices, which can get stable monitoring data, device-free means more uncontrollable factors. Users may switch back and forth between a WiFi connection and a cellular data connection. The second is the mapping of each action's unique characteristics to the wireless signal. Wireless signals are unstable in their own right and are susceptible to multi-path effects.

To handle these challenges, AppSense has adopted a number of specific strategies. For the first one, we consider two typical different scenarios where smartphones were connected directly to the router or there are other signal transmission links around the phone, our systems could operate effectively in both cases. For the second challenge, AppSense filter the original signal and utilize machine learning method to mapping signal and operations. We deploy and evaluate the performance of AppSense in a realistic environment with off-the-shelf WiFi devices. For the action recognition of the operating cell phone, the result of cross-verification by multiple experimenters is 86.43%.

The rest of this paper is organized as follows. We introduce some background and preliminaries in Sect. 2. The system design is described in Sect. 3. Then, we implement and evaluate experiments in Sect. 4. Related work is proposed in Sect. 5. Finally, we conclude our work in Sect. 6.

2   Background and Preliminary

2.1   RSS and CSI

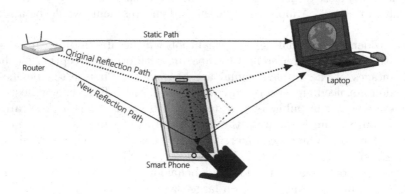

Fig. 1. A signal propagation model when using smart phone.

Earlier studies about WiFi mainly use the information of Received Signal Strength Indicator (RSSI), i.e., the received power of all signal transmit paths. It can be formulated as [24]:

$$RSS = 10log2(|H|^2) \qquad (1)$$

$$H = \sum_{K=1}^{n} \|H_k\| e^{j\theta_k} \qquad (2)$$

where $\|H_k\|$ and θ_k denote amplitude and frequency, respectively, of the k-th path among all multi-path effect. As an example of manipulating a touch phone in signal propagation environment shown in Fig. 1, propagation paths can be divided into static and dynamic. The change in the propagation path caused by the finger sliding screen belongs to the latter, which is the primary cause of the change in signal strength at the receiving end. RSSI is a kind of coarse-grained information in MAC layer. In practice, users generally only need to use the WLAN function of the smartphone to scan the WiFi access point (AP) in the environment and get the RSSI of each access point, without the need to establish any connection. Although some research uses RSSI for target localization or movement identification [11], the accuracy is low or unstable because RSSI cannot describe the multi-path effect.

Since some WiFi standards (e.g., IEEE 802.n/ac) support Orthogonal Frequency Division Multiplexing (OFDM) and Multiple-Input Multiple-Output (MIMO), we can get the Channel State Information (CSI) in the physical layer, which can better capture multipath channel features. Theoretically, we can get the phase and amplitude information for each propagation path in Fig. 1. Specifically, CSI can be expressed in a manner of channel frequency response (CFR) as follows [16]:

$$H(f,t) = \sum_{k=1}^{n} h_k(f,t)e^{-j\theta_k(f,t)} \qquad (3)$$

where $H(f,t)$ represents the complex value of CFR. It characterizes the channel performance with the amplitude and phase of sub-carrier frequency f measured at time t. We let h_k denote the amplitude that characterizes the attenuation, and $e^{-j\theta_k(f,t)}$ is the phase shift on the k-th path caused by propagation delay. We can get CSI from commodity wireless interface network cards (INC) like Intel 5300 or Atheros 9580 with corresponding CSI tool installed under Linux system. Different WiFi channel bandwidth has different number of subcarriers, 20 MHz has a maximum of 56 sub-carriers and 40 MHz up to 114.

2.2   Preliminary Experiments

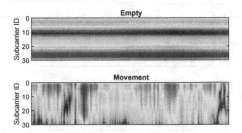

Fig. 2. Movement influence on all CSI subcarriers.

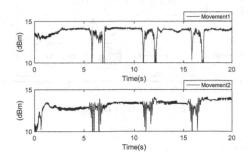

Fig. 3. Movements influence on CSI subcarriers 1

We conduct some preliminary experiments to show the feasibility of detecting mobile application usage. The equipment contains two mini PCs equipped with

Intel Network Interface Card (NIC) 5300 that works at the frequency of 5 GHz.
One of the NIC is equipped with an external antenna as the sender, the other
was connected with three antennas as the receiver. We conduct experiments in
a lab room, which contains some normal furniture like computer desks, chairs,
refrigerator, and microwave oven. Beside the experimental region, other people
just work as normal. By collecting and analyzing 30 subcarriers' information in
static and different movements of operating smartphone, we have the following
observations.

- The received signals changes as we conduct different operations. As shown
  in Fig. 2, signals are quite stable without any actions. But they show strong
  fluctuation when we are using some Apps on smartphones.
- Different operations have different influence on signals. We conduct two operations several times and observe different signal patterns as shown in Fig. 3.
  Moreover, the results show that the same movement almost has the same
  signal pattern.

In summary, our experimental results have confirmed the fact that different
operations have distinct effects on WiFi signals.

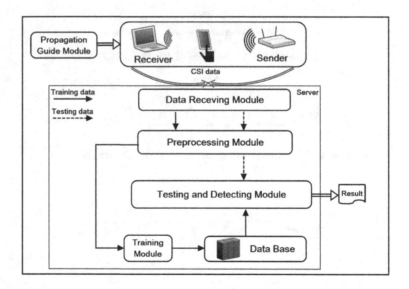

Fig. 4. System design.

3   System Design

The overview of the system design is shown in Fig. 4. Before identification, we
develop a module of data receiving which including different use scenes. Then
the received data was sent to the pre-processing module for denoising. The final
step is for training and testing module to analyze patterns for different feature
and match corresponding operate from the database.

3.1 Data Receiving Module

Users can sometimes face complex usage situations, which means mobile phones automatically switch between WiFi network connections and base station data connections in order to get better communication quality. In order to better cope with different scenarios, AppSense can work under two different modes. As shown in Fig. 5(a), in the AP mode, the smartphone directly connects to the laptop. In the monitor mode as shown in Fig. 5(b), the smartphone is covered by the signals transmitted between a WiFi router and laptop. In either case, the touch action of the finger will have a corresponding effect on the signal. Most of the previous researches just focus on one mode, but the real application environment is very complicated, and both models are needed. Our system can work well in both of the them.

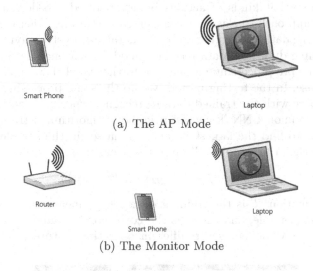

Smart Phone

Laptop

(a) The AP Mode

Router

Laptop

Smart Phone

(b) The Monitor Mode

Fig. 5. Two typical scenes

3.2 Pre-processing Module

Assuming there are N transmitters and M receivers, then we can collect $N \times M \times 30$ CSI streams. To reduce computational complexity, we first average 30 subcarriers to reduce the number of the streams to $N \times M$. For each stream, we natural choose Butter worth low-pass filter. In fact, the frequency of our sliding and clicking mobile phones will not 40 Hz, which is the low frequency part of the spectrum, and the high frequency part is mostly the noise. Since AppSense set the sampling rate as $F_s = 1000$ packages per second, the cut-off frequency of the Butter worth filter is set to $\omega_c = \frac{2\pi * f}{F_s} = \frac{2\pi * 40}{1000} \approx 0.25$ rad/s. Figure 6 conmfares the signals before and after the filting, we can see the low-pass filter removes most of the high-frequency noises and preserves the information of action details.

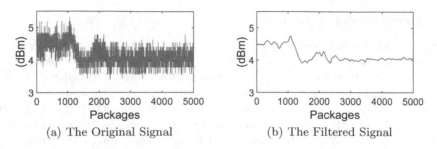

(a) The Original Signal   (b) The Filtered Signal

Fig. 6. Low pass filter

3.3   Testing and Detecting Module

In order to infer what kinds of actions being operated, we design a machine learning based approach to classify touch screen operations. There are two data flows, i.e., training data and testing data. For database construction period, after we collect training data with data receiving module, scavenge data and extract features with the pre-processing module, we further label them, and store them into the database. In the testing period, we do the same processing to the test data and compare with the trained data to recognize specific operations.

We choose common k-NN (k-nearest neighbors) algorithm to train the model. Its basic idea is to find the largest number of classes in the samples k nearest neighbors, and then the sample will be in the same class.

$$T = \left\{ (x_1, y_1), (x_2, y_2), ..., (x_N, y_N) \right\} \tag{4}$$

In the above equation, T is the training data set, x_i means the eigenvector of the i-th training sample, and the y_i is the corresponding label. The maximum value of N is 7 (we've defined seven different operating gestures).

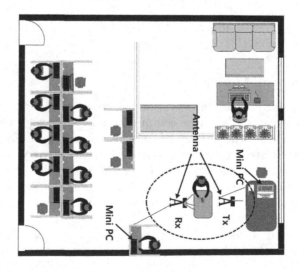

Fig. 7. Experiment environment

4 Implementation and Evaluation

4.1 Implementation

[**Environment**]. We complete the experiment in a $7 \times 10\,\mathrm{m}^2$ room as shown in Fig. 7. There are some commonly used furnishings, such as tables and chairs In the room, and except experimental region, other students work as normal.

[**Equipment**]. We setup AppSense on two mini-PCs with Intel Link 5300 NICs at 5 GHz frequency, and the operating system is Ubuntu 12.04. One of the mini-PCs linked with one antenna and the others equipped with three. We choose a Huawei G660 smartphone with a 5.0-in. touchscreen.

[**Operations and States**]. Like in Fig. 8, we choose seven common mobile operations including click, long-press, cross-slip, longitudinal-slip, double-click, power-button and static. There's a brief pause between each action so we can extract each action with the method we present before [3]. Through the identification of these actions on a time series, we further identify four app usage scenarios, etc., web browsing, chatting, gaming, and video watching.

[**Participants**]. We convene 11 experimenters, including 4 female and 7 male. We first ask them to do each operation 20 times and then they browse the Web, chat, play games and watch the video on their mobile phones in a natural state, each usage lasts five minutes.

[**Settings**]. In the monitor model, we set the sampling rate at 1000 packets/second, and can collect 3 CSI streams. In the AP model, since the performance is not as stable as the monitor model in practice, we use a smartphone as the hotspot and set the sampling rate to 300 packets/second, and can get two CSI streams simultaneously.

[**Process**]. We use Butter worth filter to reduce the noises of collected data and the touch gestures were classified with k-NN.

(a) Click   (b) Long-press   (c) Cross-slip   (d) Longitudinal-slip   (e) Double-click   (f) Power-button   (g) Static

Fig. 8. Seven different operations.

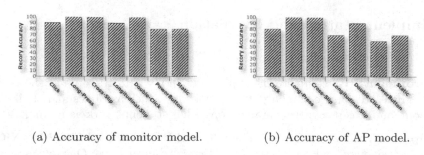

(a) Accuracy of monitor model.   (b) Accuracy of AP model.

Fig. 9. Accuracy in different model about propagation analyze

4.2 Evaluation

The evaluation is divided into two parts, the first part is about validating the detection efficiency of operating gestures in the monitor model and the AP model, to verify the effectiveness of our proposed propagation analyze. The second part focuses on the multi-person experiments in monitor model.

Evaluation of Propagation Analysis. To verify the effective of proposed propagation model, we have done numbers of experiments in different conditions with a single person.

Under the monitor mode, we change the distance between transmit antenna and receive antenna from 40 cm to 120 cm. We test in both LOS and NLOS paths under each distance. We find that the average recovery accuracy is larger than 80%. In the case of daily life, the laptop can be a receiver and the router can be considered as a transmitter. The distance between the two devices would not be far away. Therefore, we set the distance of the antenna pair at 100 cm and use the smartphone in both LOS and NLOS paths. As shown in Fig. 9(a), each operation has an accuracy of more than 80% and the average accuracy is 91.43%. The accuracy of the static state is low because the effect of our breath or other micro motion may be amplified while we do not use the smartphone.

Under the AP model, we also let the smartphone be a transmitter with different distances from the receiver. The average accuracy is always large than 75%, which means that the AP model is not as stable as Monitor model. When we select a distance of 100 cm, the recovery accuracy is showed in Fig. 9(b). The accuracy of PowerButton and static are lower than others, which is similar with results under the monitor model. The average accuracy is 81.43%.

Table 1. Confusion matrix of seven operations

	Click	Long-press	Cross-slip	Longitudinal-slip	Double-click	Power-button	Static
Click	**83.18%**	1.82%	5.91%	2.27%	2.73%	0.91%	3.18%
Long-press	2.27%	**84.09%**	6.36%	1.82%	0.91%	0.45%	4.10%
Cross-slip	4.09%	2.73%	**87.27%**	0.45%	0.45%	0.46%	4.55%
Longitudinal-slip	1.36%	2.27%	5.46%	**82.27%**	3.64%	1.36%	3.64%
Double-click	0%	3.18%	0.91%	5.91%	**86.36%**	0%	3.64%
Power-button	0.45%	1.82%	3.64%	0.91%	2.73%	**83.63%**	6.82%
Static	0.45%	0%	0.45%	0%	0.46%	0.46%	**98.18%**
Avg.							**86.43%**

Evaluation of Large-Scale Experiments. Since we confirm the effect of the identification with a single person, we further focus on a common and specific scene in monitor model with multi experimenters, to verify the effective and stability of AppSense.

For operations classify, the average accuracy is 86.43% like in Table 1. An interesting phenomenon is that the recognition rate of static has instead become the highest, even reaching 98%. The longitudinal-slip is the lowest, 82.27%, but there's actually not a big gap between it and the other five moves. We speculate that individual differences lead to the mixing of the characteristics of other movements, thus highlighting the differences in the characteristics of the static.

Summary. The results of AppSense verifies that it is reasonable and feasible to using WiFi signals to continuously monitor smartphone operations. We can also expect the potentials of AppSense in health monitoring and mobile sensing fields.

5 Related Work

Wireless WiFi signal based movement detection and identification have been extensively studied in the light of its outstanding advantages. We will then introduce the related work in the relevant fields according to the whole research trend from RSSI to CSI and action granularity from coarse to fine.

5.1 RSSI Based Work

As we mentioned before, RSSI is the coarse-grained information, and people use it at an early stage to identify relatively large movements. ActPhone [11] scan and collect signal strength info of nearby WiFi, and utilize training methods to divide the environment into activity, empty and hold mobile phones. F. Soldovieri et al. [12] put forward an improvised motion detection system (IMDS), which associate radio signal strength variations with human activities. Nonetheless, the performance is unstable due to LOS condition limited. PAWS [2] present an fusion algorithm with two features to identify six daily activities including sleeping, sitting, standing, walking, fallen and running, the average result is about 72%.

There are also jobs that try to dig deep into the properties of RSSI so that it can be used to identify smaller movements. In [10], S. Sigg et al. gather and analyze RSSI's features on a mobile phone and try to sense hand motions like up and down. However, the average recognition rate of 56% is not a particularly good performance.

5.2   CSI Based Work

Compare to RSSI, CSI based work is more abundant in number, application range and action amplitude resolution. [8,23] focus on indoor human orientation and tracking. Former built a position fingerprint database and the latter established a geometric quantify model for precise moving speed and direction estimate. Daily activities are certainly another hot spot. [20] carried out a fall detection work related to the guardianship of the elderly, to be closer to practical applications, E-eyes [19] combine activity identification with location situation. For instance, kitchen is the place we usually do cooking. CARM [18] turn the pattern based work to model based. CSI-Speed model and CSI-Activity model were utilized to recognize running, walking, sitting, etc. Come to more subtle gesture recognition, [4] recognize 9 digits gestures from American Sign Language. It turns to another 8 special designed signs in WiFinger [14], 7 in WiGeR [1] and 6 in WiAG [17]. More information like phase also be used in [15] to rebuild the trajectory of moving hand.

6   Conclusion and Future Work

In this paper, we present a wireless mobile sensing system, AppSense, a mobile using behavior and sensing system with off-the-shelf WiFi devices. Through realistic analyze, we propose the perception scenarios including both AP model and Monitor model. We further utilize filter to remove the noise, and classify operation gestures with k-NN. We prototype AppSense in the real environment and the experimental results demonstrate its effectiveness and robustness.

Our future work can split into two sides including data derivative and application derivative. For the previous, more data from more people need to gather and new method like neural network could have a try. Slid window based template matching method also deserve to apply if it doesn't need any pause between each gesture. For the latter, first, we can analyze people's traits of character and emotion status with big data method in long-time continuous monitoring. Second, we can use the system to learn different people's using habit and connect with commercial popularizing to better meet user needs. Last but not least, the system result could combine with health monitoring in the psychological field.

References

1. Al-qaness, M.A.A., Li, F.: WiGeR: WiFi-based gesture recognition system. ISPRS Int. J. Geo Inf. **5**(6), 92 (2016)

2. Gu, Y., Ren, F., Li, J.: PAWS: passive human activity recognition based on WiFi ambient signals. IEEE Internet Things J. **3**(5), 796–805 (2015)

3. Gu, Y., Zhan, J., Ji, Y., Li, J., Ren, F., Gao, S.: MoSense: an RF-based motion detection system via off-the-shelf WiFi devices. IEEE Internet Things J. **4**(6), 2326–2341 (2017)

4. Li, H., Yang, W., Wang, J., Xu, Y., Huang, L.: WiFinger: talk to your smart devices with finger-grained gesture. In: Proceedings of the 2016 ACM International Joint Conference on Pervasive and Ubiquitous Computing, pp. 250–261 (2016)

5. Li, M., et al.: When CSI meets public WiFi: inferring your mobile phone password via WiFi signals. In: Proceedings of the 2016 ACM SIGSAC Conference on Computer and Communications Security, pp. 1068–1079 (2016)

6. Liu, J., Wang, Y., Kar, G., Chen, Y., Yang, J., Gruteser, M.: Snooping keystrokes with mm-level audio ranging on a single phone. In: Proceedings of the 21st Annual International Conference on Mobile Computing and Networking, pp. 142–154 (2015)

7. Liu, X., Zhou, Z., Diao, W., Li, Z., Zhang, K.: When good becomes evil: keystroke inference with smartwatch. In: Proceedings of the 22nd ACM SIGSAC Conference on Computer and Communications Security, pp. 1273–1285 (2015)

8. Qian, K., Wu, C., Yang, Z., Yang, C., Liu, Y.: Decimeter level passive tracking with WiFi. In: Proceedings of the 3rd Workshop on Hot Topics in Wireless, pp. 44–48 (2016)

9. Shukla, D., Kumar, R., Serwadda, A., Phoha, V.V.: Beware, your hands reveal your secrets! In: Proceedings of the 2014 ACM SIGSAC Conference on Computer and Communications Security, pp. 904–917 (2014)

10. Sigg, S., Blanke, U., Tröster, G.: The telepathic phone: frictionless activity recognition from WiFi-RSSI. In: 2014 IEEE International Conference on Pervasive Computing and Communications (PerCom), pp. 148–155. IEEE (2014)

11. Sigg, S., et al.: Passive, device-free recognition on your mobile phone: tools, features and a case study. In: Stojmenovic, I., Cheng, Z., Guo, S. (eds.) MindCare 2014. LNICST, vol. 131, pp. 435–446. Springer, Cham (2014). https://doi.org/10.1007/978-3-319-11569-6_34

12. Soldovieri, F., Gennarelli, G.: Exploitation of ubiquitous Wi-Fi devices as building blocks for improvised motion detection systems. Sensors **16**(3), 307 (2016)

13. Sun, L., Sen, S., Koutsonikolas, D., Kim, K.H.: WiDraw: enabling hands-free drawing in the air on commodity WiFi devices. In: Proceedings of the 21st Annual International Conference on Mobile Computing and Networking, pp. 77–89 (2015)

14. Tan, S., Yang, J.: WiFinger: leveraging commodity WiFi for fine-grained finger gesture recognition. In: Proceedings of the 17th ACM International Symposium on Mobile Ad Hoc Networking and Computing, pp. 201–210 (2016)

15. Tian, Z., Wang, J., Yang, X., Zhou, M.: WiCatch: a Wi-Fi based hand gesture recognition system. IEEE Access **6**, 16911–16923 (2018)

16. Tse, D., Viswanath, P.: Fundamentals of Wireless Communication. Cambridge University Press, New York (2005)

17. Virmani, A., Shahzad, M.: Position and orientation agnostic gesture recognition using WiFi. In: Proceedings of the 15th Annual International Conference on Mobile Systems, Applications, and Services, pp. 252–264 (2017)

18. Wang, W., Liu, A.X., Shahzad, M., Ling, K., Lu, S.: Understanding and modeling of WiFi signal based human activity recognition. In: Proceedings of the 21st Annual International Conference on Mobile Computing and Networking, pp. 65–76 (2015)

19. Wang, Y., Liu, J., Chen, Y., Gruteser, M., Yang, J., Liu, H.: E-eyes: device-free location-oriented activity identification using fine-grained WiFi signatures. In: Proceedings of the 20th Annual International Conference on Mobile Computing and Networking, pp. 617–628 (2014)
20. Wang, Y., Wu, K., Ni, L.M.: WiFall: device-free fall detection by wireless networks. IEEE Trans. Mob. Comput. **16**(2), 581–594 (2016)
21. Website: Apple (2018). https://www.apple.com/cn/ios/ios-12/
22. Website: Pew research center (2018). http://www.pewglobal.org/interactives/
23. Xiao, J., Wu, K., Yi, Y., Wang, L., Ni, L.M.: Pilot: passive device-free indoor localization using channel state information. In: 2013 IEEE 33rd International Conference on Distributed Computing Systems, pp. 236–245. IEEE (2013)
24. Yang, Z., Zhou, Z., Liu, Y.: From RSSI to CSI: Indoor localization via channel response. ACM Comput. Surv. (CSUR) **46**(2), 1–32 (2013)
25. Zhang, D., Wang, H., Wu, D.: Toward centimeter-scale human activity sensing with Wi-Fi signals. Computer **50**(1), 48–57 (2017)
26. Zhang, J., et al.: Privacy leakage in mobile sensing: your unlock passwords can be leaked through wireless hotspot functionality. Mob. Inf. Syst. **2016** (2016)
27. Zhu, T., Ma, Q., Zhang, S., Liu, Y.: Context-free attacks using keyboard acoustic emanations. In: Proceedings of the 2014 ACM SIGSAC Conference on Computer and Communications Security, pp. 453–464 (2014)

A Distributed Computation Offloading Strategy for Edge Computing Based on Deep Reinforcement Learning

Hongyang Lai[1], Zhuocheng Yang[1], Jinhao Li[1], Celimuge Wu[2(✉)] ⓘ, and Wugedele Bao[3]

[1] University of Electronic Science and Technology of China, Chengdu, China
[2] The University of Electro-Communications, Tokyo, Japan
celimuge@uec.ac.jp
[3] Hohhot Minzu College, Hohhot, China

Abstract. Mobile edge computing (MEC) has emerged as a new key technology to reduce time delay at the edge of wireless networks, which provides a new solution of distributed computing. But due to the heterogeneity and instability of wireless local area networks, how to obtain a generalized computing offloading strategy is still an unsolved problem. In this research, we deploy a real small-scale MEC system with one edge server and several smart mobile devices and propose a task offloading strategy for one subject device on optimizing time and energy consumption. We formulate the long-term offloading problem as an infinite Markov Decision Process (MDP). Then we use deep Q-learning algorithm to help the subject device to find its optimal offloading decision in the MDP model. Compared with a strategy with fixed parameters, our Q-learning agent shows better performance and higher robustness in a scenario with an unstable network condition.

Keywords: Mobile edge computing · Computation offloading · Markov Decision Process · Deep reinforcement learning

1 Introduction

With the development of Internet of Things (IoT) technology, the number of smart devices increases explosively. These IoT devices have the functions of sensing, computation, and communication which can be connected to the Internet and collaboratively implement various applications, such as home automation, health monitoring, automated industry, and smart transportation. By 2025, it is estimated there will be an installed base of 75.44 billion IoT connected devices worldwide [1].

Since IoT devices are usually limited by computing and storage capabilities. In traditional methods, most computing tasks are offloaded to the cloud, which is called mobile cloud computing (MCC) [7]. However, due to the relatively large

© ICST Institute for Computer Sciences, Social Informatics and Telecommunications Engineering 2022
Published by Springer Nature Switzerland AG 2022. All Rights Reserved
C. T. Calafate et al. (Eds.): MONAMI 2021, LNICST 418, pp. 73–86, 2022.
https://doi.org/10.1007/978-3-030-94763-7_6

distance between IoT devices and cloud servers, this leads to high transmission delays and affects delay-sensitive applications [14]. In the past decade, through the rapid development of artificial intelligence (AI) technologies such as computer vision and natural language processing, the number of delay-sensitive intelligent applications largely increases. But the latency of public cloud providers usually exceeds 100 milliseconds, which is unacceptable [12]. Mobile edge computing (MEC) has emerged as new architecture and a key technology for IoT networks to face this problem. MEC [9,16] can provide computing services at the edge of wireless networks with low latency. Therefore, in recent years, we have witnessed a paradigm shift from centralized MCC to MEC. Compared with MCC, MEC can provide lower latency and computational agility in computational offloading. For each smart mobile device (SMD), it can migrate its computing tasks to edge nodes or cloudlets [17]. However, computing power means high expenses and energy consumption, which is not economically friendly. In addition, computational offloading can cause greater interference in ultra-dense networks and unexpected transmission delays [4]. Therefore, offloading all the computing tasks to the MEC server is not always the optimal strategy.

In a multi-user MEC scenario, computing offloading involves three parts: application partitioning, task allocation, and task execution [13]. In general, an offloading decision is to make a viable task allocation decision, which may result in any of the three types of offloading strategies: local execution, full offloading, and partial offloading, which is a trade-off result between time and energy consumption. To minimize the weighted sum of tasks completion time and energy consumption, a SMD should determine not only whether and how much to offload, but also offloading target. Such a problem can be generally formulated as integer programming problems due to the existence of binary offloading variables.

Many related engineering models for offloading decision problems and resource allocation problems in MEC networks show attractive theoretical results. Lei [11] considered it as a dynamic programming problem and formulated it into a continuous-time Markov decision process model. Chen [3] proposed a game theory for multi-user situations and made a trade-off between energy consumption and time delay, trying to achieve a Nash equilibrium. Dinh [5] also modeled it with game theory and extended the problem to a practical scenario, where the number of processed CPU cycles is time-varying and unknown. In this case, he applied Q-learning to learn SMDs' long-term offloading strategies to maximize their long-term utilities.

In most of the related works, the MEC system is stable and fixed, where it is uncomplicated to calculate the time consumption. However, a real MEC network is heterogeneous and flexible, whose structure may change at any time, and therefore it is impossible to reach a general solution. Hence, existing integer programming algorithms are not suitable for making real-time offloading decisions in a real MEC network. To improve the real-time performance, it is more practical to design a multi-user offloading mechanism, where SMDs can learn and adjust their offloading strategy at any time based on the reward and network information observed after each offloading action. In addition, most researches are based on simulations and analytical evaluations, which are not rigorous enough. The processing time for the same task varies from one SMD to another, which is not linear additive while offloading.

In this paper, we deploy a real small-scale multi-user MEC system, which has unique characteristics and topological network structure. All the SMDs have a certain ability of communication and computation and have the option to process computing tasks received from other SMDs. For instance, we use the Raspberry Pi as a SMD and apply YOLO algorithm to perform image analysis on multiple photos taken by the camera and offload the photos from SMD (Raspberry Pi) to MEC server connected to AP or other SMDs (other Raspberry Pi). To simulate the time variation and instability of a MEC system, we manually connect or disconnect SMDs at a random time. We measure the authentic processing time and calculate its power consumption according to its offloading strategy. Then, for the MEC system, the offloading process is formulated as a Markov decision process (MDP) model. Iterative methods such as Q-learning can be used to solve the above-mentioned MDP model. However, a challenge known as the curse of dimensionality [15] lies in the convergence of Q-table when simply applying Q-learning. To overcome the problem of dimensionality, we apply a better estimation alternative is to adopt a neural network which is known as Deep Q-Network (DQN). Eventually, the optimized offloading time and energy consumption can be obtained by employing the DQN to solve the MDP.

There are three main contributions of this article as follows.

1) The proposed offloading strategy not only includes local computing and MEC servers but also takes the computing ability of other SMDs into account, which contributes to practical optimization in industrial applications.
2) We consider both time delay and energy consumption and apply Deep Q-Network to solve the MDP model, giving a general offloading strategy for different scenarios.
3) Unlike most related works using simulation software to verify the offloading scheme, we build an actual MEC network system. In this case, the network structure and communication reliability may vary at any time. Besides, each offloading decision affects the whole MEC system, for example, CPU using rate of another SMD. In our work, we provide real data to evaluate its performance.

The remainder of this paper is organized as follows. In Sect. 1, the system model including network model and computation model will be introduced. Section 2 presents the offloading time and energy optimization according to MDP model and DQN strategy. Experiment settings and results are discussed in Sects. 3 and 4. Section 5 concludes the paper.

2   MEC System Model and Problem Formulation

2.1   MEC Network Model

We deploy a real MEC system for the IoT application, in which a MEC server connected to the access point (AP) provides service for N smart mobile devices (SMD) in an ad-hoc network as shown in Fig. 1, where the N is a flexible number because other SMDs may be offline at any time except for the subject smart mobile device (SSMD) in blue color. We choose Raspberry Pi as the smart mobile devices comprised of computing, communication, and storage modules. Considering a scenario of computer vision, the main task of this system is to analyze images using YOLO [2] in a real-time monitoring system. We suppose that the SSMD has several pictures to be processed as the original data, which is the basic task unit that cannot be divided anymore. However, Raspberry pi has a limited computing capability while a monitoring system is usually time-sensitive. Also, in the real-time monitoring system, since it is designed to operate constantly, the energy consumption cannot be ignored. To meet the demands for shorter delay and energy saving, the original data can be offloaded to the MEC server connected to AP or other SMDs for remote computing, to improve time efficiency and reduce energy consumption. The decision on computation process for executing tasks can be described as an action a.

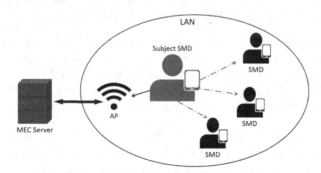

Fig. 1. Network model. (Color figure online)

$$a = \begin{cases} 0, & \text{computing locally} \\ 1, & \text{offloading to MEC server} \\ 2, & \text{offloading to another SMD} \\ 3, & \text{standby} \end{cases} \tag{1}$$

For example, $a = 1$ represents offloading the task to MEC server and $a = 2$ means offloading to another SMD. When offloading, the original data are transmitted and then the processed data will be sent back.

2.2   Computation Model

In the proposed network model, when SSMD has to complete i_{th} computation task $\tau = \{d_i, c_i\}$, where d_i is the size of data under processing and c_i represents the total number of CPU cycles required to complete the computing task. As for SSMD, it can choose either to execute all the tasks locally or to offload them to another SMD or the MEC server to execute remotely or remains in the standby state.

(1) Local Computing: We consider that the CPU in SSMD is operating at frequency f^L. While executing locally on SSMD, the computation time delay t^L is

$$t^L = \frac{c_i}{f^L} \tag{2}$$

The energy consumption of SSMD can be calculated as

$$e^L = \kappa (f^L)^3 t^L \tag{3}$$

where κ is a coefficient that depends mostly on the chip architecture and $\kappa = 10^{-26}$ [6,19].

(2) Edge Computing: In the transmission process of offloading, the achievable uplink transmission rate can be expressed as

$$r = log_2 (1 + \frac{P^T * h}{\sigma^2}) \tag{4}$$

where P^T is the transmission power and h is the channel gain between SSMD and MEC server or SSMD and another SMD. σ^2 is the noise power. Let f^C denotes the number of CPU cycles frequency of the MEC server connected to AP or another SMD. In this case, the total time delay consists of transmission time and computation time, which can be expressed as

$$t^E = \frac{d_i}{r} + t^C \tag{5}$$

where $t^C = c_i / f^C$ means the computation time in MEC server or another SMD. The energy consumption of the MEC server or another SMD can be calculated as

$$e^E = P^T * \frac{d_i}{r} + P^C * t^C \tag{6}$$

where P^C is the computation power consumption of the MEC or another SMD.

(3) Standby: We consider there is a standby mode for CPU in SSMD, which means no offloading and computation actions will be performed. In this case, the total standby time is t^S and the energy consumption during standby state is

$$e^S = t^S * P^S \tag{7}$$

where we consider P^S is a small value shows the basic power consumption of idle CPU in SSMD. The introduction of the standby state is based on the instability and latency of the proposed network. When the last task is already offloaded, since the communication time is much lower than the computation time, the current calculation progress is unknown until SSMD obtains the returned result. So it may not be the optimal way to continue to perform task offloading or computation, then SSMD turns to the standby state to wait and reduce power consumption.

2.3 Problem Formulation

When making offloading decisions, both the total execution time of the task and the total power consumption need to be taken into consideration. To make a trade-off between those two factors, we define a weighting factor $w(w \in [0, 1])$ to indicate the degree of importance to time delay and power consumption. To meet the needs of specific scenarios, the weighting factor can be adjusted to emphasize a certain aspect [8].

According to (2) and (3), the weighted sum G^L of time and energy consumption in the process of computing locally, can be defined as

$$G^L = wt^L + (1 - w)e^L \tag{8}$$

Similarly, according to (5) and (6) the energy consumption and time delay in the MEC server and in another SMD can be calculated respectively as

$$G_M^E = wt_M^E + (1 - w)e_M^E \tag{9}$$

$$G_A^E = wt_A^E + (1 - w)e_A^E \tag{10}$$

Lastly, according to (7), the weighted sum G^S of energy and time consumption in the standby state, can be defined as

$$G^S = wt^S + (1 - w)e^S \tag{11}$$

Therefore, the overhead of the subject SMD can be obtained by

$$\begin{aligned} G = w(\sum^{s_1} t^L + \sum^{s_2} t_M^E + \sum^{s_3} t_A^E + \sum^{s_4} t^S) \\ + (1 - w)(\sum^{s_1} e^L + \sum^{s_2} e_M^E + \sum^{s_3} e_A^E + \sum^{s_4} e^S) \\ = w(T^L + T_M^E + T_A^E + T^S) + (1 - w)(E^L + E_M^E + E_A^E + E^S) \\ = wT + (1 - w)E \end{aligned} \tag{12}$$

where s_1, s_2, s_3, s_4 are the counters for recording the number of actions the trade-off has performed in order to complete all the tasks of SSMD and T, E represent the total sum of time and energy consumption in executing all the tasks of SSMD.

Then in the designated network model, to investigate the tradeoff between energy and time consumption for SSMD, we can formulate the optimization problem as follows.

$$\min \quad w_1 \frac{T - T_{Exp}}{T_{Exp}} + w_2 \frac{E - E_{Exp}}{E_{Exp}}$$

$$\text{s.t.} \quad C1 : 0 \leq T_{Exp} \leq T^{max}$$

$$C2 : 0 \leq E_{Exp} \leq E^{max}$$

$$C3 : w_1 + w_2 = 1 \tag{13}$$

Here we introduce the expected minimum of total delay T_{Exp} and total energy consumption E_{Exp} to normalize the objective function. Constraint $C1$ and $C2$ limit the range of those manually giving value. Constraint $C3$ restricts the sum of weight factors to 1.

3   Offloading Time and Energy Optimization

In this section, we use MDP to represent the task execution and offloading process of the entire MEC system and use a deep reinforcement learning algorithm to solve the optimization problem.

3.1   MDP Model Formulation

In this section, we will analyze the stochastic process of the system state and formulate a Markov Decision Process (MDP) problem to minimize the normalized weighted sum of total time delay and power consumption in offloading process. When SSMD makes an offloading decision, it not only considers the current state but also considers the impact of the current decision on the future total reward. MDP considers the immediate and delayed rewards brought about by current decisions, and makes the expected optimal action under uncertain circumstances. There are five crucial elements in our MDP model: decision epoch, state, action, state transition probability, and reward function. Considering our MEC system model and offloading process, the details are as follows.

Decision Epochs: The period SSMD making offloading decision is called an epoch [18]. In the continuous decision epochs, time is described as sequence T, consisting of K discrete time slots, where K denotes the number of executing tasks.

$$T = \{1, 2, ..., t, ..., K\}, t \in T \tag{14}$$

States: A state includes the communication quality, the number of returned results, the number of remaining tasks, the number of tasks being processed, and the operating frequency of all the SMDs and the MEC server. The state vector S involves all possible states during the offloading process for the MEC system and is defined as follows.

$$S = N_{all} \times CQ \times RR \times RT \times PT \times f \tag{15}$$

where $\times$ represents the Cartesian product. N_{all} includes all the nodes of the proposed network, $N_{all} = \{N_{SSMD}, N_{MEC}, N_{ASMD}\}$. CQ denotes the communication quality by the possibility of channel failure. RR, RT and PT represent the numbers of returned results, tasks that remain and are under processing, respectively. f denotes the operating frequency of SMDs and the MEC server. All the states values can be normalized and range from $[0, 1]$. In this case, for any certain decision epoch t in (14), the current state can be described as s, a 3×5 dimension vector. An example state table is shown in Table 1.

Table 1. An example table of the current state.

	CQ	RR	RT	PT	f
SSMD	0.9	0.5	0.5	0.1	0.5
MEC	0.8	0.7	0.4	0.2	0.6
ASMD	0.7	0.4	0.2	0.2	0.7

Actions: For each epoch, SSMD needs to select a corresponding action in the action space (1), where $a_t = \{0, 1, 2, 3\}$. $a_t = 0$ denotes that for the i_{th} computation task it is executed locally in SSMD. $a_t = 1$ denotes offloading to the MEC server. $a_t = 2$ denotes offloading to another SMD (ASMD). $a_t = 3$ denotes that SSMD turns into standby state. The set of all actions selected to complete the task is defined as A.

$$A = \{a = (a_1, a_2, ..., a_t)\} \qquad (16)$$

Transition Probability: The probability of Markov state may transfer from s to state s' by selecting action a. In our case, the state is 3×5 dimension vector. In order to simplify the model of transition probability, we take the MEC server node as the focus node from all the nodes and its operating frequency is also fixed. The transition probability of MEC server node is derived by

$$P(s'|s, a) = \begin{cases} P(RR'|RR)P(RT'|RT)P(PT'|PT), & CQ' = CQ \\ \rho, & CQ' \neq CQ \end{cases}$$

where $\rho \in [0, 1]$ represents the failure probability that the channel between MEC server and SSMD. P(RR'—RR) denotes the probability of the number of returned results in the next state. P(RR'—RR) is described by

$$P(RR'|RR) = \begin{cases} \eta, & RR' = RR \\ \xi, & RR' \neq RR \end{cases}$$

where η represents the probability of the number of returned results staying at the same number, $0 \leq \eta \leq 1$. Alternatively, ξ denotes the probability of the number of returned results changes to another number, and ξ is expressed as follows

$$\xi = (1 - \eta)/RT \qquad (17)$$

P(RT′—RT) denotes the probability of the number of remaining tasks in the next state. P(RT′—RT) is described by

$$P(RT'|RT) = \begin{cases} \phi, & RT' = RT \\ \varphi, & RT' \neq RT \end{cases}$$

where ϕ represents the probability of the number of remaining tasks staying at the same number, $0 \leq \phi \leq 1$. Alternatively, φ denotes the probability of the number of remaining tasks changes to another number, and φ is expressed as follows

$$\varphi = (1 - \phi)/(RT - 1) \tag{18}$$

P(PT′—PT) denotes the probability of the number of processing tasks in the next state. P(PT′—PT) is described by

$$P(PT'|PT) = \begin{cases} \lambda, & PT' = PT \\ \mu, & PT' \neq PT \end{cases}$$

where λ represents the probability of the number of processing tasks staying at the same number, $0 \leq \lambda \leq 1$. Alternatively, μ denotes the probability of the number of processing tasks changes to another number, and μ is expressed as follows:

$$\mu = (1 - \lambda)/(RT + PT - 1) \tag{19}$$

Based on the above equations, the transition probability of the focus node and then all the nodes can be calculated and formulated as a state vector.

Reward Function: In order to evaluate the instant benefit of choosing an action in the current state, we introduce the reward function $r(s, a)$, which reflects the instant reward when SSMD makes an offloading decision in the current MEC system state. According to the objective optimization function (13) mentioned before, the reward function $r(s, a)$ is defined as follows

$$r(s, a) = \begin{cases} G^L, & a = 0 \\ G_M^E, & a = 1 \\ G_A^E, & a = 2 \\ G^S, & a = 3 \end{cases}$$

where $\{G^L, G_M^E, G_A^E, G^S\}$ are already defined by (8–11), respectively.

In our case, iterative methods such as Q-learning can be used to solve the above-mentioned MDP model. Therefore, we will discuss the use of Q-learning and Deep Q-Network in solving MDP model as follows.

3.2   Deep Q-Network

In the Q-learning algorithm, a Q-table is used to store Q-values of all state-action pairs [10]. According to Bellman equation, Q-learning $Q(s_t, a_t)$ can be expressed as

$$Q(s_t, a_t) = Q(s_t, a_t) + \alpha[r(s_t, a_t) + \gamma(\max_{a'} Q(s_{t+1}, a') - Q(s_t, a_t))] \qquad (20)$$

where α is the learning rate, γ is the discount factor. In traditional Q-learning, we use a table to record Q-value $Q(s, a)$ of all the state-action pairs as shown in (20). However, there are too many latent states of our practical MEC system to fit in the Q-table, which is generally known as the curse of dimensionality [15]. Therefore, we can't store states through tables. It is necessary for us to compress the dimensions of the state. One solution is to approximate the value function approximation. Then a neural network is built for fitting and regression, approximate the Q-values function of different state-action pairs via prediction.

The discrete action mentioned above is Q-value function, where the value function Q here is not a specific value, but a set of vectors. In the neural network, the weight of the network is θ, which is represented by a Q-value function $Q(s, a, \theta)$, and the θ after the final neural network converges is the value function. Therefore, the core of the whole process determines the θ to approximate the value function. We adopt the most classic method, gradient descent, to minimize the loss function to continuously adjust the network weight θ. The loss function is defined as

$$L_i(\theta_t) = E_{(s,a,r,s^t)}[(r(s_t, a_t) + \gamma \max_{a'} Q(s', a'; \theta') - Q(s, a; \theta))^2] \qquad (21)$$

θ_i' denotes the target network parameter of the i_{th} iteration and θ_i denotes the network parameter of evaluation network. The next step is to find the gradient of θ, as follows

$$\frac{\partial L_t(\theta_t)}{\partial \theta_t} = E_{(s,a,r,s^t)}[(r(s_t, a_t) + \gamma \max_{a'} Q(s', a'; \theta') - Q(s, a; \theta))^2] \qquad (22)$$

In addition, during the learning process, trained quadruple is stored in a replay memory, where the training network structure is read by mini-batch during the learning process, which is called the experience replay. In this scenario, the reason we add experience replay is that the states are monitored consecutively under the MEC system, so the relevance of the samples is too large. Without experience replay, a problem that the gradient descent will be in the same direction with a continuous period occurs. In this condition, the gradient may not converge under the same step size. Therefore, experience replay is to randomly select some experience from a memory pool and then find the gradient, thus avoiding this underlying problem.

The target network and evaluation network share the same structure with different parameters, both of which consist of two fully connected layers. The structure of the DQN is shown in Fig. 2.

As shown in Algorithm 1, we first initialize the MEC system and all the network parameters. A few pre-train steps are set to get some experiences through random actions stored in the experience pool, and the training of the Q-evaluation network is completed in the pre-training stage. During training, it extracts minibatch experience from the experience pool every step to train the Q network. Eventually, update the parameters of the target network with the evaluation network's every C steps.

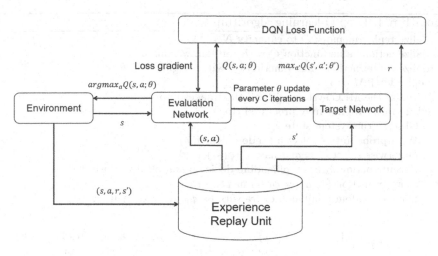

Fig. 2. DQN structure.

4 Experiment

4.1 Experiment Settings

In this part, we deploy a real MEC system to conduct the experiment. The experimental network model consists of one SSMD, three other SMDs, and the MEC server. We use Raspberry Pi 4b (Broadcom BCM2711, Quad core Cortex-A72 (ARM v8) 64-bit SoC @ 1.5 GHz) as smart mobile devices, and its power consumption is at 6.4w for regular operating and, at 2.7w for idle mode. The MEC server offers a GPU of Geforce GTX 1650 Ti. All the mobile devices are deployed in one ad-hoc based on IEEE 802.11ac in a scattered way in a radius of about 1.5 m. To simulate a real-time monitoring system, 16 unprocessed 256 * 256 images are generated in the SSMD per second as one episode. We have tested that all the SMDs and the MEC server satisfy the requirement of running YOLO algorithm to perform image analysis.

4.2 Experiment Results

To simulate a long-term unstable scenario, we set the episode number with 650, DQN memory batch size with 200, and keep the communication quality and computation stability of SMDs varying. The normalized reward value shows as Fig. 3(a). The figure illustrates a dynamic approach to the optimal strategy for this long-term dynamic MEC system, whose expected reward value increases monotonically over episodes and converges to about 0.67. Besides, it shows that the reward value declines quite frequently and with large amplitude in the early stage, indicating the learning and adapting period of DQN. To show its robustness, we set another comparing group with manual parameters that fix the current system well. It seems to be stable at first, but as the MEC system status

---

Algorithm 1. Deep Q-learning algorithm

Initialize replay memory D to capacity N
Initialize action-value function Q with random weights θ
Initialize target action-value function Q' with weights $\theta' = \theta$
for episode=1,M **do**
   Initialize the MEC system with all the images unprocessed
   while tasks are not fully processed **do**
      Observe the system state s_t
      With probability ϵ select a random action a_t
      Otherwise select $a_t = arg\max_a Q(\phi(s_t), a; \theta)$
      Execute action a_t as an offloading decision and observe reward r_t
      Store transition $(s_t, a_t, r_t, \phi_{t+1})$ in D
      Sample random minibatch of transitions $\phi_j, a_j, r_j, \phi_{j+1}$ from D

$$\text{Set } y_j = \begin{cases} r_j, & \text{if episode terminates at } j+1 \\ r_j + \gamma \max_{a'} Q'(\phi_{j+1}, a'; \theta'), & \text{otherwise} \end{cases}$$

      Perform a gradient descent step on the loss $Q(s_i, a_i; \theta_t) - y_i)^2$ with respect to
      the network parameter θ
      Reset $Q' = Q$ every $r(s_t, a_t)C$ steps
   end while
end for

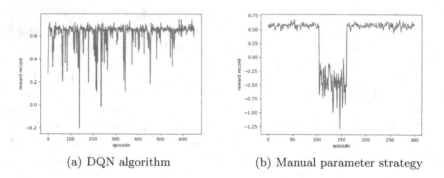

(a) DQN algorithm   (b) Manual parameter strategy

Fig. 3. Performance comparison.

change goes beyond its scope at around 100 episodes, the whole strategy crashed. Due to its fixed parameter, the agent cannot make any proper decision until we set new parameters at around episode 160. Without preset parameters, our DQN agent can choose appropriate offloading actions corresponding to MEC system states after sufficient working episodes. With the prolonged working episodes under the same system, the decisions made are more precise and less likely to be interfered by other random interferences.

5   Conclusion

In this paper, we design a practical MEC system with computation time and energy taken into account and propose an offloading strategy based on MDP model. We formulate a minimization problem that minimizes the weighted sum of the average delay and power consumption of the subject smart mobile device. We apply Deep Q-learning algorithm to learn from the offloading experience of a certain past period to improve its offloading action and predict viable decisions under unknown circumstances through regression. Compared with other traditional computation strategies, our method shows higher robustness. Especially even though the MEC system is flexible, the algorithm can make adjustments and offloading decisions in time. In our future work, we may design a larger-scale network with multiple MEC servers and take the resource allocation problem into consideration.

Acknowledgement. This research was supported in part by the National Natural Science Foundation of China under Grant No. 62062031, in part by Inner Mongolia natural science foundation grant number 2019MS06035, and Inner Mongolia Science and Technology Major Project, China, in part by ROIS NII Open Collaborative Research 21S0601, and was supported in part by JSPS KAKENHI grant numbers 18KK0279, 19H04093, 20H00592, and 21H03424.

References

1. Ahmad, I.: Discover Internet of Things editorial, inaugural issue. Disc. Internet Things **1**(1), 1–4 (2021). https://doi.org/10.1007/s43926-021-00007-6
2. Bochkovskiy, A., Wang, C.Y., Liao, H.Y.M.: YOLOv4: optimal speed and accuracy of object detection. arXiv preprint arXiv:2004.10934 (2020)
3. Chen, X., Jiao, L., Li, W., Fu, X.: Efficient multi-user computation offloading for mobile-edge cloud computing. IEEE/ACM Trans. Netw. **24**(5), 2795–2808 (2015)
4. Deng, M., Tian, H., Lyu, X.: Adaptive sequential offloading game for multi-cell mobile edge computing. In: 2016 23rd International Conference on Telecommunications (ICT), pp. 1–5 (2016). https://doi.org/10.1109/ICT.2016.7500395
5. Dinh, T.Q., La, Q.D., Quek, T.Q., Shin, H.: Learning for computation offloading in mobile edge computing. IEEE Trans. Commun. **66**(12), 6353–6367 (2018)
6. Guo, S., Liu, J., Yang, Y., Xiao, B., Li, Z.: Energy-efficient dynamic computation offloading and cooperative task scheduling in mobile cloud computing. IEEE Trans. Mob. Comput. **18**(2), 319–333 (2018)
7. Guo, S., Xiao, B., Yang, Y., Yang, Y.: Energy-efficient dynamic offloading and resource scheduling in mobile cloud computing. In: IEEE INFOCOM 2016 - The 35th Annual IEEE International Conference on Computer Communications, pp. 1–9 (2016). https://doi.org/10.1109/INFOCOM.2016.7524497
8. Guo, S., Xiao, B., Yang, Y., Yang, Y.: Energy-efficient dynamic offloading and resource scheduling in mobile cloud computing. In: IEEE INFOCOM 2016-The 35th Annual IEEE International Conference on Computer Communications, pp. 1–9. IEEE (2016)
9. Hu, Y.C., Patel, M., Sabella, D., Sprecher, N., Young, V.: Mobile edge computing-a key technology towards 5g. ETSI White Paper **11**(11), 1–16 (2015)

10. Iqbal, A., Tham, M.L., Chang, Y.C.: Double deep q-network-based energy-efficient resource allocation in cloud radio access network. IEEE Access **9**, 20440–20449 (2021)
11. Lei, L., Xu, H., Xiong, X., Zheng, K., Xiang, W.: Joint computation offloading and multiuser scheduling using approximate dynamic programming in NB-IoT edge computing system. IEEE Internet Things J. **6**(3), 5345–5362 (2019)
12. Li, A., Yang, X., Kandula, S., Zhang, M.: CloudCmp: comparing public cloud providers. In: Proceedings of the 10th ACM SIGCOMM Conference on Internet Measurement, IMC 2010, pp. 1–14. Association for Computing Machinery, New York (2010). https://doi.org/10.1145/1879141.1879143
13. Lin, L., Liao, X., Jin, H., Li, P.: Computation offloading toward edge computing. Proc. IEEE **107**(8), 1584–1607 (2019). https://doi.org/10.1109/JPROC.2019.2922285
14. Pan, J., McElhannon, J.: Future edge cloud and edge computing for internet of things applications. IEEE Internet Things J. **5**(1), 439–449 (2018). https://doi.org/10.1109/JIOT.2017.2767608
15. Peng, S.: Stochastic Hamilton-Jacobi-Bellman equations. SIAM J. Control. Optim. **30**(2), 284–304 (1992)
16. Satyanarayanan, M.: The emergence of edge computing. Computer **50**(1), 30–39 (2017). https://doi.org/10.1109/MC.2017.9
17. Satyanarayanan, M., Chen, Z., Ha, K., Hu, W., Richter, W., Pillai, P.: Cloudlets: at the leading edge of mobile-cloud convergence. In: 6th International Conference on Mobile Computing, Applications and Services, pp. 1–9. IEEE (2014)
18. Yang, G., Hou, L., He, X., He, D., Chan, S., Guizani, M.: Offloading time optimization via Markov decision process in mobile-edge computing. IEEE Internet Things J. **8**(4), 2483–2493 (2020)
19. Zhang, W., Wen, Y., Guan, K., Kilper, D., Luo, H., Wu, D.O.: Energy-optimal mobile cloud computing under stochastic wireless channel. IEEE Trans. Wirel. Commun. **12**(9), 4569–4581 (2013). https://doi.org/10.1109/TWC.2013.072513.121842

Advanced Technology in Edge and Fog Computing

How to Select SF and BW for 2.4 GHz LoRa Ad-Hoc Communication: From Energy Consumption Perspective

Haibo Luo[1,2,3]($\boxtimes$), Lianghui Xiao[1,3], Lingxin Wu[4], Zhiqiang Ruan[1,3], and Wen Lin[1,3]

[1] College of Computer and Control Engineering, Minjiang University, Fuzhou 350108, China
robhappy@mju.edu.cn
[2] Digit Fujian Internet-of-Things Laboratory of Environmental Monitoring, Fujian Normal University, Fuzhou 350117, China
[3] Electronic Information and Control of Fujian University Engineering Research Center, Fuzhou 350108, China
[4] College of Mathematics and Computer Science, Fuzhou University, Fuzhou 350108, China

Abstract. LoRa modulation is a narrowband, long-range wireless communication technology. At present, Sub-GHz LoRa is mainly used to build LoRaWAN and is applied to data collection of Internet of Things. However, the latest 2.4 GHz LoRa can be applied to point-to-point and self-organizing networks. In this paper, the impacts of bandwidth (BW) and spreading factor (SF) on the energy consumption is evaluated for the first time. In general, to reach the target transmission distance, a larger SF or a smaller BW can be selected to reduce transmitting power (but the ToA time will increase in this case), or the desired transmission distance can be achieved by increasing the transmitting power and keeping a smaller SF or a larger BW. obviously, both of them will increase the power consumption of transmission. We analyze which method is more energy-efficient by constructing an energy consumption model for LoRa communication. The energy model is suitable for the adaptive data rate (ADR) of LoRa and establishes the foundation for building low-energy node-to-node and Ad-hoc LoRa networks.

Keywords: 2.4 GHz LoRa · Energy consumption · Node to node communication

1 Introduction

LoRa is a new low-rate modulation technology for wireless communication, which uses spread spectrum communications to increase the transmission distance. It can dynamically adjust the data rate and efficient transmission distance by adjusting the spreading factor (SF) and bandwidth (BW). The existing sub-GHz LORA network is used for campus networking and coverage of LoRaWAN standard protocol network through the deployment of terminals, gateways and Network Servers (NS). For example, we can use Semtech's SX1276 chip to build a 470 MHz terminal device, use the SX1301 chip to set a gateway, and deploy a network server in the cloud. Sub-GHz LoRa relies on multiple

© ICST Institute for Computer Sciences, Social Informatics and Telecommunications Engineering 2022
Published by Springer Nature Switzerland AG 2022. All Rights Reserved
C. T. Calafate et al. (Eds.): MONAMI 2021, LNICST 418, pp. 89–99, 2022.
https://doi.org/10.1007/978-3-030-94763-7_7

parallel channels inside the SX1301 and can receive and parse up to 8 LoRa signals with different spreading factors simultaneously, thus enlarging the system capacity. In LoRaWAN networks, NS must be deployed in the cloud platform, in which protocols run. NS dynamically adjusts the parameters of terminals such as BW, SF and transmission power by issuing commands [1]. The standard LoRaWAN network is a star topology, with its gateway the central node through which other nodes must pass messages, as shown in Fig. 1(a).

To simplify network deployment and save the cost of deployment and maintenance, some applications can directly use LoRa point-to-point communication or multi-hop network communication, without deploying LoRaWAN gateways, NS and LoRaWAN networking. For example, Fig. 1(b) shows (1) Point-to-point communication: remote control device; (2) Multi-hop relay; (3) Self-organizing multi-hop ad-hoc network. Through the LoRa ad-hoc network, the coverage of LoRa can be further expanded, such as monitoring oil pipelines of tens of kilometers or wild rivers without any cellular signal. The preceding networking methods are more private and flexible, which can use LoRa as a physical layer technology to build MAC, transmission protocols and application topologies suitable for specific applications.

In particular, besides the well-known sub-GHz LoRa communication technology, Semtech has recently introduced LoRa technology and chip (SX1280) that work in the 2.4 GHz ISM frequency band [2]. The application scenarios of 2.4 GHz LoRa technology will be more inclined to use self-organizing methods for networking. Compared with sub-GHz LoRa, 2.4 GHz LoRa will be very conducive to constructing global universal Internet of Things (IoT) solutions.

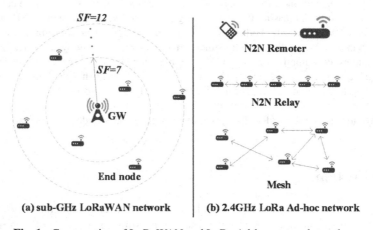

(a) sub-GHz LoRaWAN network   **(b) 2.4GHz LoRa Ad-hoc network**

Fig. 1. Comparation of LoRaWAN and LoRa Ad-hoc network topology

2 LoRa Technology and Related Works

The rapid development of the IoT has put forward higher requirements for wireless communication technology. The low-power Wide-Area Network (LPWAN) specially designed for low-bandwidth, low-power, long-distance, and massively connected IoT applications is also rapidly emerging. LoRa, which is an ultra-long-distance and low-power data transmission technology below 1 GHz, is a wireless communication technology dedicated to long distance and low power. It uses chirp-spread-spectrum modulation technology, which not only maintains the same low power consumption characteristics as Frequency-Shift Keying (FSK) modulation, but also significantly increases the communication distance, while improving network efficiency and eliminating interference. It means that terminals with different spreading sequences will not interfere with each other even if they use the same frequency to send signals simultaneously. Therefore, the Concentrator/Gateway developed on it can parallelly receive and process data from multiple nodes, which markedly expands the system capacity. The data transmission rate of LoRa is dynamically adjustable and decreases with the increase of its SF ranging from 6 to 12. The receiving sensitivity of LoRa communication has reached an astonishing −148 dbm. Compared with other advanced sub-GHz chips in the industry, its highest receiving sensitivity is improved by more than 20 db, ensuring a reliable network connection. Meanwhile, its link budget is as high as 157 db, making its communication distance up to 15 km (related to the environment), while its receiving current is only 10 mA, and its sleeping current is 200 nA, which greatly extends the battery life. Now LoRa mainly operates on free frequency bands (unlicensed frequency bands) all over the world, including 433, 868, 915 MHz, with different standards different countries and regions.

With the rapid development of the IoT, researchers pay increasing attention to LPWANs technology. Firstly, in terms of LoRa basic performance, Ruben M. Sandoval et al. [3] proposed that the average throughput per node of LoRa-based network has been mathematically formulated and the optimal network level configuration has been derived. Zhijin Qin et al. [4] investigated the uplink transmission performance of low-power-wide-area (LPWA) networks with regards to coexisting radio modules and showed how the performance of LPWA networks could be enhanced by adjusting the density of LoRa nodes around each LoRa receiver. Orestis Georgiou et al. [5] analyzed and formulated unique peculiarities of LoRa, showing that the coverage probability drops exponentially as the number of end-devices grows due to interfering signals using the same spreading sequence. Jansen C. Liando et al. [6] proposed that LoRa is capable of communicating over 10 km under line-of-sight environments. Kais Mek ki et al. [7] gave a comprehensive analysis of the LoRa modulation, including the data rate, frame format, spreading factor, and receiver sensitivity. Secondly, in terms of energy consumption, Binbin Su et al. [8] investigated energy efficiency for uplink LoRa, and formulated a nonconvex optimization problem for maximizing the system energy efficiency. Taou fik Bouguera et al. [9] presented a sensor node energy model using LoRa technology which allowed estimating the consumed power and the battery life of the sensor node for a target application. Lastly, in terms of positioning and ranging, Emanuele Goldoni et al. [10] presented a complete experimental data set of received signal strength indicator (RSSI) measurements collected in different indoor and outdoor environments using LoRa radios. However, these studies mainly focused on the basic performance of LoRa (such as optimal parameter configuration of the network, communication coverage ability, positioning and ranging capabilities, etc.) and the power consumption of nodes under the LoRaWAN network, without in-depth study on the LoRa self-organizing network.

LoRa is widely used now. To meet the requirements of long range, a small amount of data transmission, low power, and low cost of the IoT in actual applications, a low-power wide-area network information monitoring approach based on NB-IoT and LoRa was proposed by Xihai Zhang et al. [11]. Dario Madeo et al. [12] discussed the architecture of a low-cost unmanned surface vehicle (USV) to be employed for the collection of crucial parameters about water quality in rivers, lakes, or seas. Fan Wu et al. [13] presented a hybrid wearable sensor network system for the IoT connected with safety and health monitoring applications. Mauricio de Castro Tomé et al. [14] studied the application of Lora technology in smart meters, using LoRa module to send the average power required by their families in a given time. He sheng Zhang et al. [15] studied the well-covered monitoring device based on Lora and accelerometer and designed a 433-MHz whip antenna to overcome the shield of manhole cover and the absorption of electromagnetic waves of the earth. Shengwei Lin et al. [16] proposed a new mechanism to collect and transmit monitoring information based on LoRa technology. In summary, at present, most of these applications are developed on LoRaWAN networks constructed by sub-GHz LoRa, with few studies on 2.4 GHz LoRa applications.

Semtech has released a Long Range (LoRa) chipset which operated at the globally available 2.4 GHz frequency band, on top of the existing sub-GHz and km-range offer, enabling hardware manufacturers to design region-independent chipsets. Compared with sub-GHz LoRa technology, 2.4 GHz LoRa has a wider range of SF from 5 to 12, but it has only four optional BW, namely 203 kHz, 406 kHz, 812 kHz and 1625 KH, which is not as flexible as sub-GHz LoRa. Table 1 is the Receiver Sensitivity of 2.4 GHz LoRa under different SF and BW conditions.

Table 1. Receiver Sensitivity [dBm] when using 2.4 GHz LoRa (in Low Power Mode, coding rate is 4/5), taken from [2].

BW	SF							
	5	6	7	8	9	10	11	12
203 kHz	−109	−111	−115	−118	−121	−124	−127	−130
406 kHz	−107	−110	−113	−116	−119	−122	−125	−128
812 kHz	−105	−108	−112	−115	−117	−120	−123	−126
1625 kHz	−99	−103	−106	−109	−111	−114	−117	−120

Due to the advantages of 2.4 GHz LoRa, researchers have also begun to study it. Thomas Janssen et al. [17] investigated the maximum communication range of LoRa in three different scenarios. Free space, indoor and urban path loss models were used to simulate the propagation of the 2.4 GHz LoRa modulated signal at different spreading factors and band widths. Frederik Rander Andersen et al. [18] determined the ranging capabilities of LoRa 2.4 GHz and the optimal settings for the SX1280 transceiver, depending on the distance.

However, no previous study has analyzed the energy consumption of 2.4 GHz LoRa in point-to-point and self-organizing networks, especially the impacts on energy consumption when choosing different SF and BW.

The main contributions of this paper are:

(1) According to the characteristics of LoRa communication, we modify the existing energy consumption model and propose a new one that is more suitable for the assessment; (2) For the potential point-to-point and self-organizing networking applications of 2.4 GHz LoRa, the impacts of choosing different SF and BW on energy consumption are evaluated for the first time.

3 Energy Model for LoRa N2N Communication

3.1 The Problem of Existing Energy Model

Existing works are usually based on the following energy consumption model:

$$
\begin{cases}
E_t = \left(E_T + E_{amp} \times d^\tau\right) \times k \\
E_r = E_R \times k
\end{cases}
\tag{1}
$$

where E_T is the basic energy consumption of the node (such as the basic energy consumption of the MCU control unit), E_{amp} is the energy consumption of the radio frequency circuit, and E_R is the energy consumption of the receiving node. These three parameters are related to the hardware performance of the circuit. d is the transmission distance, k is the number of transmitted bits, and τ is the attenuation factor of the channel with a value range of 2–4.

The premise of using this energy consumption model is: (1) The air transmission rate of the radio frequency hardware is constant; (2) And the power amplifier circuit of the radio frequency transmission can be continuously and linearly adjusted according to the transmission distance. Transmission power of most RF chips including LoRa can only be set to several gears. For example, TI's CC2530 only defines 17 adjustment gears for transmission power: −28 dbm–+4.5 dbm [19]. However, LoRa can dynamically adjust the rate by setting SF and BW and changing the transmission distance accordingly. At the same time, its settable transmission power gear is also discrete-the sub-GHz SX1276 can be divided into 20 transmission power levels (−4 dbm–+15 dbm) and 17 transmission power levels (+2 dbm–+17 dbm and 20 dbm [20]) according to different radio frequency pins; While the 2.4 GHz SX1280 has 32 transmit power levels (−18 dbm–+12.5 dbm [2]). Obviously, neither of the premises mentioned above is satisfied.

3.2 Improve Energy Model for LoRa N2N Communication

Considering that LoRa communication can dynamically adjust the transmission data rate [21], combined with adjustment of the discrete gear on the transmission power, the above energy consumption model formula can be redefined as follows:

$$
\begin{cases}
E_t = \left(P_T + P_{amp}\right) \times ToA \\
E_r = P_R \times ToA
\end{cases}
\tag{2}
$$

where P_T and P_R are the basic circuit power for sending and receiving, P_{amp} is the power of the radio frequency transmission circuit, and *ToA* is the air flight time of the data packet. In view of the preamble, CRC and spreading coefficients in wireless communication, it is more accurate and close to the actual situation to use Time on Air (ToA) to express the transmission time.

Calculation of P_{amp}. P_{amp} is the transmission power of the sending node. Under the same parameters, the longer the distance, the more the power is required. To determine the minimum transmission power required when the transmission distance is D, and considering the receiving sensitivity of LoRa modulation, the received signal energy needs to meet:

$$P_k g(d) \geq (S_{th}|sf, bw) \tag{3}$$

$g(d) = \lambda^2 / (4\pi d)^2$ represents the attenuation of the signal. For simplicity, this paper assumes that the environment is ideal, the gain of the receiving antenna is 1, and λ is the wavelength of the signal carrier. S_q represents the receiving sensitivity at a specific SF and BW, which is the lowest threshold of the signal reached. So the above formula can be transformed into:

$$P_k \geq \frac{S_{th} \times (4\pi d)^2}{\lambda^2} \tag{4}$$

Calculation of ToA. For LoRa communication, Time on Air for sending kbit data is the sum of preamble time and data load time:

$$T_{packet} = T_{preamble} + T_{payload} \tag{5}$$

According to the SX1280 data manual, the ToA calculation formula for 2.4 GHz LoRa is as follows (With CR as Legacy Coding Rate (ie. not Long Interleaving)):

$$T_{packet} = \begin{cases} \left[n_{preamble} + 6.25 + 8 + ceil\left(\frac{max(8PL - 4SF + 16CRC - 20H, 0)}{4 \times SF} \right) \times (CR + 4) \right] \times T_s \quad SF < 7 \\ \left[n_{preamble} + 4.25 + 8 + ceil\left(\frac{max(8PL - 4SF + 8 + 16CRC - 20H, 0)}{4 \times SF} \right) \times (CR + 4) \right] \times T_s \quad SF \in [7 - 10] \\ \left[n_{preamble} + 4.25 + 8 + ceil\left(\frac{max(8PL - 4SF + 8 + 16CRC - 20H, 0)}{4 \times (SF - 2)} \right) \times (CR + 4) \right] \times T_s \quad SF > 10 \end{cases} \tag{6}$$

where T_s is the symbol time, which satisfies:

$$T_s = 2^{SF} / BW \tag{7}$$

$n_{preamble}$ is the preamble length set by the system, and PL is the number of bytes in the payload. H is 0 in the explicit header and 1 in the implicit header. CR stands for encoding rate. The values of CR are 1, 2, 3 or 4, representing encoding rates of 4/5, 4/6, 4/7 or 4/8 respectively. CRC is the tail CRC check. If the check is turned on, $CRC = 1$, otherwise $CRC = 0$.

Combining the calculation of P_{amp} and ToA, we minimize the value of E_t by selecting SF and BW, which means making the transmission energy consumption of the sending node of LoRa reach the lowest. Obviously, it can be seen that for the receiving node, the receiving power consumption only depends on the ToA. The faster the rate, the smaller the ToA and the lower the receiving power consumption.

4   Performance Evaluation

We use Matlab to analyze the impact of SF and BW on energy consumption. Simulation parameters are set according to real hardware settings: packet payload length (PL) is 64, we choose the explicit header mode where H is 0, CRC is 1 to enable CRC verification, CR is 1 and coding rate is set to 4/5. Besides, we choose the corresponding SF (5–12) and BW (203 kHz, 406 kHz, 812 kHz, each 1625 kHz) to calculate the transmission energy consumption in different parameter settings. For ease of description, the form of (x, y) parameter group is used below to indicate that SF is currently set as x and BW is y.

In the energy consumption evaluation, according to the requirements for receiving sensitivity when setting different SF and BW values in Table 1, then, calculating the minimum transmitting power of the starting node satisfying the communication distance according to Eq. (4), we can see that, if the minimum transmit power required is greater than the maximum value that the system can set (12.5 dBm), the current (SF, BW) setting is invalid and cannot meet the communication distance.

First, we set the communication distance d to 3000 m, and calculated and analyzed the transmission energy consumption of each (SF, BW) setting (E_t), as shown in Fig. 2 and Fig. 3 below. Figure 2 shows the minimum transmission energy consumption of different (SF, BW) configurations under theoretical parameter conditions (The corresponding energy consumption can be calculated according to the minimum receiving sensitivity value required by formula (4)). It can be seen from the figure that: (1) For the same BW, with the increase of SF, the overall trend of transmission energy consumption first drops and then rises, and the minimum energy consumption value is between 7 and 8. This indicates that when the BW is constant, although increasing SF increases ToA, the receiving sensitivity will also be improved at the same time, and sequentially, a smaller transmission power can be set, thus making a contribution to reducing the overall transmission energy consumption. But as SF continues to increase, ToA will grow rapidly, thus leading to an increase in overall transmission energy consumption; (2) In case of the same SF, with the increase of BW, the overall trend of transmission energy consumption also goes downward. But what is interesting is that when the BW reaches the maximum value of 1625 kHz, energy consumption faces a great increase, for the receiving sensitivity decreases markedly and the increase in the transmission power will seriously affect the overall power consumption when the BW reaches 1625 kHz. The above two points show that under ideal parameter conditions, large or small SF and BW are not conducive to reducing power consumption.

Then we used the actual power parameters of the module composed of SX1280 chip and MCU to simulate. Here we not only considered the minimum transmission energy consumption required for data transmission, but also the basic energy consumption required for the normal operation of the transmission module. The result is shown in Fig. 3. It can be seen from the figure that: (1) In case of the same BW, the transmission energy consumption continues to increase with the increase of SF; (2) In case of the same SF, the transmission energy consumption also continues to increase as the BW decreases. Therefore, it can be concluded that the basic energy consumption of the module plays a decisive role in the overall energy consumption. For formula (2), when the basic circuit power (P_T) is significantly greater than the gear adjustment power of power amplifier (P_{amp}), the transmission power of LoRa communication is mainly affected by ToA.

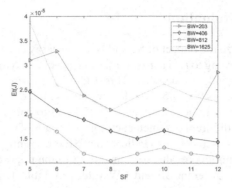

Fig. 2. Transmission power consumption using model parameters

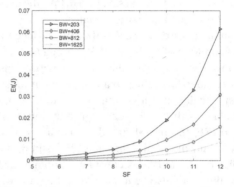

Fig. 3. Transmission power consumption using chip parameters

Secondly, the communication distance d was also set as 3000 m, but it was equally divided into 1–6 segments, and a LoRa node was added at each bisection point as a relay for forwarding data to form a multi-hop topology network. In case of different segments, two adjacent relay nodes set an (SF, BW) value that can minimize the transmission power according to the segment distance. Next, we counted and analyzed the energy (E_t) required by all nodes at different hops, as shown in Fig. 4 and Fig. 5 below.

Figure 4 shows the results under the theoretical parameter conditions. The best (SF, BW) value for different hop counts are marked on the top of the histogram. It can be seen from the figure that: (1) The overall transmission energy consumption will decrease as the number of hop counts increases; (2) Under the premise that the communication distance is 3000 m, the parameter SF of the lowest transmission energy consumption is 7 or 8, and the BW is 812 kHz, which is consistent with the result in Fig. 2 above. It is clear that the more the network hops, the lower the overall energy consumption of the network.

Figure 5 shows the results under the actual operating parameters of the module. We not only considered the minimum transmission power required to transmit data, but also took into account the receiving power of each node (including relay nodes and receiving nodes) and the basic circuit power of the module to maintain the normal operation. It can be seen from the figure that as the number of hops increases, the overall energy consumption continues to increase. Besides, the best (SF, BW) value for all hops is (5, 1625 kHz), which is consistent with the result shown in Fig. 3.

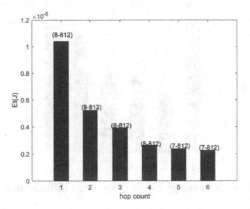

Fig. 4. Transmission power consumption under different hops (model parameters)

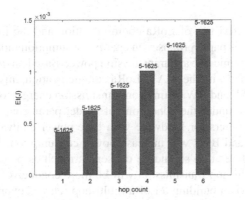

Fig. 5. Power consumption under different hops (chip parameters)

To further analyze the influence of distance and hop number on power consumption under actual working parameters, we fixed the communication distance as 10,000 m, and the remaining test conditions were consistent with the above working parameters. The total energy consumption for different hop counts was counted and analyzed, as shown in Fig. 6. It can be seen from the figure that: (1) The total energy consumption of the network is the smallest when the transmission is divided into three hops; (2) The energy consumption for different hop counts reaches the lowest when the SF is set to a lower value (5, 6 or 7) and the BW is set to 1625 kHz, which can ensure a faster transmission rate and reduce ToA.

In addition, comparing Fig. 5 with Fig. 6, we can come to an interesting conclusion: as the total transmission distance increases, the basic energy consumption of nodes is no longer a decisive factor that determines the total energy consumption of the network, which will also be affected by the transmission distance and the number of hops between single-hop transceivers.

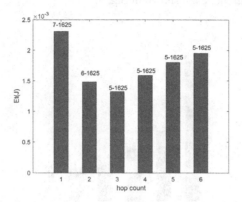

Fig. 6. Total energy consumption under different hops

5 Conclusion

Considering the characteristics of LoRa communication and the limitations of actual hardware conditions, this paper proposes an energy consumption model suitable for discrete adjustment of dynamic rate and transmission power. Based on the energy consumption model and combined with the ToA of LoRa communication, this paper analyzes the influence of different SF and BW settings on transmission energy consumption, as well as energy consumption under the conditions of model parameters and actual parameters. For model parameters (or hardware with base power equivalent to PA power), larger or smaller SFs and BWs will increase power consumption. For actual parameters, a faster rate configuration should be chosen as much as possible to shorten the ToA. Besides, the multi-hop transmission will be more conducive to reducing overall energy consumption when building a LoRa multi-hop relay network, especially when the distance is long. These conclusions can not only provide a reference for 2.4 GHz LoRa-based self-organizing networks but also be used for the potential applications of sub-GHz LoRa-based self-organizing networks.

Acknowledgement. This work was supported by the National Nature Science Foundation of China (Grant number: 61902167, 61871204, 61901207), the Nature Science Foundation of Fujian Province, China (Grant number: 2021J011015), Digit Fujian Internet-of-Things Laboratory of Environmental Monitoring Research Fund (Fujian Normal University) (Grant number: 202006). Educational Research Projects of Young and Middle-aged Teachers in Fujian Province (Grant number: JAT200432).

References

1. LoRa Alliance incorporated: LoRaWAN Specification V1.0.2. LoRa Alliance incorporated, San Ramon (2016)

2. Semtech: SX1280/SX1281 Data Sheet Rev 2.0, February 2018. https://www.semtech.com/uploads/documents/DS_SX1280-1_V2.0.pdf
3. Sandoval, R.M., Garcia-Sanchez, A.-J., et al.: Optimizing and updating LoRa communication parameters: a machine learning approach. IEEE Trans. Netw. Serv. Manage. **16**(3), 884–895 (2019)
4. Qin, Z., Liu, Y., et al.: Performance analysis of clustered LoRa networks. IEEE Trans. Veh. Technol. **68**(8), 7616–7629 (2019)
5. Georgiou, O., Raza, U.: Low power wide area network analysis: can LoRa scale? IEEE Wirel. Commun. Lett. **6**(2), 162–165 (2017)
6. Liando, J.C., Gamage, A., et al.: Known and unknown facts of LoRa: experiences from a large-scale measurement study. ACM Trans. Sens. Netw. **15**(2), 1–35 (2019)
7. Mekki, K., Bajic, E., et al.: A comparative study of LPWAN technologies for large-scale IoT deployment. ICT Express **5**(1), 1–7 (2019)
8. Su, B., Qin, Z., et al.: Energy efficient resource allocation for uplink LoRa networks. IEEE Trans. Commun. **68**(8), 4960–4972 (2018)
9. Bouguera, T., Diouris, J.-F., et al.: Energy consumption modeling for communicating sensors using LoRa technology. In: IEEE Conference on Antenna Measurements and Applications, pp. 1–4. IEEE, Vasteras (2018)
10. Goldoni, E., Prando, L., Vizziello, A., et al.: Experimental data set analysis of RSSI-based indoor and outdoor localization in LoRa networks. Internet Technol. Lett. **2**(1), 1–6 (2017)
11. Zhang, X., Zhang, M., et al.: A low-power wide-area network information monitoring system by combining NB-IoT and LoRa. IEEE Internet Things J. **6**(1), 590–598 (2019)
12. Madeo, D., Pozzebon, A., et al.: A low-cost unmanned surface vehicle for pervasive water quality monitoring. IEEE Trans. Instrum. Meas. **69**(4), 1433–1444 (2020)
13. Wu, F., Wu, T., et al.: An Internet-of-Things (IoT) network system for connected safety and health monitoring applications. Sensors **19**(1), 1–21 (2019)
14. de Castro Tomé, M., Nardelli, P.H.J., et al.: Long-range low-power wireless networks and sampling strategies in electricity metering. IEEE Trans. Ind. Electron. **66**(2), 1629–1637 (2019)
15. Zhang, H.-S., Li, L., et al.: Development and test of manhole cover monitoring device using LoRa and accelerometer. IEEE Trans. Instrum. Meas. **98**(5), 2570–2580 (2020)
16. Lin, S., Ying, Z., et al.: Design and implementation of location and activity monitoring system based on LoRa. Ksii Trans. Internet Inf. Syst. **13**(4), 1812–1824 (2019)
17. Janssen, T., BniLam, N., et al.: LoRa 2.4 GHz communication link and range. Sensors **20**(16), 1–12 (2020)
18. Andersen, F.R., Ballal, K.D., Petersen, M.N., Ruepp, S.: Ranging Capabilities of LoRa 2.4 GHz. In: 2020 IEEE 6th World Forum on Internet of Things (WF-IoT), pp. 1–5, June 2020
19. Texas Instruments Incorporated: CC2530 Data Sheet, February 2011. http://www.ti.com.cn/cn/lit/ds/symlink/cc2530.pdf
20. Semtech: SX1276-7-8-9 Data Sheet Rev 7.0, May 2020. https://www.semtech.com/uploads/documents/DS_SX1276_V7.0.pdf
21. Ayoub, W., Samhat, A.E., et al.: Internet of mobile things: overview of LoRaWAN, DASH7, and NB-IoT in LPWANs standards and supported mobility. IEEE Commun. Surv. Tutor. **21**(2), 1561–1581 (2019)

FSE-MV: Compressed Domain Video Information Assisted Hybrid Real-Time Vehicle Speed Estimation

Yangjie Cao[1], Qi Wu[1], Bo Zhang[1(✉)], Zhi Liu[2], and Junfeng Li[1]

[1] Zhengzhou University, Zhengzhou, China
{caoyj,zhangbo2050,lijfimp}@zzu.edu.cn, wq1996@gs.zzu.edu.cn
[2] The University of Electro-Communications, Chofu, Japan
liu@ieee.org

Abstract. Vehicular speed estimation is a vital component in intelligent transportation systems. With the recent development of smart cameras and computer vision technologies, video-based vehicle speed estimations have been widely studied. However, facing the huge volume of pixel-domain information, conventional methods are computationally intensive, and often fail to deliver estimation results in real-time. In this paper, we target the video-based real-time vehicle speed estimation problem. For data volume reduction, we utilize the compressed domain video information and propose a hybrid real-time vehicle speed estimation method termed FSE-MV. FSE-MV first segments vehicles using motion vector (MV) information in the compressed domain. The pixel information of the segmented vehicles is then retrieved through decoding. Feature points of each vehicle are extracted for multi-object matching and pixel domain displacement calculation. The speed of the target vehicle is finally calculated through spatial coordinate transformation. Experiments over the public dataset demonstrate that FSE-MV is able to process 1080p traffic video data in real-time (~30 frames per second) with a high estimation accuracy (~93.09%).

Keywords: Speed estimation · ITS · Feature matching · Compressed domain

1 Introduction

Vehicle speed estimation is one of the vital components of intelligent transportation systems (ITS) [1,2]. Effective and accurate real-time speed estimation offers unparalleled capabilities for ITS to subsequently monitor and diminish traffic accidents caused by speeding, thereby fully utilize traffic infrastructures as well as protect commuters' assets and lives.

This work is supported by Collaborative Innovation Major Project of Zhengzhou under Grant 20XTZX06013, the Research Foundation Plan in Higher Education Institutions of Henan Province under Grant 20A520037.

© ICST Institute for Computer Sciences, Social Informatics and Telecommunications Engineering 2022
Published by Springer Nature Switzerland AG 2022. All Rights Reserved
C. T. Calafate et al. (Eds.): MONAMI 2021, LNICST 418, pp. 100–114, 2022.
https://doi.org/10.1007/978-3-030-94763-7_8

Current mainstream vehicle speed estimation systems often involve sensors such as inductive loop detectors, laser meters, and Doppler radars [3]. The inductive loop detectors require complex installation and maintenance. Laser meters and Doppler radars often incur a high cost and suffer from environmental restrictions.

With the advancement of digital cameras in terms of both data quality and cost-effectiveness, as well as the development of computer-vision techniques, both academia and industry shift their attentions to video-based speed estimation [3–9]. It is inevitable for all video-based vehicle speed estimation techniques to first detect the vehicles from captured frames. Vehicle detection is often addressed by either modeling [4,9], background subtraction [5,6,8] or Neural Networks [7,10,11]. Vehicle matching is then performed to calculate the pixel displacement of the vehicle. Finally, the pixel displacement is converted into real-world position displacement for speed calculation. Depending on the camera deployed, the method of spatial coordinate conversion can be divided into monocular-based approaches [4,5] and stereo-based approaches [7–9]. Monocular cameras require additional parameters to obtain the spatial position of objects in the video. A binocular camera, simulating human eyes, can itself retrieve the spatial position of the video object, but doubles the amount of video data compared to the monocular camera.

Video data is generally encoded into the compressed form prior to transmission or storage [12–15]. Traditional video analysis methods need to scan every pixel of each video frame for object detection. The whole video therefore must be fully decoded for pixel information retrieval. For traffic surveillance servers where multiple incoming live video streams are to be processed, decoding and per-pixel analysis often lead to an unbearably long delay. In contrast, compressed domain methods do not require full video decoding by avoiding the pixel-level calculation of the entire frame for every frame of the video [15–20]. However besides the absence of texture information, compressed domain information also often exhibits high encoding noises. We, therefore, consider combining the strengths of both compressed domain and pixel domain information to achieve fast and accurate speed estimation. In this paper, we propose Fast Speed Estimation based on MV (FSE-MV). FSE-MV utilizes compressed domain information for vehicle segmentation, to avoid per-pixel processing. We focus only on the moving part and not the whole frame. Contributions of this work are summarized as follows:

- We propose FSE-MV, a hybrid real-time vehicle speed estimation method with the highly accuracy and efficiency. The method uses compressed domain information to assist the pixel domain to reduce the computational complexity.
- FSE-MV includes an effective denoising method, region of interest (ROI) segmentation and object track base on the compressed domain, feature matching base on compressed and pixel domains, and a commonly coordinate translation.
- This paper tests FSE-MV on real-world surveillance video data, confirming that the method, running on a personal laptop with modest computational capacity, can process 1080p video format and perform estimation at 93.09% accuracy, with the processing speed of up to 30fps.

The remainder of this article is as follows: In Sect. 2, we discuss the related work. In Sect. 3, we introduce FSE-MV in detail. In Sect. 4, we demonstrate and analyze the experiment result. The conclusion is placed in Sect. 5.

2   Related Works

In this section, we will introduce compressed domain segmentation approaches and the pixel-based vehicle speed estimation methods respectively.

2.1   Compressed Domain Target Segmentation

The compressed domain methods require only partial decoding of the sparse cues such as motion vectors (MV), transform coefficients, quantization parameters (QP), macro-block partition modes, etc. [16]. Poppe et al. [21] proposed a background model based on the macro-block (MB) sizes within a frame, predicting that moving objects generally involve more bits in MB than the background. However, the number of encoded bits of complex regions is also higher, affecting the foreground segmentation accuracy. Ma et al. [22] introduced a motion target detection algorithm. The algorithm uses both MV and QP as features. They construct a Markov Random Field (MRF) model for foreground and background differentiation. The system only works when *QP adaptation* is enabled at the encoder. Chen et al. [23] proposed to use an eight-parameter model to compute frame-level global motion and compensate the MV field before performing motion segmentation. Their method shows good accuracy for videos with moving cameras. However, the proposed iterative approach accumulates error over time.

2.2   Vehicle Speed Estimation

Most speed estimation methods involve a background/foreground segmentation step to detect region of interest, such as modeling [4], background subtraction [6,8], and Neural Networks [7].Vehicle speeds are measure by tracking vehicle features. Luvizon et al. [4] proposed to use *Motion History Image* (MHI) to detect vehicles and use the *FIND-HILLS* routine to determine vehicle boundaries. They then used a license plate detector to locate the license plate. Speed is calculated by tracking the features of the license plate. Afifah et al. [6] used background subtraction to determine the vehicle location and form the vehicle contour. They first acquire the complete background by accumulating images without vehicles. Then the background is Gaussian filtered to obtain the foreground mask. Morphological filtering is performed to remove the noise from the foreground mask to form the target profile. Vehicles are then tracked from the distance of centers from one frame to another frame. Yang et al. [7] used the stereo cameras for speed estimation. Their system uses an optimized single shot multi-box detector network that can efficiently detect license plates, which are then used for vehicle matching as well as speed calculation. Bouziady et al. [8]

presented a technique to estimate vehicle speed on the highway using stereo images. They use stereo cameras to capture images and determine the vehicle by subtracting the background. Finally, they use feature point matching to calculate the speed.

Most existing video-based speed estimation methods require locating vehicles in the pixel domain of the entire frame. We instead consider using compressed domain information to reduce the complexity introduced by the pixel domain. MVs exist in a variety of standards with commonality. Therefore, FSE-MV using MV is more versatile. Our analysis in the compressed domain avoids iteration and is confined only in adjacent frames. In this case, the error accumulation is also avoided.

3   FSE-MV: Fast Speed Estimation Based on MV

In this section, we describe the proposed FSE-MV in detail.

Table 1. Major symbols used in this paper

Symbol	Denotation
MV_i	The motion vector of MB_i
$MVx_i \& MVy_i$	The horizontal and vertical coordinate of MV_i
E_i	The energy of MV_i
ηMV	Projection motion vector
H	Homography matrix
α	Feature point removal threshold
S_i	Displacement of a matching pair of points
V	Speed of current frame

3.1   Overview of FSE-MV

The overall process of FSE-MV is summarized in Fig. 1. MVs of a given video are first extracted and pre-processed for target segmentation and ROI determination. ROIs are then tracked across adjacent frames to obtain ROI pairs. Feature points of ROI pairs are extracted and matched. Through coordinate transformation, we map the pixel-level displacement to real-world displacement. The actual speed of objects can then be calculated.

FSE-MV includes the following steps: MV extraction, MV pre-processing, target detection and segmentation, target tracking, and speed estimation with coordinate transformation. We next describe each step in detail. Major symbols used in this work are summarized in Table 1.

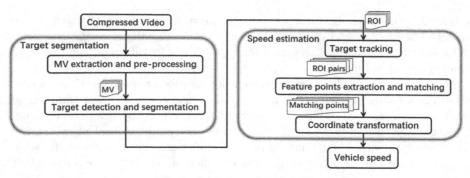

Fig. 1. Overview of FSE-MV.

3.2 MV Extraction

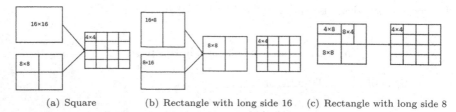

(a) Square   (b) Rectangle with long side 16   (c) Rectangle with long side 8

Fig. 2. Example of macro-block normalization

Motion vector (MV) is a two-dimensional vector with a horizontal parameter x and a vertical parameter y in the compressed domain. In the widely applied H.264 coding standard, the smallest coding, macro-block (MB), is assigned with one MV. The sizes of MBs are adaptive from 16×16 through 4×4 pixels. FSE-MV uses FFmpeg [24,25] to extract the MVs, before MB normalization and MV replication. We normalize the sizes of MBs to 4×4. A square MB is directly split into 4×4 blocks as in Fig. 2(a). Otherwise, the MB is first divided into square MBs before splitting, as shown in Fig. 2(b) and 2(c). All MVs of little MBs are given by large MBs. The extraction result is called the MV field.

3.3 MV Pre-processing

MVs are mainly generated for coding efficiency. The MV field is therefore severely affected by noise. We propose to utilize the continuous and smooth property of actual motion for noise removal. The pre-processing of MVs includes three steps: filtering, MV spatial noise removal, and MV temporal noise removal.

Filtering. FSE-MV filters the MV field to remove zero-MV. Zero-MV is the MV with 0 energy. The energy of MV_i is defined as E_i, given by Eq. (1). MBs with zero-MV are skipped in the subsequent processing.

$$E_i = (MVx_i)^2 + (MVy_i)^2. \tag{1}$$

MV Spatial Noise Removal. FSE-MV uses spatial noise removal to eliminate isolated MVs, since they rarely represent actual moving objects. The spatial noise removal process is shown in Algorithm 1. For each MV in the MV field, if for all its surrounding MVs, less than half (50%) are zero-MV, then this MV is deemed useful MV, and is added into the result (lines 2–7).

Algorithm 1. MV Spatial Noise Removal

INPUT: MV field F

OUTPUT: Spatially denoised MV field F'

1: $F' = \emptyset$
2: **for** $f \in F$ **do**
3:     S_f is the set of surrounding blocks of f
4:     **if** count($i \in S_f \& E_i = 0$)$\leq 50\%$ len(S_f) **then**
5:         $F' = F' \cup \{f\}$
6:     **end if**
7: **end for**
8: **return** F'

MV Temporal Noise Removal. FSE-MV uses Algorithm 2 to remove residual fake MVs through temporal analysis. Each block f is reversely mapped to location b_f of the preceding frame according to its MV_f (lines 3–4). If b_f has non-zero MV, MB f is considered as a useful block and stored in F_t'' (lines 5–6). Otherwise, we map position of f to location b_f in the subsequent frame (lines 8–9). If b_f has non-zero MV, f is considered as a useful block and stored in F_t'' (lines 10–12). The returned MV field is then used for motion analysis.

Algorithm 2. MV Temporal Noise Removal

INPUT: Previous frameF_{t-1}', Current frame F_t', Next frame F_{t+1}'

OUTPUT: Temporal denoised MV field F_t''

1: $F_t'' = \emptyset$
2: **for** $f \in F_t'$ **do**
3:     Calculate the best match block $b_f \in F_{t-1}'$
4:     b_f's coordinates $=f$'s coordinates $+MV_f$
5:     **if** $E_{b_f} \neq 0$ **then**
6:         $F_t'' = F_t'' \cup \{f\}$
7:     **else**
8:         Calculate the best match block $b_f \in F_{t+1}'$
9:         b_f's coordinates $=f$'s coordinates $-MV_f$
10:         **if** $E_{b_f} \neq 0$ **then**
11:             $F_t'' = F_t'' \cup \{f\}$
12:         **end if**
13:     **end if**
14: **end for**
15: **return** F_t''

3.4   Target Detection and Segmentation

FSE-MV now determines the region of moving objects in each frame based on these MVs. A binary mask is first constructed to marks the pre-processed MVs (set to white) and isolates vehicles from the background.

FSE-MV performs morphological filtering on the vehicle mask to remove voids or gaps and then checks the connectivity of the white area to form the ROI. FSE-MV obtains pixel domain information of the ROI and analyzes only this information.

3.5   Target Tracking

Algorithm 3. Target Tracking

INPUT: ROI $A(x, y, w, h)$, Next frame ROI $M(m_1, m_2...m_i)$
OUTPUT: Tracking target m_t
1: $IOU_{max} = 0$
2: Calculate ηMV by Eq. (3)
3: Move A with ηMV to obtain $A'(x', y', w, h)$
4: $x' = x - \eta MV_x$
5: $y' = y - \eta MV_y$
6: **for** $m_i \in M$ **do**
7:     $IOU_{max} = Max\{IOU_{max}, IOU(A', m_i)\}$
8:     **if** IOU_{max} is changed **then**
9:         $m_t = m_i$
10:     **end if**
11: **end for**
12: **if** $IOU_{max} = 0$ **then**
13:     **for** $m_i \in M$ **do**
14:         Calculate the center-of-mass distance between A' and m_i
15:         **if** distance is smaller than current minimum value **then**
16:             $m_t = m_i$
17:         **end if**
18:     **end for**
19: **end if**
20: **return** m_t

Tracking. The ROI of each vehicle needs to be tracked across multiple frames before speed calculation. The tracking is carried out as Algorithm 3. Among the input parameters, (x, y) is the upper-left corner coordinates of the ROI, w and h are ROI's width and height. M contains all ROIs in the subsequent frame. MVs in A are synthesized as the projected $MV(\eta MV)$ in lines 2. Then A is moved by ηMV to the next frame to get A' (lines 3–5). A' is then matched with each ROI in this frame by the IOU method (lines 6–11). The one with the largest intersection ratio is used as the tracking object of A (lines 7–9). If there is no intersecting target, the algorithm sets the spatially closest one as the tracking object (lines 12–19). Let N denote the number of MVs in the ROI, the IOU and ηMV formulas are as follows:

$$IOU(A, B) = \frac{A \bigcap B}{A \bigcup B}, \tag{2}$$

$$\eta MV(x, y) = \frac{\sum_{i=1}^{N} MV_i(x, y)}{N}. \tag{3}$$

Feature Point Matching. FSE-MV obtains the displacement of the same target between frames by feature point matching. We utilize SURF [26], a common feature matching approach, instead of using the ROI center to calculate speed. Compared with other feature point description operators, SURF remains stable in translation and rotation [8,9,27].

The matching is carried out as follows. Feature points are extracted from the ROI. Euclidean distance of feature points is calculated. FSE-MV uses the nearest neighbor distance ratio(NNDR) matching strategy [26] to obtain the best match pairs. Matching points are ranked by the ratio between the shortest and the second shortest distances. If this ratio is less than a preset threshold, they are retained as good matching points. The threshold value is set to 0.7 according to [26]. The tracking is considered failed, if no such matching point is found.

3.6   Speed Estimation with Coordinate Transformation

Coordinate Transformation. By feature matching, we get the matched pixel points. Matching points describe the pixel-level displacement of the vehicle. For real-world speed calculation, FSE-MV requires a coordinate transformation to obtain the actual displacement. FSE-MV uses the homography matrix for coordinate transformation. The homography matrix H may be obtained by associating four points in the image to known coordinates in the real-world plane [4]. Let real-world position coordinates are $(x', y', 1)$ and the pixel coordinates are $(x, y, 1)$, then the conversion equation is:

$$\begin{bmatrix} x' \\ y' \\ 1 \end{bmatrix} = H \begin{bmatrix} x \\ y \\ 1 \end{bmatrix}, H = \begin{bmatrix} h_{11} & h_{12} & h_{13} \\ h_{21} & h_{22} & h_{23} \\ h_{31} & h_{32} & h_{33} \end{bmatrix}. \tag{4}$$

We set $h_{33} = 1$ for H normalization. The other 8 parameters in the matrix H are calculated by solving eight equations through at least two matching point pairs. Matrix H is calculated by marked points in advance.

The coordinates of the matching points belong to the current ROI. The matrix H is for the frame. To unify the coordinate system, coordinates need to be compensated. Let $P_{1i}(x_{1i}, y_{1i})$ be one matching point in ROI. The compensation value (x_0^{ROI}, y_0^{ROI}) is the point of the upper-left corner of the ROI in the frame. The pixel coordinates in the frame are therefore $(x_{1i} + x_0^{ROI}, y_{1i} + y_0^{ROI})$. The real-world coordinates $P_{1r}(x_{1r}, y_{1r})$ then are calculated by Eq. (4).

We get the real-world points of tracking object $p_{1r}(x_{1r}, y_{1r})$ and $p_{2r}(x_{2r}, y_{2r})$ similarly. The real-world displacement can then be calculated by:

$$S = \sqrt{(x_{1r} - x_{2r})^2 + (y_{1r} - y_{2r})^2}. \tag{5}$$

Speed Estimation. The obtained matching points contain noise, i.e., incorrect matches, leading to incorrect displacement calculation. FSE-MV uses trimmed mean to eliminate the effect of incorrect values. We calculate and sort the speeds of all matching points. Then the index of the median of this list is found as *med*. Suppose the number of speeds is *length*. FSE-MV sets a threshold α for extreme value removal. FSE-MV retains the speed values in the interval $[med - \alpha length, med + \alpha length]$. After this, we calculate the instantaneous speed of the vehicle V as follows:

$$V = \frac{\sum_i^N S_i}{Nt}, \tag{6}$$

where S_i is displacements of matching points in current ROI, N is the number of retained displacements, t is obtained from the frames per second.

Our final result should be the average speed of the vehicle over a period of time. So FSE-MV keeps tracking the target vehicle and stops tracking at the stop line, and the average of all estimation speeds is calculated as our result.

4   Experiment

This section presents the results of our experiments. We first introduce the experiment setup including hardware environment and dataset, followed by a step-wise algorithm demonstration, before discussing quantitative results.

4.1   Setup

Dataset and Environment. The system was tested on full HD quality sequences [4] with the true value of vehicle speed measured by a high precision system of inductive loop detectors. This dataset is annotated with the ground truth displacement. We used two environments for comparison experiments. The CPU environment consists of one 2.8 GHz Intel Core i7 CPU with 8 GB of RAM. The GPU environment includes one RTX 2080Ti graphic card with 12 GB of RAM.

Evaluation Metrics and Comparison Schemes. We evaluate the delay and accuracy of FSE-MV. Delay is defined as the average estimation time required per frame. As for accuracy, an acceptable measurement should be within the $[-3, +2]$ km/h error interval according to [4]. The results lying within this interval are therefore considered to be accurate. For comparison schemes, we substitute *compressed-domain vehicle segmentation* of FSE-MV with YOLOv4 [10] and Fast R-CNN [11] to generate comparing schemes FSE-YOLO and FSE-RCNN. We further compared FSE-MV with Luvizon et al.'s method [4] and Yang et al.'s method [7].

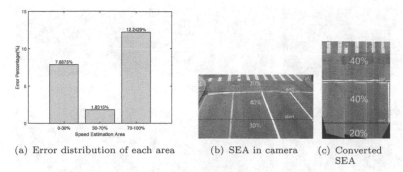

<table>
<tr><td>(a) Error distribution of each area</td><td>(b) SEA in camera</td><td>(c) Converted SEA</td></tr>
</table>

Fig. 3. Set speed estimation area

Speed Estimation Area. Due to the dips of the camera, there may be an area of the captured frame that is more suitable for speed estimation. The optimal speed estimation area (SEA) can be determined by learning. We use the instantaneous speed of the vehicle in different areas to find the mean error of the speed in that area. By continuously dividing the areas, we obtain an area with a minimum mean error for the sequences. As shown in Fig. 3, the average error in the middle part is smaller. As in Fig. 3(c), we converted the original image to show that the scale in the original image is unevenly distributed in reality. This situation is caused by the dips of the camera. This may be one of the reasons why the error in the middle part is smaller. For the sequences used in this paper, we set the bottom of the middle area as the start line and the top as the stop line as in Fig. 3(b).

4.2 Step-Wise Demonstration

In this section, we demonstrate the per-step workflow of FSE-MV. MV noises can be clearly observed in Fig. 4(a), 4(b), and 4(c), where frame 4, frame 30 and frame 165 represent the case of no-vehicle, single-vehicle, and multi-vehicles respectively. FSE-MV performs spatial and temporal noise removal to obtain clean MV maps as shown in Fig. 4(d), 4(e), and 4(f).

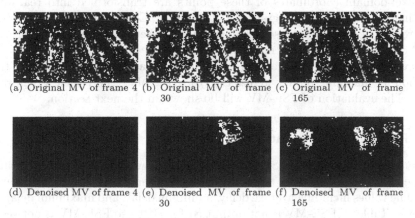

(a) Original MV of frame 4 (b) Original MV of frame 30 (c) Original MV of frame 165

(d) Denoised MV of frame 4 (e) Denoised MV of frame 30 (f) Denoised MV of frame 165

Fig. 4. The effect of MV noise removal

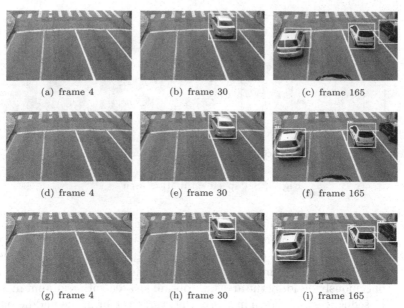

(a) frame 4	(b) frame 30	(c) frame 165
(d) frame 4	(e) frame 30	(f) frame 165
(g) frame 4	(h) frame 30	(i) frame 165

Fig. 5. The effect of vehicle segmentation. (a–c) FSE-MV. (d–f) FSE-YOLO. (g–i) FSE-RCNN

We then segment the vehicle using the MV filed. As can be seen from Fig. 5, the neural network approaches, learning pixel information, result in more reliable segmentation. However, FSE-MV avoids full decoding and thus results in much faster segmentation, as will be discussed later. In our experiment, if its distance is closer than 0.7 times distance of the second nearest neighbor, a matching pair is detected. Matching points are shown in Fig. 6. FSE-MV uses the trimmed mean to remove outliers. We studied the effect of different settings of α. From Fig. 7, it is found that setting 30% has the smallest error. So we set α to 30% for the experiment.

After two ROIs of the same car are matched according to matching points, the pixel-domain coordinates of these points are transformed into real-world coordinates using the homography matrix H. FSE-MV calculates the H for each road lane to facilitate such transform. We are now able to retrieve real-world displacements of these matching points.

Now that we have obtained the real-world displacement together with time duration for matching points, we use Eq. (6) to calculate the vehicle's real-world speed. The evaluation of FSE-MV will be shown in the next section.

4.3   Performance Evaluation

We first analyze the delay of FSE-MV. Figure 8(a) shows the mean delay per frame. The delay is composed of the target segmentation part and the speed estimation part. The values including average delay, minimum delay, and maximum delay are shown in Table 2. FSE-MV is not optimized for GPU, so FSE-MV is not tested

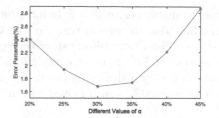

Fig. 6. SURF feature points matching

Fig. 7. Estimation error vs. different values of α

in the GPU environment. Since FSE-RCNN has a delay of more than one second in the CPU environment, we choose not to show it. FSE-MV's speed estimation method has the lowest delay. The delay of the speed estimation depends on the area of the ROI. ROI size in Table 2 shows the percentage of ROI against the frame. FSE-MV has a small ROI size and reduces the time delay.

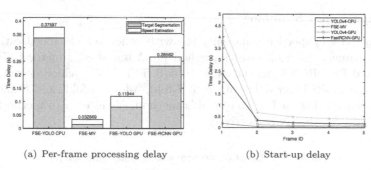

(a) Per-frame processing delay   (b) Start-up delay

Fig. 8. Real-time performance

Table 2. Time delay comparison

Method	Target segmentation (s)	Speed estimation (s)	Total (s)			ROI size (%)
			Min	Mean	Max	
FSE-YOLO CPU	0.3364	0.0396	0.3533	0.3760	0.4049	9.7750
FSE-YOLO GPU	0.0793	0.0401	0.0952	0.1194	0.1379	
FSE-RCNN GPU	0.2325	0.0331	0.2417	0.2656	0.3042	8.3578
FSE-MV	0.0145	0.0184	0.0212	0.0329	0.0387	6.8411

We also compared the start-up delay, as shown in Fig. 8(b). Start-up is performed only once, so we compared the start-up delay separately. Neural network based algorithms require model loading and thus need more time for the start-up.

Furthermore, we calculated the speed of the vehicles in the sequences. The results are shown in Fig. 9. FSE-MV is able to reach an accuracy of 93.09%.

The estimation error is mainly introduced by the instability of the feature point matching due to camera tilt. We compared FSE-YOLO and FSE-RCNN under the same condition, results show that they have higher accuracy than FSE-MV. Their target box is more complete, allowing more accurate feature points for matching when calculating the velocity. But FSE-MV still achieves an accuracy rate of over 90%, which is well within the acceptable range.

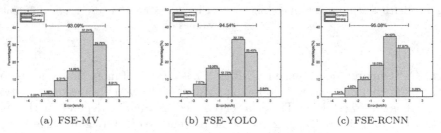

(a) FSE-MV   (b) FSE-YOLO   (c) FSE-RCNN

Fig. 9. Speed estimation error distribution

4.4 Experiment Summary

We compared the speed estimation error with other vehicle speed estimation methods, namely, Luvizon et al.'s method [4], Yang et al.'s method [7], FSE-YOLO, and FSE-RCNN, as shown in Table 3. FSE-MV's achieved comparable error with a much lower delay of up to 7-fold, 5-fold, 4-fold, and 8-fold delay reduction comparing to Luvizon et al.'s method, Yang et al.'s method, FSE-YOLO, and FSE-RCNN respectively.

Table 3. Estimation accuracy and delay summary.

Method	RMSE (km/h)	Max error (km/h)	Delay (ms)
Luvizon et al. [4]	1.36	[−4.68,+6.00]	244.8(4.1FPS)
Yang et al. [7]	0.65	[−1.6,+1.1]	185.2(5.4FPS)
FSE-YOLO	0.94	[−3.2,+2.93]	119.4(8.3FPS)
FSE-RCNN	1.25	[−3.69,+2.49]	265.6(3.7FPS)
FSE-MV	1.15	[−2.85,+2.98]	32.9(30.4FPS)

5   Conclusion

In this paper, we studied the video-based vehicle speed estimation method. To address the computational intensiveness of traditional pixel-information based approaches, we propose a hybrid method called FSE-MV that utilizes both pixel domain information and compressed domain information. The system was tested on full HD quality video. Experiments show that FSE-MV is able to achieve an average estimation accuracy of 93.09%, with an overall estimation delay of about 32.9 ms.

References

1. Zhou, P., Chen, X., Liu, Z., Braud, T., Hui, P., Kangasharju, J.: DRLE: decentralized reinforcement learning at the edge for traffic light control in the IoV. IEEE Trans. Intell. Transp. Syst. **22**(4), 2262–2273 (2020)
2. Wu, C., Liu, Z., Liu, F., Yoshinaga, T., Ji, Y., Li, J.: Collaborative learning of communication routes in edge-enabled multi-access vehicular environment. IEEE Trans. Cogn. Commun. Netw. **6**(4), 1155–1165 (2020)
3. Llorca, D.F., Martínez, A.H., Daza, I.G.: Vision-based vehicle speed estimation for its: a survey. arXiv preprint arXiv:2101.06159 (2021)
4. Luvizon, D.C., Nassu, B.T., Minetto, R.: A video-based system for vehicle speed measurement in urban roadways. IEEE Trans. Intell. Transp. Syst. **18**(6), 1393–1404 (2016)
5. Famouri, M., Azimifar, Z., Wong, A.: A novel motion plane-based approach to vehicle speed estimation. IEEE Trans. Intell. Transp. Syst. **20**(4), 1237–1246 (2018)
6. Afifah, F., Nasrin, S., Mukit, A.: Vehicle speed estimation using image processing. J. Adv. Res. Appl. Mech. **48**(1), 9–16 (2019)
7. Yang, L., Li, M., Song, X., Xiong, Z., Hou, C., Qu, B.: Vehicle speed measurement based on binocular stereovision system. IEEE Access **7**, 106628–106641 (2019)
8. El Bouziady, A., Thami, R.O.H., Ghogho, M., Bourja, O., El Fkihi, S.: Vehicle speed estimation using extracted surf features from stereo images. In: 2018 International Conference on Intelligent Systems and Computer Vision (ISCV), pp. 1–6. IEEE (2018)
9. Jiang, J., Mi, C., Wu, M., Zhang, Z., Feng, Y.: Study on a real-time vehicle speed measuring method at highway toll station. In: 2019 International Conference on Sensing and Instrumentation in IoT Era (ISSI), pp. 1–5. IEEE (2019)
10. Bochkovskiy, A., Wang, C.Y., Liao, H.Y.M.: Yolov4: optimal speed and accuracy of object detection. arXiv preprint arXiv:2004.10934 (2020)
11. Girshick, R.: Fast r-CNN. In: Proceedings of the IEEE International Conference on Computer Vision, pp. 1440–1448 (2015)
12. Guo, C., Cui, Y., Liu, Z.: Optimal multicast of tiled 360 VR video. IEEE Wireless Commun. Lett. **8**(1), 145–148 (2018)
13. Liu, Z., Cheung, G., Chakareski, J., Ji, Y.: Multiple description coding and recovery of free viewpoint video for wireless multi-path streaming. IEEE J. Sel. Top. Sign. Process. **9**(1), 151–164 (2014)
14. Zhou, H., Wang, X., Liu, Z., Ji, Y., Yamada, S.: Resource allocation for svc streaming over cooperative vehicular networks. IEEE Trans. Veh. Technol. **67**(9), 7924–7936 (2018)
15. Liu, Z., et al.: Point cloud video streaming in 5G systems and beyond: challenges and solutions. In: IEEE Network (2021)
16. Babu, R.V., Tom, M., Wadekar, P.: A survey on compressed domain video analysis techniques. Multimedia Tools Appl. **75**(2), 1043–1078 (2014). https://doi.org/10.1007/s11042-014-2345-z
17. Jaballah, S., Larabi, M.C.: Fast object detection in H264/AVC and HEVC compressed domains for video surveillance. In: 2019 8th European Workshop on Visual Information Processing (EUVIP), pp. 123–128. IEEE (2019)
18. Zhao, L., He, Z., Cao, W., Zhao, D.: Real-time moving object segmentation and classification from HEVC compressed surveillance video. IEEE Trans. Circuits Syst. Video Technol. **28**(6), 1346–1357 (2016)

19. Zhang, B., Liu, Z., Chan, S.H.G., Cheung, G.: Collaborative wireless freeview video streaming with network coding. IEEE Trans. Multimedia **18**(3), 521–536 (2016)
20. Liu, Z., Zhan, C., Cui, Y., Wu, C., Hu, H.: Robust edge computing in UAV systems via scalable computing and cooperative computing. IEEE Wireless Commun. **28**(5), 36–42 (2021)
21. Poppe, C., De Bruyne, S., Paridaens, T., Lambert, P., Van de Walle, R.: Moving object detection in the H 264/AVC compressed domain for video surveillance applications. J. Vis. Commun. Image Represent. **20**(6), 428–437 (2009)
22. Ma, M., Song, H.: Effective moving object detection in H 264/AVC compressed domain for video surveillance. Multimedia Tools Appl. **78**(24), 35195–35209 (2019)
23. Chen, Y.M., Bajic, I.V.: A joint approach to global motion estimation and motion segmentation from a coarsely sampled motion vector field. IEEE Trans. Circuits Syst. Video Technol. **21**(9), 1316–1328 (2011)
24. Tomar, S.: Converting video formats with FFmpeg. Linux J. **2006**(146), 10 (2006)
25. FFmpeg Developers: FFmpeg tool (Version 4.4) [Software] (2021). http://ffmpeg.org/
26. Bay, H., Tuytelaars, T., Van Gool, L.: SURF: speeded up robust features. In: Leonardis, A., Bischof, H., Pinz, A. (eds.) ECCV 2006. LNCS, vol. 3951, pp. 404–417. Springer, Heidelberg (2006). https://doi.org/10.1007/11744023_32
27. Zhu, Y., Cheng, S., Stanković, V., Stanković, L.: Image registration using BP-sift. J. Vis. Commun. Image Represent. **24**(4), 448–457 (2013)

WiMPP: An Indoor Multi-person Positioning Method Based on Wi-Fi Signal

Pengsong Duan, Biao Ye, Chenfei Jiao, Weixing Zhang$^{(\boxtimes)}$, and Chao Wang

School of Software, Zhengzhou University, Zhengzhou 450002, China
{duanps,rjwxzhang}@zzu.edu.cn

Abstract. In the era of Internet of things, convenient and high-precision location service is of great importance for the connection among things. In recent years, the indoor positioning technology based on Wi-Fi devices has developed rapidly, but there is still space for the improvement of accuracy in multi-target positioning. In this paper, a multi person positioning method named WiMPP based on Wi-Fi signal is proposed for the high-precision positioning in indoor scenes. WiMPP first collects the Wi-Fi sensing signals in environment with only one pair of transmit and receive antennas, and then estimates AOA, TOF and other parameters using two-dimensional MUSIC algorithm; Then, the estimated parameters are constructed as a heat map which is then inputted into a two-dimensional convolution neural network for training and classification such that the positioning of targets can be obtained. The experimental results show that WiMPP can achieve high precision positioning accuracy (average error distance is 6 cm, median error distance is 8 cm) under the condition that two persons are in the indoor scene. Compared with other location methods based on Wi-Fi signal, WiMPP not only can position multiple persons, but also improves the location accuracy to a certain extent.

Keywords: Indoor multi-person positioning · Wi-Fi sensing · MUSIC algorithm · CNN

1 Introduction

With the rapid development of computer technology and mobile communication technology, human society is experiencing the change of information technology. Smart life and smart city have become hot topics. More convenient and easier interaction with the surrounding environment and equipment has gradually become people's primary need. With the huge growth in the number of wirelessly connected devices, wireless signals are everywhere. These signals interact with people and objects in the environment and imply information about various properties of the surroundings Therefore, using wireless signals to sense surrounding environment has aroused great interest among researchers. For example, many attempts have been made to use wireless signals for positioning [1, 2], health detection [3, 4], motion recognition [5, 6], identity recognition [7], and gesture recognition [8–10]. In particular, passively locate multiple people walking in an

© ICST Institute for Computer Sciences, Social Informatics and Telecommunications Engineering 2022
Published by Springer Nature Switzerland AG 2022. All Rights Reserved
C. T. Calafate et al. (Eds.): MONAMI 2021, LNICST 418, pp. 115–126, 2022.
https://doi.org/10.1007/978-3-030-94763-7_9

area, without relying on any equipment carried by participants, this is a very challenging problem, and has important significance in many applications, such as elderly life monitoring, intrusion detection and retail analysis.

At present, indoor positioning technologies include Radio Frequency Identification (RFID) positioning technology [11], Ultra-Wideband (UWB) positioning technology [12], Bluetooth positioning technology [13], Ultrasonic positioning technology [14], Infrared positioning technology [15], ZigBee technology [16] and various other positioning technologies. After years of research and exploration, significant progress has been made. However, these positioning technologies usually require special hardware equipment or special deployment, which leads to high application cost and popularization difficulty. Wi-Fi network has been widely used in indoor positioning system research because of its high penetration rate and low cost. Therefore, Wi-Fi signal-based indoor positioning technology has become the mainstream of current indoor positioning technology. In this paper, the main problem we want to deal with is to achieve multiple targets passive localization in a specific environment.

In this paper, we propose a localization method that uses only few Wi-Fi resources to achieve passive in-region multi-person localization.

- We use two-dimensional MUSIC algorithm to estimate parameters such as AoA and ToF contained in received Wi-Fi signals and generate a heat map. Then, a two-dimensional convolutional neural network is constructed to classify the parametric heat map obtained after signal processing for target localization.
- We conduct experiments to validate our proposed multi-person localization method in a test environment, and test the localization results for the 2-person case. The results show that high-precision localization for two people can be achieved in the target environment with an average error distance of 6 cm and a median error distance of 8 cm.

2 Related Work

2.1 Related Research Review

In this section, we review the latest developments in passive target location using wireless signals. We first discuss the work that only focuses on single-target positioning. Then summarized the work of realizing passive multi-target positioning. A detailed comparison of the different proposed methods (including ours) for single and multiple target tracking is shown in Table 1.

Single-Target Positioning. In [17], an indoor fingerprint recognition system based on CSI was proposed, which uses the ownership value of the deep neural network as the weight of fingerprint training layer by layer. The average distance error tested in the living room is about 0.95 m.

The Widar system measures the relationship between CSI information and the user's position and speed without using statistical learning techniques, and can reach an error distance of 38 cm [18].

Yin Zhendong proposed a positioning scheme UWB-IP based on Wavelength Division Multiple Access (WDMA), which achieves centimeter-level positioning accuracy with a second-level response, and can also achieve an error within 10 cm in a noisy environment [19]. In [20], a UWB positioning algorithm based on the attention mechanism was proposed. This method can reduce positioning errors caused by multipath effects and non-line-of-sight in a dynamic environment. Experimental results show that the error distance can reach 0.0012 m [20].

Multi-target Positioning. In [21], a two-person positioning method based on channel state information (CSI) is proposed. Two kinds of resolution fingerprint libraries are constructed in the offline phase. In the online matching stage, it matches with the fingerprint database to obtain accurate positioning results. Through experimental verification, the minimum positioning error of this method is 1.12 m.

In [22], a multi-parameter indoor passive positioning technology is proposed. First, the relationship between user motion and channel state information (CSI) is quantified through the parameter model of the angle of arrival (AoA), time of flight (ToF) and Doppler frequency shift (DFS), and the generalized expectation maximization algorithm (Alternating Generalized Expectation Maximization algorithm (SAGE) refines the wrong original parameters to a certain precise range, and finally outputs the target position.

Table 1. Comparison with the technologies in target positioning using RF signals

Paper	Number of targets	Bandwidth	Number of devices used	Positioning error
DeepFi,	Single	Narrowband	2 WiFi NICs	0.95 m
Widar	Single	Narrowband	2 WiFi NICs	0.38 m
[19]	Single	UWB radar	1 UWB radar	0.1 m
[20]	Single	UWB radar	1 UWB radar	0.01 m
[21]	Multiple (2)	Narrowband	2 WiFi NICs	1.12 m
[22]	Multiple (5)	Narrowband	2 WiFi NICs	0.8 m–1.3 m
This paper	Multiple (2)	Narrowband	2 WiFi NICs	0.08 m

3 System Design

3.1 2D MUSIC Algorithm

In this section, we use the two-dimensional multi-signal classification algorithm to estimate the value of the parameters (AoA, ToF) related to the target position, because it has the advantage of high resolution.

Consider a scenario where the receiving array contains M and the distance between antennas A is *dant*. The antenna of the array samples the received signal for *Twin* length at a rate of $1/T$ (sample per second). Therefore, the number of samples in space and time is M_A and $M_T = Twin / Ts$, respectively. Use C to represent the $M_A \times M_T$ matrix of the square of the magnitude in the space-time window:

$$C = \begin{bmatrix} |c_{1,1}|^2 & |c_{1,2}|^2 & \cdots & |c_{1,M_T}|^2 \\ |c_{2,1}|^2 & \ddots & & \vdots \\ \vdots & & \ddots & \vdots \\ |c_{M_A,1}|^2 & \cdots\cdots & & |c_{M_A,M_T}|^2 \end{bmatrix} \tag{1}$$

$c_{i,j}$ are channel state information. We express C as the following mathematical model:

$$C = AS + N \tag{2}$$

Where N is the noise, A is the steering vector of the signal, S is the incident signal:

$$S = [S_1(t), S_2(t), \ldots S_n(t)]^T \tag{3}$$

Rc is the correlation matrix of vector C:

$$R_c = E\left[CC^H\right] = AR_S A^H + R_N \tag{4}$$

Where $R_S = E[SS^H]$, $R_N = \sigma^2 I$, E is the expectation, σ^2 is the noise power, and I is the identity matrix.

The feature vector of Rc is divided into a signal subspace (its dimension is equal to the rank of Rs) and a noise subspace (which is orthogonal to all direction vectors corresponding to the N signal paths to the receiving array). Therefore, we can define the frequency spectrum as:

$$P\left(\psi^M, \psi^A\right) = \frac{1}{a^H(\psi^M, \psi^A)E_n E_n{}^H a(\psi^M, \psi^A)} \tag{5}$$

Where E_N is a matrix composed of various noise eigenvectors. a is the guiding vector.

The denominator in this formula is the inner product of the signal vector and the noise matrix, because the signal subspace is orthogonal to the noise subspace. Therefore, when ψ^M and ψ^A are equal to the position corresponding to the target, the denominator gets 0, where the spectrum takes a maximum value. Generally, we can obtain the correlation value (θ and τ) of the target's position parameters (AoA and ToF) by searching for the peak of the spectrum peak.

However, in the actual environment, because of the coherence of the signals of different targets, the correct position cannot be obtained through spectral search. Although the frequency spectrum does not directly reflect the final result, it contains sufficient multi-object spatial features. Therefore, our method uses deep learning techniques to train a model, extract features from the spectrum and predict the location of the target. After calculation, a set of (AoA, ToF) parameter estimates can be obtained, which are displayed on a high-resolution heatmap, as shown in Fig. 1, so that we can sort them in the network model in next section.

The performance and estimation accuracy of the MUSIC algorithm mentioned above are affected by the number of sources, so at present this article can only estimate the motion parameters of two targets when only a pair of transceiver devices are used.

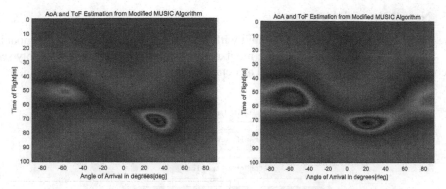

Fig. 1. Examples of heat maps processed by MUSIC algorithm. The highlighted part in the figure is the estimation of the parameter value pair containing the target position information

3.2 Convolutional Neural Network

In this section, we show how to input the heat map obtained by processing the original CSI data through the MUSIC algorithm into a convolutional neural network we proposed to locate the target. Its overall structure is shown in Fig. 2.

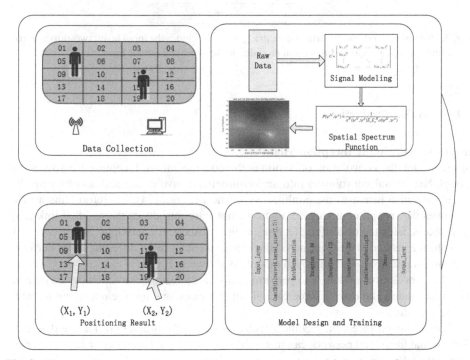

Fig. 2. The overall structure diagram of the neural network model. Including four parts, data acquisition, signal modeling, construction of spatial spectrum function, target positioning.

3.3 Neural Network Structure

The model structure of this article is built with Keras, and the parameters of the model, the size of the convolution kernel, the number of model layers, etc. are reasonably set according to the experimental needs. The detailed model structure is shown in Fig. 3.

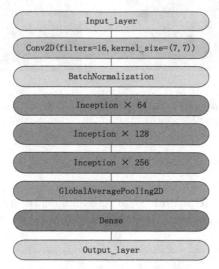

Fig. 3. Neural network model structure diagram, which includes the input layer, two-dimensional convolutional layer, improved Inception module, dense layer and output layer.

3.4 Module Introduction

Improvements in the Inception Module

In the model, the convolution operation is the core operation. Inception V3 solves the GoogleNet spatial convolution into an asymmetric convolution, and accelerating the calculation also increases the nonlinearity of the network [24]. Therefore, this article improves the Inception module on its basis, not only introduces the residual link [25] on its basis, adds the underlying features to the subsequent operations; and uses 1×1 convolution instead of the Concatenate layer to make features of different scales Perform a linear combination. The improved module is shown in Fig. 4:

The convolution module is to perform preliminary feature extraction on the data of the input model, and extract some overall data features, and use them as input to enter the next module.

The improved Inception module effectively solves the problem of feature degradation, so that the neural network can reach a deeper level and better deal with features of different scales.

Classifier

According to the definition of the problem, the input of the model is a heat map, denoted by X, and the output is the coordinates of the positions of two people, denoted by Y. The function of the model is to predict the position category Y of the two persons through the input X. The number of monitored locations in the location problem studied in the paper is greater than 2, so the problem is determined to be a multi-classification problem. The Softmax function can be used for multiple classifications, so this article chooses the Softmax function to distinguish the action categories. The expression formula is as follows:

$$P(y|X) = \frac{\exp(z_y)}{\sum_{y=1}^{r} \exp(z_y)}, y \in [1, r] \tag{6}$$

In the formula, r is the number of categories of y, which represents the result of the global average pooling operation, and represents the posterior probability of the model input X predicted belonging to the y category.

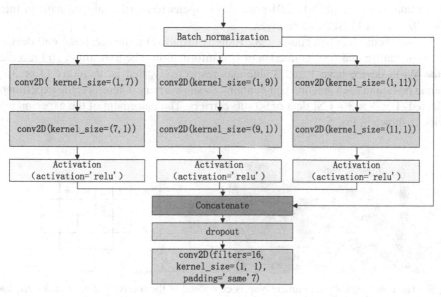

Fig. 4. The improved Inception module structure diagram, which combines residual linking and asymmetric convolution.

4   Experiment and Result Analysis

4.1   Evaluation Index

This paper uses Average Distance Error, Median Distance Error, and CDF (Cumulative Distribution Function) curves to evaluate the classification effect of the model. Among them, the average distance error is defined as:

$$\text{Average Distance Error} = \frac{\sum_{i=1}^{m} \sqrt{(x_i - p_i)^2 + (y_i - q_i)^2}}{m} \tag{7}$$

Where m is the number of test points, (x_i, y_i) is the predicted coordinates of the i-th test point, and (p_i, q_i) is the true coordinate of the i-th test point.

The Median Distance Error is the median obtained from the sum of the error distances.

CDF (Cumulative distribution function) curve refers to the sum of the probability of occurrence of all values less than or equal to a for a continuous function. That is, $F(a) = P(x< = a)$.

4.2 Experimental Setup

We choose a relatively empty laboratory for multi-person positioning experiments. In each experiment, two targets are invited to be located in the detection area on the side of the Wi-Fi device. A total of 2000 pieces of CSI data in a two-person environment were collected as the training set and the test set.

The experimental equipment is composed of a TP_LINK AC1750 wireless router as a transmitter and a ThinkPad X201 portable computer terminal equipped with an Intel 5300 802.11n Wi-Fi NIC as a receiver.

Among them, the open source CSI Tools is installed on the receiving end device, which can realize real-time collection of CSI information. The transmitter and receiver of the Wi-Fi device have 1 and 3 antennas respectively, that is, there are (1×3) 3 antenna pairs, and each antenna pair contains 30 sub-carriers. Therefore, the experiment collected $(1 \times 3 \times 30)$ CSI data of 90 sub-carriers. The placement of the experimental device is shown in Fig. 5.

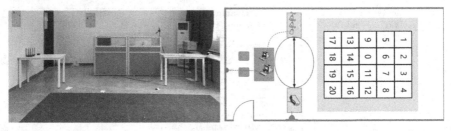

Fig. 5. The experimental environment map is composed of the receiving device area (left) and the positioning area (right). The positioning area is divided into 20 sub-areas of the same size, numbered starting from 1. When positioning data is collected, the inspected person is stationary in the 20 sub-areas.

There are 90 CSI data streams collected in this experiment, and all experiments are done at 5 GHz frequency to ensure the integrity and accuracy of the data. The sampling rate of the CSI data packet is set to 1000 data packets per second at the receiving end. In order to extract more feature information, the sliding step length d = 200 and the sliding window T = 600 ms are set. The sliding step length and the overlap between the windows ensure the continuity of the data after segmentation. Based on this, the sample data was constructed and different heat maps were generated.

In the selection of deep learning tools, the deep learning framework of this article uses Keras, and the model construction is implemented in Python. The collected CSI data is labeled with the positions of two persons, and the proposed neural network is used to supervise and learn the heat map of the localized target. The data of the data set is divided into two parts: training data and test data. Among them, training data accounts for 90% of all collected CSI data, and the remaining 10% is used as test data. The test set is used to evaluate the positioning effect after training. At present, the verification and evaluation of the model are based on the data set collected by our team.

4.3   Experimental Results

Analysis of Experimental Results
In order to verify the positioning effect of our model, this article designed a comparative experiment using different models in this scenario. In terms of model selection, we chose the classic LSTM and VGG16 [26] to compare with this experimental model, using the above The detailed comparison results of the proposed evaluation methods are as shown in Table 2 (Fig. 6).

Table 2. Comparison table of experimental results of different models.

Index model	ADE (m)	MDE (m)	Parameters	GFLOPs	Duration (ms)
LSTM	0.76	0.76	572,244	4.4	7571.22
VGG	0.33	0.39	138,357,544	15.5	5962.71
This paper	0.08	0.06	2,541,974	7.6	2771.56

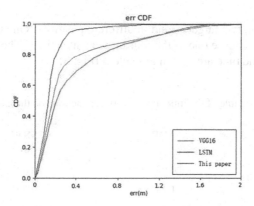

Fig. 6. The cumulative distribution function graph of the error in the experimental results of different neural network models.

LSTM is an excellent variant model of RNN. It inherits most of the characteristics of RNN models and at the same time solves the problem of gradient disappearance caused by the gradual reduction of the gradient backpropagation process. Therefore, LSTM is suitable for dealing with problems that are highly related to time series. It performs poorly in the image classification problem of this experiment. The VGG16 model is composed of several convolutional layers and pooling layers to form a deeper network structure. The depth of the layer makes the feature map wider and more suitable for large data sets, but the 16-layer network structure now looks It is not very deep, the fitting effect is not as good as our 23-layer model, and VGG has a very large number of parameters, resulting in too long training time. After updating the Inception module, the network model we proposed adds residual links, which can overcome the problem of feature degradation, thereby making the model more in-depth and improving the processing of data with different scale features. Therefore, the performance is the best in the comparison test, and the parameter quantity is moderate. This not only ensures the model fitting ability, but also enables the training time to meet actual needs.

The Impact of Movement on Positioning Results

In order to verify the influence of the action of the tested person on the positioning result in the experiment, we collected different actions in the same indoor environment and the same deployment. We additionally collected four different actions of the target which including the up, down, left, and right actions of the target in the same position grid, as shown in Fig. 7.

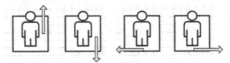

Fig. 7. Four different actions of the target in the same position grid, which include the up, down, left, and right actions of the target.

In this experiment, two targets stand in different positions. One target is stationary, and the other one can choose one of the four movement actions. The results of locating two targets at the same time are shown in Table 3 (Fig. 8):

Table 3. Comparison table of the influence of different actions on the experimental results

Index prerequisite	ADE (m)	MDE (m)
Static & Static	0.06	0.08
Static & Up	1.74	0.09
Static & Down	1.58	0.08
Static & Left	2.19	0.08
Static & Right	2.38	0.09

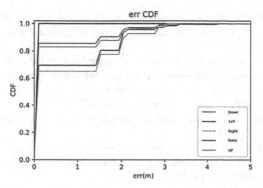

Fig. 8. The cumulative distribution function graph of the error of different action experiment results, the influence of different target actions on the experiment.

5 Conclusion

This paper proposes a new positioning method. First, we use the MUSIC method to process the signal, estimate the position parameter (AoA, ToF) of the positioning target and generate heatmaps. Then building a neural network to classify the images to achieve the purpose of positioning. In view of the feature degradation and poor effect of traditional deep neural networks for deep network structures, our neural network model effectively solves the feature degradation problem, enabling the neural network to reach deeper levels and better handle features of different scales. Experimental results show that the average error distance is only 8 cm and the median error distance is only 6 cm for simultaneous positioning of two persons in an indoor environment. In the future, we will study multi-person positioning for more than two persons. And to realize the trajectory tracking of the targets, so as to further improved the practical value of positioning under the Wi-Fi signal.

References

1. Li, Q.Y., et al.: AF-DCGAN: amplitude-feature deep convolutional GAN for fingerprint construction in indoor localization system. IEEE Trans. Emer. Top. Comput. Intell. **5**(3), 468–480 (2021)
2. Ding, Y.L., Sun, D.G., Yang, S.J.: Research on positioning technology of wireless sensor network based on ZigBee. In: Information Technology and Informatization, pp.187–188 (2021)
3. Lin, N., et al.: Contactless body movement recognition during sleeping via WiFi signal. IEEE Int. Things J. **7**(3), 2028–2037 (2020)
4. Gu, Y., Wang, Y.T., Liu, Z., Liu, J., Li, J.: SleepGuardian: an RF-based healthcare system guarding your sleep from Afar. IEEE Network **34**(2), 164–171 (2020)
5. Duan, P., Li, H., Zhang, B.: APFNet: Amplitude-Phase Fusion Network for CSI-Based Action Recognition. Mobile Netw. Appl. **26**, 2024–2034 (2021)
6. Gu, Y., Zhang, X., Liu, Z., Ren, F.J.: BeSense: leveraging WiFi channel data and computational intelligence for behavior analysis. IEEE Comput. Intell. Mag. **14**(4), 31–41 (2019)

7. Gu, Y., et al.: WiONE: one-shot learning for environment-robust device-free user authentication via commodity WiFi in man-machine system. IEEE Trans. Comput. Soc. Syst. **8**(3), 630–642 (2021)
8. Wang, C.: Research and implementation of Wi-Fi signal gesture recognition technology based on multi-modality. Beijing University of Posts and Telecommunications (2020)
9. Wang, X.: Research on Gesture Recognition Based on Improved EMA in Wi-Fi Environment. Beijing University of Posts and Telecommunications (2020)
10. Zhang, K.Q., Huang, Q.: Context-Aware Wireless Based Cross Domain Gesture Recognition. IEEE Int. Things J. (2021)
11. Cui, D., Zhang, Q.: The RFID data clustering algorithm for improving indoor network positioning based on LANDMARC technology. Clust. Comput. **22**(3), 5731–5738 (2017). https://doi.org/10.1007/s10586-017-1485-0
12. Zhang, K., Shen, C., Zhou, Q., Wang, H., Gao, Q., Chen, Y.: A combined GPS UWB and MARG locationing algorithm for indoor and outdoor mixed scenario. Clust. Comput. **22**(3), 5965–5974 (2018). https://doi.org/10.1007/s10586-018-1735-9
13. Kalbandhe, A.A., Patil, S.C.: Indoor positioning system using Bluetooth low energy. In: Proceedings of the 2016 International Conference on Computing, Analytics and Security Trends, pp. 451–455 (2016)
14. Paredes, J.A., Alvarez, F.J., Aguilera, T.: 3D indoor positioning of UAVs with spread spectrum ultrasound and time-of-flight cameras. Sensors **18**(1), 89 (2017)
15. Martin-gorostiza, E., Garcia-Garrido, M.A., Pizarro, D.: An indoor positioning approach based on fusion of cameras and infrared sensors. Sensors **19**(11), 2519 (2019)
16. Hahnloser, R.H.R., Sarpeshkar, R., Mahowald, M.A.: Digital selection and analogue amplification coexist in a cortex-inspired silicon circuit. Nature **405**(6789), 947–951 (2020)
17. Wang, X., Gao, L., Mao, S., Pandey, S.: DeepFi: deep learning for indoor fingerprinting using channel state information. In: IEEE Wireless Communications and Networking Conference (WCNC), pp. 1666–1671 (2015)
18. Qian, K., Wu, C.S., Yang, Z., Liu, Y.H., Jamieson, K.: Widar: decimeter-level passive tracking via velocity monitoring with commodity Wi-Fi. In: Proceedings of the 18th ACM International Symposium on Mobile Ad Hoc Networking and Computing. Association for Computing Machinery (2017)
19. Yin, Z., Jiang, Z., Yang, Z., Zhao, N., Chen, Y.: WUB-IP: a high-precision UWB positioning scheme for indoor multiuser applications. IEEE Syst. J. **13**(1), 279–288 (2019)
20. Ye, X.T., Zhang, Y., Song, J.D.: UWB indoor positioning algorithm based on attention mechanism. Computer Applications and Software, pp. 198–201,(2021)
21. Dang, X.C., Cao, Y, Hao, Z.J., Duan, Y.: A two-person positioning method based on CSI. J. Sens. Technol. (2019)
22. Wang, Y.Y., Chang, J., Wu, H.: Research on multi-parameter optimization of indoor WiFi positioning technology. Comput. Eng., 128–135 (2021)
23. Karanam, C.R., Korany, B., Mostofi, Y.: Tracking from One Side - Multi-Person Passive Tracking with WiFi Magnitude Measurements. In: 18th ACM/IEEE International Conference on Information Processing in Sensor Networks (IPSN), pp. 181–192 (2019)
24. Szegedy, C., Vanhoucke, V., Ioffe, S.: Rethinking the inception architecture for computer vision. In: Proceedings of the IEEE Conference on Computer Vision and Pattern Recognition, pp. 2818–2826 (2016)
25. He, K., Zhang, X., Ren, S.: Deep residual learning for image recognition. In: IEEE Conference on Computer Vision and Pattern Recognition (CVPR) (2016)
26. Simonyan, K., Zisserman, A.: Very deep convolutional networks for large-scale image recognition. In: International Conference on Learning Representations (2015)

Task Scheduling and Resource Management in MEC-Enabled Computing Networks

Jie Feng[1,2,3], Wenjing Zhang[4], Lei Liu[1,2(✉)], Jianbo Du[3], Ming Xiao[5], and Qingqi Pei[1]

[1] State Key Laboratory of ISN, School of Telecommunication Engineering, Xidian University, Xi'an, Shaanxi, China
qqpei@mail.xidian.edu.cn
[2] Guangzhou Institute of Technology, Xidian University, Xi'an, China
tianjiaoliulei@163.com
[3] Shaanxi Key Laboratory of Information Communications, Xi'an University of Posts and Telecommunications, Xi'an 710121, China
[4] University of Guelph, Guelph, ON N1G2W1, Canada
wzhang25@uoguelph.ca
[5] Division of Information Science and Engineering, KTH Royal Institute of Technology, Stockholm, Sweden
ming.xiao@ee.kth.se

Abstract. The rapid development of the fifth generation (5G) promotes a variety of new applications, which will pose a huge challenge to the computing resources of networks. Computing networks is a promising technology, which can provide ubiquitous computing resources for applications in 5G. However, resource optimization in computing networks is still an open problem. In this paper, we propose a novel resource allocation framework for computing networks to investigate the energy consumption minimization problem in terms of delay constraint. To tackle the problem, we propose a dynamic task scheduling and resource allocation algorithm to utilizing the Lyapunov optimization method, which doesn't need to know any prior knowledge of networks. In order to reduce the complexity of solving the problem, we decompose the original problem into several sub-problem to solve. Particulary, the solutions of transmit power and subcarrier assignment are obtained by using the Lagrangian dual decomposition method. The solutions of computation time, postponing time, and CPU-cycle frequency are achieved in the closed form. Simulation results show that the performance of the proposed algorithms and can achieve the tradeoff between the average delay and the average energy consumption.

Keywords: Mobile edge computing (MEC) · Total cost saving · Network stability · Resource allocation

© ICST Institute for Computer Sciences, Social Informatics and Telecommunications Engineering 2022
Published by Springer Nature Switzerland AG 2022. All Rights Reserved
C. T. Calafate et al. (Eds.): MONAMI 2021, LNICST 418, pp. 127–137, 2022.
https://doi.org/10.1007/978-3-030-94763-7_10

1 Introduction

The fifth-generation (5G) network is paramount for supporting a multitude of emerging applications that require rich data communication in both directions, such as artificial intelligence (AI) [1,2] and virtual reality (VR) [3,4]. This is because it has the considerable capability to deliver high bandwidth and speed to enable high-reliability and rich two-way communication of high-volume data and high-definition video. Particularly, 5G technology creates enormous opportunities for the Internet of vehicles (IoV). With the rapid advancements of autonomous driving, the demand for computing power in the IoV services and applications has increased sharply.

Nevertheless, the proliferation of computing performance in 5G needs to be accelerated to keep up with these emerging applications that consume considerable amount of computing power [5]. Consequently, cloud computing [6] has become a popular paradigm aiming at providing on-demand availability of data storage and computing power [7]. Even though cloud computing has made data processing to be much more efficient, a major limitation is that it can cause large communication delay since the cloud center might be far away from users' devices [8].

As a more efficient alternative computing framework, Multi-access edge computing (MEC) is introduced to address the concern of communication latency [9–13], which has received widespread attention from both academia and industries. In terms of academic research, recent works studied multiple deployment approaches [14], joint radio-and-computational resource management [15], and applications which could take advantage of MEC [16–18]. In the industry side, several MEC based architectures have been developed, such as ThinkAir [19] and EdgeGallery [20].

In fact, how to achieve efficient computing power allocation and collaboration remains to be a big challenge in the deployment of MEC. To address this challenge, we aim of establishing deep integration between MEC and networking, i.e., building the Multi-access edge computing networks (MECN). The concept of a MECN is to use a ubiquitous network to connect distributed heterogeneous computational power, and provide personalized computational services for diverse upper layer services through unified management and on-demand scheduling [5,21]. However, the research on computing networks is still in early stage.

In this paper, we focus on jointly optimize transmit power, subcarrier assignment, computation time, postponing time, and CPU-cycle frequency to minimize the average energy consumption of the MEC-enabled computing networks. By using the Lyapunov optimization method, we develop a dynamic resource allocation algorithm to solve the minimum problem.

The main contributions of the paper are as follows:

– We propose a dynamic resource allocation scheme in MEC-enabled computing network to study the average energy consumption minimization problem, where transmit power, subcarrier assignment, computation time, postponing time, and CPU-cycle frequency are jointly optimized to stabilize the network.

- To resolve the problem, we design a dynamic radio and computation resource allocation algorithm, which does not need prior knowledge of the network. To improve the efficiency of the algorithm, we decompose the original problem into several sub-problems to obtain the optimal network control policy.
- In the simulation, we estimate the performance of the proposed algorithms. Observed from the simulation results, the proposed algorithm can achieve the trade off between the average delay and the average energy consumption.

The rest parts of this paper are organized as follows. In Sect. 2, The system model is described. We formulate the average energy consumption minimization problem in Sect. 3. In Sect. 4, an algorithm design framework is introduced. We design the network control policies in Sect. 5. In Sect. 5, we present the simulation results. Finally, the summary of the paper is given in Sect. 6.

2   System Model

We consider an MEC-enabled computing network that is composed of an MEC server and a set of applications. We assume that the MEC server is regarded as a computing provider medium installed at a base station (BS). Consequently, it can be accessed by applications through wireless communications to obtain the corresponding computing service. In the system, time is assumed to be slotted. We let N_t denote the number of tasks arriving in time slot t and $\mathcal{N}_t = \{1, 2, ..., N_t\}$ represent the index set of tasks. We consider two types of tasks, delay-intolerant and delay-tolerant tasks. Denoted by $\tau_n(t)$ the required service time for each task $n \in \mathcal{N}_t$. Let $k_n(t)$ represent the maximum delay allowed for each task from its arrival time t to completion, where $k_n(t) \geq \tau_n(t)$. Let $s(t) = (s_n(t))$ denote the optimal "postponing" time for task n in time slot t. Assuredly, we have to $s_n(t) = 0$ for the delay-intolerant tasks.

2.1   Computation Offloading Model

We consider a non-interference communication environment in the system. There are M subcarriers, where $N_t \leq M$, and the bandwidth of each subcarrier is B. Let $\boldsymbol{P}(t) = (P_{n,m}(t))$ and $\boldsymbol{G}(t) = (G_{n,m}(t))$ represent the transmit power and the channel gain of task n on subcarrier m, respectively. Then, the transmit rate of task n on subcarrier m is given by

$$r_{n,m}(t) = B \log_2(1 + \frac{P_{n,m}(t)g_{n,m}(t)}{\sigma_n^2(t)}), \tag{1}$$

where $\sigma_n^2(t)$ is the noise power.

Consequently, the sum transmit rates and the total transmit power of task n are respectively expressed as $R_n(t)$ and $P_n(t)$.

We assume that the transmit time of task n is set to $T_n(t)$. Therefore, the amount of offloading task n to MEC server is denoted by $D_n^o(t) = T_n(t)R_n(t)$. The energy consumption of the task n is expressed as $E_n^o(t) = T_n(t)P_n(t)$.

We set that the power consumption of task n in idle state is $P^{id}(t)$, which is a variable that changes over time. Then the energy consumed while the task n is given by

$$E_n^s(t) = s_n(t)P^{id}(t). \tag{2}$$

Note that $E_n^s(t)$ relies on the decision made.

2.2 MEC Server Computation Model

After receiving the task n, the computation time of the MEC server is set to $e(t) = (e_n(t))$. Let $f(t) = (f_n(t))$ denote the CPU-cycle frequency of task n in time slot t. The data size of the task n executed by the MEC server is given by

$$D_n^m(t) = \frac{f_n(t)e_n(t)}{c_n}, \tag{3}$$

where c_n is the CPU cycles required by the MEC server to process 1-bit computing task n. Then the energy consumed by the MEC server to process the task n in time slot t is given by

$$E_n^m(t) = \kappa f_n(t)^3 e_n(t), \tag{4}$$

where κ is the effective switched capacitance of the MEC server.

2.3 Task and Computation Queueing Models

We denote that $A(t) = (A_n(t))$ is the amount of arriving task n at the beginning of the time slot t, which is assumed to an independent and identically distributed (i.i.d) over slots. The arrival rate is $\lambda(t) = (\lambda_n(t))$, and $\mathbb{E}\{A(t)\} = \lambda(t)$. We assume that the dynamic update of all queues is based on the First-In-First-Out (FIFO) principle. Thus, each task in the system is equally important. Let $Q^o(t) \triangleq [Q_1^o(t), Q_2^o(t), ...Q_n^o(t)]$ denote the backlog of the task buffers at time slot t. Then, the queue length of the task n in the network evolves according to

$$Q_n^o(t+1) = \max\{Q_n^o(t) - R_n(t)(\tau_n(t) - e_n(t)), 0\} + A_n(t), n \in \mathcal{N}_t. \tag{5}$$

Usually, the MEC server stores that the tasks offloaded but not yet processed by the server in a task buffer. The capacity of the MEC server is assumed to be sufficiently large. Denote by $Q(t)$ the queue length of the task buffer at the MEC server at slot t. Then, the evolution of the queue length $Q(t)$ on the MEC server is given by

$$Q(t+1) = \max\{Q(t) - \sum_{n=1}^{N_t} D_n^m(t), 0\} + D_{in}(t), \tag{6}$$

where $D_{in}(t) = \sum_{n=1}^{N_t} D_n^o(t)$. We note that $0 \leq D_n^m(t) \leq Q(t)/N_t$.

3   Problem Formulation

In the paper, we focus on the total energy consumption of the task processing in the system, including the energy consumed by transmission, the energy consumed while waiting, and the energy consumption of the MEC server. Then the time average energy consumption of task n is given by

$$\bar{E}_n = \limsup_{T \to \infty} \frac{1}{T} \sum_{t=0}^{T-1} \mathbb{E}\{E_n(t)\}, \forall n \in \mathcal{N}_t, \tag{7}$$

where $E_n(t) = E_n^o(t) + E_n^s(t) + E_n^m(t)$.

Therefore, the average energy consumption of the system is equal to

$$\bar{E} = \sum_{n \in \mathcal{N}_t} \bar{E}_n. \tag{8}$$

We denote the system operation at time slot t as $A(t) \triangleq [P(t), \rho(t), s(t), e(t), f(t)]$. Therefore, the average energy consumption minimization problem can be formulated as

$$\min_{A(t)} \quad \bar{E} = \sum_{n \in \mathcal{N}_t} \bar{E}_n$$

$$\text{s.t.} \quad (C1): \sum_{m=1}^{M} \rho_{n,m}(t) r_{n,m}(t) \geq R_n^{req} \forall n,$$

$$(C2): \sum_{n=1}^{N_t} \rho_{n,m}(t) \leq 1, \forall m,$$

$$(C3): \rho_{n,m}(t) \in \{0,1\}, \forall n, m,$$

$$(C4): \sum_{m=1}^{M} \rho_{n,m}(t) P_{n,m}(t) \leq P_{n,max}, \forall n,$$

$$(C5): s_n(t) + e_n(t) \leq k_n(t) - T_n(t), \forall n, \tag{9}$$

$$(C6): \limsup_{T \to \infty} \frac{1}{T} \sum_{t=1}^{T} \sum_{n=1}^{N_t} \overline{y_n^t(s_n(t))} \leq \alpha$$

$$(C7): f_{n,min} \leq f_n(t) \leq f_{n,max}, \forall n,$$

$$(C8): P_{n,m}(t) \geq 0, f_n(t) \geq 0, \forall n,$$

$$(C9): \frac{f_n(t) e_n(t)}{c_n} \leq Q(t)/N_t, \forall n,$$

$$(C10): \overline{Q}_n < \infty, \overline{Q} < \infty, \forall n,$$

where R_n^{req} and $P_{n,max}$ denote the required transmission rate and the maximum transmission power of task n, respectively. $f_{n,min}$ and $f_{n,max}$ are respectively the minimum and the maximum CPU-cycle frequency for executing task n. We note that the value of $y_n^t(s_n(t))$ is different for diverse tasks.

4   Algorithm Design Framework

In this section, we propose a dynamic energy consumption minimum algorithm to solve the stochastic optimization problem (9) by employing the Lyapunov optimization method.

4.1   The Lyapunov Optimization-Based Algorithm

Firstly, we introduce the concept of virtual queue to deal with the average dissatisfaction constraint (C6) in (9). Particularly, the virtual queue is defined as $Q^v(t)$ with $Q^v(0) = 0$ and the update equations is defined as

$$Q^v(t+1) = \max\{Q^v(t) + \sum_{n=1}^{N_t} y_n^t(s_n(t)) - \alpha, 0\}. \tag{10}$$

Then solving problem (9) is transformed into minimizing the following problem.

$$\min_{\boldsymbol{X}(t)} \Phi(\boldsymbol{X}(t))$$
$$\text{s.t.} \ (C1)-(C5), (C7)-(C9), \tag{11}$$

where

$$\Phi(\boldsymbol{X}(t)) = V \sum_{n=1}^{N_t}(\tau_n(t) - e_n(t)) \sum_{m=1}^{M} \rho_{n,m}(t) P_{n,m}(t) - \sum_{n=1}^{N_t}(Q_n^o(t) - Q(t))(\tau_n(t) - e_n(t))$$

$$\sum_{m=1}^{M} \rho_{n,m}(t) B \log_2(1 + \frac{P_{n,m}(t)g_{n,m}(t)}{\sigma_n(t)^2}) + \sum_{n=1}^{N_t}\{V(\kappa f_n(t)^3 - P_n(t)) - [R_n(t)(Q_n^o(t)$$

$$-Q(t)) + Q(t)\frac{f_n(t)}{c_n}]\}e_n(t) + Q^v(t) \sum_{n=1}^{N_t} y_n^t(s_n(t)) + V \sum_{n=1}^{N_t} s_n(t) \sum_{j=0}^{\tau_n - 1} P^{id}(j + t + s_n(t)),$$

$$V \sum_{n=1}^{N_t} \kappa f_n(t)^3 e_n(t) - Q(t) \sum_{n=1}^{N_t} \frac{f_n(t)e_n(t)}{c_n}$$

To solve (9), we develop a dynamic resource allocation algorithm, shown in Algorithm 1.

Algorithm 1. Dynamic Resource Allocation Algorithm

1: Monitor the current queue states $\boldsymbol{Q}^o(t)$, $\boldsymbol{Q}(t)$, $\boldsymbol{Q}^v(t)$ and the channel condition $\boldsymbol{G}(t)$ at each time slot t, respectively;
2: Obtain the network control policy, including power allocation, subcarrier assignment, computation time, postponing time, and CPU-cycle frequency accordingly to problem (11);
3: Update $\boldsymbol{Q}^o(t)$, $\boldsymbol{Q}(t)$, $\boldsymbol{Q}^v(t)$ according to (8), (9), and (14) based on the above obtained control policy.

---

5   Design of Control Strategies

In this section, we first develop an algorithm for power allocation and subcarrier assignment. We then obtain computation time allocation, the postponing time, and CPU-cycles frequency, respectively.

5.1   Power Allocation and Subcarrier Assignment

For a given $e(t)$, the problem of the power allocation and subcarrier assignment is given by

$$\min_{P(t),\rho(t)} \Phi_1(P(t),\rho(t))$$
$$\text{s.t.}\ \ (C1)-(C4),(C8)' : P_{n,m}(t) \geq 0. \tag{12}$$

To solve (12), we first relax $\rho_{n,m}(t)$ to interval $[0,1]$, then introduce a new variable $x_{n,m}(t) = \rho_{n,m}(t)P_{n,m}(t)$, where let $x(t) = (x_{n,m}(t))$. We set $\rho_{n,m}(t)B\log_2(1 + \frac{P_{n,m}(t)g_{n,m}(t)}{\sigma_n(t)^2}) = 0$ when $\rho_{n,m}(t) = 0$. Therefore, (12) is rearranged as

$$\min_{x(t),\rho(t)} \Phi_1(x(t),\rho(t))$$
$$\text{s.t.}\ \ (C1),(C2),(C3),(C4),(C8). \tag{13}$$

It is easy to prove that optimization problem (13) is a convex optimization problem. Therefore, we can easily obtain the solution of (13).

5.2   Computation Time Allocation

For a given $P(t), \rho(t), f(t)$, and $s(t)$, the optimization problem of computation time allocation is given by

$$\min_{e(t)} \Phi_2(e(t))$$
$$\text{s.t.}\ \ (C5) : e_n(t) \leq k_n(t) - T_n(t) - s_n(t), \forall n, \tag{14}$$
$$(C9) : e_n(t) \leq \frac{Q(t)c_n}{N_t f_n(t)}, \forall n.$$

We can observe that (14) is a standard linear programming, so the optimal computation time is denoted as $e_n^*(t)$.

5.3   Postponing Time Allocation

For a given computation time $e(t)$, the optimization problem of postponing time allocation is given by

$$\min_{s(t)} \Phi_3(s(t))$$
$$\text{s.t.}\ \ (C5) : s_n(t) \leq k_n(t) - T_n(t) - e_n(t), \forall n. \tag{15}$$

Since the objective function of (15) is convex and its constraint is linear, (15) is a convex optimization problem. so the optimal postponing time is given by

$$s_n^*(t) = \arg \min_{0 \le s_n(t) \le k_n(t) - T_n(t) - e_n(t)} Q^v(t) y_n^t(s_n(t)) + V \sum_{j=0}^{\tau_n - 1} P^{id}(j + t + s_n(t)). \quad (16)$$

5.4 Optimal CPU-Cycle Frequency

For a given computation time $e(t)$, the optimization problem of CPU-cycle frequency is given by

$$\min_{\boldsymbol{f}(t)} \Phi_4(\boldsymbol{f}(t))$$

$$\text{s.t.} \quad (C7)' : f_{n,min} \le f_n(t) \le \min\{f_{n,max}, \frac{c_n Q(t))}{N_t e_n(t)}\}, \forall n. \quad (17)$$

In (17), we can observe that both its objective function and constraint are convex, so (17) is convex optimization problem. Then, the optimal solution of CPU-cycle frequency for any user n is denoted as $f_n^*(t)$.

6   Simulation Results

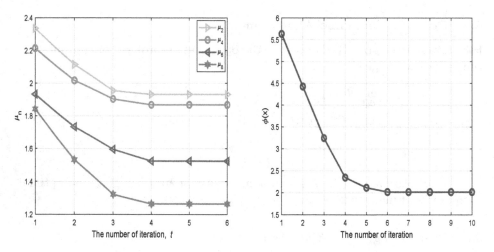

Fig. 1. Convergence of Algorithm 2.   **Fig. 2.** Convergence of Algorithm 3.

In this section, we show simulation results to analyze the proposed algorithms. There are $N = 8$ users located at the central of BS. We assume that the arrival process of all tasks obeys follows Poission process with different intensity λ_n. In the simulation process, we consider two types of applications, delay-tolerant tasks and delay-tolerant tasks. The arrival intensities for the tasks are 2.5, 1.5, 0.2, and 40, respectively. The functions of dissatisfaction are assumed to be $y(x) = x^2 + x$. The maximum CPU computation capacity f_{max} is set to be 2 GHz. The parameter α of the average dissatisfaction constraint is set to be 5000, and we set the control parameter $V = 200$. To evaluate the performance of the proposed algorithms, we give two schemes as comparison scheme. The first scheme is that the variables of power allocation, computation time, and CPU-cycle frequency allocation are separately optimized (Policy A). The second scheme only optimize power allocation and CPU-cycle frequency allocation (Policy B).

In Fig. 1, we give the performance evaluation of Algorithm 2. Peculiarly, the trend of the dual variables $\boldsymbol{\mu}(t) = (\mu_n(t)), n \in N_t$ is regards as the judgment target. Observed from Fig. 1, we can find that the convergence rate of Algorithm 2 is fast. Figure 2 shows the convergence rate of Algorithm 3. It is observed that it has also a fast convergence rate. Therefore, we can conclude that the proposed algorithm is highly efficient.

Figure 3 shows the comparison of the average energy consumption and control parameter V. The average energy consumption deceases as V increase for a given arrival rate $\lambda_n(t)$. Besides, observed from Fig. 3, we can see that the average energy consumption increases as arrival rate $\lambda_n(t)$ for a given control parameter V.

In Fig. 4, we display the average energy consumption of with the variation of maximum transmit power $P_{n,max}$. The average energy consumption deceases as maximum transmit power $P_{n,max}$ increase for a given control parameter $V = 100$. By comparing the two schemes (Policy A and Policy B), we can conclude

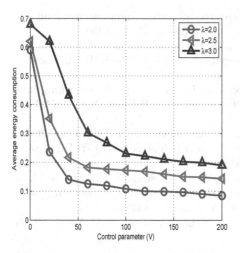

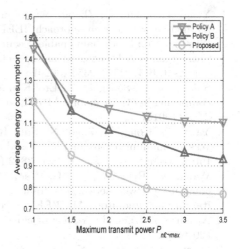

Fig. 3. Average energy consumption vs. control parameter V.

Fig. 4. Average energy consumption vs. maximum transmit power $P_{n,max}$.

that the proposed scheme consumes the least energy, followed by Policy B, and finally Policy A.

7 Conclusion

In this paper, we have researched the average energy consumption minimization problem, where jointly optimize transmit power allocation, subcarrier assignment, computation time, postponing time, and CPU-cycle frequency for MEC-enabled computing networks. We propose an algorithm that does not require prior knowledge of the network in advance. Particulary, the solutions of transmit power and subcarrier assignment were obtained by using the Lagrangian dual decomposition method. The solutions of computation time, postponing time, and CPU-cycle frequency were achieved in the closed form. Simulation results shown that the performance of the proposed algorithms and can achieve the tradeoff between the average delay and the average energy consumption.

Acknowledgment. This work is supported by the National Key Research and Development Program of China (No. 2020YFB1807500), the National Natural Science Foundation of China (NO. 6210070336, No. 62001357), the Key Research and Development Programs of Shaanxi (No. 2021ZDLGY06-03, No. 2019ZDLGY13-07), the Guangdong Basic and Applied Basic Research Foundation (2020A1515110496, 2020A1515110079), and the Fundamental Research Funds for the Central Universities (No. XJS210105, XJS210107). Finally, thank Xinyi Tang for all her hard work in organizing the related materials, participating in the academic discussion.

References

1. Yang, T., Chen, J., Zhang, N.: Ai-empowered maritime Internet of Things: a parallel-network-driven approach. IEEE Network **34**(5), 54–59 (2020)
2. Liu, L., et al.: Blockchain-enabled secure data sharing scheme in mobile-edge computing: an asynchronous advantage actor-critic learning approach. IEEE Internet Things J. **8**(4), 2342–2353 (2020)
3. Sukhmani, S., Sadeghi, M., Erol-Kantarci, M., El Saddik, A.: Edge caching and computing in 5G for mobile AR/VR and tactile internet. IEEE MultiMedia **26**(1), 21–30 (2018)
4. Yang, T., Kong, L., Zhao, N., Sun, R.: Efficient energy and delay tradeoff for vessel communications in SDN based maritime wireless networks. IEEE Trans. Intell. Transp. Syst. **22**(6), 3800–3812 (2021)
5. Wang, X., Ren, X., Qiu, C., Cao, Y., Taleb, T., Leung, V.C.: Net-in-AI: a computing-power networking framework with adaptability, flexibility and profitability for ubiquitous AI. IEEE Network **35**(1), 280–288 (2020)
6. Armbrust, M., et al.: A view of cloud computing. Commun. ACM **53**(4), 50–58 (2010)
7. Montazerolghaem, A., Yaghmaee, M.H., Leon-Garcia, A.: Green cloud multimedia networking: NFV/SDN based energy-efficient resource allocation. IEEE Trans. Green Commun. Networking **4**(3), 873–889 (2020)

8. Shi, W., Dustdar, S.: The promise of edge computing. Computer **49**(5), 78–81 (2016)
9. Taleb, T., Samdanis, K., Mada, B., Flinck, H., Dutta, S., Sabella, D.: On multi-access edge computing: a survey of the emerging 5G network edge cloud architecture and orchestration. IEEE Commun. Surv. Tutorials **19**(3), 1657–1681 (2017)
10. Feng, J., Yu, F.R., Pei, Q., Chu, X., Du, J., Zhu, L.: Cooperative computation offloading and resource allocation for blockchain-enabled mobile-edge computing: a deep reinforcement learning approach. IEEE Internet Things J. **7**(7), 6214–6228 (2019)
11. Mao, S., Wu, J., Liu, L., Lan, D., Taherkordi, A.: Energy-efficient cooperative communication and computation for wireless powered mobile-edge computing. IEEE Syst. J. 1–12 (2020). https://doi.org/10.1109/JSYST.2020.3020474
12. Feng, J., Yu, F.R., Pei, Q., Du, J., Zhu, L.: Joint optimization of radio and computational resources allocation in blockchain-enabled mobile edge computing systems. IEEE Trans. Wirel. Commun. **19**(6), 4321–4334 (2020)
13. Liu, L., Chen, C., Pei, Q., Maharjan, S., Zhang, Y.: Vehicular edge computing and networking: a survey. Mobile Networks Appl. **26**(3), 1145–1168 (2021)
14. Beck, M.T., Werner, M., Feld, S., Schimper, S.: Mobile edge computing: a taxonomy. In: Proceedings of the Sixth International Conference on Advances in Future Internet, pp. 48–55. Citeseer (2014)
15. Mao, Y., You, C., Zhang, J., Huang, K., Letaief, K.B.: A survey on mobile edge computing: the communication perspective. IEEE Commun. Surv. Tutorials **19**(4), 2322–2358 (2017)
16. Yi, S., Li, C., Li, Q.: A survey of fog computing: concepts, applications and issues. In: Proceedings of the 2015 Workshop on Mobile Big Data, pp. 37–42 (2015)
17. Yang, T., Qin, M., Cheng, N., Xu, W., Zhao, L.: Liquid software-based edge intelligence for future 6G networks. IEEE Network (2021, to appear)
18. Du, J., Yu, F.R., Lu, G., Wang, J., Jiang, J., Chu, X.: MEC-assisted immersive VR video streaming over terahertz wireless networks: a deep reinforcement learning approach. IEEE Internet Things J. **7**(10), 9517–29 (2020)
19. Kosta, S., Aucinas, A., Hui, P., Mortier, R., Zhang, X.: Thinkair: dynamic resource allocation and parallel execution in the cloud for mobile code offloading. In: Proceedings IEEE Infocom, pp. 945–953. IEEE (2012)
20. Edgegallery. https://www.edgegallery.org/en/
21. Mao, S., et al.: Computation rate maximization for intelligent reflecting surface enhanced wireless powered mobile edge computing networks. IEEE Trans. Veh. Technol. **7**, 1 (2021). https://doi.org/10.1109/TVT.2021.3105270

Unlicensed Assisted Ultra-Reliable and Low-Latency Transmission

Qiqi Xiao[1]([✉]), Jiantao Yuan[2], Rui Yin[2], Wei Qi[2], Celimuge Wu[3], and Xianfu Chen[4]

[1] School of Information Science and Electronic Engineering, Zhejiang University, Hangzhou 310027, China
`xiaoqiqi@zju.edu.cn`
[2] School of Information and Electrical Engineering, Zhejiang University City College, Hangzhou 310015, China
`{yuanjt,yinrui,qiw}@zucc.edu.cn`
[3] Graduate School of Informatics and Engineering, The University of Electro-Communications, Tokyo 182-8585, Japan
`celimuge@uec.ac.jp`
[4] VTT Technical Research Centre of Finland, Oulu 90570, Finland
`xianfu.chen@vtt.fi`

Abstract. The *ultra-reliable and low-latency communication* (URLLC) has many potential applications in the *Internet of Things* (IoTs). This paper exploits both the licensed and unlicensed spectrums to support the URLLC transmissions, alleviating the lack of licensed spectrum resources, and adopts the *duty-cycle muting* (DCM) to ensure fair coexistence with the WiFi network. The user grouping scheme, mini-slot frame structure, and finite block length regime are used to guarantee low latency and high reliability. Meanwhile, to reduce the power consumption at the URLLC devices, we establish a minimum power optimization model and provide the globally optimal solutions. Simulation results are presented to verify the feasibility and effectiveness of the proposed scheme, which can not only reduce the power consumption at the devices, but also improve the system spectrum efficiency.

Keywords: URLLC · Finite block length regime · Unlicensed band · DCM · Spectrum allocation · Power allocation

This work was supported in part by the National Natural Science Foundation of China (Grant No. 61771429), in part by The Okawa Foundation for Information and Telecommunications, in part by G-7 Scholarship Foundation, in part by JSPS KAKENHI grant numbers 18KK0279, 19H04093, 20H00592, and 21H03424, in part by the Zhejiang Lab Open Program under Grant 2021LC0AB06, in part by the Academy of Finland under Grant 319759.

© ICST Institute for Computer Sciences, Social Informatics and Telecommunications Engineering 2022
Published by Springer Nature Switzerland AG 2022. All Rights Reserved
C. T. Calafate et al. (Eds.): MONAMI 2021, LNICST 418, pp. 138–151, 2022.
https://doi.org/10.1007/978-3-030-94763-7_11

1   Introduction

The *International Telecommunication Union-Radiocommunication Sector* (ITU-R) has proposed three major application scenarios for 5G: the *enhanced mobile broadband* (eMBB) aspires to obtain higher transmission data rates, the *massive machine type communication* (mMTC) aims to provide millions of connections for the *Internet of Things* (IoTs), and the *ultra-reliable and low-latency communication* (URLLC) supports millisecond level low latency and ultra-reliable communications.

According to the 3GPP standard [1], URLLC requires the user plane delay of transmitting a 32-byte data packet to be less than 1 ms and requests the block error rate to be less than 10^{-5}, that is, the reliability reaches no less than 99.999%. However, in 4G *long term evolution* (LTE) technology, the user plane delay is required to be less than 10 ms and the packet error rate is less than 10^{-2}, that is, the reliability reaches 99%. Due to the strict latency and reliability conditions of URLLC, URLLC is applied to critical communication scenarios. The main potential applications include [2,3]:

- Emergency communication: remote diagnosis, remote surgery.
- Industrial automation: factory automation, smart grid, automatically distribute power grid energy, detect and restore grid faults.
- Intelligent transportation: intelligent transportation systems, autonomous driving, and *vehicle-to-vehicle* (V2V).
- Other applications: augmented reality and virtual reality.

With the wide application of IoTs like industrial automation, the limited channel capacity of the licensed bands will bring transmission congestion to URLLC transmissions. Besides, factories need to pay operators to use the licensed bands, and require to meet strict latency and reliability requirements for URLLC, which will bring enormous costs. Therefore, deploying URLLC on unlicensed band has attracted attention. The unlicensed band contributes to increasing the network capacity of URLLC and facilitates the deployment of wireless devices. It also improves cost-effectiveness due to its advantages of low cost, high flexibility and a large quantity of the available bandwidth.

However, there exist some problems with URLLC accessing the unlicensed bands, and there are a few researches of URLLC on unlicensed band currently. Due to the discontinuity of the unlicensed bands, which will bring challenges to achieve strict low latency conditions for URLLC. A multi-channel multi-transmission mechanism has been adopted to reduce channel access delay [4,5]. A new channel access priority has been proposed for URLLC services in the *listen-before-talk* (LBT) mechanism, which guarantees the low latency constraint of 1 ms [6]. The authors in [7] have proposed a wireless access technology based on MulteFire which uses a grant-free uplink scheduling mechanism to reduce the uplink delay. Besides, the URLLC system needs to consider fair coexistence with other wireless systems on unlicensed band. So that URLLC can reduce interference to other systems and improve its reliability. Nowadays, the commonly used unlicensed bands are 2.4 GHz and 5 GHz, which deploy WiFi, ZigBee, Bluetooth, and other wireless systems. We mainly consider the fair coexistence of URLLC and WiFi systems. Since the 5G NR estimates that it is essentially an extension of 4G LTE [5], the deployment of the NR-U in 5 GHz also follows the relevant regulations of LTE-U. The commonly used LTE-U and WiFi coexistence mechanisms are the LBT and *duty-cycle muting* (DCM). We adopt the DCM to guarantee the harmonious coexistence between URLLC and WiFi system.

In this paper, the URLLC system uses the unlicensed bands to reduce costs and increase network capacity. Since most of the terminal devices are battery-powered, it is necessary to minimize the power consumption of the transmitters and extend the service life of the devices. Therefore, our goal is to propose a spectrum and power resource allocation scheme for joint licensed and unlicensed bands to improve *spectrum efficiency* (SE) and *energy efficiency* (EE). We focus on minimizing total power consumption while satisfying the strict latency and reliability requirements. Firstly, the DCM mechanism is adopted to access unlicensed bands and ensure fair coexistence with URLLC and WiFi systems. Based on the estimated WiFi traffic loads, we can calculate the unlicensed time fraction for URLLC. Then, we employ the user grouping scheme and mini-slot frame structure to meet low latency requirement. We also establish an optimal power allocation model to minimize the total power consumption. Finally, the Lagrangian multiplier method is used to acquire the globally optimal solutions of the spectrum and power allocation. Simulation results verify that the proposed scheme effectively improves the SE and EE of the URLLC system.

The rest of this paper is organized as follows. In Sect. 2, we first introduce the system model and delay model. Then, the DCM mechanism is used to ensure fair coexistence between the URLLC and WiFi system. The user grouping scheme, mini-slot frame structure, and finite block length regime are adopted to guarantee low latency and high reliability. Meanwhile, we analyze the URLLC available transmission data rates. In Sect. 3, a minimum power optimization model is established. We propose an optimization algorithm for spectrum and power allocation. In Sect. 4, simulation results and performance analysis of the proposed scheme are provided. Finally, this paper is concluded in Sect. 5.

2   System Model

In the paper, the scenario where the NR-U cellular systems use both licensed and unlicensed spectrums to serve URLLC devices is studied. As depicted in Fig. 1, a NR-U *base station* (BS) serves I URLLC devices which are denoted as a set of $\mathcal{U} = \{U_1, U_2, \cdots, U_i, \cdots U_I\}$. In addition, there are K WiFi *access points* (APs) using K different unlicensed channels, denoted as a set of $\mathcal{W} = \{W_1, W_2, \cdots, W_k, \cdots W_K\}$, in the coverage of the BS. The devices are in charge of sensing the unlicensed channels, estimating the WiFi traffic load, and feeding back information to the BS. Then, the BS decides the available time fraction on the corresponding unlicensed channels and adopts the DCM mechanism to share the unlicensed spectrum with the WiFi APs. Accordingly, the BS may use both licensed and unlicensed channels to serve the uplink transmission for URLLC devices. Moreover, on licensed spectrum, the OFDM technique is applied to divide the licensed bands into J subchannels which have the same bandwidth.

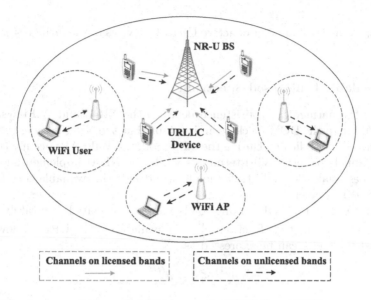

Fig. 1. A coexistence model between the URLLC and WiFi system.

2.1 Delay Model and Latency Guarantee

According to the 3GPP standard [1], the user plane latency is defined as the time spent on successfully delivering an application layer packet/message from the radio protocol layer 2/3 *service data unit* (SDU) ingress point to the radio protocol layer 2/3 SDU egress point via the radio interface in both uplink and downlink directions, which is given by

$$T = T^{(qe)} + T^{(bp)} + T^{(fa)} + T^{(tx)} + T^{(mp)} + t \cdot T^{(rx)}, \qquad (1)$$

where $T^{(qe)}$ represents the queuing delay for the data packets to wait for transmission in the buffer. $T^{(fa)}$ stands for the frame alignment delay which is between 0 and TTI [8], and $T^{(tx)}$ is the transmission delay. $T^{(bp)}$ and $T^{(mp)}$ are defined as the processing delay at the BS and the URLLC devices, respectively. In the 5G NR system, with the development of integrated circuits, the processing delay will be much less than a few milliseconds. Therefore, it can be ignored [9,10]. $T^{(rx)}$ represents the retransmission delay, which allows devices and the BS to use 3 symbols when the subcarrier spacing is between 15 and 30 kHz, and use 9 symbols when the subcarrier spacing is between 60 and 240 kHz, t is the number of retransmissions.

To meet the low latency requirement, the user grouping scheme in [11] is applied while reducing the control signaling overheads. That is, we disperse a group of N users into M consecutive time slots. The number of users in a group can be expressed as

$$N = \sum_{m=1}^{M} N_m, \tag{2}$$

where N_m is the total number of active URLLC devices in the mth $(1 \leq m \leq M)$ time slot.

2.2 Available Unlicensed Spectrum

To ensure the harmonious coexistence between the NR-U and WiFi system on unlicensed band, the DCM mechanism is adopted at the NR-U, where the NR-U turns "on/off" periodically. During the off period, the WiFi APs occupy the unlicensed channels to serve WiFi terminals while the NR-U implementing carrier sensing to estimate the WiFi traffic loads and decide the available time fraction on unlicensed channels.

Based on [12], the WiFi traffic loads can be estimated accurately. Then, according to [13], the time fraction, $\theta_k^{(U)}$, is available to the URLLC devices on unlicensed channel k can be expressed as

$$\theta_k^{(U)} \leq 1 - d_k^{(U)}, \tag{3}$$

where $d_k^{(U)}$ represents the time fraction occupied by the WiFi users on unlicensed channel k, defined as $d_k^{(U)} = \frac{\hat{R}_k^{(\max)}}{\hat{R}_k}$, $\hat{R}_k$ stands for the average WiFi throughput achieved on the unlicensed spectrum when $1 - \theta_k^{(U)}$ time fraction on the unlicensed spectrum is used by the WiFi systems, $\hat{R}_k^{(\max)}$ indicates the maximum achievable average throughput of the WiFi system when there are only WiFi users using the unlicensed spectrum, $\theta_k^{(U)} \in [0, 1]$. Both $\hat{R}_k$ and $\hat{R}_k^{(\max)}$ can be achieved by the scheme used in [12].

2.3 Data Rates Analysis

Since the URLLC devices can use licensed spectrum and share unlicensed spectrum with the WiFi network, the achievable data rates can be divided into two parts, including the data rates on licensed and unlicensed spectrums. Moreover, to satisfy the low latency and high reliability requirements, the finite data block length is employed in the URLLC system as described in [14,15]. However, the finite data block length will bring about the loss on data rates and the Shannon channel capacity is no longer applicable. In order to meet the latency and reliability constraints while satisfying minimum data rate, it is necessary to trade off the relationship between the transmission data rate, the finite block length, and the transmission error probability.

According to the above analysis, the achievable data rates of URLLC device i on licensed subchannel j is given by

$$R_{i,j}^{(L)} = \xi_{i,j}^{(L)} W^{(L)} \left(\log(1 + \gamma_{i,j}^{(L)}) - \sqrt{\frac{V_{i,j}^{(L)}}{l}} \frac{Q^{-1}(\varepsilon)}{\ln 2} \right), \tag{4}$$

where $\xi_{i,j}^{(L)}$ represents the bandwidth fraction allocated to device i on licensed subchannel j, $W^{(L)}$ is the licensed bandwidth, $\gamma_{i,j}^{(L)}$ stands for the *signal to interference plus noise* (SINR) experienced at the device i on licensed subchannel j, defined as $\gamma_{i,j}^{(L)} = \frac{p_{i,j}^{(L)} h_{i,j}^{(L)}}{\xi_{i,j}^{(L)} W^{(L)} N_0}$, $p_{i,j}^{(L)}$ is the transmission power allocated to the device i on licensed subchannel j, $h_{i,j}^{(L)}$ indicates the channel power gain between the BS and device i on licensed subchannel j, N_0 is the noise power spectrum density of *additive white Gaussian noise* (AWGN), $V_{i,j}^{(L)}$ stands for the channel dispersion of device i on licensed subchannel j, defined as $V_{i,j}^{(L)} = 1 - (1 + \gamma_{i,j}^{(L)})^{-2}$, $Q^{-1}(\varepsilon)$ represents the inverse of complementary Gaussian cumulative distribution function, ε is the transmission error probability, $Q(x) = \int_x^\infty \frac{1}{\sqrt{2\pi}} e^{-t^2/2} dt$, l is the block length. It is noteworthy that $V \approx 1$, when the SINR experienced on the channel is higher than 10 dB.

When the BS transmits on the unlicensed channels, the downlink data rates of the URLLC device i on unlicensed channel k can be expressed as

$$R_{i,k}^{(U)} = \theta_{i,k}^{(U)} W^{(U)} \left(\log(1 + \gamma_{i,k}^{(U)}) - \sqrt{\frac{V_{i,k}^{(U)}}{l}} \frac{Q^{-1}(\varepsilon)}{\ln 2} \right), \tag{5}$$

where $\theta_{i,k}^{(U)} \in [0,1]$, represents the time fraction allocated to device i on unlicensed channel k, $W^{(U)}$ is the unlicensed channel bandwidth, $\gamma_{i,k}^{(U)}$ stands for the SINR experience on unlicensed channel k of device i, defined as $\gamma_{i,k}^{(U)} = \frac{p_{i,k}^{(U)} h_{i,k}^{(U)}}{N_0 W^{(U)}}$, $p_{i,k}^{(U)}$ indicates the transmission power allocated to i on unlicensed channel k, $h_{i,k}^{(U)}$ is the channel power gain between BS and device i on unlicensed channel k, $V_{i,k}^{(U)}$ stands for the channel dispersion of device i on unlicensed channel k, defined as $V_{i,k}^{(U)} = 1 - (1 + \gamma_{i,k}^{(U)})^{-2}$.

Based on the above analysis, the total achievable data rates at URLLC device i can be expressed as

$$R_i = \sum_{j=1}^{J} R_{i,j}^{(L)} + \sum_{k=1}^{K} R_{i,k}^{(U)}. \tag{6}$$

2.4   Power Consumption

The power consumption of each URLLC device mainly contains three parts. The first and second parts are the transmission power consumed by the device on licensed and unlicensed channels, respectively. The third part is the sensing power consumption on unlicensed channels at the device. Accordingly, the power consumption of URLLC device i can be expressed as

$$P_i = \sum_{j=1}^{J} p_{i,j}^{(L)} + \sum_{k=1}^{K} \theta_{i,k}^{(U)} p_{i,k}^{(U)} + \sum_{k=1}^{K} (1 - \theta_{i,k}^{(U)}) p_s^{(U)}, \tag{7}$$

where $p_s^{(U)}$ is the power consumed on sensing the unlicensed channel k, which is a constant.

The total power consumed by the URLLC devices in the uplink transmission can be written as

$$P^{(tot)} = \sum_{i=1}^{N} P_i \tag{8}$$

3   Power Consumption Minimization

In consideration of the limited power capacity, our objective is to minimize the power consumption at the BS and devices while guaranteeing the strict low latency and high reliability requirements. Accordingly, the optimization problem can be formulated as

$$\min_{\{p_{i,j}^{(L)}, p_{i,k}^{(U)}, \xi_{i,j}^{(L)}, \theta_{i,k}^{(U)}, l\}} P^{(tot)}, \tag{9}$$

subject to

$$R_i \geq r, \ \forall i \tag{9a}$$

$$\sum_{i=1}^{N} \xi_{i,j}^{(L)} \leq 1, \ \forall j, \tag{9b}$$

$$\sum_{i=1}^{N} \theta_{i,k}^{(U)} \leq 1 - d_k^{(U)}, \ \forall k, \tag{9c}$$

$$\sum_{i=1}^{N} \theta_{i,k}^{(U)} p_{i,k}^{(U)} \leq p_t^{(U)}, \ \forall k, \tag{9d}$$

$$\sum_{j=1}^{J} p_{i,j}^{(L)} + \sum_{k=1}^{K} \theta_{i,k}^{(U)} p_{i,k}^{(U)} + \sum_{k=1}^{K} (1 - \theta_{i,k}^{(U)}) p_s^{(U)} \leq P^{(max)}, \ \forall i, \tag{9e}$$

$$p_{i,j}^{(L)} \geq 0, p_{i,k}^{(U)} \geq 0, \xi_{i,j}^{(L)} \geq 0, \theta_{i,k}^{(U)} \geq 0, \ \forall i, j, k, \tag{9f}$$

where the objective function (9) aims to minimize the total power consumption, constraint (9a) is to satisfy the minimum transmission data rate requirements of each device to guarantee the QoS, constraint (9b) guarantees the allocated licensed spectrum bandwidth is less than $W^{(L)}$, (9c) ensures that the allocated unlicensed spectrum is less than or equal to the available one, $\sum_{i=1}^{N} \theta_{i,k}^{(U)}$ is the time fraction allocated to the devices on the unlicensed channel k, (9d) is to limit the transmission power of the devices on the unlicensed channels, (9e) is the total power constraint of each device.

3.1 Joint Power and Spectrum Allocation

Obviously, problem (9) is a non-convex optimization problem. Let $A_{i,k}^{(U)} = \theta_{i,k}^{(U)} \cdot p_{i,k}^{(U)}$, the objective function and constraint (9a) can be converted into convex functions through mathematical derivation. Accordingly, problem (9) can be converted into a convex optimization problem with respect to $p_{i,j}^{(L)}$, $A_{i,k}^{(U)}$, $\xi_{i,j}^{(L)}$, and $\theta_{i,k}^{(U)}$. Then, we use the Lagrangian multiplier method to solve the problem and obtain the globally optimal power and spectrum allocation. Hence, we minimize the total power consumption and improve the SE and EE of the URLLC system. The constructed Lagrangian function can be expressed as

$$
\begin{aligned}
& f\left(p_{i,j}^{(L)}, A_{i,k}^{(U)}, \xi_{i,j}^{(L)}, \theta_{i,k}^{(U)}, \alpha_j, \beta_k, \psi_i, \mu_k, \lambda_i\right) \\
& = P^{(tot)} + \sum_{i=1}^{N} \lambda_i(r - R_i) \\
& + \sum_{j=1}^{J} \alpha_j\left(\sum_{i=1}^{N} \xi_{i,j}^{(L)} - 1\right) + \sum_{k=1}^{K} \beta_k\left(\sum_{i=1}^{N} A_{i,k}^{(U)} - p_t^{(U)}\right) \\
& + \sum_{i=1}^{N} \psi_i\left(\sum_{j=1}^{J} p_{i,j}^{(L)} + \sum_{k=1}^{K} A_{i,k}^{(U)} + \sum_{k=1}^{K}(1 - \theta_{i,k}^{(U)})p_s^{(U)} - P^{(max)}\right) \\
& + \sum_{k=1}^{K} \mu_k\left(\sum_{i=1}^{N} \theta_{i,k}^{(U)} - 1 + d_k^{(U)}\right),
\end{aligned}
\tag{10}
$$

where λ_i, α_j, β_k, ψ_i, and μ_k are the Lagrangian multipliers.

Based on the KKT conditions, we can derive the globally optimal solutions of the spectrum and power allocation for the URLLC device i on licensed and unlicensed channels.

$$
p_{i,j}^{(L)} = \xi_{i,j}^{(L)} W^{(L)}\left(\frac{\lambda_i}{\psi_i} - \frac{N_0}{h_{i,j}^{(L)}}\right)^+,
\tag{11}
$$

$$
\xi_{i,j}^{(L)} = \frac{\lambda_i R_{i,j}^{(L)} - \psi_i p_{i,j}^{(L)}}{\alpha_j},
\tag{12}
$$

$$
p_{i,k}^{(U)} = W^{(U)}\left(\frac{\lambda_i}{\beta_k + \psi_i} - \frac{N_0}{h_{i,k}^{(U)}}\right)^+,
\tag{13}
$$

$$
\theta_{i,k}^{(U)} = \frac{\lambda_i R_{i,k}^{(U)}}{\mu_k - \psi_i p_s^{(U)} - p_s^{(U)} + (\beta_k + \psi_i) A_{i,k}^{(U)}},
\tag{14}
$$

where $(a)^+$ represents $\max(a, 0)$, α_j and μ_k are the Lagrangian multipliers of the constraints (9b) and (9c) on licensed and unlicensed spectrum restrictions respectively, β_k and ψ_i are the Lagrangian multipliers of the unlicensed band power limitation and total power limitation of the constraints (9d) and (9e), respectively. We can see that the closed-form expressions of $p_{i,j}^{(L)}$ and $p_{i,k}^{(U)}$ are similar to the power allocation of the water injection algorithm. It is clear that $p_{i,j}^{(L)}$ is related to $\xi_{i,j}^{(L)}$. Defined as $A_{i,k}^{(U)} = \theta_{i,k}^{(U)} \cdot p_{i,k}^{(U)}$, according to Eqs. (13) and (14), $p_{i,k}^{(U)}$ is also related to $\theta_{i,k}^{(U)}$.

3.2 Optimal Algorithm Development

Based on the above analysis, the detail of the algorithm steps to solve the optimization problem (9) can be summarized as in Algorithm 1. Firstly, according to equation (3), we can estimate the WiFi traffic load by the number of WiFi users and calculate the unlicensed time fraction for URLLC. Next, according to Eqs. (11), (12), (13), and (14), the Lagrangian multiplier method is adopted to obtain the globally optimal solutions of the optimization problem (9). Thus, we can acquire the optimal power and spectrum allocation for URLLC devices on licensed and unlicensed spectrums.

Algorithm 1. Adaptive channel access algorithm in the coexistence of URLLC and WiFi systems

---

1: **Initialize** : NR-U BS determines the available licensed bandwidth fraction, $\xi_{i,j}^{(L)}$, obtains the available unlicensed time fraction, $1 - d_k^{(U)}$, initializes block length l.

2: **if** $1 - d_k^{(U)} = 0$ **then**

3:     The URLLC system only accesses licensed channels, and obtains the optimal solutions of $p_{i,j}^{(L)}$ and $\xi_{i,j}^{(L)}$ according to (11) and (12).

4: **else if** $0 < 1 - d_k^{(U)} < 1$ **then**

5:     The URLLC system simultaneously accesses licensed and unlicensed channels.

6:     According to (11), (12), (13), and (14), use the Lagrangian multiplier method to obtain the optimal solutions of $p_{i,j}^{(L)}$, $\xi_{i,j}^{(L)}$, $p_{i,k}^{(U)}$, and $\theta_{i,k}^{(U)}$.

7: **else**

8:     The URLLC system only accesses unlicensed channels, and obtains the optimal solutions of $p_{i,k}^{(U)}$ and $\theta_{i,k}^{(U)}$ according to (13) and (14).

9: **end if**

10: **return** the globally optimal solution $P = \{p_{i,j}^{(L)}, \xi_{i,j}^{(L)}, p_{i,k}^{(U)}, \theta_{i,k}^{(U)}\}$, $\forall i, j, k$.

---

4   Simulation Results

In this section, we provide numerical simulation results to demonstrate the effectiveness of the proposed URLLC power and spectrum allocation scheme for joint licensed and unlicensed bands. We first evaluate the performance of the URLLC system. Next, we analyze the impact of the available unlicensed spectrum resources.

In the simulation scenario, we consider a URLLC network with a BS. There are I URLLC devices randomly distribute within 50 m coverage of BS, and the arrival of data packets for all URLLC devices obeys a Poisson distribution. The mini-slot frame structure is adopted with the subcarrier of 30 kHz and 2 symbols. At the same time, we estimate the WiFi traffic load to calculate the unlicensed time fraction based on the number of WiFi users accessing the unlicensed bands. In addition, the licensed and unlicensed bandwidths are both 20 MHz. The licensed and unlicensed channels are Rayleigh fading channels. Other main simulation parameters are shown in Table 1.

Table 1. Simulation parameters.

Parameters	Value
Maximum transmission power of each device, $P^{(max)}$	33 dBm
Transmission power on unlicensed band, $p_t^{(U)}$	23 dBm
AWGN noise power, N_0	−95 dBm (over 20 MHz BW)
Bandwidth on licensed and unlicensed, $W^{(L)}$, $W^{(U)}$	20 MHz
Path loss model on licensed band (dB)	$-15.3 - 37.6\log_{10}(d(m))$
Path loss model on unlicensed band (dB)	$-15.3 - 50\log_{10}(d(m))$
Maximum allowed transmission error probability, ε	10^{-5}
Delay requirement for URLLC	1 ms

4.1   Performance Evaluation of the URLLC System

Figure 2 demonstrates the achievable SE of the URLLC system with different available time fractions on each unlicensed channel, $1 - d_k^{(U)}$, and data block length, with $L = 50$, 200, 500, and 800. As $1 - d_k^{(U)}$ increases, the SE of the system improves as well. Therefore, the more opportunities the system has to use the unlicensed spectrum resources, the higher SE the system can achieve.

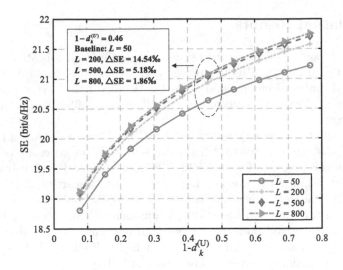

Fig. 2. The SE with different data block lengths and unlicensed time fractions.

Besides, as L increases, the proportion of control signaling overheads reduces and the effective data information increases, which would improve the SE. However, when L increases to 500, the SE improves only a little if continuing to increase the block length. We define a spectrum efficiency growth rate with $L = 50$ as the baseline, $\triangle SE = \frac{SE - SE_{50}}{SE_{50}}$. When $1 - d_k^{(U)}$ is about 0.46 and L increases from 50 to 200, the SE improves 14.54‰. Then, when L increases from 200 to 500, the SE improves 5.18‰. When L increases from 500 to 800, the SE only improves 1.86‰. It is because that L is related to the transmission delay D_t and bandwidth W as follows, $L = D_t W$ [15]. If continuing to increase L, it will bring more transmission delay or require more bandwidth. Thus, we compromise the transmission delay, channel bandwidth, and data rate of the URLLC system. It can be seen that $L = 500$ is the optimal block length in this simulation. In the subsequent simulations, L is selected to be 500 for other simulation analyses of optimal power and spectrum allocation.

Figure 3 depicts the total power consumption with different available time fractions and required minimum data rates, $r = 25, 30, 35$, and 40 Mbps. The increase on $1 - d_k^{(U)}$ implies that the available unlicensed spectrum resources for the URLLC devices increase. Therefore, the power consumption for listening to unlicensed channels to estimate the WiFi traffic loads decreases. In addition, Algorithm 1 optimizes the power and spectrum allocation, further reducing power consumption. However, as r increases, more transmission power is required to meet the rise on the data rate requirements.

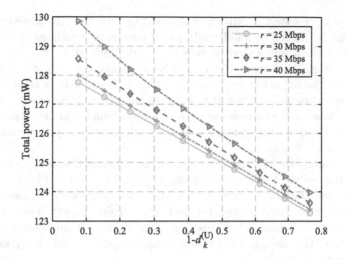

Fig. 3. The total power consumption with different unlicensed time fractions and minimum data rates.

4.2 Impact of the Available Unlicensed Spectrum Resource

Figure 4(a) shows the effect of Algorithm 1 on the EE achieved on licensed channels. When the available unlicensed spectrum resources increase, URLLC devices can release the pressure on licensed spectrum by using unlicensed channels and acquire more channel capacity. Therefore, the devices can use the licensed spectrum more efficiently by Algorithm 1 to improve the EE on licensed channels. On the contrary, as r increases, the power consumption increases to satisfy the high transmission rate requirements, and the average EE decreases.

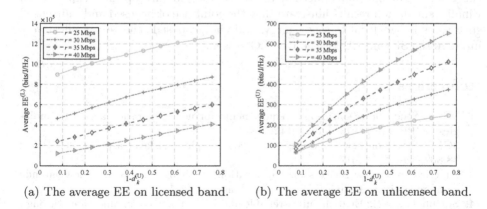

(a) The average EE on licensed band.   (b) The average EE on unlicensed band.

Fig. 4. The average EE with different unlicensed time fractions and minimum data rates.

Figure 4(b) presents the impact of Algorithm 1 on the EE achieved on unlicensed channels. As the available unlicensed spectrum resources are close to 0,
the EE achieved on unlicensed channels with different data rate requirements
tends to 0. The EE improves with the increase of unlicensed spectrum resources.
Different from the EE achieved on licensed channels, the EE increases when the
data rate requirements increase. It is because the available unlicensed spectrum
resources increase as the increase on data rate requirements of devices. Therefore,
there is more freedom in frequency domain to decrease the power consumption
by the proposed scheme.

It is noteworthy that the average EE on the unlicensed spectrum is generally
lower than that of the licensed spectrum, as demonstrated in Fig. 4(a) and (b).
That is because that the power consumption on unlicensed channels includes
not only the transmission power, but also the sensing power. Thus, the power
consumption on unlicensed channels is greater than that on licensed channels.
In consequence, the average EE on unlicensed channels is relatively lower than
that on licensed channels.

5   Conclusion

In this paper, we propose an optimal power and spectrum allocation scheme for
the URLLC system. In order to reduce the power consumption, the unlicensed
spectrum is exploited to serve the URLLC devices, and the DCM mechanism is
adopted to ensure fair coexistence with the WiFi network. Moreover, we combine
the user grouping scheme and mini-slot frame structure to make the URLLC
system satisfy the low latency requirement. The finite block length regime is
also employed to trade off the transmission data rate, finite block length, and
transmission error probability. Then, we establish a power minimization model
which meets the requirements of low latency and high reliability, and apply
the Lagrangian multiplier method to derive the globally optimal expressions.
Finally, simulation results illustrate that the joint use of licensed and unlicensed
spectrums is beneficial to save energy, and the proposed scheme can effectively
improve the SE and EE for the URLLC system.

References

1. 3GPP: Study on scenarios and requirements for next generation access technologies. 3GPP TR 38.913, V16. 0.0 (2020)
2. 3GPP: Study on new radio access technology; physical layer aspects. 3GPP TR
   38.802, V14. 2.0 (2017)
3. Americas, G.: New services and applications with 5g ultra-reliable low latency
   communications. Technical Report, 5G Americas (2018)
4. Sutton, G., et al.: Enabling ultra-reliable and low-latency communications through
   unlicensed spectrum. IEEE Network **32**(2), 70–77 (2018)
5. Zeng, Y., Wang, Y., Sun, S., Yang, K.: Feasibility of URLLC in unlicensed spectrum. In: 2019 IEEE VTS Asia Pacific Wireless Communications Symposium
   (APWCS), pp. 1–5. IEEE (2019)

6. Le, T.K., Salim, U., Kaltenberger, F.: Channel access enhancements in unlicensed spectrum for NR URLLC transmissions. In: GLOBECOM 2020-2020 IEEE Global Communications Conference, pp. 1–6. IEEE (2020)
7. Cuevas, R.M., Rosa, C., Frederiksen, F., Pedersen, K.I.: Uplink ultra-reliable low latency communications assessment in unlicensed spectrum. In: 2018 IEEE Globecom Workshops (GC Wkshps), pp. 1–6. IEEE (2018)
8. Pocovi, G., Pedersen, K.I., Mogensen, P.: Joint link adaptation and scheduling for 5G ultra-reliable low-latency communications. IEEE Access 6, 28912–28922 (2018)
9. Pocovi, G., Pedersen, K.I., Soret, B., Lauridsen, M., Mogensen, P.: On the impact of multi-user traffic dynamics on low latency communications. In: 2016 International Symposium on Wireless Communication Systems (ISWCS), pp. 204–208. IEEE (2016)
10. Shafi, M., et al.: 5G: a tutorial overview of standards, trials, challenges, deployment, and practice. IEEE J. Sel. Areas Commun. 35(6), 1201–1221 (2017)
11. Yuan, J., Yu, G., Yin, R., Qu, F., Zeng, R.: Group-based data transmission protocol for small-sized URLLC services. IEEE Wirel. Commun. Lett. 9(9), 1432–1436 (2020)
12. Yin, R., Zou, Z., Wu, C., Yuan, J., Chen, X., Yu, G.: Learning-based WiFi traffic load estimation in NR-U systems. IEICE T. Fund. Electr. 104(2), 542–549 (2021)
13. Yin, R., Zou, Z., Wu, C., Yuan, J., Chen, X.: Distributed spectrum and power allocation for D2D-U networks: a scheme based on NN and federated learning. Mobile Netw. Appl. 1–14 (2021)
14. Polyanskiy, Y., Poor, H.V., Verdú, S.: Channel coding rate in the finite blocklength regime. IEEE Trans. Inf. Theor. 56(5), 2307–2359 (2010)
15. She, C., Yang, C., Quek, T.Q.: Radio resource management for ultra-reliable and low-latency communications. IEEE Commun. Mag. 55(6), 72–78 (2017)

Relay-Assisted Task Offloading Optimization for MEC-Enabled Internet of Vehicles

Heli Zhang[1(✉)], Haonan Zhang[1], Xun Shao[2], and Yusheng Ji[3]

[1] Beijing University of Posts and Telecommunications, Beijing 100876, China
zhangheli@bupt.edu.cn
[2] Kitami Institute of Technology, Kitami 0908507, Hokkaido, Japan
[3] National Institute of Informatics (NII), Chiyoda City, Tokyo, Japan

Abstract. Mobile edge computing (MEC)-enabled Internet of Vehicles (IoV) is a promising way to provide low latency and high computation functions to smart vehicles. Owing to the mobility of vehicles and unpredicted distribution of computation-intensive tasks, computational resources at the edge may be utilized with only low efficiency. To solve this problem, this study investigates a relay-supported task offloading scheme in MEC-enabled IoV. In this scheme, computational tasks produced by vehicles are predictively offloaded to MEC nodes through relays to improve the allocation of computational resources. A combinational problem is used to model relay selection for vehicles connected to the MEC. To solve the corresponding problem, a low-complexity algorithm that combines the Hungarian and the Greedy algorithms is designed. Simulation results show that the proposed scheme achieves better performance than existing schemes in terms of overall efficiency and offloading time.

Keywords: Vehicular network · MEC · Predictive offloading · Multihop relay

1 Introduction

With the development of the Internet of Vehicles (IoV), the number of vehicles connected to the network has been increasing exponentially. Considering the complexity of the traffic environment, wireless channel status, and user demand, dealing with the growth in vehicular services with high accuracy and making automatic decisions with low latency are major challenges [1].

Because IoV tasks are computation-intensive, mobile edge computing (MEC) technology has emerged as a promising tool to provide high computational capacity nearer to vehicle devices [2–4]. MEC can reduce the burden of the wireless backhaul and core network [5]. In MEC-enabled vehicular networks, tasks are offloaded to MEC nodes via the Vehicle-to-Infrastructure (V2I) mode. Owing to the instability of the wireless link and resource starvation, relay-assisted offloading schemes are widely used. Relay-assisted schemes are designed to optimize the offloading performance by transmitting a task to a better location. Recent research has identified and studied some key features in the realization of vehicular network architectures as well as solutions for some key

© ICST Institute for Computer Sciences, Social Informatics and Telecommunications Engineering 2022
Published by Springer Nature Switzerland AG 2022. All Rights Reserved
C. T. Calafate et al. (Eds.): MONAMI 2021, LNICST 418, pp. 152–164, 2022.
https://doi.org/10.1007/978-3-030-94763-7_12

challenges. For instance, a mobility-aware strategy was developed to realize resource sharing among servers in MEC-enabled vehicular networks [6]. Another study used the effective connectivity of vehicles, mobile devices, and infrastructure to overcome the adverse effects of mobility on reliable data transmission and introduced this concept into IoV applications using millimeter wave (mmWave) technology [7]. An autonomous hybrid edge/cloud framework for vehicular edge computing was proposed to significantly increase the computational capacity by utilizing the available computational resources in surrounding vehicles, roadside units (RSUs), and the cloud via multiaccess networks [8]. However, this model did not consider the relay mode. Another study considered a three-node relaying MEC system and an adapted transport protocol for realizing better energy performance [9]. From the abovementioned studies, it is obvious that selecting favorable servers in an offloading scheme remains a challenging task. As a vehicle moves, multiple RSUs are connected to different MEC servers. Existing studies rarely considered MEC server overload or downtime in a certain region. Because upgrading onboard units and realizing wider coverage of MEC servers requires a longer period of time, MEC-enabled vehicular networks may be unable to respond to a surge in demand for data processing; in other words, some vehicle tasks cannot be offloaded in time because of the low network scalability. Furthermore, low expansibility results in some vehicles suffering high delays. Thus, the present authors proposed a relay-assisted task offloading scheme to optimize the total latency and improve the scalability of the network. The present study describes the whole mission arrival process and defines it as a composite process in which task forecasting is relayed to a specified location and offloaded for computation. When the accessed server is busy, the vehicle terminal cannot receive calculation results in time. Therefore, multihop relay vehicles on its way are selected to offload the task data to a resource-rich server. Further, a joint selection algorithm is proposed to identify appropriate relay nodes for a part of the vehicles used in the proposed scheme. This study aims to minimize the total offloading latency of the terminals in the current area through reasonable matching between the source vehicles and each-hop relay vehicles.

The remainder of this paper is organized as follows. Section 2 describes the system model and problem formulation. Section 3 describes the developed optimal offloading scheme and joint selection algorithm. Section 4 presents the simulation results and discussions. Finally, Section 5 presents the conclusions of this study.

2 Introduction

This section describes the proposed relay-assisted MEC-enabled vehicular network system and discusses both the transmission model and the computation model.

2.1 Network Model

Figure 1 shows the vehicular network equipped with a continuous MEC server considered in this study. Typically, the RSUs installed along the unidirectional road collocate with the MEC server so that vehicle terminals can access the computing resources of the MEC server by communicating with the RSU. The coverage radius of each RSU is L.

For clarity, Fig. 1 shows only one routing path; in reality, multiple parallel paths will exist simultaneously. Vehicles with tasks are called source vehicles (SVs) and those acting as relay nodes traveling in the same direction are called relay vehicles (RVs).

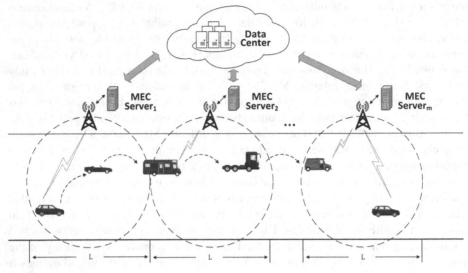

Fig. 1. System model

Analogous to cellular network users in communication systems, a connected vehicle determines whether the MEC server is idle by communicating with the current RSU [10]. One-to-one correspondence is used to satisfy the requirements of reducing signal interference and excessive resource overheads; in other words, each RV can serve only one SV through the Vehicle-to-Vehicle (V2V) mode, and each SV can only be served by one RV.

2.2 Transmission Model

The transmission model can also be interpreted as a communication model consisting of a direct connection and a multihop relay connection. This study considers environments where scatterers are sparse, such as suburban or expressway scenarios. As in similar studies in this area, signal fading caused by non-line-of-sight is ignored, and the influence of the relative distance between the vehicles on the signal strength of data transmission is considered. Pass loss is positively correlated with the distance between different devices and is given by

$$L(d(t)) = L(d_0) + 10\alpha \log_{10}\left(\frac{d(t)}{d_0}\right) \tag{1}$$

where $d(t)$ is the distance between the terminals; $L(d_0)$ is a path loss constant due to factors such as frequency, weather, and geology; and α is the path loss index from which the path loss L can be obtained [11].

1) **Direct Connection**

A task is offloaded from a vehicle terminal or a relay node to the RSU. The path-loss channel model is used for the link gain. For a given transmission power P_s and received power P_r,

$$L(d(t)) = 10\log_{10}\left(\frac{P_s}{P_r}\right) \tag{2}$$

This equation can be rewritten in terms of P_r as follows:

$$P_r = \frac{P_s}{10^{\frac{L(d(t))}{10}}} \tag{3}$$

N_0 is the Gaussian white noise power. The instantaneously available information transmission rate can be expressed as

$$R(t) = \log_2\left(1 + \frac{P_s 10^{-\frac{L(d(t))}{10}}}{N_0}\right) \tag{4}$$

The vehicle communicates with the RSU through the V2I mode based on the Long-Term Evolution Advanced specification. Let B_{V2I} denote the channel bandwidth and $d_{i,R}$, the distance between the vehicle carrying task i and the RSU. Then, the data rate is given by

$$R_{V2I}(t) = B_{V2I}\log_2\left(1 + \frac{P_t 10^{-\frac{L(d_{i,R}(t))}{10}}}{N_0}\right) \tag{5}$$

2) **Multihop Relay Connection**

The V2V model can support multihop relay connections. Moving vehicles can share communication, computational, and storage resources with other nearby vehicles by using dedicated short-range communication (DSRC) technology following the IEEE 802.11p specification 8. The task requester in SVs are considered able to exchange position, velocity, and driving status information with RVs. Moreover, according to the DSRC link feature, the vehicle can update the status table in real time, including the variety of information obtained from nearby vehicles. Obviously, the vehicle may estimate the distance on the basis of its table as follows:

$$d_{i,j}(t) = \sqrt{\left(X_{i,j}(t)\right)^2 + \left(Y_{i,j}(t)\right)^2} \tag{6}$$

$$X_{i,j}(t) = X_{i,j}(0) + \left(v_j - v_i\right)t \tag{7}$$

$X_{i,j}$ is the parallel distance to the road between vehicles i and j at time t, and $Y_{i,j}$ is the lateral distance perpendicular to the road between the two vehicles and is assumed to be fixed. Given that the maximum communication distance according to the DSRC standard and actual link conditions between any two vehicles is D,

$$0 \le d_{i,j}(t) \le D \tag{8}$$

Then, within the communication distance, the end-to-end reachable information rate of $i \ni SV$ and $j \ni RV$ is

$$R_{i,j}(t) = B_{V2V} \log_2 \left(1 + \frac{P_t 10^{-\frac{L(d_{i,j}(t))}{10}}}{N_0} \right) \tag{9}$$

2.3 Computation Model

For task i, c_i is the number of cycles required for completing task i, and d_i is the data size for transmitting it from the transmitter to the receiver. The tolerance delay for each task is $t_{i,local} > t_{i,max}$. Briefly, the initial information of task i can be clearly denoted as $T_i = \{c_i, d_i, t_{i,max}\}$. In addition, let f_i and f_m respectively be the CPU operating frequency at the vehicle terminal and at a MEC server (unit: number of CPU cycles per second). When the computing power of the SV is insufficient to complete the task calculation within the delay tolerance, that is,

$$t_{i,local} > t_{i,max} \tag{10}$$

the MEC server is requested to assist in the calculation. $t_{i,local}$ is the time required to complete the task locally. When the vehicle leaves the RSU radio coverage area or the MEC is not expected to provide part of the computational resources for SVs, the next or even a later MEC server can be accessed through multihop V2V relay transmission. An analysis of this model shows that the total task processing delay involves three parts: transmission delay through the DSRC link, latency to offload to the MEC, and task execution time. In most task types, the amount of data obtained through the analysis is often much smaller than the input raw data; therefore, the delay in returning the calculation result is ignored in previous research.

3   Optimal Offloading Scheme and Joint Selection Algorithm

Based on the MEC-enabled IoV model discussed in Sect. 2, an optimal offloading scheme is designed to achieve the desired performance. Subsequently, a joint selection algorithm is used to solve the relay node selection problem of multiple vehicles.

3.1   Optimal Offloading Scheme

The offloading problem is considered for all vehicles in the area in light of the area covered by one of the RSUs as an example. First, under the influence of the computational task complexity ρ, the delay required by the vehicle's onboard unit to process the current task is calculated as

$$t_{i,local} = \frac{\rho c_i}{f_i} \tag{11}$$

Then, whether the computational capacity of the vehicle's onboard unit satisfies this task's delay requirement is judged using (10)–(11). If the task delay tolerance is met, the local mode is used as the first choice.

In the opposite case, the proposed multi-relay-assisted offloading scheme is applied for the uplink network shown in Fig. 1. Within the delay limit, the N_i - th RSU on which task i can be offloaded to the farthest continuous MEC is calculated as

$$\left\lfloor \frac{v_i t_{i,\max}}{L} \right\rfloor = N_i \tag{12}$$

where $\lfloor \cdot \rfloor$ means rounding down, and v_i is the velocity of the requester carrying task i. Because the vehicle transmits task data for a short time, the velocity change problem is not considered during the task offloading process.

The unique identifier of the source vehicle, N_i, and other information should be attached to task i. After the vehicle determines that the onboard unit fails to satisfy the needs, a resource is requested from the MEC, and the multihop relay connection process is used when the current server has no idle resources. According to the joint selection algorithm, a suitable RV is selected as the first-hop relay node. Let RV1 be the collection of first-hop relay terminals to which j belongs. Define a pairing $\theta = \{\theta_{i,j}\}_{SV \times RV}$ consisting of binary elements $\theta_{i,j} \in \{0, 1\}$ for $i \in SV$ and $j \in RV$. Specifically, if SV i is paired with RV j, $\theta_{i,j} = 1$; otherwise, $\theta_{i,j} = 0$. Each RV can only be paired with one SV and vice versa; therefore,

$$\begin{cases} \sum_{i=1}^{n_{SV}} \theta_{i,j} = 1, \ \forall i = 1, \ldots, SV \\ \sum_{j=1}^{n_{RV}} \theta_{i,j} = 1, \ \forall j = 1, \ldots, RV \\ \theta_{i,j} = 0, \quad otherwise \end{cases} \tag{13}$$

The time required for transmitting the task from i to j is $t_{i,j}$:

$$t_{i,j} = \frac{d_i}{R_{i,j}} \tag{14}$$

When task i reaches the relay node of the first-hop terminal, that terminal is reassigned to V_i and whether the connected MEC can support offloading is checked. As noted in [14] and [15], if it can support offloading, the offloading delay $t_{i,up}$ and the computing delay $t_{i,ex}$ are given by

$$\begin{cases} t_{i,up} = \frac{d_i}{R_{V2I}} \\ t_{i,ex} = \frac{c_i}{f_m} \end{cases} \tag{15}$$

$$t_i = \theta_{i,j} t_{i,j} + t_{i,up} + t_{i,ex} \tag{16}$$

If the MEC service is still unavailable, the second-hop relay process is continued and the abovementioned judgment conditions are rechecked and calculation methods are repeated. However, the limitation of N_i must be considered. Owing to the problem of communication distance, for more than N_i relay hops, the task can reach the coverage of the N_i-th MEC server. When an idle MEC server is still not found after N_i relay hops, the task has to be queued for calculation and offloading. Therefore, the maximum number of hops is set to N_i to ensure that the task is offloaded before the source vehicle arrives.

This scheme aims to minimize the total latency when the requester completes the application in an area where MEC computational resources cannot be obtained. The problem can be mathematically formulated as (17), where $C1$ is a prerequisite for relay offloading. hop_k indicates the k - th hop relay, and $k \leq N_i$ limits task i to pass the $t_{i,j,k} = +\infty$ jump at most. $t_{keep}^{i \to j}$ records the connectable time between the source vehicle and the relay vehicle. $C2$ and $C3$ ensure that tasks can be transmitted to the relay vehicle. $C4$ limits the one-to-one correspondence of V2V. $C5$ guarantees that the task is completed within the time delay requirement. By solving problem P1, the total latency is optimized.

$$P1 : \min_{\theta_{i,j}} \sum_{i=1}^{n_{sv}} \sum_{k=1}^{N_i} t_i^{hop_k}$$

$$\text{s.t.} \begin{cases} C1 : t_{i,local} > t_{i,max}, \forall i \in \text{SV} \\ C2 : t_{keep}^{i \to j, hop_k} = \underset{t}{argmin}\left\{d_{i,j}^{hop_k}(t) \leq D\right\}, \\ \quad \forall i \in \text{SV}, \forall j \in \text{RV}, \forall k \in N_i \\ C3 : t_{keep}^{i \to j, hop_k} > t_{i,j}^{hop_k} \\ C4 : \sum_{i=1}^{n_{SV}} \sum_{j=1}^{n_{RV}} \theta_{i,j} = 1 \\ C5 : \sum_{i=1}^{n_{SV}} \sum_{k=1}^{N_i} t_i^{hop_k} \leq t_{i,max} \end{cases} \quad (17)$$

3.2 Joint Selection Algorithm

When more than one choice is available between SVs and RVs, Algorithm 1 is proposed to generate the optimal vehicle combination for relaying. All requesters of SVs monitor the nearby vehicle status information. First, when generating a new offloading program, the requester can apply for a RV vehicle. At the same time, surrounding vehicles will also connect with others and send relaying requests to them. Then, if a request is sent to multiple RVs, one of the requests will be selected using the proposed joint selection algorithm shown below. At the same time, the request should notify other RVs to disconnect. Ultimately, as soon as a trunk connection is established, one RV immediately stops announcing its availability until the service is terminated or disconnected.

In this light, an efficient and low-complexity scheduling algorithm is designed to solve problem 1, as shown below. This algorithm involves the following four steps. The delay is calculated for all $i = 1 , \cdots, SV$ required to transfer task data between each requester and the relay node it can connect to. Let the vehicle carrying the task i be V_i and the next hop relay node be V_j. The greedy algorithm and the quick sorting method will rapidly select the optimal vehicle j to join the RV set under the constraints of low complexity. When different requesters select the same relay vehicle, the vehicle V_j that can obtain a suboptimal delay is added to the RV, and so on. The optimal problem considered is for all requesters, in which case P1 is reduced to

$$\min_{\theta_{i,j}} \sum_{i=1}^{n_{SV}} \sum_{k=1}^{N_i} \theta_{i,j} t_i^{hop_k} \tag{18}$$

$$\text{s.t. } n_{SV} = n_{RV}.$$

Then, $W^{hop_k} = \{t_{i,j,k}\}_{n_{SV} \times n_{RV}}$, $i.e.$,

$$W^{hop_k} = \begin{bmatrix} t_{1,1,k} & t_{1,2,k} & \cdots & t_{1,j,k} \\ t_{2,1,k} & t_{2,2,k} & \cdots & t_{2,j,k} \\ \vdots & \vdots & \ddots & \vdots \\ t_{i,1,k} & t_{i,2,k} & \cdots & t_{i,j,k} \end{bmatrix} \tag{19}$$

where element $t_{i,j,k}$ indicates the transmission delay between V_i and V_j at the k - th hop. When V_i and V_j have no communication relationship, $t_{i,j,k} = +\infty$. This problem is then equivalent to minimizing the sum of delays by selecting exactly one element in each row and column of W, where each V_i is only permitted to operate only one V_j. This is an assignment problem that can be solved as follows [17]. When task i does not get the opportunity to offload after the k-hop relay, it satisfies $t_{i,up}^{hop_k} = t_{i,ex}^{hop_k} = 0$, and $t_{i,up}^{hop_k}$ increases the relaying time of V_i to V_j in the k - th hop. Therefore, flag$_i = 0$ is set to indicate that it is not offloaded; otherwise, flag$_i = 1$ is set and the total latency t_i for task i is found when it finishes offloading after the k - th hop relay or reaches the upper limit of N_i - th hops. This can be expressed as

$$t_i = t_{i,wait} + \sum_{k=1}^{N_i} t_{i,up}^{hop_k} + t_{i,ex}^{hop_k} + t_{i,j}^{hop_k} \tag{20}$$

where $t_{i,wait}$ indicates the time when the task is queued for offloading when task i reaches the maximum number of relay hops.

This predictive offloading method can also prevent the pressure of the requester from driving to the wireless network through the wireless backhaul link owing to the fact that the requester has left the area covered by the RSU after the local queuing calculation is offloaded. When task i ends, a matching matrix W is reformed in the new one-hop relay until all tasks are offloaded. W is a square matrix. The assignment problem can be solved by the Hungarian algorithm [15] whose complexity is $\mathcal{O}(N^3)$. The proposed joint selection algorithm is shown below in Algorithm 1.

Table 1. Joint selection algorithm process

Algorithm 1 Joint Selection Algorithm
1: Initialization:
a) Request vehicles $\mathbf{SV} = \{1, \cdots, i, \cdots n_{SV}\}$
b) Maximal hops N_i
c) Distance between V_i and V_j
d) Set $\text{flag}_i = 0$, $i = \{1, 2, \cdots n_{SV}\}$;
2: **for** V_i in **SV do**
3:     Choose V_j and form $\mathbf{RV} = \{1, \cdots, j, \cdots n_{RV}\}$
4:     **for** V_j in **RV do**
5:        Calculate $t_{i,j}^{hop_1}$
6:     **end for**
7:     Set $\mathbf{W}^{hop_1}$
8:     Calculate $t_{i,up}^{hop_1}, t_{i,ex}^{hop_1}, t_i^{hop_1}$
9: **end for**
10: **while** $\mathbf{W} \neq 0$ **do**
11:    Set new V_j in hop_k , $V_j \in \mathbf{RV}_k^*$
12:    Update distance between $V_i \in \mathbf{SV}_k^*$ and $V_j \in \mathbf{RV}_k^*$
13:    Calculate $t_{i,up}^{hop_k}$ and update $\mathbf{W}^{hop_k}$
14:    **for** i in $n_{SV,k}^*$ **do**
15:       **if** $k = N_i$ or task i satisfy constraint (21) **then**
16:       Set $\text{flag}_i = 1$ and calculate t_i
17:       **end if**
18:       **if** $\text{flag}_i = 0$ **then**
19:         Set $t_{i,up}^{hop_k} = t_{i,ex}^{hop_k} = 0$
20:       **end if**
21:    **end for**
22:    $k = k+1$
23: **end while**
24: Output: relay selection $\mathbb{RV} = \{\mathbf{RV}_1^*, \mathbf{RV}_2^*, \cdots, \mathbf{RV}_k^*\}$ and the optimal total latency.

4   Simulation Result and Discussion

This section presents some simulation results to illustrate the performance of the optimal offloading scheme and joint selection algorithm. A vehicular network in which SVs and RVs move along a unidirectional straight road is simulated. Each RSU is mounted at a position 15 m away from the curb, and it can cover a range of 200 m [12]. The wireless channel is modelled as a Rayleigh fading channel with V2I and V2V path-loss

models given by [11], $L_{V2I}(d(t)) = 100.7 + 23.5 \log_{10}\left(\frac{d(t)}{d_0}\right)$, $L_{V2V}(d(t)) = 63.3 +$
$17.7 \log_{10}\left(\frac{d(t)}{d_0}\right)$, respectively. $P_t = 1.3$ W is set for a wireless bandwidth of 1 MHz
to transmit data. The background noise is $N_0 = -100$ dBm, DSRC coverage radius is
$D = 150$ m and $\beta = 1.05$. The computational capacities of f_m and f_v are considered to
be randomly distributed on the intervals $\left[10^6, 10^8\right]$ cycles/s and $\left[10^5, 10^7\right]$ cycles/s.
For a given vehicle, the velocity is randomly selected in the range of 10–30 m/s.

To evaluate the proposed relay algorithm, two approaches are compared in the simulations: V2I offloading and partial V2V offloading. Partial V2V offloading is performed
by splitting the computing tasks into different vehicle calculations. Figure 5 shows the
performance of exhaustive search; the proposed scheme can optimize the total delay in
multivehicle or multitasking situations compared to the other methods.

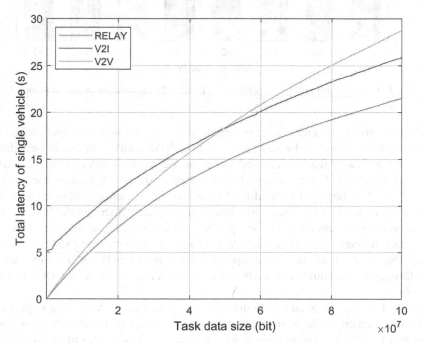

Fig. 2. Comparison of V2I and V2V optimal offloading schemes in terms of latency.

Figures 2 and 3 show comparisons of the delay gap under a single task request to more
clearly analyze the effect. Figure 2 shows the total delay of the three offloading methods
when the task data volumes are different. The data volume ranges from 10^5–10^8 bits.
Because the local MEC server is busy in the considered scenario, even when the amount
of task data is very low, the popular V2I mode still needs to be queued for offloading or
be rejudged when entering the next RSU coverage, resulting in poor performance. As
the amount of task data increases, the V2V mode needs to assign tasks to more vehicle
calculations, resulting in increased delays. The other two unloading methods calculate
that the total delay is relatively stable. Considering the fact that the vehicle velocity

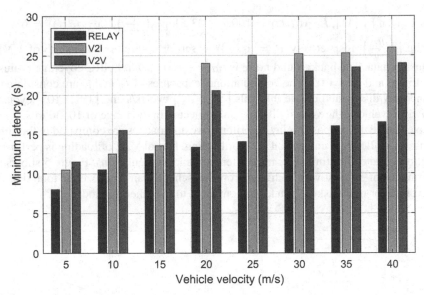

Fig. 3. Latency with vehicular speed for V2I and V2V optimal offloading schemes.

has always been an important factor in vehicle networks, the impact of mobility on the proposed scheme is analyzed with a task volume of 50M as an example. Figure 3 shows that when the velocity reaches a critical value, the V2I mode is offloaded in the current RSU, and the vehicle leaves the area before returning the result, causing the delay to rise suddenly. Similarly, the possibility of vehicles with assisted calculations returning the result to the SV in time is reduced when increasing the velocity in the V2V mode.

The proposed scheme does not occupy the computational resources of the relay car as long as communication factors such as connectivity are considered so as to achieve a lower total delay. In addition, the proposed scheme performs better and more consistently throughout the simulation, in line with the expectations that it increases network scalability.

Figure 4 shows the latency with the RSU coverage radius. According to previous simulation parameters, the vehicle velocity is in the range of 10–30 m/s. This figure shows that the delay is the minimum for a coverage radius of 200 m. Subsequently, because the coverage radius is much larger than the DSRC communication distance and the connection time with the current RSU is long, the computing task queues to offload. Then, the total delay for completing the task reaches a peak and tends to become stable as the coverage radius increases.

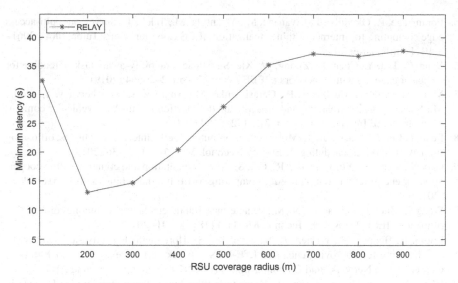

Fig. 4. Latency with RSU radius in proposed scheme.

5 Conclusion

In this study, the predictive offloading is investigated under the assistance of relay in MEC-enhanced vehicular networks. An optimal offloading scheme is proposed to reduce the total latency of computing tasks. And furthermore, a joint solution with greedy and hungarian algorithms is proposed to improve the scalability of vehicular networks. The proposed algorithm can help multiple vehicles select appropriate relay nodes to achieve higher completion efficiency of task processing. Simulation results demonstrated that our proposed optimal offloading scheme can work well. Compared with V2I and V2V without relaying, our algorithm can reduce the latency with 20%–40%.

Acknowledgement. This work is supported by ROIS NII Open Collaborative Research 2021 (21FA03).

References

1. Ma, M., He, D., Wang, H., Kumar, N., Choo, K.R.: An efficient and provably secure authenticated key agreement protocol for fog-based vehicular ad-hoc networks. IEEE Internet Things J. **6**(5), 8065–8075 (2019)
2. Zhang, K.,Mao, Y., Leng, Y., He, Y., Zhang, Y.: Mobile-edge computing for vehicular networks: a promising network paradigm with predictive off-loading. IEEE Veh. Technol. Mag. **12**(2),36–44 (2017)
3. Zheng, C., Feng, D., Zhang, S., Xia, X., Qian, G., Li, G.Y.: Energy efficient V2X-enabled communications in cellular networks. IEEE Trans. Veh. Technol. **68**(1), 554–564 (2019)
4. Tran, T.X., Hajisami, A., Pandey, P., Pompili, D.: Collaborative mobile edge computing in 5g networks: new paradigms, scenarios, and challenges. IEEE Commun. Mag. **55**(4), 54–61 (2017)

5. Porambage, P., Okwuibe, J., Liyanage, M., Ylianttila, M., Taleb, T.: Survey on multi-access edge computing for internet of things realization. IEEE Commun. Surv. Tutor. **20**(4), 2961–2991, Fourthquarter 2018
6. Yang, C., Liu, Y., Chen, X., Zhong, W., Xie, S.: Efficient mobility-aware task offloading for vehicular edge computing networks. IEEE Access **7**, 26652–26664 (2019)
7. Moltchanov, D., Kovalchukov, R., Gerasimenko, M., Andreev, S., Koucheryavy, Y., Gerla, M.: Socially inspired relaying and proactive mode selection in mmWave vehicular communications. IEEE Internet Things J. **6**(3), 5172–5183 (2019)
8. Feng, J., Liu, Z., Wu, C., Ji, Y.: Mobile edge computing for the internet of vehicles: offloading framework and job scheduling. IEEE Veh. Technol. Mag. **14**(1), 28–36 (2019)
9. Cao, X., Wang, F., Xu, J., Zhang, R., Cui, S.: Joint computation and communication cooperation for energy-efficient mobile edge computing. IEEE Internet Things J. **6**(3), 4188–4200 (2019)
10. Wang, Z., Zhong, Z., Zhao, D., Ni, M.: Vehicle-based cloudlet relaying for mobile computation offloading. IEEE Trans. Veh. Technol. **67**(11), 11181–11191 (2018)
11. Luoto, P., Bennis, M., Pirinen, P., Samarakoon, S., Horneman, K., Latva-aho, M.: Vehicle clustering for improving enhanced LTE-V2X network performance. In: 2017 European Conference on Networks and Communications (EuCNC), Oulu, pp. 1–5, June 2017
12. Wang, H., Li, X., Ji, H., Zhang, H.: Federated Offloading Scheme to Minimize Latency in MEC-Enabled Vehicular Networks 2018 IEEE Globecom Workshops (GC Wkshps), pp. 1–6. Abu Dhabi, United Arab Emirates (2018)
13. Guo, H., Liu, J., Zhang, J.: Efficient computation offloading for multi-access edge computing in 5G HetNets. In: 2018 IEEE International Conference on Communications (ICC), Kansas City pp. 1–6, May 2018
14. Guo, H., Liu, J.: Collaborative computation offloading for multiaccess edge computing over fiber-wireless networks. IEEE Trans. Veh. Technol. **67**(5), 4514–4526 (2018)
15. Desikan, K.E.S., Kotagi, V.J., Murthy, C.S.R.: Smart at right price: a cost efficient topology construction for fog computing enabled iot networks in smart cities. In: 2018 IEEE 29th Annual International Symposium on Personal, Indoor and Mobile Radio Communications (PIMRC), Bologna, pp. 1–7, September 2018

Emerging Technologies and Applications in Mobile Networks and Management

WiMTAR: A Contactless Multi-target Activity Recognition Model

Pengsong Duan[1], Chen Li[1], Chenfei Jiao[1], Wenning Zhang[2,3(⊠)], and Jinsheng Kong[1]

[1] School of Software, Zhengzhou University, Zhengzhou 450000, Henan, China
[2] Software College, Zhongyuan University of Technology, Zhengzhou 450000, Henan, China
zhangwn@zut.edu.cn
[3] State Key Laboratory of Mathematical Engineering and Advanced Computing,
Zhengzhou 450000, Henan, China

Abstract. At present, most Wi-Fi based sensing researches aim at single target scene, due to the difficulties in separation of mixed signals. In this paper, a Wi-Fi based model for multi-target activity recognition is proposed. A diverse dataset of sufficient volume for multi-target activity recognition is first collected in our paper. After blind source separation algorithm (FastICA) processing, the dataset is input to the proposed signal sort algorithm named CC-ICA for efficient and accurate signal sort according to CSI correlation coefficient. Experimental results show that CC-ICA algorithm can effectively solve the problem of random order caused by FastICA. Separated CSI data is input into a neural network consisting of ABiGRU and TCN for training and multi-target recognition evaluation. The experiments demonstrate that accuracy of WiMTAR is improved by 26% after CSI data is processed by CC-ICA for multi-target recognition, and accuracy of WiMTAR is also more than 2.6% higher than that of other single target recognition schemes.

Keywords: Wi-Fi sensing · Multi-target · Blind source separation · Deep learning

1 Introduction

In the era of artificial intelligence, how to sense target behavior more conveniently and efficiently in human-computer interaction has always been the focus of academic and industrial circles. Recently, with the rapid development of Internet of Things technology, human activity sensing technology [1] has been initially applied in behavior analysis [2], smart home [3, 4], medical monitoring [5] and other aspects.

Common sensing technology can be divided into computer vision-based, special sensor-based and wireless signal-based according to different acquisition equipment. Computer vision-based technology is to collect image or video information of human activity and use computer image processing technology to extract human activity information for recognition. Such technology has high accuracy and wide application range.

© ICST Institute for Computer Sciences, Social Informatics and Telecommunications Engineering 2022
Published by Springer Nature Switzerland AG 2022. All Rights Reserved
C. T. Calafate et al. (Eds.): MONAMI 2021, LNICST 418, pp. 167–181, 2022.
https://doi.org/10.1007/978-3-030-94763-7_13

However, it is easy to be affected by light and obstacles, and may cause invasion of user privacy. Special sensors-based technology uses special sensors or wearable devices to collect activity data, and then realizes human activity sensing through relevant analysis, which can be used for human activity recognition such as running and walking. This method achieves high recognition accuracy, but it is difficult to be widely deployed due to the high cost, poor convenience and so on. Wireless signal-based technology utilizes the theory that different human behaviors have different perturbations to wireless signals and achieves contactless perception based on perturbation data analysis, attracting extensive attention in recent years.

The sensing technology based on wireless signal can be divided into two kinds, including special radio frequency (RF) signal based and Wi-Fi signal based. RF signal-based technology needs special customized equipment, which costs a lot in installation and maintenance, is not conducive to large-scale use. In recent years, with the extensive deployment of Wi-Fi devices, Wi-Fi signal based human activity recognition has been widely researched. In 2011, Halperin et al. released the CSI Tool [6], which greatly facilitates the extraction of CSI based on physical layer from commercial off-the-shelf Wi-Fi devices. CSI describes how a signal propagates from a transmitter to a receiver and reflects the combined multipath effects such as scattering, reflection, diffraction, etc. of surrounding objects. CSI contains abundant attenuation and phase shift information, which enables to be applied in finer-grained human activity monitoring and recognition systems, such as sleep monitoring [7–9], fall detection [10, 11], gesture recognition [12, 13], vital sign monitoring [14, 15], activity recognition [16–18], etc.

At present, Wi-Fi sensing technology mainly focuses on single person activity recognition, and there are few researches on multi-person activity recognition. In a multi-person scene, the received signals contain not only the changes caused by the activity of the targets but also the signals reflected from the targets to each other due to multipath effect. Therefore, direct recognition on such mixed signals cannot ensure enough accuracy and generalization ability. In 2018, Wi-Run [19] and WIMU [20] made the first attempt to solve the problem of multi-person activity recognition. Wi-Run used Canonical Polyadic (CP) decomposition to separate signals of multiple persons' activity, and achieved recognition accuracy rate of 88.25%. However, only when the mixed signal was sinusoidal can the Wi-Run effectively decomposed the signal, which limited its application. WIMU used random combination of single gesture to generate a virtual sample of multi-person mixed gestures, and then compared it with the real multi-person mixed sample to identify them. The accuracy rates of 2, 3, 4, 5 and 6 simultaneously executed gestures were 95.0%, 94.6%, 93.6%, 92.6% and 90.9%, respectively. However, due to the different data generated by human gestures in different positions, WIMU needed to collect action samples from all positions in advance, which led to high training cost and limited scalability. Although there have been researches on multi-person activity recognition, effective separation of mixed data and accuracy of multi-person activity recognition still are needed to be improved.

To solve the above problems, this paper uses FastICA, which is one of blind source separation algorithms, and deep learning method to realize Wi-Fi based multi-person activity recognition. The contributions of this paper are as follows:

- This paper proposes a sorting algorithm CC-ICA based on subcarrier relevance mechanism to solve the problem of random signal sequence after being separated by FastICA algorithm. Experimental results demonstrate the effectiveness of CC-ICA.
- This paper proposes a hybrid neural network model, named as Multi-Target Activity Recognition (WiMTAR), which integrates attention mechanism. The model takes the separated data as input, and then features of the data are fully extracted by fusing attention mechanism based Bi-directional Gate Recurrent Unit (ABiGRU) and Temporal Convolutional Network (TCN).

2 Basic Theory

2.1 Problem Definition

Assume that subcarrier frequency is f, then relationship between transmitter signal $T(f, t)$ and receiver signal $R(f, t)$ is formalized as:

$$R(f, t) = H(f, t)T(f, t) \tag{1}$$

where $H(f, t)$ represents Channel Frequency Response (CFR) of the carrier. In Wi-Fi environment, transmission of wireless signals is always hindered by various objects between receiver and transmitter, which cause multipath effect in transmission process of signals. Signals on different paths may have delay, fading and frequency diffusion, leading to signal distortion. As shown in the Fig. 1, when collecting multi-target data in the Wi-Fi environment, the signal in transmission will be reflected due to existence of fixed objects such as walls and furniture. We name the reflected signal and the signal on Line-of-Sight (LoS) path between receiver and transmitter as static signal. The influence of human body movement on the signal in transmission is called dynamic signal. Therefore, CFR obtained during data acquisition is a superposition of static signal and dynamic signal, which can be expressed as:

$$H(f, t) = \sum_{n} a_n e^{-j2\pi f \tau_n} + \sum_{m} a_m \xi(f) e^{-j2\pi f \tau_m(t)} \tag{2}$$

where $\sum_{n} a_n e^{-j2\pi f \tau_n}$ represents CFR in static signal, and $\sum_{m} a_m \xi(f) e^{-j2\pi f \tau_m(t)}$ represents dynamic CFR changing with time t.

CSI is the result of sampling CFR, and can be used to approximate influence of environment on channel. We take CSI data as the analysis source and realize multi-person activity detection by feature recognition of data from different activities. CSI matrix contains abundant mixed information of static signals and dynamic signals. CSI information carried by each subcarrier is expressed as:

$$X = [H_{1,k} \ H_{2,k} \cdots H_{j,k}]^T \tag{3}$$

where $H_{j,k}$ represents CSI data on the kth subcarrier at time j.

To simplify problem definition, a CSI data set with different activity labels is represented as $D = \{(X_i, Y_i)\}_{i=1}^I$, where data set D contains I CSI sequences and corresponding labels. Therefore, multi-target recognition problem can be summarized as a mapping model construction problem to predict corresponding activity label Y according to input CSI data matrix X.

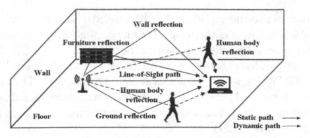

Fig. 1. Collecting multi-target data in the Wi-Fi environment.

2.2 Frequency Energy Graph

When processing single subcarrier sequence data, only activity features reflected by the CSI data within subcarriers can be extracted, while activity features among subcarriers are insufficient. 30 subcarriers of different frequencies obtained during data acquisition have different sensitivities to actions. Therefore, CSI data can be constructed into a two-dimensional matrix to convert original time series form into frequency energy graph (FEG) as follow:

$$\mathbf{X}=\begin{bmatrix} A_{1,1} & A_{1,2} & \cdots A_{1,k} & \cdots & A_{1,K} \\ A_{2,1} & A_{2,2} & \cdots A_{2,k} & \cdots & A_{2,K} \\ \vdots & \vdots & \vdots & & \vdots \\ A_{j,1} & A_{j,2} & \cdots A_{j,k} & \cdots & A_{j,K} \\ \vdots & \vdots & \cdots & & \vdots \\ A_{J,1} & A_{J,2} & \cdots A_{J,k} & \cdots & A_{J,K} \end{bmatrix} \quad (4)$$

where $A_{j,k}$ represents the amplitude of CSI data on the kth subcarrier at time j. We simplify formula (4) as $X = [x_1, x_2, \ldots, x_j, \ldots, x_J]^T j \in J$, where x_j represents CSI data at time j.

FEG not only visually demonstrates energy attenuation of wireless signals, but also contains more activity information. FEG takes activity duration and the number of subcarriers as horizontal and vertical coordinates. A visual FEG is shown in Fig. 2.

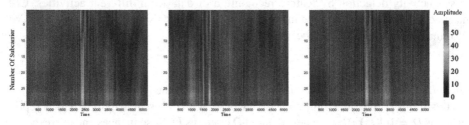

Fig. 2. Frequency energy graph.

2.3 CC-ICA Algorithm

Blind source separation refers to a series of algorithms that separate source signal according to the received mixed signal without information of source signal and transmission channel. Current blind source separation algorithms include JADE [21], FastICA [22], and SOBI [23]. FastICA algorithm is widely used in the fields of sound signal separation, ECG denoising and wireless source signal separation. Among various blind source separation algorithms, FastICA converges faster and has a better application prospect in large-scale data sets.

In order to provide more accurate target activity feature, this paper selects FEG as data reconstruction mechanism. The FEG in this paper is a two-dimensional matrix containing $N_t \times N_c$ pixels, where N_c is the number of subcarriers and N_t is the number of sampling timestamps. Figure 3 is a FEG of two persons running and sitting in the same environment respectively.

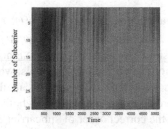

Fig. 3. Frequency energy graph of running and sitting.

Single target feature separation of mixed data is essential for realizing multi-target activity recognition. In this paper, CSI data of each subcarrier is decomposed by FastICA algorithm, and the number of decomposed targets is consistent with the number (i.e. two in this paper) of targets known in advance. Then, the two groups of decomposed subcarriers are reconstructed into two FEGs, as shown in Fig. 4.

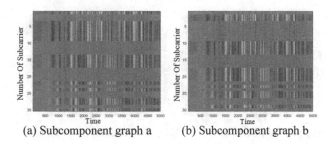

(a) Subcomponent graph a   (b) Subcomponent graph b

Fig. 4. Separation results of FastICA.

As shown in Fig. 4, result of direct separation is not ideal. Positions of multiple subcarriers in the two images are misjudged. The reason is that result of blind source separation algorithms is fuzzy. For FastICA algorithm, the fuzziness of the separation results is mainly manifested in two aspects which are amplitude and order. The essential reason is that blind source separation algorithm requires the independence of source signals, and amplitude and order of signals do not affect the independence of the components. FastICA carries out blind source separation on each subcarrier in turn, which leads to disorder of subcomponents in the reconstruction process, resulting in poor performance of activity recognition.

In a multiple-input-multiple-output (MIMO) based Wi-Fi system, signals between adjacent subcarriers are highly correlated, which can be used as the basis for reconstruction of FEG. Inspired by this property, we propose a sorting algorithm CC-ICA based on signal correlation coefficient. Concept of correlation coefficient is introduced to measure correlation degree of two subcarriers, and its definition is as follow:

$$\rho_{xy} \stackrel{def}{\Rightarrow} \frac{c_{xy}}{\sigma_x \sigma_y} = \frac{E\left[x(t)y^H(t)\right]}{\sqrt{E\left[|x(t)|^2\right]E\left[|y(t)|^2\right]}} \tag{5}$$

where c_{xy} represents cross covariance of signal $x(t)$ and $y(t)$, σ_x^2 and σ_y^2 represent variance of $x(t)$ and $y(t)$, respectively. According to Caucht-Schwartz inequality, $0 \le |\rho_{xy}| \le 1$. Correlation coefficient gives similarity degree between signal $x(t)$ and $y(t)$. ρ_{xy} close to 0 indicates a smaller correlation between the two signals, while it close to 1 indicates a greater correlation between the two signals. This paper calculates correlation coefficient between a subcarrier and its previous one to determine whether the subcarrier is adjacent to the previous subcarrier, so the correct order of subcarrier could be determined. After CC-ICA algorithm, blind source separation results of the finally decomposed FEG are shown in the Fig. 5.

Compared with the results of direct separation in Fig. 4, subcarriers processed by CC-ICA return to normal order, indicating effectiveness of CC-ICA in solving sequential fuzziness problem of FastICA. Figure 5 demonstrates that different decomposed subcomponents have better independence and correlation between adjacent subcarriers in the same FEG is high. Experimental results show that CC-ICA algorithm could effectively sort the subcarriers, thus achieving multi-target activity recognition.

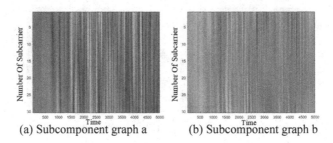

(a) Subcomponent graph a   (b) Subcomponent graph b

Fig. 5. Result of CC-ICA algorithm.

3 WiMTAR Architecture

This paper establishes a multi-target activity recognition model, WiMTAR, on the sort results of CC-ICA algorithm. Taking an indoor scenario as an example, the overall process of WiMTAR is shown in Fig. 6, including data acquisition module, data processing module and activity recognition module. This section mainly introduces the detailed design of activity recognition module.

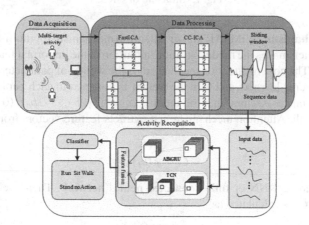

Fig. 6. WiMTAR architecture.

3.1 ABiGRU

ABiGRU adopts Bi-directional Gate Recurrent Unit (BiGRU) and attention mechanism to extract the activity information from FEG, which includes past and future information and focuses attention on crucial information.

BiGRU. Traditional Recurrent Neural Networks (RNN) and its variants such as Long-Short Term Memory (LSTM) [24] can only remember the past information while extracting feature of time series data. For multi-target activity recognition task, activity is a continuous action, thus feature extraction of past and future is very important. Therefore, BiGRU with Gate Recurrent Unit (GRU) [25] as the basic neuron is adopted in WiMTAR to extract the past and future information of activity data to enrich feature information and thus improve model recognition performance.

As shown in Fig. 7, update gate z_t is used to control the extent to which the state information of the previous time t is carried into the state of the current time t in GRU. The larger value of update gate is, the more state information is brought in at time $t - 1$. Reset gate controls how much state information is written to candidate set for the current time t at time $t - 1$. r_t represents reset gate, the smaller value of r_t is, the less the state information at time $t - 1$ is written.

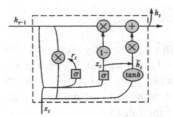

Fig. 7. Structure of GRU.

Attention Mechanism. WiMTAR utilizes attention mechanism for multi-target activity recognition, which makes the model pay more attention to the important feature information of activity. The core of attention mechanism is the weight of parameters. Importance of each parameter is learned, and then the weight is assigned to each parameter according to its importance. Assume that the input is $b_t = [b_1, b_2, \cdots, b_n]$, $(0 < t \leq T)$, n is sequence length. Attention mechanism first extracts feature vectors from the input as follow:

$$C_t = f(b_t) \tag{6}$$

where $f(\cdot)$ could be RNN or fully connected neural network. Then, weight vector of each feature in C_t is calculated as:

$$w_t = \frac{\exp(C_{ti})}{\sum_{i=1}^{n} \exp(C_{ti})} \tag{7}$$

Finally, the input data b_t is multiplied by its weight vector w_t, and summed to get the final output as:

$$o = \sum b_t \bullet w_t \tag{8}$$

3.2 TCN

TCN has been proved to be effective in [26] for extracting feature of time series data. Multi-target activity data is also a kind of time series data, so this paper adds TCN to WiMTAR. In TCN, let $X_t \in R^{F_0}$, $(0 < t \leq T)$ be input feature vector with the length of F_0 at time t. In this paper, time T is fixed and set as 800, which is consistent with the length of sliding window. The true label of each time series is given by $p_i \in \{1, \cdots, c\}$, where c is the number of categories. Assume that the network contains L convolutional layers, with each convolution layer using a set of one-dimensional convolution kernels to extract the variation feature of activity data in the time dimension. Each convolution kernel is parameterized by weight tensor $W^l \in R^{F_l \times d \times F_{l-1}}$ and bias $b^l \in R^{F_l}$, in which L is layer index and D is convolution kernel size. Output of the lth convolutional layer $E_{i,j}^l \in R^{F_l}$ is function of input matrix $E_{i,j}^{l-1} \in R^{F_{l-1} \times T}$ from previous layer. The function is as:

$$E_{i,j}^l = f_{relu}\left(b_i^l + \sum_{r=1}^{d} W_{i,\tau}^l, E_{i,t+d-\tau}^{l-1}\right), \tag{9}$$

where $\langle \bullet \rangle$ represents correlation function and $f_{relu}(\bullet)$ represents activation function Rectified Linear Unit (ReLU).

TCN conducts a layered approach to extract multi-target activity data features on a time scale. In this paper, TCN can fully mine the relationship among multi-target data features, so as to improve model performance.

3.3 Activity Recognition Network

Figure 8 shows overview of activity recognition network. Data processed by CC-ICA algorithm pass through TCN network and ABiGRU network respectively for activity feature extraction. Then the activity features extracted from the two networks are fused and finally input to SoftMax classifier for classification. Because the datasets in this paper are about two-target activities, the model designed is more suitable to two-target activity recognition.

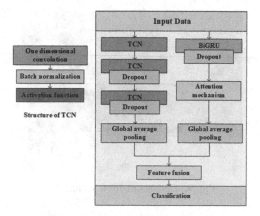

Fig. 8. Activity recognition network.

TCN network is composed of three TCN blocks, each of which contains a one-dimensional convolutional layer, a normalized layer and an activation layer. We abandon Dropout layer in the first TCN block, thus low-level features can be retained to the maximum extent to prevent feature loss. Whereas the Dropout layer in other two TCN blocks is retained to avoid overfitting. In order to fix data distribution after one-dimensional convolution, model uses batch normalization to process the data, which is then entered into the activation layer for nonlinear transformation, and then into the Dropout layer. Finally, we add a global average pooling layer to prevent overfitting and reduce the number of network parameters.

ABiGRU network consists of two parts. GRU neuron based BiGRU is used to extract the past and future features of activity data. Then the features are input into Dropout layer. We introduce attention mechanism to assign weights for each feature, so as to distinguish the importance of different features to the current activity. Global average pooling is used to adjust data dimensions to facilitate feature fusion in the next step. To realize attention mechanism, we first utilize fully connected layer for features extraction, and then calculate the weight vector by SoftMax function. Finally, the input data is multiplied by its weight vector and summed to get the output result.

4 Experimental Results and Analysis

4.1 Experimental Setup

In the field of Wi-Fi multi-target activity recognition, there is currently no available open dataset for use. Therefore, self-collected data sets are needed for model validation. In order to construct a typical activity dataset and avoid the influence of environmental factors such as indoor layout. At present, only an empty indoor room, as shown in Fig. 9, is chosen as data acquisition scenario in this paper. When the model has high accuracy, data in multiple scenario will be collected to enhance the robustness of the model. Detailed experimental parameters are shown in Table 1.

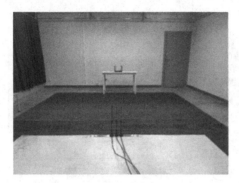

Fig. 9. Data acquisition scenario.

To ensure objectivity and universality of data set, 10 volunteers are distributed between the ages of 18 and 30 and divided into 5 different groups. During data acquisition, activity data of two volunteers are collected each time. The two volunteers walk back and forth along the direction perpendicular to LoS path at the same time, and they are guaranteed to cross LoS path only once. In the process of data acquisition, in order to effectively capture multi-person activities, two experimenters are required to repeat different activities simultaneously, and 5 s of data fragments are collected each time as a data sequence. In this dataset, five daily activities (no action, walk, sit down, stand up and run) are collected from five groups of volunteers, as well as all possible combinations of two of these activities. The actual activities of each target are recorded as labels during collection. After processing, there are 2500 valid data in this dataset. In order to promote faster development of Wi-Fi sensing research, this paper will publish the dataset late.

4.2 Experimental Results

In order to fully evaluate the performance of WiMTAR, this paper conducts comparative experiments in various aspects.

Table 1. Detailed configuration of experimental equipment and parameters.

Index	Name	Parameter
1	Transmitter	TP_LINK AC1750 wireless router
2	Receiver	Intel 5300 NIC
3	Number of transmitting antenna	1
4	Number of receiving antenna	3
5	Number of subcarriers	30
6	Work frequency	5 GHz
7	Sampling frequency	1 kHz
8	Sampling duration	5000 ms
9	Sliding window size	800 ms
10	Sliding step length	200 ms

Validation of CC-ICA Algorithm. To verify the effectiveness of CC-ICA algorithm, performance of WiMTAR model before and after using CC-ICA will be compared in this paper. On the one hand, the multi-target data are pre-processed by CC-ICA algorithm. Then, input into activity recognition module of WiMTAR for training and recognition. On the other hand, a control group is experimentally set up, and it is trained by using the same model structure, but the training data are not processed by CC-ICA algorithm, and multi-person labels as a whole are coded as a single category in one-hot form. For classification results of the two groups, the four evaluation indicators introduced above are used to evaluate respectively, and the results are shown in Fig. 10.

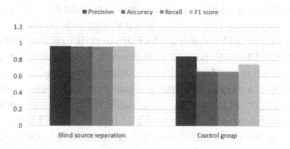

Fig. 10. Performance comparison of blind source separation.

It can be seen that after using CC-ICA algorithm, performance of WiMTAR in the four evaluations metrics has been significantly improved. The reason is that when mixed signals of multi-target activities are recognized as a whole, there are too many combinations of activity labels (10 combinations for 5 activities), and mixed information contains not only environmental noise but also interference factors among the targets, leading to poor recognition performance. Confusion matrix of recognition results in both cases is shown in Fig. 11.

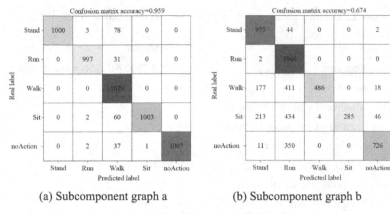

(a) Subcomponent graph a   (b) Subcomponent graph b

Fig. 11. Confusion matrix contrast.

As can be seen from Fig. 11, after CC-ICA algorithm, although the signals corresponding to each target activity have been separated, a small number of recognition errors exist due to mutual interference existing among the targets that is still difficult to completely eliminate. For direct recognition, because the overall recognition introduces more interference factors, identification error items also increase significantly. Since sitting action is larger in magnitude than other actions, it greatly affects recognition of other activities without feature separation, leading to a decrease in performance. CC-ICA algorithm, however, sorts the features after separation, which better solves problem of multi-target activity recognition.

Comparison of Different Models. Experiment will firstly use CC-ICA algorithm to separate and sort the collected data, transform multi-target activity recognition problem into multiple single-target activity recognition problems, and then carry out comparative experiments with existing similar models. Since the input of WiMTAR model is time-series data, GRU and ABLSTM models, which are usually excellent at processing time-series data, are selected for comparison in this paper. In addition, since convolutional neural networks are used in WiMTAR, classical neural network FCN [27] is also selected for comparison. GRU is a model with timing signal as input which is composed of three GRU layers in this paper. FCN is a model suitable for computer vision field, and the one used in our experiment contains three CNN layers. ABLSTM is a relatively new network structure for Wi-Fi based activity recognition in existing studies. ABLSTM used in comparison experiments in this paper has the same network structure as that in the published papers. Results of comparison experiments are shown in Fig. 12.

As can be seen from Fig. 12, the accuracy of WiMTAR, ABLSTM, GRU and FCN reaches 95.9%, 93.3%, 92.3% and 92.2%, respectively. Classification accuracy of WiMTAR is at least 2.6% higher than the other three models, indicating structural superiority and stronger feature extraction capability of WiMTAR. In addition, since the four models are all tested on the basis of the separated dataset in this chapter, it can be seen that CC-ICA has a wide validity in the multi-target recognition tasks. The technical route of

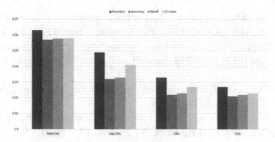

Fig. 12. Accuracy of different models.

independent feature extraction is not only applicable to WiMTAR, but also achieve high performance combining with other models.

5 Conclusion

This paper mainly proposes a multi-target activity recognition model based on Wi-Fi sensing. The proposed model contains three modules including data acquisition, data processing and activity recognition. In this paper, CC-ICA algorithm proposed is used for sort data after blind source separation to obtain independent single target data. Activity recognition module takes the sorted activity data as input, and after being trained by the specially designed neural network model (i.e. mainly composed of ABiGRU and TCN), multi-target activity recognition can be realized. Experimental results show that WiMTAR performs better in multi-target activity recognition scenarios.

In the future, WiMTAR will be further improved in the following three aspects: (1) Try to use the phase information from CSI information. (2) Increase the number of simultaneous targets in the experimental scenario (two people in this paper). (3) Improve generalization ability of the model in different environments.

References

1. Lu, Y.: Research review of human behavior sensing technology based on wi-fi signals. Chin. J. Comput. **42**(02), (2019)
2. Gu, Y., Zhang, X., Liu, Z., Ren, F.J.: BeSense: leveraging Wi-Fi channel data and computational intelligence for behavior analysis. IEEE Comput. Intell. Mag. **14**(4), 31–41 (2019)
3. Gu, Y., et al.: WiONE: One-shot learning for environment-robust device-free user authentication via commodity Wi-Fi in man-machine system. IEEE Trans. Comput. Soc. Syst. **8**(3), 630–642 (2021)
4. Li, Q.Y., et al.: AFDCGAN: amplitude-feature deep convolutional GAN for fingerprint construction in indoor localization system. IEEE Transactions on Emerging Topics in Computational Intelligence, vol. 5, no. 3, pp. 468–480 (2021)
5. Gu, Y., et al.: EmoSense: computational intelligence driven emotion sensing via wireless channel data. IEEE Trans. Emerg. Topicsin Comput. Intell. **4**(3), 216–226 (2020)

6. Halperin, D., Hu, W., Sheth, A., et al.: Tool release: gathering 802.11n traces with channel state information. ACM SIGCOMM Comput. Commun. Rev. **41**(1), 53 (2011)

7. Liu, X., Cao, J., Tang, S., Wen, J.: Wi-Sleep: contactless sleep monitoring via wi-fi signals. In: Proceedings of the IEEE 35th IEEE Real-Time Systems Symposium. Rome, pp. 346–355 (2014)

8. Lin, N., et al.: Contactless body movement recognition during sleeping via Wi-Fi signal. IEEE Internet Things J. **7**(3), 2028–2037 (2020)

9. Gu, Y., Wang, Y.T., Liu, Z., Liu, J., Li, J.: SleepGuardian: an RF-based healthcare system guarding your sleep from afar. IEEE Netw. **34**(2), 164–171 (2020)

10. Han, C., Wu, K., Wang, Y., et al.: WiFall: device-free fall detection by wireless networks. In: IEEE INFOCOM (2014)

11. Maheshwari, S., Tiwari, A.K.: Ubiquitous fall detection through wireless channel state information. In: International Conference on Computing and Network Communications (CoCoNet). IEEE (2015)

12. He, W., Wu, K., Zou, Y., et al.: WiG: Wi-Fi-based gesture recognition system. In: 2015 24th International Conference on Computer Communication and Networks (ICCCN). IEEE (2015)

13. Li, H., Yang, W., Wang, J., et al.: WiFinger: talk to your smart devices with finger-grained gesture. In: Proceedings of the 2016 ACM International Joint Conference on Pervasive and Ubiquitous Computing. ACM (2016)

14. Abdelnasser, H., Harras, K.A., Youssef, M.: UbiBreathe: a Ubiquitous non-Invasive WiFi-based breathing estimator (2015)

15. Nguyen, P., Zhang, X., Halbower, A.: Continuous and fine-grained breathing volume monitoring from afar using wireless signals. In: IEEE INFOCOM 2016 - IEEE Conference on Computer Communications. IEEE (2016)

16. Gao, Q., Wang, J., Ma, X.: CSI-based device-free wireless localization and activity recognition using radio image features. IEEE Trans. Veh. Technol. 66, 10346–10356 (2017)

17. Chen, Z., Zhang, L., Jiang, C.: WiFi CSI based passive human activity recognition using attention based BLSTM. IEEE Trans. Mobile Comput. 18, 2714–2724 (2018)

18. Duan, P., Li, H., Zhang, B.: APFNet: amplitude-phase fusion network for CSI-based action recognition. Mobile Netw. Appl. **26,** 2024–2034 (2021)

19. Zhang, L., Liu, M., Lu, L., Gong, L.: Wi-run: Multi-runner step estimation using commodity wi-fi. In: 2018 15th Annual IEEE International Conference on Sensing, Communication, and Networking (SECON), pp.1–9. IEEE (2018)

20. Venkatnarayan, R.H., Page, G., Shahzad, M.: Multi-user gesture recognition using wifi. In: Proceedings of the 16th Annual International Conference on Mobile Systems, Applications, and Services, pp. 401–413. ACM (2018)

21. Guo, K., Chen, L., Chen, H.: Research on blind separation of random noise from seismic data based on JADE algorithm. Earth Sci. Front. **18**(3), 302–309 (2011)

22. Mahajan, A., Birajdar, G.: Blind source separation using modified contrast function in fast ICA algorithm. Int. J. Comput. Appl. **6**(4), 14–17 (2010)

23. Wang, Y.: Research on blind signal processing method in mechanical noise monitoring. Kunming University of Science and Technology (2010)

24. Hochreiter, S., Schmidhuber, J.: Long short-term memory. Neural Comput. **9**(8), 1735–1780 (1997)

25. Schuster, M., Paliwal, K.K.: Bidirectional recurrent neural networks. IEEE Trans. Signal Process. **45**(11), 2673–2681 (1997)

26. Wang, Z., Yan, W., Oates, T.: Time series classification from scratch with deep neural networks: a strong baseline. In: Proceedings of the International Joint Conference Neural Network (IJCNN), pp. 1578–1585 (2017)
27. Long, J., Shelhamer, E., Darrell, T.: Fully convolutional networks for semantic segmentation. In: Proceedings of the IEEE Conference on Computer Vision and Pattern Recognition, pp. 3431–3440 (2015)

WiBFall: A Device-Free Fall Detection Model for Bathroom

Pengsong Duan, Jingxin Li, Chenfei Jiao, Yangjie Cao[✉], and Jinsheng Kong

School of Software Engineering, Zhengzhou University, Zhengzhou 450002, China
{duanps,caoyj,jskong}@zzu.edu.cn

Abstract. Falling detection, especially for elderly people in confined areas such as bathrooms is vital for timely rescue. The mainstream vision-based fall detection approaches however are not applicable here for strong privacy concerns. It is therefore necessary to design a privacy-preserving fall detection model that utilizes other signals such as widely existed Wi-Fi for this scenario. Existing Wi-Fi based fall detection approaches often suffer from environment noise removal, resulting in moderate accuracy. In this paper, a Wi-Fi based fall detection model for bathroom environment, termed WiBFall, is proposed. Firstly, time series CSI data is reconstructed into a two-dimensional frequency energy map structure to obtain more feature capacity. Secondly, the reconstructed CSI data stream is filtered by Butterworth filter for noise elimination. Finally, the filtered data is used to train the established deep learning network to get a high accuracy fall detection model for bathroom. The experimental results show that the WiBFall not only reaches a fall detection accuracy of up to 99.63% in home bathroom environment, but also enjoys high robustness comparing to other schemes in different bathroom settings.

Keywords: Fall detection · Channel state information · Deep neural network

1 Introduction

At present, falling has become the leading cause of death due to injury for people over 65 years old in China [1]. Among many falling scenes, bathroom poses a serious threat to the life and health of the elderly due to the high privacy and strong closure, resulting in poor timely assistance after a fall. Therefore, how to achieve efficient and convenient fall detection in such scenarios has attracted widespread attention from academia and industry.

Generally speaking, fall detection methods mainly include computer vision, wearable devices and so on, but these methods have some limitations in practical use. Computer vision is susceptible to illumination and obstruction and has poor privacy, while wearable devices are expensive and inconvenient to install and carry, so neither of which is suitable

Supported by National Natural Science Foundation of China under Grant 61972092, Collaborative Innovation Major Project of Zhengzhou under Grant 20XTZX06013,the Research Foundation Plan in Higher Education Institutions of Henan Province under Grant 21A520043

© ICST Institute for Computer Sciences, Social Informatics and Telecommunications Engineering 2022
Published by Springer Nature Switzerland AG 2022. All Rights Reserved
C. T. Calafate et al. (Eds.): MONAMI 2021, LNICST 418, pp. 182–193, 2022.
https://doi.org/10.1007/978-3-030-94763-7_14

for fall detecting in the bathroom scene. In contrast, Wi-Fi perception technology has become an emerging direction of perception research with its advantages of low cost, contactless, non-light influence, and good privacy. Wi-Fi sensing technology works by sensing the disturbance of the signal caused by human movements. In 2000, Bahl et al. [2] first proposed Radar, a system which uses Wi-Fi signals for sensing, and realized the use of Wi-Fi signal strength information (Received Signal Strength, RSS) for indoor positioning. Subsequently, RSS gradually became the signal carrier in the Wi-Fi perception field for perception recognition. Since RSS can only realize coarse-grained perception, people had been looking for signal carriers that can realize fine-grained perception. In 2011, Halperin et al. [3] released the CSI tool to extract Channel State Information (CSI) from commercial network cards, which greatly facilitates the process of obtaining CSI information from commercial Wi-Fi devices, and also makes using more to perceive has become a new research hotspot. Nowadays, fine-grained CSI has become the mainstream carrier in the Wi-Fi perception field, and CSI-based gait recognition [3–5], sleep monitoring [6–8], fall detection [9–13], etc. have appeared.

In the existing fall detection research based on Wi-Fi perception, traditional machine learning algorithms are mostly used. They have problems such as insufficient feature extraction and complex extraction process, which affect the accuracy of model recognition. In addition, the existence of multipath effects makes the recognition model less robust. Existing researches on fall detection mainly focus on indoor scenes such as meeting rooms and bedrooms, while there are few studies on fall detection in bathroom environment. To this end, this article proposes a fall detection model suitable for bathroom environments using Wi-Fi perception technology and deep learning method, hoping to contribute to the bathing safety of people, especially for the elderly. The main contributions of this paper are summarized as follows.

(1) The one-dimensional time series data is reconstructed into a two-dimensional multi-carrier data stream, which is filtered by Butterworth filter. In this way, the method enhances the data feature capacity while remove environmental noise effectively.
(2) A lightweight fall detection model, WiBFall, based on deep learning, was proposed for bathroom scenes with an accuracy of 99.63%. The experimental results show that, compared with the existing similar algorithms, WiBFall has higher accuracy.

2   Related Work

According to the types of wireless signals, the existing fall detection work can be divided into three categories: radar-based, infrared-based, and Wi-Fi-based.

2.1   Radar-Based

The radar emits electromagnetic waves to irradiate the human body's actions and receives the echoes, thus collecting the unique radar characteristics of the human body falling. Jin et al. [14] propose mmFall - a novel fall detection system, which comprises of millimeter-wave (mmWave) radar sensor to collect the human body's point cloud along with the body centroid, and a Hybrid Variational RNN Auto Encoder (HVRAE) to compute the anomaly level of the body motion based on the acquired point cloud. Experimental results show that the detection accuracy rate is 98% in 50 falls. Su et al. [15] proposed a fall detection method that integrates the fall characteristics collected by two Doppler radars installed in the center of the ceiling and the horizontal position of the torso. Experimental results show a 10-fold reduction in false alarm rate and a 100% correct detection rate compared to the radar at the ceiling position alone.

2.2 Infrared-Based

Infrared-based fall detection uses infrared to image the human body, which can meet the perception and recognition in low-light scenes. Chen et al. [16] proposed a fall detection method based on support vector machine-based infrared-ultrasonic sensor fusion, and experimentally studied the fall actions of standing, sitting, bending, falling forward, and falling sideways to simulate the daily activities of the elderly. Experimental results show that for discrete data recordings, the accuracy rate of fall detection reaches 96.7%. For continuous data recordings, the accuracy rate of fall detection reaches approximately 96.7%. Fan et al. [17] proposed a fall detection system using infrared array sensors and multiple deep learning methods (LSTM, GRU, etc.) is proposed.

2.3 Wi-Fi-Based

At present, there have been some research results of fall detection using Wi-Fi sensing technology. The WiFall [9] system uses amplitude transformation of channel state information in Wi-Fi signals, and then uses SVM and random forest algorithms to achieve single-person fall detection with accuracy rates of 90% and 94%, respectively. RT-Fall [10] uses the phase and amplitude of the channel state information to extract more effective features, achieving 100% accuracy and better than WiFall. Fallsense [11] uses the amplitude transformation of the channel state information and then uses the dynamic time warping algorithm to achieve 95% fall detection accuracy, and the complexity is lower than WiFall. Ramezani et al. [12] proposed a new type of Sensing-Fi system that uses Wi-Fi channel state information (CSI) and ground-mounted accelerometers to detect floor vibrations for fall detection. The test results showed that the fall detection accuracy rate of the system is 95%. PALIPANA et al. [13] proposed a CSI fall detection method, which used the traditional short-time Fourier transform (STFT) to extract time-frequency features, and used sequential forward selection algorithm to pick out features that were resilient to environmental changes. Test results showed that the system had a detection accuracy of 93%.

Compared with the first two wireless sensing technologies, Wi-Fi-based sensing technologies are more versatile and easier to deploy. However, the current research on fall detection based on Wi-Fi sensing technology is mainly focused on the daily life environment. There is no effective research result for fall detection in the special environment like bathroom. Therefore, this paper proposes a method for fall detection in bathroom scene using Wi-Fi sensing technology.

3   Preliminaries

3.1   Problem Definition

Under the premise that the Wi-Fi signal covers the bathroom environment, a fall of the human body will cause disturbance to the Wi-Fi signal, which in turn causes a change in channel state. The schematic diagram of bathroom fall detection based on Wi-Fi perception is shown in Fig. 1.

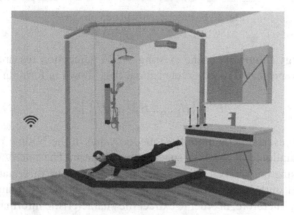

Fig. 1. Schematic diagram of bathroom fall detection

In widely used OFDM systems, CSI provides more multipath information than RSS, with different signal strength and phase in different subcarriers [18, 19]. Commercial Wi-Fi devices are usually Multiple Input Multiple Output (MIMO), and the CSI data of each antenna pair contains multiple subcarrier information [20]. If we use Nt and Nr to represent the transmitting and receiving antennas, and m as the number of subcarriers for each antenna pair, CSI can be constructed via the following equation.

$$H(f_k) = ||H(f_k)||e^{j\angle H(f_k)}k \in [1, K]. \tag{1}$$

where $H(f_k)$ is the complex number representation of the k-th subcarrier, $||H(f_k)||$ and $\angle H(f_k)$ represents the amplitude and phase respectively, and K is the number of subcarriers. Since the phase information is susceptible to interference, only amplitude information is used in this paper.

3.2   Feature Reconstruction

Accurate feature characterization methods can obtain features with a high degree of recognition, which in turn can improve the recognition performance of the model. Therefore, based on the feature reconstruction strategy of the previous frequency energy map [21], this paper selects Butterworth filter to remove noise. The complete feature reconstruction process is shown in Fig. 2.

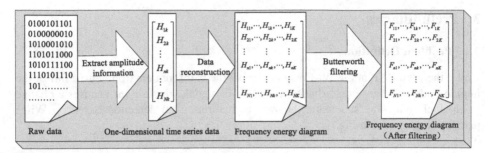

Fig. 2. Feature reconstruction process

Frequency Energy Diagram. In the existing Wi-Fi perception research, most of the CSI sequence is represented by one-dimensional data shown in formula (2) [22,23]

$$H_k = \left[H_k^1, ..., H_k^n, ..., H_k^N \right]. \tag{2}$$

where H_k represents the amplitude sequence value in the N time period, and H_k^n represents the amplitude of the k-th subcarrier at time n. The one-dimensional time sequence processing method can only extract the characteristic information in the sub-carriers and the disturbance of different sub-carrier amplitudes by human behavior is different [24, 25]. Therefore, in order to extract the characteristic information within and between subcarriers at the same time, this paper reconstructs the one-dimensional time series data in the N time period into the two-dimensional matrix form shown in formula (3), where Hnk is the CSI amplitude value of the k-th subcarrier at time n.

$$X = \begin{bmatrix} H_H, ..., & H_{1k}, ..., & H_{1k} \\ H_{21} & H_{2K} & H_{2K} \\ \vdots & \vdots & \vdots \\ H_{n1}, ..., & H_{nk}, ..., & H_{nk} \\ \vdots & \vdots & \vdots \\ H_{N1}, ..., & H_{NK}, ..., & H_{NK} \end{bmatrix} \tag{3}$$

According to the data reconstruction method shown in formula (3), the corresponding frequency energy map can be generated after proper coloring design.

Butterworth Filtering. The raw selected data may contain abnormal samples caused by background noise or hardware glitches and thus should be filtered [26]. The dynamic noise source of the bathroom scene is mainly shower water, and the frequency response curve of the passband of the Butterworth filter is smooth [10], it can effectively filter the bathroom noise. The signal fluctuations caused by human behaviors usually are at the low-frequency band, while the background noises induced by hardware and environment tend to focus on the high-frequency band [27]. Therefore, this article chooses it as the filtering method. In previous works, we found that the frequency f of CSI change caused by falling action is 10–40 Hz [10, 28]. In this article, the sampling frequency Fs of the

CSI data is set to 1000 Hz, and the frequency of the CSI time series change is set to 40 Hz. The construction process of the Butterworth filter is as follows:

First, calculate the cut-off frequency w_c by Eq. (4).

$$w_c = \frac{2 \times f}{F_s} \tag{4}$$

Secondly, the butter function in Matlab is called to calculate the coefficients b and a of the Butterworth filter, as shown in formula (5), where N is the order of the filter, *low* represents low-pass filtering, w_c represents the cut-off frequency. Then b and a represent the coefficient vectors of the numerator and denominator polynomials of the Butterworth filter system function.

$$[b, a] = butter(N, w_c, 'low'); \tag{5}$$

Finally, we use the filtfilt function in Matlab to construct a Butterworth filter, as shown in formula (6), where *Signal* represents the reconstructed perceptual information, and *Signal_Filter* represents the filtered perceptual information.

$$Signal\_Filter = filtfilt(b, a, Signal); \tag{6}$$

4 System Design

The flow chart of WiBFall is given in Fig. 3. There are mainly two modules in the process.

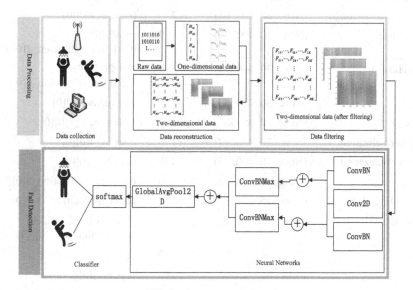

Fig. 3. System overview

Data Processing module mainly collects and preprocesses the perception data, including data collection, data reconstruction and data filtering.

Fall Detection module inputs the processed perception data into a designed neural network model to extract features. Then the detection result is calculated through the SoftMax layer. After training with a large amount of effective data, WiBFall can realize effective fall detection in bathroom scenes.

Table 1. The structure table of the neural network for fall detection

Layer	Output shape	Param	Connected to
input_1	[(None, 30, 400, 3)]	0	
conv2d_1	(None, 30, 400, 64)	640	input_1[0][0]
conv2d_5	(None, 30, 400, 64)	640	input_1[0][0]
batch_normalization	(None, 30, 400, 64)	256	conv2d_1[0][0]
batch_normalization_4	(None, 30, 400, 64)	256	conv2d_5[0][0]
conv2d_2	(None, 30, 400, 64)	12352	batch_normalization[0][0]
conv2d_6	(None, 30, 400, 64)	12352	batch_normalization_4[0][0]
batch_normalization_1	(None, 30, 400, 64)	256	conv2d_2[0][0]
batch_normalization_5	(None, 30, 400, 64)	256	conv2d_6[0][0]
conv2d_3	(None, 30, 400, 64)	36928	batch_normalization_1[0][0]
conv2d_7	(None, 30, 400, 64)	36928	batch_normalization_5[0][0]
conv2d	(None, 30, 400, 32)	128	input_1[0][0]
batch_normalization_2	(None, 30, 400, 64)	256	conv2d_3[0][0]
batch_normalization_6	(None, 30, 400, 64)	256	conv2d_7[0][0]
Concatenate	(None, 30, 400, 96)	0	conv2d[0][0] batch_normalization_2[0][0]
concatenate_1	(None, 30, 400, 96)	0	conv2d[0][0] batch_normalization_6[0][0]
conv2d_4	(None, 30, 400, 32)	27680	concatenate[0][0]
conv2d_8	(None, 30, 400, 32)	27680	concatenate_1[0][0]
batch_normalization_3	(None, 30, 400, 32)	128	conv2d_4[0][0]
batch_normalization_7	(None, 30, 400, 32)	128	conv2d_8[0][0]
max_pooling2d	(None, 15, 200, 32)	0	batch_normalization_3[0][0]
max_pooling2d_1	(None, 15, 200, 32)	0	batch_normalization_7[0][0]
concatenate_2	(None, 15, 200, 64)	0	max_pooling2d[0][0] max_pooling2d_1[0][0]
gap2d	(None, 64)	0	concatenate_2[0][0]
dense	(None, 3)	195	gap2d[0][0]

4.1 Network Structure

This paper builds a neural network module for fall detection based on the Keras Platform. For the methodology of this paper, it takes the filtered two-dimensional frequency energy map as input, and combines the characteristics of wireless sensing signals in bathroom scenes with the basic theory of image convolution. The sliding step length determines the overlap percentage between adjacent sliding windows, which increases the CSI data volume and as a result, enhances movement feature extraction [7]. Considering the instantaneous nature of the fall action, the sliding window size was set to 400 ms and the sliding step size to 100 ms when generating the frequency energy map. The detailed model structure is shown in Table 1.

4.2 Classifier

According to the problem definition, the input of the model is a filtered frequency energy map, denoted by X, and the output is a action category, denoted by Y. In a typical classifier, the sigmoid function is usually used for two classifications, while the SoftMax function is usually used for multiple classifications. Therefore, this article chooses the SoftMax function to distinguish the action categories. The expression formula is as follows:

$$p(y|X) = \frac{\exp(z_y)}{\sum_{y=1}^{r} \exp(z_y)}, y \in [1, r] \tag{7}$$

In the formula, r represents the number of categories of y, z_y represents the result of global average pooling, and $P(y|X)$ represents the posterior probability of class y predicted by the model input X.

5 Experimental Results

In order to make the model more convincing, this paper designs comparative experiments using different filtering methods and models to comprehensively evaluate the recognition effect of the model, and analyze the experimental results in detail.

5.1 Experimental Setting

After investigation, there is no public Wi-Fi sensing bathroom fall data set at home and abroad currently. In order to verify the correctness of the model, this paper chooses the home bathroom environment for fall detection data collection. The actual environment of the home bathroom is shown in Fig. 4.

The experimental equipment is composed of TP_LINK AC1750 wireless router as transmitter (T) and ThinkPad X201 portable computer terminal as receiver (R) equipped with Intel 5300 802.11n Wi-Fi NIC network card. Among them, the opensource CSI Tool is installed on the receiving end device, which can realize real-time collection of CSI information. The transmitter has one antenna and the receiver has three antennas, forming three pairs (1 × 3) antennas, each pair containing 30 subcarriers. Therefore, the

Fig. 4. The exterior (left) and interior (right) of bathroom

data files collected by each receiving end contain 90 (1 × 3 × 30) sub-carrier CSI data [29].

In the home bathroom environment, a total of 5 volunteers' normal bathing and falling motion CSI data and empty environment data were collected. The age of the volunteers is between 18 and 30, which can fully guarantee the diversity and representativeness of the data. In the data collection stage, one volunteer was invited to perform normal bathing and falling movements at a time. Due to the instantaneous nature of the falling action, each data acquisition was performed for 1 s and repeated 60 times to accurately obtain its characteristics.

For the collected data set, manually add no-action, shower, waterfall three action labels, and we divide them into training set and test set according to the ratio of 4:1. This experiment is based on a data set built by ourselves. The model focuses on the classification of predefined activities. There is no need to train different models for different people.

5.2 Comparison of Different Models

To verify the effectiveness of the model for fall detection in the home bathroom scene, the data before and after filtering was compared, and the classic methods like WiNet [21], FCN [30] and ResNet34 [31] were selected for model selection. WiBFall was compared with the experimental model and the results are shown as follows (Fig. 5).

It can be seen from the graphs that the area of the home bathroom environment is small, the signal propagation path is relatively simple, and there are fewer obstacles. On the dataset before filtering, the WiBFall model performed well, with a recognition accuracy of 94.78%. The frequency energy graph containing time and space information is used to accurately describe the action characteristics, but there is still some noise interference information that has not been removed. Therefore, to further improve the accuracy of the model, a Butterworth filtered frequency energy graph was introduced. Experimental results show that the model performs better on the filtered data set, and the recognition accuracy rate reaches 99.63%.

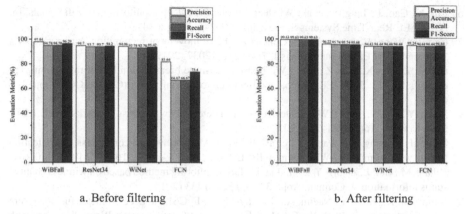

a. Before filtering   b. After filtering

Fig. 5. Comparison of evaluation indicators of different models

6 Conclusions

WiBFall proposed in this paper is a contactless fall detection model for bathroom. There are mainly two modules in WiBFall, data processing module and fall detection module. The filtered frequency energy map is used to reconstruct the CSI data to contain more kinds of features. Deep learning method is employed in fall detection module to accurately extract the features of target action. The experimental results show that t WiBFall has a high accuracy rate for fall detection in home bathroom scenes.

Future research work will start from the following aspects: (1) we will try to extract effective phase difference information to improve the accuracy of WiBFall. (2) We will enhance WiBFall's robustness to make it can adapt to different bathroom scenes.

References

1. Liu, K., Chen, Y., Gao, Z., et al.: The effect of plantar perception training on the balance ability and fall risk of elderly people with a history of falls. Chin Gen. Pract. **023**(012), 1504–1508 (2020)
2. Bahl, P., Padmanabhan, V.: Radar: an in-building RF-based user location and tracking system. In: Proceedings IEEE INFOCOM 2000. Conference on Computer Communications. Nineteenth Annual Joint Conference of the IEEE Computer and Communications Societies (Cat. No. 00CH37064), vol. 2, pp. 775–784 (2000)
3. Zeng, Y., Pathak, P., Mohapatra, P.: WiWho: wifi-based person identification in smart spaces. In: 2016 15th ACM/IEEE International Conference on Information Processing in Sensor Networks (IPSN), pp. 1–12 (2016)
4. Wang, W., Liu, A., Shahzad, M.: Gait recognition using wifi signals. In: Proceedings of the 2016 ACM International Joint Conference on Pervasive and Ubiquitous Computing, pp. 363–373 (2016)
5. Zhang, J., Wei, B., Hu, W., et al.: Wifi-id: Human identification using wifi signal. In: 2016 International Conference on Distributed Computing in Sensor Systems (DCOSS), pp. 75–82 (2016)

6. Liu, X., Cao, J., Tang, S., et al.: Wi-sleep: Contactless sleep monitoring via wifi signals. In: 2014 IEEE Real-Time Systems Symposium, pp. 346–355 (2014)
7. Cao, Y., Wang, F., Lu, X., et al.: Contactless body movement recognition during sleep via WiFi signals. IEEE Internet Things J. **7**(3), 2028–2037 (2019)
8. Gu, Y., Zhang, X., Liu, Z., et al.: WiFi-based real-time breathing and heart rate monitoring during sleep. In: 2019 IEEE Global Communications Conference (GLOBECOM), pp. 1–6 (2019)
9. Wang, Y., Wu, K., Ni, L.: Wifall: Device-free fall detection by wireless networks. IEEE Trans. Mob. Comput. **16**(2), 581–594 (2016)
10. Wang, H., Zhang, D., Wang, Y., et al.: RT-Fall: A real-time and contactless fall detection system with commodity WiFi devices. IEEE Trans. Mob. Comput. **16**(2), 511–526 (2016)
11. Huang, M., Liu, J., Zhang, Y., et al.: Passive fall monitoring method based on wireless channel status information. J. Comput. Appl. **39**(5), 1528–1533 (2019)
12. Ramezani, R., Xiao, Y., Naeim, A.: Sensing-Fi: Wi-Fi CSI and accelerometer fusion system for fall detection. In: 2018 IEEE EMBS International Conference on Biomedical & Health Informatics (BHI), pp. 402–405 (2018)
13. Palipana, S., Rojas, D., Agrawal, P., et al.: FallDeFi: Ubiquitous fall detection using commodity Wi-Fi device. Proc. ACM Interact. Mobile Wearable Ubiquit. Technol. **1**(4), 1–25 (2018)
14. Jin, F., Sengupta, A., Cao, S.: MmFall: fall detection using 4-D MmWave Radar and a Hybrid Variational RNN AutoEncoder. IEEE Trans. Auto. Sci. Eng. 1–13 (2020)
15. Su, B.Y., et al.: Radar placement for fall detection: signature and performance. J. Ambient Intell. Smart Environ. **10**(1), 21–34 (2018)
16. Chen, Z., Wang, Y., et al.: Infrared-ultrasonic sensor fusion for support vector machine-based fall detection. J. Intell. Mater. Syst. Struct. **29**(9), 2027–2039 (2018)
17. Fan, X., Zhang, H., Leung, C., Shen, Z.: Fall detection with unobtrusive infrared array sensors. In: Lee, S., Ko, H., Oh, S. (eds.) MFI 2017. LNEE, vol. 501, pp. 253–267. Springer, Cham (2018). https://doi.org/10.1007/978-3-319-90509-9_15
18. Li, Q., Qu, H., Liu, Z., et al.: AF-DCGAN: Amplitude feature deep convolutional GAN for fingerprint construction in indoor localization systems. IEEE Trans. Emerg. Topics Comput. Intell. **5**(3), 468–480 (2021)
19. Gu, Y., Wang, Y., Liu, T., et al.: EmoSense: computational intelligence driven emotion sensing via wireless channel data. IEEE Trans. Emerg. Topics Comput. Intell. **4**(3), 216–226 (2019)
20. Yang, Z., Zhou, Z., Liu, Y.: From RSSI to CSI: indoor localization via channel response. ACM Comput. Surv. **46**(2), 1–32 (2013)
21. Duan, P., Zhou, Z., Wang, C., et al.: WiNet: A gait recognition model suitable for wireless sensing scenes. J. Xi'an Jiaotong Univ. **54**(07), 187–195 (2020)
22. Xin, T., Guo, B., Wang, Z., et al.: Freesense: Indoor human identification with Wi-Fi signals. In: 2016 IEEE Global Communications Conference, IEEE, pp. 1–7 (2016)
23. Chen, Z., Zhang, L., Jiang, C., et al.: WiFi CSI based passive human activity recognition using attention based BLSTM. IEEE Trans. Mob. Comput. **18**(11), 2714–2724 (2018)
24. Ohara, K., Maekawa, T., Matsushita, Y.: Detecting state changes of indoor everyday objects using Wi-Fi channel state information. Proc. ACM Interact. Mobile Wear. Ubiquit. Technol. **1**(3), 1–28 (2017)
25. Pokkunuru, A., Jakkala, K., Bhuyan, A., et al.: NeuralWave: gait-based user identification through commodity WiFi and deep learning. In: IECON 2018–44th Annual Conference of the IEEE Industrial Electronics Society, IEEE, pp.758–765 (2018)
26. Gu, Y., Zhang, X., Liu, Z., et al.: BeSense: leveraging WiFi channel data and computational intelligence for behavior analysis. IEEE Comput. Intell. Mag. **14**(4), 31–41 (2019)

27. Gu, Y., Yan, H., Dong, M., et al.: WiONE: one-shot learning for environment-robust device-free user authentication via commodity Wi-Fi in man-machine system. IEEE Trans. Comput. Soc. Syst. **8**(3), 630–642 (2021)
28. Yu, Z., Xia, Z., Wang, Z., et al.: User identification method based on action sequence monitoring in indoor WiFi environment. Northwestern Polytechnical University, China. CN201710608840.X (2020)
29. Cao, Y., Wang, F., Lu, X., et al.: Contactless body movement recognition during sleep via WiFi signals. IEEE Internet of Things J. **7**(3), 2028–2037 (2019)
30. Duan, P., Li, H., Zhang, B., et al.: APFNet: Amplitude-phase fusion network for CSI-based action recognition. Mobile Netw. Appl. **6**, 1–11(2021)
31. Long, J., Shelhamer, E., Darrell, T.: Fully convolutional networks for semantic segmentation. In: Proceedings of the IEEE Conference on Computer Vision and Pattern Recognition, pp. 3431–3440 (2015)
32. He, K., Zhang, X., Ren, S., et al.: Deep residual learning for image recognition. In: Proceedings of the IEEE Conference on Computer Vision and Pattern Recognition, pp. 770–778 (2016)

A Decentralized Scheduling Function for TSCH-Based Wireless Networks

Wei Yang[1]([✉]), Yuanlong Cao[1], Xun Shao[2], Hao Wang[1], Zhiming Zhang[1], and Qinghua Liu[1]

[1] School of Software, Jiangxi Normal University, Nanchang, China
yw@jxnu.edu.cn
[2] School of Regional Innovation and Social Design Engineering, Kitami Institute of Technology, Kitami, Japan

Abstract. Time-Slotted Channel Hopping (TSCH) is the emerging standard for industrial automation and process control low-power and lossy networks. Scheduling function is very crucial in the TSCH-based wireless networks, which defines the packets select which cells to send/receive. But the current industrial wireless standard does not define the function how to adds/deletes/relocates cells between neighbors. In this paper, we propose a decentralized scheduling function, which fully consider the use probability and distance of cell rather than simple random selection. We implement a decentralized scheduling function in 6TiSCH simulator and evaluate its performance experimentally in different cases. The experimental results show that our proposed scheme can reach lower end-to-end latency, as well as no extra costs.

Keywords: Time-slotted channel hopping (TSCH) · Decentralized scheduling · Wireless sensor network

1 Introduction

Industrial wireless sensor networks will be widely used in the field of industrial process automation in the future [1, 2]. The technology can greatly improve the efficiency and quality of industrial production. Industrial automation applications have strict requirements for low power consumption, high reliability and real-time performance of wireless network. These demands have been difficult to fulfill until the introduction of the Time-Synchronized Mesh Protocol (TSMP) [3] in 2008. Industrial wireless standards such as WirelessHART (2008) [4] and ISA100.11a (2011) [5] adopt TSMP technology. In April 2012, time-slotted channel hopping (TSCH), which is based on TSMP technology, became an important medium access control (MAC) layer protocol of the IEEE802.15.4e standard [6].

In TSCH-based wireless networks, all nodes keep high-precision time synchronization. Parts of nodes in the networks can cooperatively go to sleep at the same time when they have no data to send. It can achieve a low-power wireless network and

© ICST Institute for Computer Sciences, Social Informatics and Telecommunications Engineering 2022
Published by Springer Nature Switzerland AG 2022. All Rights Reserved
C. T. Calafate et al. (Eds.): MONAMI 2021, LNICST 418, pp. 194–200, 2022.
https://doi.org/10.1007/978-3-030-94763-7_15

prolong network life, which is very important in the battery-powered industrial applications. External interference and multi-fading seriously affects the reliability of wireless communication. The nodes in TSCH-based wireless networks, adopt channel hopping technology to combat the challenge. Research has proved it can reach 99.9% reliability [7, 8], which can be equip to the reliability of wired industrial networks. IEEE.802.15.4e standard defines time-slotted communication mechanisms for a pair of nodes exchanging packet in a cell (see Fig. 1). The communication of nodes happens at a [slotOffset, channelOffset] location according to the network schedule. However, it does not provide policies pertaining to the time for adding/deleting cells or the cells to select. Therefore, the scheduling function is crucial for solving the problems above.

The existing scheduling algorithms in TSCH-based wireless networks can be classified into two categories: centralized scheduling and distributed scheduling. Centralized scheduling algorithms (e.g., traffic aware scheduling algorithm (TASA) [9] and adaptive multi-hop scheduling (AMUS) [10]) rely on a center node to compute the schedule of all nodes in the networks. It is only suitable for static networks. However, numerous mobile nodes exist in industrial wireless applicants, and the nodes traffic are not fixed. Most scheduling algorithms for 6TiSCH networks involve distributed scheduling (e.g., on-the-fly (OTF) [11], SF0 [12], low latency scheduling function (LLSF) [13], recurrent low-latency scheduling function (ReSF) [14]).

However, the current distributed scheduling algorithms are affected by some challenges. First, the end-to-end latency in a multi-hop network is excessively high and uncertain. Some packets such as the alarm information in industrial process control systems must be transmitted to the border router in a timely manner. It requires the scheduling algorithms to coordinate a low latency multi-hop path. Second, schedule collisions often occur in distributed scheduling algorithms. Two pairs of neighbor nodes are scheduled in the same cell to send/receive data. Schedule collisions can further affect the performance of the network (e.g., reliability, power, and latency). Therefore, an efficient schedule function for TSCH-based wireless industrial networks must be identified. In the paper, we will propose our scheduling function for TSCH-based wireless networks.

The remainder of this article is organized as follows. Section 2 proposes a decentralized scheduling function for TSCH-based wireless networks. Section 3 evaluates the performance of the proposed scheme. Finally, Sect. 4 concludes this paper and presents future work.

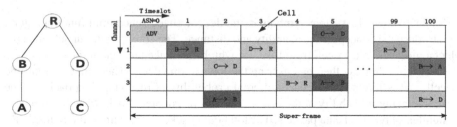

Fig. 1. Example of communication in TSCH-based wireless networks.

2 Decentralized Scheduling Function

Industrial wireless networks have strict requirements for real-time and reliability. The goal of resource scheduling algorithm is to provide low-latency end-to-end delay and no conflict communication. The new node joins and synchronizes to the TSCH-based wireless networks after receiving the EB packets from the multiple neighbor nodes. It may choose a prefer neighbor node as its parent according to the JP value, which is contained in the EB packets. Then the preferred parent node will allocate first Tx and Rx negotiated cells to the new joining node by 6P command. The autonomous cells are only used to send EB and DIO packets. The new node need to add Tx and Rx cells with its preferred parent after it continuously generate packets. Therefore, when to add or delete timeslots and which timeslots to select is a critical problem in the scheduling algorithm.

According to the latest 6TiSCH minimal scheduling function documentation, it specifies when to add or delete timeslots such as adapting to traffic, switching parent and handling schedule collisions. But it did not define how to select timeslots. The SF0 [12] which is proposed by 6TiSCH working group just used simple random timeslots selection. Time slot selection is very important in the resource scheduling algorithm, and it will directly affect the end-to-end delay and reliability of network. The goal of our scheme is to minimize the end-to-end packet transmission delay. It selects a suitable cell from the available cell list based on the use probability and distance of cell, which is different from random timeslot selection in SF0 [12] and LLSF [13].

Table 1. System symbols.

Symbol	Description
List_Tx	Available Tx cell
List_Rx	Available Rx cell
P_{ti}	Packet transmission probability of the i-th Tx cell
P_{ri}	Packet receiving probability of the i-th Rx cell
D_{ri}	The distance between the i-th Rx cell and the selected Tx cell
Slotframe_length	The length of slotframe

Table 1 shows the system symbols in the decentralized scheduling function. Here, we introduce the concepts of probability and distance. The core idea of our scheme is to select a most suitable Tx cell from List_Tx, which can make the sum of the distances to all Rx cell the shortest, thereby ensuring the lowest time delay. There may be multiple Rx cell, and different Rx cell have different probability of receiving data packets. The packet receiving probability of the i-th Rx cell can be counted. Each Rx cell will record the number of received data packets. The total data packet is the sum of the multiple Rx cell from the same source node, and the probability P_{ri} is the ratio of the received data packet of the i-th Rx cell to the total data packet. Each Tx cell and Rx cell has an ASN value (typical one ASN value represents 15 ms). The distance between the Tx cell and Rx cell can be calculated by the Eq. (1). Assuming the number of available Rx cell in the

List_Rx is k, we can calculate the sum of the distances from the one selected Tx cell to all Rx cell based on the Eq. (2). Repeating the above method, we can calculate the distance of all the available Tx cell in the List_Tx. Finally, we select the smallest distance from the calculation results, and can easily deduce which Tx cell is. In the following, we will take an example to further illustrate.

$$D_r = \begin{cases} T_x\_ASN - R_x\_ASN, \ T_x\_ASN > R_x\_ASN \\ Slotframe\_length + T_x\_ASN - R_x\_ASN, \ T_x\_ASN < R_x\_ASN \end{cases} \quad (1)$$

$$Sum\_D_r = P_{r1} * D_{r1} + P_{r1} * D_{r2} + ... + P_{rk} * D_{rk}, \ P_{r1} + P_{r2} + ... + P_{rk} = 1; \quad (2)$$

Assuming the networks consisting of 5 nodes and slotframe_length is 23, the node R is root. Here, taking node B as an example, it describes how the decentralized sched-uling function adds and deletes a Tx cell. Node B will periodically receive data pack-ets from node A, and usually there will be one packet per slotframe. The node B has 3 Rx cells from A (timeslot 4, 9 and 16), which is shown in Fig. 2. In order to be able to forward data packets from node A to the root node R, node B needs to add a Tx cell. Currently, node B has 3 available Tx cells (timeslot 8, 14 and 18). In our scheme, the node B should select one suitable Tx cell to minimize the end-to-end packet transmission delay. The sum of the distance from the one selected Tx cell to all Rx cell is shortest. And the calculation method of distance can refer to Eq. (2). Assum-ing the selected Tx cell is timeslot 14, we can calculate the distance Dr1 is 10, Dr2 is 5 and Dr3 is 21 based on the Eq. (1). Further assuming the probability Pr1 is 0.3, Pr2 is 0.6 and Pr3 is 0.1, we can calculate the sum of distance is 8.1 based on the Eq. (2). Using the same method, we can calculate the sum of distance value under different Tx cell. If the selected Tx cell is timeslot 8, the sum of distance value is 15.9. And if the se-lected Tx cell is timeslot 18, the sum of distance value is 9.8. By comparison, we can infer that the shortest distance can be achieved by selecting Tx timeslot 14.

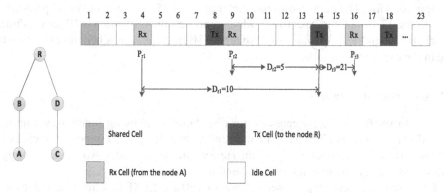

Fig. 2. Example of scheduling an Tx cell in the node B.

During a certain period of network running, the network traffic of node B is lower than the capacity. The node B determines to delete one of the Tx cells. Figure 4 depicts the general process of deleting Tx cells. Node B has 3 Rx cells from node A (timeslot

4, 9 and 16) and 4 Tx cells to node R (timeslot 8, 11, 14 and 18). To each Tx cell, node B counts the number of sending packets. It is easy to derive Pti, which is the packet transmission probability of the i-th Tx cell. Here, the Tx cell with the lowest packet transmission probability needs to be deleted. In Fig. 3 the Tx cell (timeslot 11) need to remove.

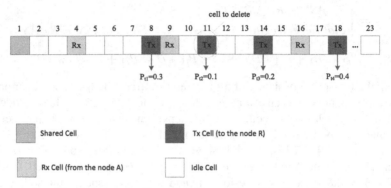

Fig. 3. Example of unscheduling an Tx cell in the node B.

3 Simulation Setup and Results

3.1 Simulation Setup

We adopt 6TiSCH open-source simulator [15] to evaluate our decentralized scheduling function. The 6TiSCH simulator is a discrete-event simulator written in Python, which is fully support TSCH protocol stack. The experiment parameters can be easily set in the configuration file. The num_Motes parameter is set to 25. The app_pkPeriod parameter is set to 6 s, 12 s and 60 s respectively, which represent the traffic rate is 10 packets/min, 5 packets/min and 1 packet/min. And we repeat 30 runs for each scheduling function to obtain the experiment results.

3.2 Experimental Results

In order to verify the effectiveness of our distributed scheduling function, we implemented our scheme on 6TiSCH simulator. End to end delay is an important metrics in distributed resource scheduling algorithm. Here we mainly consider two metrics: average end-to-end latency and maximum end-to-end latency.

First, we compared our proposed scheme to SF0 and LLSF in terms of average end-to-end delay. Average end-to-end delay is the main metrics of performance evaluation in the resource scheduling algorithm. As shown in Fig. 4 (a), the average end-to-end delay of our proposed scheme is much lower than that of SF0 and LLSF in the different traffic rate cases. When the network traffic rate is 1 packets/min, the average end-to-end delay of our proposed scheme is only about 0.75 s. At the same time, the average end-to-end delay of SF0 and LLSF reached 2.89 s and 1.81 s. Compare to SF0 and LLSF, the average end-to-end delay of our proposed scheme has dropped significantly. Fig. 4 (b) shows that the maximum end-to-end latency of our proposed scheme is much lower than SF0 and LLSF.

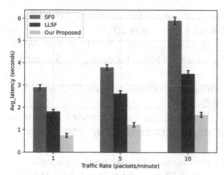 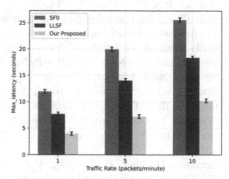

（a）The average end-to-end latency   （b）The maximum end-to-end latency

Fig. 4. The average and maximum end-to-end latency of SF0, LLSF and Our Proposed Function in different cases.

4 Conclusion

In this paper, we presented an efficient decentralized scheduling function for TSCH-based wireless networks. Our paper has three novel contributions. First, we proposed a cell selection method which fully consider the use probability and distance of cell. It can solve the problem of high latency in the current scheduling functions. Second, we proposed a cell deletion method which fully consider packet transmission probability. It can reduce network energy consumption. Finally, we implemented our proposed scheme and verified its performance through experimentation on the 6TiSCH simulator. The experimental results show that our proposed scheme can reach lower average and maximum end-to-end latency than the SF0 and LLSF scheduling functions. In our future work, we will deploy our proposed scheme in a real-world 6TiSCH wireless networks to further verify its performance.

Acknowledgments. This work is supported by the National Natural Science Foundation of China under Grant No. 62002143 and the Natural Science Foundation of Jiangxi Province under Grant No. 20192BAB217007.

References

1. Khan, W., Rehman, M., Zangoti, H., et al.: Industrial internet of things: recent advances, enabling technologies and open challenges. Comput. Electr. Eng. **81**(11), 1065–1087 (2020)

2. Huang, X.: Intelligent remote monitoring and manufacturing system of production line based on industrial Internet of Things. Comput. Commun. **150**(1), 421–428 (2020)
3. Pister, K., Doherty, L.: TSMP: time synchronized mesh protocol. In: International Symposium on Distributed Sensor Networks (DSN), pp. 391–398 (2008)
4. WirelessHART Specification 75: TDMA Data-Link Layer, HART Communication Foundation Std., Rev. 1.1, 2008, hCF SPEC-75
5. ISA-100.11a-2011: Wireless Systems for Industrial Automation: Process Control and Related Applications, International Society of Automation (ISA) Std., May 2011
6. IEEE Standard for Local and Metropolitan Area Networks-Part 15.4: Low-Rate Wireless Personal Area Networks (LR-WPANs) Amendment 1: MAC Sublayer, IEEE Standard 802.15.4e-2012, April 2012
7. Stanislowski, D., Vilajosana, X., Wang, Q., et al.: Adaptive synchronization in IEEE802.15.4e networks. IEEE Trans. Ind. Inform. **10**(1), 795–802 (2014)
8. Watteyne, T., Tuset-Peiro, P., Vilajosana, X., et al.: Teaching communication technologies and standards for the industrial IoT? Use 6TiSCH! IEEE Commun. Mag. **55**(5), 132–137 (2017)
9. Accettura, N., Vogli, E., Palattella, M.R., et al.: Decentralized traffic aware scheduling in 6TiSCH networks: design and experimental evaluation. IEEE Internet Things J. **2**(6), 455–470 (2015)
10. Jin, Y., Kulkarni, P., Wilcox, J., et al.: A centralized scheduling algorithm for IEEE 802.15.4e TSCH based industrial low power wireless networks. In: 2016 International Conference on Wireless Communications & Networking Conference, pp. 1725–1730. IEEE (2016)
11. Palattella, M.R., Watteyne, T., Wang, Q., et al.: On-the-fly bandwidth reservation for 6TiSCH wireless industrial networks. IEEE Sens. J. **16**(2), 550–560 (2016)
12. Dujovne, D., Grieco, L., Palattella, M., Accettura, N.: 6TiSCH 6top scheduling function zero/experimental (SFX), Internet-Draft draft-ietf-6tisch-6top-sfx-00, Internet Engineering Task Force, 22 September 2017
13. Chang, T., Watteyne, T., Wang, Q., Vilajosana, X.: LLSF: low latency scheduling function for 6TiSCH networks. In: 2016 International Conference on Distributed Computing in Sensor Systems Conference, pp. 93–95 (2016)
14. Daneels, G., Spinnewyn, B., Latre, S., et al.: ReSF: recurrent low-latency scheduling in IEEE 802.15.4e TSCH networks. Ad hoc Netw. **6**(9), 100–114 (2018)
15. Esteban, M., Glenn, D., Mališa, V., et al.: Simulating 6TiSCH networks. Trans. Emerg. Telecommun. Technol. **30**(3), 1–16 (2019)

Feature Detection Based Spectrum Sensing in NOMA System

Jingyi Wu[1], Tianheng Xu[1,2], Ting Zhou[1(✉)], and Kaijie Wang[1]

[1] Shanghai Advanced Research Institute, Chinese Academy of Sciences, Shanghai 201210, China
{wujy,xuth,zhouting,wangkaijie2019}@sari.ac.cn
[2] Shanghai Frontier Innovation Research Institute, Shanghai, China

Abstract. Non-orthogonal multiple access (NOMA) technology allows multiple users to share the same spectrum resource. Meanwhile, the technology of spectrum sensing enables us to find the free time of the spectrum. Both two technologies can significantly improve spectrum efficiency. In this paper, we attempt to combine the two techniques, for meeting the higher demand of spectrum resources requirements in future communication. We propose a transceiver architecture by the combination of two techniques. And we verify the feasibility of this scheme. The experiments and obtained data reveal that the proposed method is feasible. And it manifests to have a good detection performance.

Keywords: NOMA · Spectrum sensing · Feature detection · Cyclic delay diversity

1 Introduction

In the past ten years, wireless communication technology has developed rapidly, and the fifth-generation (5G) wireless communication network is currently in use [1–3]. It is supposed to have higher transmission speeds and can handle more complex scenarios [4,5]. However, for the significant growth of spectrum demands, available spectrum resources are still insufficient [6–8]. Hence, the problem of how to improve the utilization of the spectrum is a long-term challenge.

Spectrum sensing is one of the promising schemes to improve spectrum utilization [9–11]. It aims to find the spectral idle time of the primary user (PU), and allow the secondary user (SU) to share the spectrum hole dynamically [12]. The main methods of spectrum sensing include feature detection [13], energy detection [14,15] and matched filtering detection [16]. Among them, feature detection is a method that can detect the state of multiple users [17], which is used in this paper.

Meanwhile, until 5G, orthogonal multiple access (OMA) technology is the main method of information transmission. But the next generation communication technology needs to consider a more complex transmission environment

© ICST Institute for Computer Sciences, Social Informatics and Telecommunications Engineering 2022
Published by Springer Nature Switzerland AG 2022. All Rights Reserved
C. T. Calafate et al. (Eds.): MONAMI 2021, LNICST 418, pp. 201–217, 2022.
https://doi.org/10.1007/978-3-030-94763-7_16

and better transmission performance [18,19]. Many studies have shown that non-orthogonal multiple access (NOMA) is a very promising technology [20–22]. NOMA utilizes superposition coding at the transmitters and successive interference cancellation at the receivers to enables multiple users to multiplex on the same subchannel [23–25].

Hence, both spectrum sensing and NOMA can increase resource utilization. However, by the definition of NOMA, combining spectrum sensing with it differs much from combining with OMA. How to combine NOMA with spectrum sensing, are the problems that we pay attention to. Meanwhile, most of the existing relevant studies regard edge users as PU, center users as SU, and SU plays the role of relay for PU transmission [26–28]. For instance, Jia et al. [29] let SU play the role of the user relay, and the SU adopts the energy detection technique of spectrum sensing to identify the spectrum holes. Through theoretical derivation and simulation, they prove that their scheme has higher throughput. In the work of Wang et al. [30], SUs harvest wireless energy and sense the spectrum state simultaneously, in order to maximize the energy efficiency of the network. These studies above have done meaningful work on the combination of NOMA and spectrum sensing. However, there is still lacking research that examines the transmission status of both two NOMA users by feature detection. Hence, to answer the questions above, we attempt to explore how to set the sensing threshold under the condition of NOMA. To solve these problems, we have the following contributions in this paper:

– Firstly, we propose a feature detection based spectrum sensing technology in NOMA system, and design the system framework.
– Secondly, we verify the feasibility of this scheme. We design two patterns for detection under NOMA, and deduce the relationship between false-alarm probability (P_f) and threshold. Then we analyze the performance and compare it with that of OMA.
– Finally, We have sufficient simulations and then analyze the results. We conclude that the proposed scheme is better than OMA under the same conditions.

The remainder of this paper can be organized as follows. In Sect. 2, the system model of the spectrum sensing in NOMA is set up. Section 3 presents how the receiver gets the feature of the signal and the derivation of false alarm probability. In Sect. 4, a scheme of two users with the same working state is simulated. Section 5 discusses the situation when one user keeps on transmitting. Finally, conclusions are given in Sect. 6.

2   System Model

In this paper, we consider the model of downlink NOMA with a base station (BS) and two users, as shown in Fig. 1.

We apply cyclic delay diversity (CDD) to generating the feature of the signal. CDD uses multiple antennas to obtain signal feature [31,32]. The main transmission structure is shown in Fig. 2. In our paper, a model with two transmitting antennas and a single receiving antenna is utilized.

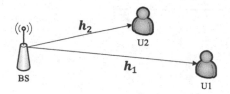

Fig. 1. The downlink system

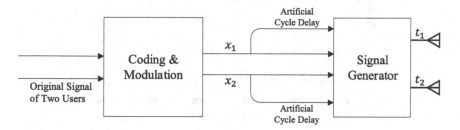

Fig. 2. Transmitter architecture for two users

We assume that x_1 and x_2 are the transmitted signals of two users respectively. The power allocation for users is α_1 and α_2, where $\alpha_1, \alpha_2 > 0$ and $\alpha_1 + \alpha_2 = 1$. The first antenna outputs two modulated signals x_1 and x_2, and the second antenna outputs x_1 and x_2 with different delays. The signals sent by two antennas are both in NOMA mode, then they pass through Rayleigh channels **h** and the signals are obtained by the receiver. The received signal by User 1 can be written as

$$r_1(n) = \mathbf{h}_1 \mathbf{t}(n) + w(n),\tag{1}$$

where $\mathbf{h}_1 = [h_{11}, h_{12}]$, $\mathbf{t}(n) = [t_1(n), t_2(n)]^T$, and $w(n)$ is the additive white Gaussian noise (AWGN) with specific power. h_{11} and h_{12} are the channel coefficients between two antennas and the receiver U1, and the difference between them is fixed. t_1 and t_2 are the signals transmitted by two antennas respectively, which can be computed by the following formulas

$$t_1(n) = \alpha_1 x_1(n) + \alpha_2 x_2(n)\tag{2}$$

and

$$t_2(n) = \alpha_1 x_1(n + d_1) + \alpha_2 x_2(n + d_2),\tag{3}$$

where d_1 and d_2 is the cyclic delay of two users respectively, which are chosen differently.

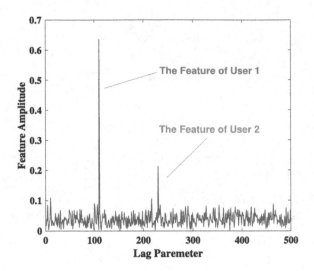

Fig. 3. The feature amplitude of NOMA signal after passing Rayleigh channel. System conditions: $SNR_1 = 0\,\mathrm{dB}$, $SNR_2 = 5\,\mathrm{dB}$, $\alpha_1 = 0.8$, $d_1 = 110$ and $d_2 = 230$.

3   The Proposed Method of Feature Detection in NOMA

3.1   Framework of the Receiver

We take the correlation between the received signal and the signal after its cyclic delay as the detection target, which is

$$R(\delta) = \frac{1}{S} \sum_{n=0}^{S-1} r(n)r^*(n+\delta),\qquad(4)$$

where S is the length of the received signal, the symbol $(\cdot)^*$ means the conjugate operation. The correlation value reaches a maximum when δ equals the delay of the users. We call this peak the amplitude of the feature.

Take a NOMA downlink model with spectrum sensing as an example. The system satisfies: $SNR_2 - SNR_1 = 5$ dB, $SNR_1 = 0$ dB and $\alpha_1 = 0.8$. And we set the delays as $d_1 = 110, d_2 = 230$. We call User 1 the strong user. Figure 3 shows the feature amplitude of this situation.

It can be seen that there are obvious peaks at the delays of the signals, meanwhile, at other δ, the amplitude fluctuates within a small range.

3.2   Principle of Feature Detection

In spectrum sensing, the sensing process needs to determine whether the correlation at the delay (d_1, d_2) is greater than the given threshold, which is a binary decision problem. If the correlation is greater than the threshold, then we can conclude that the user is at the state of transmitting signals (denoted as H_1), otherwise, the user is supposed not to be transmitting signals (denoted as H_0). The received signal can be written as

$$r(n) = \begin{cases} w(n), & H_0, \\ \mathbf{h}t(n) + w(n), & H_1. \end{cases} \tag{5}$$

The decision can be expressed as:

$$\begin{cases} \hat{H}_0 : |R| < \lambda, \\ \hat{H}_1 : |R| \geq \lambda, \end{cases} \tag{6}$$

where λ is the threshold we choose, and $\hat{H}_1$, $\hat{H}_0$ are the two possible detection results of the transmitting state. The detection probability (P_d) is the probability of correctly find the existence of the transmitter. And the false-alarm probability (P_f) is the probability of deciding the state of the transmitter to be working when it is not. Thus we have

$$\begin{aligned} P_d &= Pr(\hat{H}_1 | H_1) \\ &= Pr(|R| \geq \lambda) \\ &= Pr(|\tfrac{1}{S} \sum_{n=0}^{S-1} r(n) r^*(n+\delta)| \geq \lambda) \end{aligned} \tag{7}$$

and

$$\begin{aligned} P_f &= Pr(\hat{H}_1 | H_0) \\ &= Pr(|\tfrac{1}{S} \sum_{n=0}^{S-1} w(n) w^*(n+\delta)| \geq \lambda). \end{aligned} \tag{8}$$

3.3 False Alarm Probability Derivation

The noise is subject to Rayleigh distribution and without loss of generality, can be expressed as

$$\begin{cases} w(n) = \frac{N_0}{\sqrt{2}} w_1, \\ w(n+\delta) = \frac{N_0}{\sqrt{2}} w_2, \end{cases} \tag{9}$$

where w_1, w_2 are independent identically distributed variables subject to the standard normal distribution. To be specific,

$$\begin{cases} w_1 = x_1 + iy_1, \\ w_2 = x_2 + iy_2, \end{cases} \tag{10}$$

where x_1, x_2, y_1, y_2 satisfy

$$\begin{cases} x_1, x_2 \sim N(0, 1), \\ y_1, y_2 \sim N(0, 1). \end{cases} \tag{11}$$

Multiply w_1 and the conjugate of w_2, we get

$$F = w_1 w_2^* = (x_1 x_2 + y_1 y_2) + i(x_2 y_1 - x_1 y_2). \tag{12}$$

Let I and Q represent real and imaginary parts of F. Hence

$$\begin{cases} \mu_I = \mu_Q = 0, \\ \sigma_I^2 = \sigma_Q^2 = 2. \end{cases} \tag{13}$$

Suppose the length of the signal is S, accumulate all of the $w_1 w_2^*$. Then we have $\dot{F}$ as the function of the signal correlation

$$\dot{F} = \sum_{j=0}^{S-1}(I_j + iQ_j) = \dot{I} + i\dot{Q}, \tag{14}$$

where $\dot{I}, \dot{Q}$ are the real and imaginary part of $\dot{F}$, respectively. By Law of Large Numbers,

$$\begin{aligned} \lim_{S\to\infty} \frac{I - S\mu_I}{\sqrt{S}\sigma_I} \sim N(0,1), \\ \lim_{S\to\infty} \frac{Q - S\mu_Q}{\sqrt{S}\sigma_Q} \sim N(0,1). \end{aligned} \tag{15}$$

If the length of the received signal S is large enough, we can get

$$\dot{I}, \dot{Q} \sim N(0, 2S). \tag{16}$$

$\dot{F}$ also follows the Rayleigh distribution, let $t = |\dot{F}|$, and the probability distribution can be expressed as

$$f(t) = \frac{t}{2S} e^{\frac{-t^2}{4S}} \, (t \geq 0). \tag{17}$$

Hence, the sum of the correlations for the noise is

$$\left| \frac{1}{S} \sum_{n=0}^{S-1} w(n)w^*(n+\delta) \right| = \frac{N_0^2}{2S} |\dot{F}|. \tag{18}$$

Then the P_f can be evaluated by

$$\begin{aligned} P_f &= Pr(|\frac{1}{S}\sum_{n=0}^{S-1} w(n)w^*(n+\delta)| \geq \lambda) \\ &= Pr(\frac{N_0^2}{2S}|\dot{F}| \geq \lambda) \\ &= Pr(|\dot{F}| \geq \frac{2S\lambda}{N_0^2}) \\ &= \int_{\frac{2S\lambda}{N_0^2}}^{+\infty} e^{\frac{-t^2}{4S}} dt \\ &= e^{-\frac{S\lambda^2}{N_0^4}}. \end{aligned} \tag{19}$$

Therefore, we get the relationship between P_f and λ it as

$$\lambda = \sqrt{-\frac{lnP_f}{S}} N_0^2. \tag{20}$$

Use the formula to determine the threshold of spectrum sensing in OMA scene, and can obtain the correctness of it. We compare this result of OMA with that of our proposed method in NOMA.

Table 1. Simulation parameters.

Parameters	Values
Original signal size	4096
Channel coding	LDPC
Coding rate	449/1024
Antenna configuration	2×1
Channel model	Rayleigh fading
Modulation	QPSK
Number of multiplexed NOMA users	2
NOMA mode	Downlink
Proportion of power distribution	$\alpha_1 : \alpha_2 = 2 : 1, 4 : 1, 10 : 1$
SNR difference	$SNR_2 - SNR_1 = 5$ dB

4   Simulation Results and Performance Analysis

We considered two modes of spectrum sensing in NOMA, one of which is two users share the same transmission state, the other is keep U2 transmitting.

4.1   Mode 1: Same Transfer State

Suppose strong and weak users share the same transmission state in the NOMA-spectrum sensing system. In other words, both users are transmitting signals or neither of them. Because of this limitation, this mode is more suitable for some downlink NOMA scenarios and applications. The feature amplitude of the received signal is calculated and compared with the threshold. Then we use the Monte-Carlo simulation to calculate the probability. The basic simulation parameters are listed in Table 1.

In this paper, we use two kinds of methods to calculate SNR. The first one adds the power of the two users as the power of the signal. The other one utilizes the power of a single user for its own SNR, who called "with SNR compensation". In order to give consideration to the actual conditions and fairness of the results, and to give a more complete show of the performance of the system, both methods will be used in the simulation.

We choose three power allocation rates that are widely adopted in the NOMA system [24]. They are $\alpha_1 : \alpha_2 = 2 : 1$, $4 : 1$ and $10 : 1$.

Figure 4 shows the detection probability P_d and false-alarm probability P_f of the two users with power allocation $\alpha_1 : \alpha_2 = 2 : 1$. The U1 in figs means the strong user, and the U2 means the weak user. We can see that the P_f of two users are both stay around 0.1. Figure 4(a) describes that at system SNR, the P_d curve of U2 is clearly below that of U1. At about –5 dB, the P_d of U1 reaches 0.9, meanwhile the P_d of U2 is round 0.72. This result reveals that, when the two users are at the same environment of SNR, the detection performance of weak users

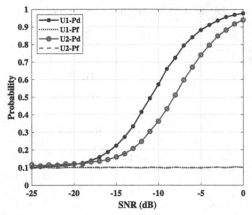

(a) The P_d and P_f of two users without SNR compensation.

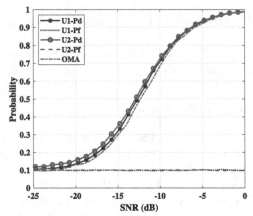

(b) The P_d and P_f of two users with SNR compensation.

Fig. 4. Downlink NOMA system with power allocation $\alpha_1 : \alpha_2 = 2 : 1$.

will be relatively weak. As we can observe from Fig. 4(b), after compensating SNR to their own SNR, both P_d of two users are almost superposed with the OMA result. It shows their P_d reach 0.9 at around –6 dB, and at 0 dB P_d nearly achieve to 1.

Then we try to simulate systems with different power allocations.

Figure 5 and Fig. 6 show the detection performance with $\alpha_1 : \alpha_2 = 4 : 1$ and $\alpha_1 : \alpha_2 = 10 : 1$, respectively. It is observed from Fig. 5(a) and Fig. 6(a) that the less power of U2 is allocated, the greater the difference between its P_d and that of the U1. When $\alpha_1 : \alpha_2 = 2 : 1$, the difference of P_d between two users is about 0.2 at most. At the same time, when $\alpha_1 : \alpha_2 = 10 : 1$, the gap can even achieve more than 0.5. It can be perceived that from either Fig. 5(b) and Fig. 6(b), after

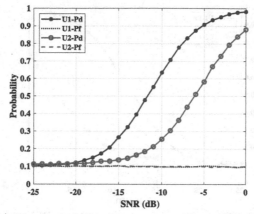

(a) The P_d and P_f of two users without SNR compensation.

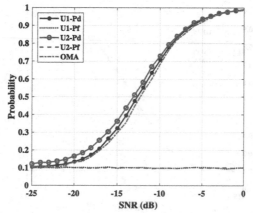

(b) The P_d and P_f of two users with SNR compensation.

Fig. 5. Downlink NOMA system with power allocation $\alpha_1 : \alpha_2 = 4 : 1$.

compensating SNR to their own SNR, in the range of approximately −8 dB to 0 dB, the detection performance of the two users remained consistent with OMA. However, when U2 is distributed less power, at low SNR, P_d of U2 will be larger than that of U1.

Combined with three groups of pictures, it can be analyzed that, transmitting with another NOMA user, the performance of U1 will not be significantly inferior to the OMA scheme. Meanwhile, the performance of U2 largely depends on the power allocation. At the same SNR, U2 is inferior to U1 as to the P_d. However, at their own SNR, the detection performance of two users is similar to that of OMA. Therefore, it is better to make the difference between α_1 and α_2 as small as possible, due to the inferiority of U2 at the same SNR.

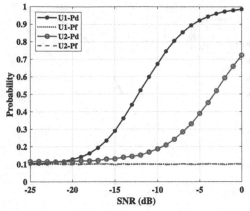

(a) The P_d and P_f of two users without SNR compensation.

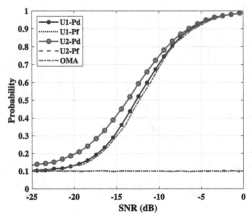

(b) The P_d and P_f of two users with SNR compensation.

Fig. 6. Downlink NOMA system with power allocation $\alpha_1 : \alpha_2 = 10 : 1$.

4.2   Mode 2: Weak User Keep Transmitting

To make the scenario more general, now keep the U2's signal always transmitting. This mode is recommended to apply to the uplink system, and we consider detecting the state of U1.

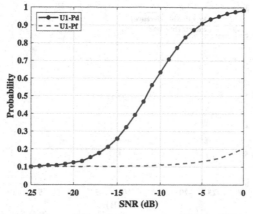

(a) The P_d and P_f of two users without SNR compensation.

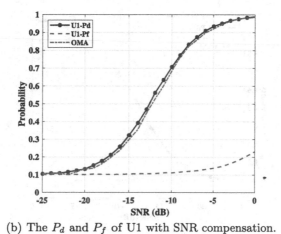

(b) The P_d and P_f of U1 with SNR compensation.

Fig. 7. Downlink NOMA system with power allocation $\alpha_1 : \alpha_2 = 4 : 1$, when U2 is keep on transmitting.

As Fig. 7 indicates, P_f starts to increase when SNR is −10 dB. And at 0 dB, P_f reaches to more than 0.2. Meanwhile, the curve of P_d is a little superior to that of OMA at some SNR.

While running the Monte-Carlo simulation, we save the mean value of the signal feature amplitude when U1 is not transmitting. Finally, output the trend of the ratio of it to the threshold when SNR changes, as is shown in Fig. 8. The straight line in the figure is the reference value of the ratio when P_f is maintained at 0.1.

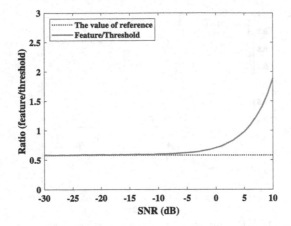

Fig. 8. The rate of the feature amplitude when U1 in H_0 condition to the threshold, with $\alpha_1 : \alpha_2 = 4 : 1$.

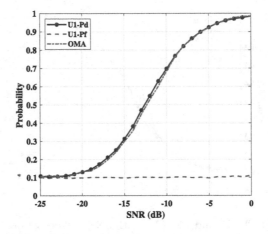

Fig. 9. Downlink NOMA system with power allocation $\alpha_1 : \alpha_2 = 4 : 1$ after threshold adjustment, when U2 is keep on transmitting.

When the power of the noise is reduced, the power of U2 is relatively increased. Therefore, Fig. 8 describes that when SNR increases, the correlation of U2 signals has a greater impact on the detection results.

We suspect that the existence of the U2 signal prevents P_f from being maintained at 0.1. In this case, not only noise but also U2 signal correlation should be considered in the P_f calculation. Hence, we need to adjust the threshold and restore P_f to 0.1.

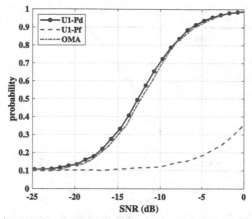

(a) The P_d and P_f of two users with SNR compensation before threshold adjustment.

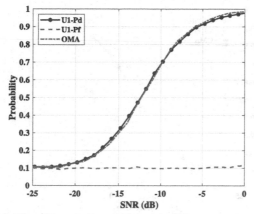

(b) The P_d and P_f of U1 with SNR compensation after threshold adjustment.

Fig. 10. Downlink NOMA system with power allocation $\alpha_1 : \alpha_2 = 2 : 1$, when U2 is keep on transmitting.

4.3   Threshold Adjustment for Mode 2

Now we come up with a numerical solution to adjust the threshold. We use the ratio of the feature amplitude when U1 in H_0 condition to the threshold to adjust the new threshold, the following three pairs of figures (Fig. 9, Fig. 10 and Fig. 11) show the result before and after adjustment.

Figure 9 shows that after threshold adjustment, the curve of P_d is still close to OMA. Especially, around -2–0 dB, the P_d value of U1 is slightly inferior to P_d of OMA. Probably because when U1 is transmitting, the feature amplitude of this situation is significantly greater than the threshold. Even if the threshold is adjusted, it is still quite small for most feature values in the case of H_1.

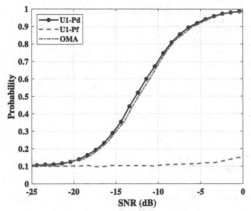

(a) The P_d and P_f of two users with SNR compensation before threshold adjustment.

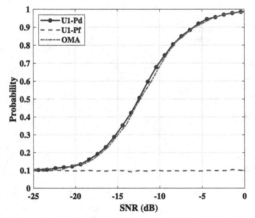

(b) The P_d and P_f of U1 with SNR compensation after threshold adjustment.

Fig. 11. Downlink NOMA system with power allocation $\alpha_1 : \alpha_2 = 10 : 1$, when U2 is keep on transmitting.

Figure 10(a) exhibits that P_f is largely influenced when more power is allocated to U2. The P_f of U1 even reaches to about 0.35 at 0 dB. The adjustment result as Fig. 10(b) indicates, when the power of U2 is relatively high, P_d will significantly decrease at high SNR, which is 0.02 less than OMA at most. When the power of U2 decreases, as shown in Fig. 11(a), P_f also fluctuates less, which is around 0.14 at 0 dB. Hence, as Fig. 11(b) indicates, there was barely changed after the adjustment. This result reveals that the less power is allocated, the less influence has the threshold adjustment on P_d is.

To sum up, this mode of keep U2 transmitting has the P_f that failed to regulate. The method presented in this chapter can solve this problem. Moreover, in this mode with threshold adjustment, the result indicates that the effect on the detection performance of U1 is not particularly obvious.

5 Conclusion

In this paper, we have investigated the application of spectrum sensing in NOMA system. We have designed the workflow and simulated it to verify the feasibility of the scheme. Considering the form of NOMA, we have designed two modes of spectrum sensing, and distinguished the downlink and uplink scenarios in the two modes. Then we have simulated the scenarios and studied the detection performance. The simulation results confirm that the proposed NOMA-spectrum sensing technology has good detection performance, which is attractive for practice.

Our future work will involve more properties of spectrum sensing based on NOMA, improvements in performance, and further applications.

Acknowledgement. The authors' work was supported in part by the Science and Technology Commission Foundation of Shanghai (No. 21511101400), Shanghai Rising-Star Program (No. 21QC1400800), the National Natural Science Foundation of China (No. 61801461) and the Youth Innovation Promotion Association of CAS.

References

1. Zhang, Z., et al.: 6G wireless networks: Vision, requirements, architecture, and key technologies. IEEE Veh. Technol. Mag. **14**(3), 28–41 (2019)
2. Ghosh, A., Maeder, A., Baker, M., Chandramouli, D.: 5G evolution: a view on 5G cellular technology beyond 3GPP release 15. IEEE Access **7**, 127639–127651 (2019)
3. Xu, T., Zhou, T., Tian, J., Sang, J., Hu, H.: Intelligent spectrum sensing: when reinforcement learning meets automatic repeat sensing in 5G communications. IEEE Wirel. Commun. **27**(1), 46–53 (2020)
4. Zou, Z., Yin, R., Wu, C., Yuan, J., Chen, X.: Distributed spectrum and power allocation for D2D-U networks. In: Monami 2020, pp. 161–180. Springer International Publishing, Chiba (2020)
5. Vitturi, S., Zunino, C., Sauter, T.: Industrial communication systems and their future challenges: next-generation ethernet, IIoT, and 5G. Proc. IEEE **107**(6), 944–961 (2019)
6. Chen, S., Zhai, D., Bai, W., Guan, H., Ma, P., Shao, W.: Resource allocation scheme design in power wireless heterogeneous networks considering load balance. In: Monami 2020, pp. 111–124. Springer International Publishing, Chiba (2020)
7. Giordani, M., Polese, M., Mezzavilla, M., Rangan, S., Zorzi, M.: Toward 6G networks: use cases and technologies. IEEE Commun. Mag. **58**(3), 55–61 (2020)
8. Zhang, J., Björnsonon, E., Matthaiou, M., Ng, D.W.K., Yang, H., Love, D.J.: Prospective multiple antenna technologies for beyond 5G. IEEE J. Select. Areas Commun. **38**(8), 1637–1660 (2020)

9. Qu, H., Xu, X., Zhao, J., Yan, F., Wang, W.: A robust hyperbolic tangent-based energy detector with gaussian and non-gaussian noise environments in cognitive radio system. IEEE Syst. J. **14**(3), 3161–3172 (2020)

10. Spooner, C.M., Mody, A.N.: Wideband cyclostationary signal processing using sparse subsets of narrowband subchannels. IEEE Trans. Cogn. Commun. Netw. **4**(2), 162–176 (2018)

11. Cabric, D., Mishra, S., Brodersen, R.: Implementation issues in spectrum sensing for cognitive radios. In: 2004 Conference Record of the Thirty-Eighth Asilomar Conference on Signals, Systems and Computers, vol. 1, pp. 772–776 (2004)

12. Salama, G.M., Taha, S.A.: Cooperative spectrum sensing and hard decision rules for cognitive radio network. In: 2020 3rd International Conference on Computer Applications Information Security (ICCAIS), pp. 1–6 (2020)

13. Sherbin, M.K., Sindhu, V.: Cyclostationary feature detection for spectrum sensing in cognitive radio network. In: 2019 International Conference on Intelligent Computing and Control Systems (ICCS), pp. 1250–1254 (2019)

14. Yasrab, T., Gurugopinath, S.: Spectral efficiency of MIMO-NOMA cognitive radios with energy-based spectrum sensing. In: 2019 IEEE International Conference on Distributed Computing, VLSI, Electrical Circuits and Robotics (DISCOVER), pp. 1–6 (2019)

15. Chin, W.L.: On the noise uncertainty for the energy detection of OFDM signals. IEEE Trans. Veh. Technol. **68**(8), 7593–7602 (2019)

16. Picciolo, M.L., Myrick, W.L., Goldstein, J.S.: A quadrature median matched filter for robust detection and estimation. In: 2019 International Radar Conference (RADAR), pp. 1–6 (2019)

17. Xu, T., Zhang, M., Hu, H., Chen, H.H.: Sliced spectrum sensing-a channel condition aware sensing technique for cognitive radio networks. IEEE Trans. Veh. Technol. **67**(11), 10815–10829 (2018)

18. Saad, W., Bennis, M., Chen, M.: A vision of 6G wireless systems: applications, trends, technologies, and open research problems. IEEE Netw. **34**(3), 134–142 (2020)

19. Yang, P., Xiao, Y., Xiao, M., Li, S.: 6G wireless communications: vision and potential techniques. IEEE Netw. **33**(4), 70–75 (2019)

20. Wang, K., Zhou, T., Xu, T., Hu, H., Tao, X.: Asymmetric adaptive modulation for uplink NOMA systems. IEEE Trans. Commun. **69**, 1–1 (2021)

21. Yang, K., Yang, N., Ye, N., Jia, M., Gao, Z., Fan, R.: Non-orthogonal multiple access: achieving sustainable future radio access. IEEE Commun. Mag. **57**(2), 116–121 (2019)

22. Maraqa, O., Rajasekaran, A.S., Al-Ahmadi, S., Yanikomeroglu, H., Sait, S.M.: A survey of rate-optimal power domain NOMA with enabling technologies of future wireless networks. IEEE Commun. Surv. Tutor. **22**(4), 2192–2235 (2020)

23. Wei, F., Zhou, T., Xu, T., Hu, H.: BER analysis for uplink NOMA in asymmetric channels. IEEE Commun. Lett. **24**(11), 2435–2439 (2020)

24. Ding, Z., Lei, X., Karagiannidis, G.K., Schober, R., Yuan, J., Bhargava, V.K.: A survey on non-orthogonal multiple access for 5G networks: Research challenges and future trends. IEEE J. Select. Areas Commun. **35**(10), 2181–2195 (2017)

25. Wang, Z., Xu, T., Zhou, T., Hu, H.: Joint tier slicing and power control for a novel multicast system based on NOMA and D2D-relay. In: GLOBECOM 2020–2020 IEEE Global Communications Conference, pp. 1–6 (2020)

26. Wang, X., Jia, M., Guo, Q.: Full-duplex cooperative non-orthogonal multiple access with spectrum sensing. In: 2020 15th IEEE International Conference on Signal Processing (ICSP), pp. 411–416 (2020)

27. Liu, X., Wang, Y., Liu, S., Meng, J.: Spectrum resource optimization for NOMA-based cognitive radio in 5G communications. IEEE Access **6**, 24904–24911 (2018)
28. Song, Z., Wang, X., Liu, Y., Zhang, Z.: Joint spectrum resource allocation in NOMA-based cognitive radio network with SWIPT. IEEE Access **7**, 89594–89603 (2019)
29. Jia, M., Wang., X., Guo, Q., Ho, I., Gu, X., Lau, F.: Performance analysis of cooperative non-orthogonal multiple access based on spectrum sensing. IEEE Trans. Veh. Technol. **68**(7), 6855–6866 (2019)
30. Wang, X., et al.: Energy efficiency optimization for NOMA-based cognitive radio with energy harvesting. IEEE Access **7**, 139172–139180 (2019)
31. Bauch, G., Malik, J.: Cyclic delay diversity with bit-interleaved coded modulation in orthogonal frequency division multiple access. IEEE Trans. Wircl. Commun. **5**(8), 2092–2100 (2006)
32. Iradukunda, N., Nguyen, H.T., Hwang, W.J.: On cyclic delay diversity-based single-carrier scheme in spectrum sharing systems. IEEE Commun. Lett. **23**(6), 1069–1072 (2019)

A Scalable IoT Data Collection Method by Shared-Subscription with Distributed MQTT Brokers

Ryohei Banno[1(✉)] and Toshinori Yoshizawa[1,2P]

[1] Kogakuin University, Tokyo, Japan
banno@computer.org
[2] VINX Corp., Osaka, Japan

Abstract. Internet of Things (IoT) systems like a smart factory and a smart city require collecting a massive amount of data from sensors. MQTT is a promising protocol for such uses due to its lightweight design and loose-coupling nature by publish/subscribe messaging model. On the other hand, there is an issue that a broker could be a performance bottleneck. Even though it is not the case, reception by a subscriber might not catch up with the amount of data from the broker. In this paper, we propose a scalable IoT data collection method with distributed MQTT brokers. By shared-subscription functionality, which appeared in MQTT version 5.0, the proposed method enables an application to receive a massive amount of IoT data. To evaluate the proposed method, we have developed a load testing tool named MQTTLoader. Experimental results show that the proposed method can improve the throughput compared to conventional ways.

Keywords: MQTT · IoT · Publish/subscribe · Distributed systems

1 Introduction

Internet of Things (IoT) has been developing in various application fields. For example, in Industrie 4.0, monitoring the condition of industrial robots enables preventive maintenance and reduces unexpected downtime [8]. It is made possible by collecting data such as operation time and enclosure temperature from industrial robots. Another example is a smart city, where sensors provide environmental data to realize various services, e.g., relieving traffic congestion and lowering damages caused by natural disasters.

For collecting data from IoT devices, MQTT [14] is a promising communication protocol. It provides loose-coupling nature by publish/subscribe messaging model [7], in addition to its small size of header that contributes to traffic reduction and power saving.

© ICST Institute for Computer Sciences, Social Informatics and Telecommunications Engineering 2022
Published by Springer Nature Switzerland AG 2022. All Rights Reserved
C. T. Calafate et al. (Eds.): MONAMI 2021, LNICST 418, pp. 218–226, 2022.
https://doi.org/10.1007/978-3-030-94763-7_17

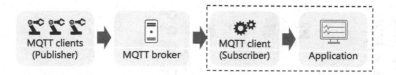

Fig. 1. Collecting IoT data by MQTT

However, an MQTT broker or a subscriber could be a performance bottleneck. Figure 1 illustrates a typical architecture of collecting data by MQTT. A massive amount of data from publishers concentrates on the broker, and thus it might not accept all published data. Even though the broker can process all the data, the subscriber might not catch up with the amount of data from the broker.

To tackle this issue, we propose a scalable IoT data collection method with distributed MQTT brokers. In the proposed method, an application can use more than one subscriber to receive data by shared-subscription functionality, which appeared in MQTT version 5.0 [16].

2   Related Work

Since an MQTT broker could be a performance bottleneck, there are existing studies to extend the performance of brokers.

muMQ [17] is a high-performance MQTT broker. It efficiently exploits multi-core CPUs by an event-driven I/O mechanism and avoids the kernel overhead by DPDK. muMQ can improve the performance of a single broker, though it does not obtain horizontal scalability and requires hardware supporting DPDK.

MQTT-ST [13] and ILDM [3,4] are methods to utilize multiple MQTT brokers by connecting them and forming a delivery tree. They are effective if the placement of publishers and subscribers has a high locality, i.e., publishers and subscribers of the same topic tend to connect to the same broker. On the other hand, considering the case to collect IoT data from all publishers as shown in Fig. 1, it is hard to obtain load distribution as well as causing high latency due to multi-hop forwarding among brokers.

Detti et al. [5] have proposed a method to reduce the traffic among brokers by making each subscriber connect to multiple brokers. It is similar to our method from the viewpoint that an application utilizes multiple connections to brokers to receive data in which it is interested. However, there is a difficulty in load distribution if a topic has a massive amount of data.

3   Scalable IoT Data Collection with MQTT Brokers

We propose a scalable IoT data collection method with distributed MQTT brokers. Figure 2 shows an overview of the proposed method. In the proposed

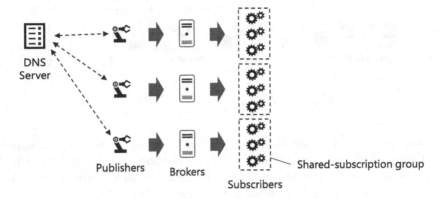

DNS
Server

Publishers   Brokers   Subscribers

Shared-subscription group

Fig. 2. Overview of proposed method

method, we use multiple brokers for load distribution. In addition, each application uses multiple subscribers to receive IoT data in parallel.

We assume a large number of publishers. Each publisher connects to one of the brokers. The broker to connect to is decided by Domain Name System (DNS) round-robin, i.e., a publisher does not need additional functionality except for specifying the broker by a domain name.

An application uses subscribers more than or equal to the number of brokers. Each subscriber connects to one of the brokers. We assume that the broker to connect to is decided as the configuration of the application by its user. Subscribers connecting to the same broker make a shared-subscription group.

Shared-subscription functionality has appeared in MQTT version 5.0 [16]. It enables to group subscribers so that they share receiving messages of a topic. That is, each message of the topic is delivered to one of the subscribers participating in the group. This could help load distribution and improve the throughput of subscribers.

Collecting data by shared-subscription is similar to the consumer group mechanism of Apache Kafka [1,11], which is proprietary software. In contrast, MQTT is an open standard protocol by OASIS [16] and an ISO recommendation [10].

4   Load Testing Tool

The performance of MQTT brokers holds interest from engineers and researchers since they could be bottlenecks, as we mentioned in Sect. 2. However, it has not been sufficiently clarified what characteristics actual MQTT brokers have and how we can appropriately measure and analyze their performance, especially for the MQTT v5.0.

To evaluate MQTT v5.0 brokers and the proposed method, we have developed a load testing tool named MQTTLoader [2,15]. It is implemented in Java. Binary files, source codes, and documents are publicly available on GitHub [15].

Figure 3a shows an overview of MQTTLoader. It generates multiple MQTT clients (publishers and subscribers) and applies a load on a broker based on specified parameter settings. Examples of parameters are listed in Table 1. Besides the list, various parameters are provided, such as QoS level, Retain flag, payload size, publish interval, ramp-up/ramp-down time, etc.

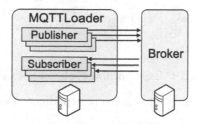

(a) Running on single-host

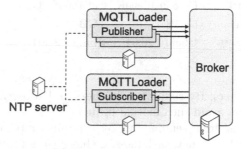

(b) Running on multi-host

Fig. 3. Overview of MQTTLoader

Table 1. Example of parameters

Parameter	Description
broker	Broker address
mqtt_version	MQTT version
num_publishers	Number of publishers
num_subscribers	Number of subscribers
shared_subscription	Enable shared-subscription
ntp	NTP server address

We can run MQTTLoader either on a single host machine or multiple host machines like Fig. 3b. Running both publishers and subscribers on a single host may cause mutual influence, e.g., receiving load of subscribers lowers the

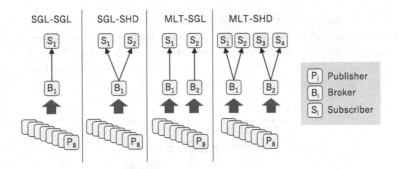

Fig. 4. Experimental configurations

Table 2. Hardware information of experimental environment

	Publisher	Broker, Subscriber
CPU	Core i9 10900K	Celeron N3350
Memory	64 GB	4 GB
OS	Ubuntu 20.04	Ubuntu 20.04

throughput of publishers. By running publishers and subscribers separately on different hosts, we can avoid such mutual influence.

Latency is the time from sending out by a publisher to receiving by a subscriber. To calculate the latency, each message has a timestamp of sending out in its payload. The latency is calculated by the difference between this timestamp and when a subscriber receives the message. In the case of running MQTTLoader on multi-hosts, MQTTLoader obtains time information from the specified Network Time Protocol (NTP) server and uses it for the calculation to avoid the influence of the time offset among the hosts.

5 Evaluation

To evaluate the proposed method, we conducted experiments to measure the following performance characteristics.

Throughput (publishers)
Average throughput between publishers and brokers.
Throughput (subscribers)
Average throughput between brokers and subscribers.
Latency
Average time from publishers to subscribers.

We use MQTTLoader v0.7.2 for publishers and subscribers. Although there are various MQTT broker products [6,9,12], we choose Mosquitto (v1.6.9 − 1) since it is widely used and known for its superior performance.

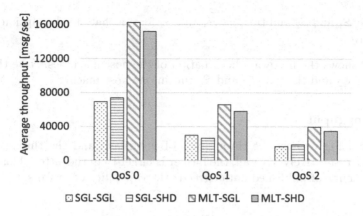

Fig. 5. Publisher throughput

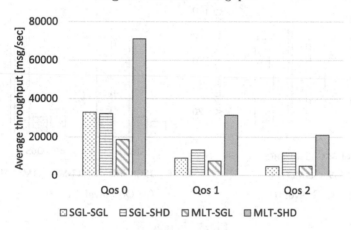

Fig. 6. Subscriber throughput

We set the number of publishers 8. Each publisher sends out messages with no interval, where each message has a 600 bytes payload. Each measurement takes 60 s and it is conducted three times repeatedly.

Regarding brokers and subscribers, we use four cases in Fig. 4 for comparison:

SGL-SGL
Using a single broker B_1 and a single subscriber S_1.

SGL-SHD
Using a single broker B_1 and two subscribers S_1 and S_2, which consists of a shared-subscription group.

MLT-SGL
Using two brokers B_1 and B_2 and two subscribers S_1 and S_2 without shared-subscription.

MLT-SHD
Using two brokers B_1 and B_2 and four subscribers S_1, S_2, S_3, and S_4.

The pair S_1 and S_2 and the pair S_3 and S_4 form a shared-subscription group, respectively.

Table 2 shows the hardware information of the host machines. Note that the pair S_1 and S_2 and the pair S_3 and S_4 run in one host machine.

5.1   Throughput

Figure 5 and Fig. 6 show the throughput of publishers and the throughput of subscribers, respectively. Overall, the former is larger than the latter. This means that the amount of published data exceeds the capability of brokers.

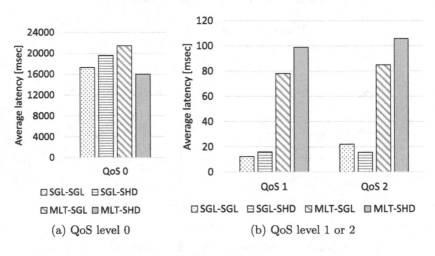

(a) QoS level 0   (b) QoS level 1 or 2

Fig. 7. Latency

When focusing on the throughput of subscribers, MLT-SHD, i.e., the proposed method, achieves the largest throughput. That is, using multiple brokers and multiple subscribers is effective for collecting a massive amount of IoT data.

On the other hand, in Fig. 5, MLT-SGL gets larger throughput than MLT-SHD. One possibility is that the load of processing shared-subscription inside each broker influences the receiving process of the broker.

5.2   Latency

Figure 7 shows the results of latency. Regardless of the four cases, QoS 0 traffic causes significantly long latency. In the case of QoS 1 and 2, MLT-SHD has the largest latency. It possibly appears in return for the high throughput.

Note that the latency could increase according to the elapsed time because the brokers are considered to be overloaded as mentioned above.

6   Conclusion

In this paper, we proposed a scalable IoT data collection method with distributed MQTT brokers. In the proposed method, each application uses multiple subscribers with shared-subscription functionality to receive IoT data in parallel. To evaluate the proposed method, we developed a load testing tool MQTT-Loader. By the experiments with Mosquitto and MQTTLoader, we found that the proposed method can improve the throughput compared to conventional ways. On the other hand, the latency of the proposed method tends to become large. Future work includes a detailed analysis of those experimental results and improvement of the latency.

Acknowledgments. This work was supported by JSPS KAKENHI Grant No. 19K20253.

References

1. Apache Kafka: https://kafka.apache.org/. Accessed 7 July 2021
2. Banno, R., Ohsawa, K., Kitagawa, Y., Takada, T., Yoshizawa, T.: Measuring performance of MQTT v5.0 brokers with MQTTLoader. In: Proceedings of the IEEE Consumer Communications & Networking Conference, pp. 1–2 (2021)
3. Banno, R., Sun, J., Fujita, M., Takeuchi, S., Shudo, K.: Dissemination of edge-heavy data on heterogeneous MQTT brokers. In: Proceedings of the IEEE International Conference on Cloud Networking, pp. 1–7 (2017)
4. Banno, R., Sun, J., Takeuchi, S., Shudo, K.: Interworking layer of distributed MQTT Brokers. IEICE Trans. Inf. Syst. **E102.D**(12), 2281–2294 (2019)
5. Detti, A., Funari, L., Blefari-Melazzi, N.: Sub-linear scalability of MQTT clusters in topic-based publish-subscribe applications. IEEE Trans. Netw. Serv. Manag. **17**(3), 1954–1968 (2020)
6. EMQ X: https://www.emqx.io/. Accessed 7 July 2021
7. Eugster, P.T., Felber, P.A., Guerraoui, R., Kermarrec, A.M.: The many faces of publish/subscribe. ACM Comput. Surv. **35**(2), 114–131 (2003)
8. FANUC Corp.: Field system. https://fanuc.co.jp/en/product/field/index.html. Accessed 7 July 2021
9. HiveMQ: https://www.hivemq.com/. Accessed 7 July 2021
10. ISO Central Secretary: Information technology - Message Queuing Telemetry Transport (MQTT) v3.1.1. Standard ISO/IEC 20922:2016, International Organization for Standardization (2016)
11. Kreps, J., Narkhede, N., Rao, J.: Kafka: A distributed messaging system for log processing. In: Proceedings of the International Workshop on Networking Meets Databases, pp. 1–7 (2011)
12. Light, R.A.: Mosquitto: server and client implementation of the MQTT protocol. J. Open Sour. Softw. **2**(13), 265 (2017)
13. Longo, E., Redondi, A.E., Cesana, M., Arcia-Moret, A., Manzoni, P.:MQTT-ST: a spanning tree protocol for distributed MQTT brokers. In: Proceedings of the IEEE International Conference on Communications, pp. 1–6 (2020)
14. MQTT: https://mqtt.org/. Accessed 7 July 2021

15. MQTTLoader: https://github.com/dist-sys/mqttloader. Accessed 7 July 2021
16. OASIS Standard: MQTT Version 5.0 (2019)
17. Pipatsakulroj, W., Visoottiviseth, V., Takano, R.: muMQ: a lightweight and scalable MQTT broker. In: Proceedings of the IEEE International Symposium on Local and Metropolitan Area Networks, pp. 1–6 (2017)

A Fog-Based IOV for Distributed Learning in Autonomous Vehicles

Pawan Subedi[✉], Beichen Yang, and Xiaoyan Hong

Computer Science, The University of Alabama, Tuscaloosa, USA
{psubedi,byang12}@crimson.ua.edu, hxy@cs.ua.edu

Abstract. Internet of Vehicles (IoVs) consist of connected vehicles and connected autonomous vehicles. With fog computing built within the IoV, it becomes promising for federated learning to be used in vehicular environments. One important application of such a fog computing system is distributed deep learning for decision-making tasks in autonomous driving. In this paper, a distributed training system building on top of the Named-Data Networking (NDN) architecture is introduced in order to combat the mobility challenges to the underlying network. The paper presents analyses on critical latency issues pertained to soliciting the worker CVs and collecting the partial updates. Further, the advantages of using NDN for the IoV are evaluated with comparisons to IP network through simulation. The results show promising performance gains for the evaluation cases.

Keywords: Internet of Vehicles · Fog computing · Connected vehicles · Federated learning · Autonomous driving

1 Introduction

With great progresses in wireless communications supporting vehicular networks, the Internet of Vehicles (IoVs) has been closer to reality. Connected vehicles (CVs), and more recently, connected autonomous vehicles (CAVs), all benefit from IoVs for various data and application services for enhancing safety, efficiency and autonomy in driving. The networked vehicles often sense, generate and consume massive amount of data for these services. At the same time, for information dissemination in vehicular fog environment, the multi-hop vehicular ad hoc network (VANET) and encounter based vehicular delay tolerant network (VDTN) have been extensively studied. The recent easiness in cloud accesses for both storage and computations have further motivated this trend. On the other hand, some of these services are the application scenarios that directly

The work is supported partly by the National Science Foundation under Grants No. 1719062. Any opinions, findings, and conclusions or recommendations expressed in this paper are those of the author(s) and do not necessarily reflect the views of the National Science Foundation.

© ICST Institute for Computer Sciences, Social Informatics and Telecommunications Engineering 2022
Published by Springer Nature Switzerland AG 2022. All Rights Reserved
C. T. Calafate et al. (Eds.): MONAMI 2021, LNICST 418, pp. 227–242, 2022.
https://doi.org/10.1007/978-3-030-94763-7_18

impact driving and utilize the vehicles to forward messages generated by them. With the latter, the networking are challenged in terms of connectivity, latency, bandwidth, throughput, and security requirements.

Along with the easiness of the cloud infrastructure, the architectures of Mobile Edge Computing and Fog Computing also have been developing for IoVs, which would enable the edge servers or the CVs (Fog Computing) to carry out equivalent service tasks traditionally carried out by the cloud. Building on vehicle networking technology, Fog Computing brings computing into the network so to further reduce the overhead from communication and networking.

On the other hand, the development of autonomous vehicles is expected to help alleviate various transportation management issues including safety, congestion, energy conservation, etc. Autonomous driving involves various critical decision-making tasks requiring artificial intelligence [1]. These sophisticated tasks require continual evolution of the models used in the AI system to guide the ever-changing scenarios of driving conditions. Therefore, the AI models need to be constantly trained and retrained. The massive aggregation of the training data and computing are mostly carried out at the central cloud.

At the same time, the recent research in distributed machine learning brings new opportunity for autonomous driving to use local and emerging new data in decision making. Federated Learning (FL), a distributed training process for Deep Neural Networks (DNN) [2], can be performed in the fog of the vehicles [3]. With federated learning, the vehicles in the fog system participate in the training process with their local data. It will bring two advantages to autonomous driving: quickly access richer dataset from distributed data sources because there is no need to transfer data to the cloud; and built-in privacy preservation because each distributed training process uses own set of data and a participating vehicle's data never leaves the owner. On top of the improvements on federated learning, the recent advances in incremental (continual) learning further lay the foundation for taking local data and enhancing an existing model [4,5]. With incremental learning, a trained model can be trained again using new data, without loosing the learned knowledge. This enables the federated learning to be more useful for the autonomous driving scenario as the learned knowledge can be integrated in an asynchronous manner without losing the previously learned knowledge of the model [6].

We envision a system that integrates federated learning with the continuum of the fog of the vehicles, the edge network, and the cloud such that the retraining of the model can happen in the fog of the vehicles, and the involvement of the edge network, and the cloud enables the aggregation of the updates coming from the fog [7–9].

Recognizing the challenges coming from the host-based network architecture, e.g., uneasy to obtain addresses, hard to maintain long-term and stable connections, dynamic network topology, routing protocol overhead, etc., the fog computing will use an information-centric networking (ICN) approach to overcome the mobility and intermittent connectivity challenges. Being on realization of ICN, Named-Data Networking (NDN) has been recognized as a promising solution for ad hoc networks and for vehicular networking [10–12]. In NDN, communications are based on data names, instead of host-to-host connections. To request data, a consumer sends an Interest packet with a data name to the network. Any provider who has the name-matching data will send it back.

The sharing nature of NDN communication model via its connection-free feature, such as multicast and in-path caching, allows effective use of wireless broadcast channel, leading to lower communication overhead. In addition, the name based data addressing scheme of NDN eliminates the burden for learning and managing the addresses of the CAVs and CVs in the vehicular scenario with constant topology changes and network disruptions [11,12]. The advantages and enhancements of NDN over VANET and VDTN are also being discussed in earlier work [10,13–16]. In addition, with NDN's name-data integrity, any participated nodes can verify that the received packets are tampered or not during transmissions. This offers security assurance to the CAVs.

In this paper, we present extensive analyses about the impact of vehicle mobility on the latency in tasks involving FL in vehicular fog. Understandings on the latency is extremely important because it reveals whether it would be feasible using FL for model enhancement under certain vehicular environments. Although many works have been done analyzing the network performance relating to mobility, most of these works do not directly address problems involving tasks in federated learning over the fog continuum. Similarly, we also present simulation results comparing IP networks with NDN for such systems.

The analyses show closed form latency distributions for the tasks in vehicular fog. Similarly, the simulation results show NDN to have better network performance in comparison to IP networks for such systems. At the same time, the simulation results also exhibit that the inclusion of fog continuum into the NDN based system as envisioned in this paper further improves the network performance.

The rest of the paper is organized as follows. Section 2 describes the networking and computing system over IoV Fog and cloud continuum. Section 3 presents the main analyses. The advantages of using NDN over IP network is presented in Sect. 4 through simulation results. Section 5 concludes the paper.

2   System Model

The vehicular fog to cloud continuum mainly consists of CVs and CAVs. It builds on top of the underlying network technologies of NDN over multihop vehicular ad hoc network (NDN-VANET) and encounter based vehicular delay tolerant network (NDN-VDTN) [10,13–15]. The vehicular fog to cloud continuum is also supported by edge servers. The edge servers serve as distributed distribution centers for the training models, which not only host initial models, but also receive model updates and forward them to the cloud. The cloud servers are responsible for the model aggregation.

On the other hand, the distributed training process involves several steps such as a CAV must have the model at the first place, be able to transfer the

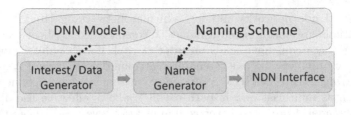

Fig. 1. System modules

model to at least one CV worker and collect at least one new update. With a proper ratio of CVs and set of NDN-VANET and NDN-VDTN protocols, a CAV can send an interest to solicit CV workers in proximity to help train a model. Multiple CVs can join as workers. The CVs, after receiving the model from the CAV, train the model so that both the environmental conditions as well as the actions taken by the driver in a CV based on these conditions can be fed to the model. After completing the training, the CAV can collect these updates. In a more general scenario, many CAVs can participate in soliciting more CVs to increase the capability of the training process. Or, many CAVs can directly benefit from the partial updates available at the workers. In addition, when considering mobility, a CAV who previous expressed an interest may move increasing away from a worker. Yet, the update may be useful for another CAV. To facilitate these situations, our proposed protocol is for a worker to send an interest to announce the available update. Interested CAVs can then collect the updates. Such a system increases the chances of finding a worker and also increases the computing efficiency by maximizing the sharing of the updates. Further, the CAV can submit the partial updates to an edge server. The edge servers are connected via internet to share the partially updated models and aggregate multiple of them. The enhanced model will be hosted by the edge servers for subsequent requests from the CAVs.

Using the NDN architecture requires a thoughtful design of the naming scheme because it determines how a piece of named-data may be retrieved through the interest-data packet pair. It can impact the overall network performance [17]. The naming scheme for the system primarily includes three major fields, reflecting hierarchical information within the names.

$$\langle model\_fields \rangle \, / \, \langle src\_id \rangle \, / \, \langle seq\_i \rangle$$

Here, the first **model_fields** is to identify a specific model. This field can contain multiple subfields. Three common subfields are: (i) *model_id:* It is the identifier of the training model; (ii) *model_version:* A training process involves multiple rounds/epochs. This field identifies the round of the model with *model_id*. It can be the incremental versioning of the trained model; and (iii) *part_number:* It identifies the part of the model that the packet carries. The second **src_id** is an optional identifier of the node looking out for the data and could include vague geographic location to help forward the packet. The last **seq_id** is the sequence number of this packet when it was created, serving as version control.

The IoV system is layered according to the dependence of functionalities. The layering consists of the function blocks for an application, here, the DNN model and the naming scheme, building on top of NDN primitives. The interplay of these function blocks and primitives is shown in Fig. 1. For the NDN primitives, *Interest/Data Generator* module handles new data pieces, be it a message, a model or a partial update. The module submits the data piece along with the metadata (e.g., version number, model Id, etc.) to the *Name Generator* for the further processing of the interest or data packet. *Name Generator* is the component responsible for creating the names for the packet in consideration. It uses the name convention when doing so. It then attaches the generated name to the data or interest piece submitted by the Data Generator module to create a complete packet. It then submits the packet to the NDN Interface Module. The *NDN Interface* is the NDN network interface that handles the forwarding and receiving of both Interest and Data packets.

3 Numerical Analysis

In this section we present analyses about the latency occurred during worker solicitation process and update collection process. The worker solicitation process decides how the computation task originated from CAVs would be distributed to the worker CVs. Meanwhile, the update collection process decides how the training results generated by CVs would be returned to CAVs. Understandings about the latency of the two processes are vital to the performance of the purposed system. Our analyses consider an area with N CAVs, M worker CVs that are willing to participate in the training process, and other CVs in the connected vehicular environments.

CAVs and CVs can communicate when they are within the transmission range of one another. The IoV fog networking environment can occur in a mix of NDN-VANET and NDN-VDTN. The former will disseminate information in a short time period via multi-hop packet relays. But with the latter, communication opportunities occur only when CVs or CAVs encounter one another. In this section, we analyze the impact of mobility of the more challenging NDN-VDTN scenario. There are certain similarity between worker solicitation process and update collection process. However, two different mathematical approaches are used in the analyses. This is due to the two different problem settings. With the worker solicitation process, the analyses starts with the case that all the CAVs have the same model waiting to be distributed, whereas with the update collection process, only a subset of the CVs have the updates ready.

3.1 Worker Solicitation Delay

Worker solicitation delay measures the time for a worker CV to receive an interest packet sent by a CAV looking for CVs to join distributed training. A worker CV receiving the interest is called a holding vehicle. After receiving the interest, it then follows up to retrieve the model. The solicitation delay is the time needed for a CAV to meet one of the holding vehicles. The delay mainly constitutes of the time needed for encountering a holding vehicle, which may take multiple encounters because only a part of the vehicles are the holding vehicles.

The encounter opportunity of two mobile nodes is one important mobility property. Earlier work has shown that the time for any pair of nodes to meet follows a Poisson distribution and thus the inter-meeting time of the pair follows an exponential distribution, Robin et al. [18]. The work shows that such a result applies to the Manhattan mobility, the random waypoint model, or simply random direction. In addition, various empirical studies on real-life mobility traces of the vehicles have also shown that exponential distribution is followed by the inter-meeting times. Thus, we assume the same for the vehicles in our scenario. Suppose $0 \leq t_{i,j}(1) < t_{i,j}(2) < \dots$ are the series of the time points when two vehicles i and $j(i \neq j)$ meet. The processes $\{t_{i,j}(n), n \geq 1\}, 1 \leq i,j \leq T, i \neq j$, is the independent Poisson processes with parameter λ. λ describes how many times can a pair of vehicle meet with each other in unit time. Further, let $\rho_{i,j}(n) = t_{i,j}(n+1) - t_{i,j}(n)$ be the n-th inter-meeting time of vehicle i and j. The random variables $\{\rho_{i,j}(n)\}_i, j, n$ are independent with each other and follow the exponential distribution with mean $1/\lambda$. $1/\lambda$ is the expected inter-meeting time before any pair of vehicles meet again with each other. A Markov Chain model is used in the analysis considering the case of a single worker CV (named W) receiving the solicitation interest in the area with total $R+1$ CVs. Let a state denotes the number of vehicles in the area that have the interest. Here we assume N AV nodes initially hold the interest, i.e., the initial state being N. Let F be the absorbing state when W receives the interest. Let $N+i$ represents the state that ith non-worker CVs have received the interest. State $N+i$ transitions to the next non-absorbing state $N+i+1$ when the interest is transmitted to another non-worker CV. State $N+i$ transitions to the absorbing state F when the interest is transmitted to W. The solicitation process finishes when W has the interest. Thus, the state space, S of the Markov chain includes $R+1$ non-absorbing states and one absorbing state F, denoted as $S = \{N, N+1, N+2, ..., N+R-2, N+R-1, N+R, F\}$.

Starting from the initial state N, one CAV encounters one of the R CVs at the rate $R\lambda$, and thus the aggregate transition rate from the state N to $N+1$ is $NR\lambda$. On the other hand, if W receives the solicitation from one of the CAVs, the aggregate rate from state N to the absorbing state F is $N\lambda$. In general, let $b_i = N+i$ be the number of vehicles having the interest at the state $N+i, i = 0, 1, ...R$, and let $d_i = (R-i)$ be the number of remaining non-worker CVs. The aggregate transition rate from ith state $N+i$ to the $(i+1)th$ state $N+i+1$ is $b_i d_i \lambda$, and the aggregate rate from state $N+i$ to the absorbing state F is $b_i \lambda$. These transition rates are shown in Fig. 2.

Let a series of state transitions from $N \to N+1 \to \cdots \to N+i \to F$ be a complete trajectory ending at the absorbing state for W. The random variable X such that $X = x_i$ describes the ith trajectory which transitioning from the

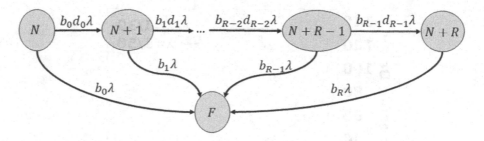

Fig. 2. Markov chain for a single worker solicitation

last state $N+i$ to F. Further, let p_{x_i} be the probability of the trajectory $X = x_i$, i.e., $P(X = x_i)$. For example, $X = x_0$ means a transition from the state N to F, and $X = x_1$ refers to the transitions from the states N to $N+1$ then to F.

At state $N+i$, there are $N+i$ number of holding vehicles, and $R-i$ non-worker CVs without the solicitation. As seen from Fig. 2, two types of transitions would happen to them. The first type happens when one of the former meets one of the latter, hence, transits to state $N+i+1$. There are $(N+i)(R-i)$ possible occurrences of this type. The other happens when one from the former meets the worker W, leading to the absorbing state. There are $N+i$ possible occurrences. Thus, the total possible events are $(N+i)(R-i)+(N+i)$. As such, the probability for transition from state $N+i$ to $N+i+1$ is $(N+i)(R-i)/(N+i)*(R-i)+(N+i) = (R-i)/(R-i+1)$, whereas the probability for transitioning from state $N+i$ to F is $(N+i)/(N+i)(R-i) + (N+i) = 1/(R-i+1)$.

The occurrence of a particular trajectory takes a series of state transitions. Its probability combines the probabilities of each horizontal transition in Fig. 2 and the transition to state F. Specifically, the probability p_{x_i} for trajectory x_i is given in Eq. 1.

$$p_{x_i} = \left[\prod_{j=0}^{i-1} \frac{(R-j)}{(R-j+1)}\right] \frac{1}{R-i+1} \tag{1}$$

Similarly, the delay along a trajectory x_i has to consider a series of times spending at each state waiting for an encounter to happen so to transit to the next state until encountering W. The latter leads to state F. Taking the aggregation factors at each state into consideration, for transitioning between horizontal states, the factor at state $N+j$ is $1/(N+j)(R-j)$; for transitioning to state F from $N+j$, the factor is $1/(N+j)$. The expected delay along trajectory x_i is the summation of the delays at each horizontal states, denoted as D_{x_i}. Recall that the expected pair-wise inter-meeting time is $1/\lambda$, D_{x_i} is given by Eq. 2.

$$E[D_{x_i}] = \left[\sum_{j=0}^{i-1} \frac{1}{(N+j)(R-j)\lambda}\right] + \frac{1}{(N+i)\lambda} \tag{2}$$

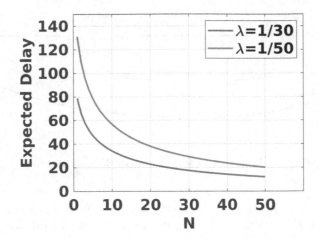

Fig. 3. Worker solicitation delay vs number of AVs with total vehicles = 100

Take trajectory $X = x_0$ as an example, the probability of N CAVs encountering W so transiting to state F, p_{x_0}, is given as $N/(RN + N) = 1/(1 + R)$, where the average delay transitioning from state N to the absorbing state F is $\frac{1}{N\lambda}$ due to the aggregation of N CAVs encountering W. Further, take trajectory $X = x_1$ as another example. Trajectory x_1 transits from state N to state $N + 1$, then F. The existence of state $N + 1$ is based on the event that one of the AVs at state N has passed the interest to one of the non-worker CVs. Thus, the probability is $RN/(RN + N) = R/(R + 1)$. At state $N + 1$, there are $N + 1$ holding vehicles, and $R - 1$ non-worker CVs plus the worker W without the interest. Thus, the probability that one of the $N + 1$ vehicles passes the interest to W is $(N + 1)/(R - 1)(N + 1) + (N + 1) = 1/R$. Combining the two probabilities, we have the probability of trajectory x_1 be $[R/(R + 1)] * (1/R) = 1/(R + 1)$. The delay of trajectory x_1 has to count the delays at states N and $N + 1$, which is given as $\frac{1}{N\lambda} + \frac{1}{(N+1)\lambda}$.

Now, with Eqs. 1 and 2, the expectation of the solicitation delay over all the trajectories is given by Eq. 3.

$$E[D] = \sum_{i=0}^{R} E[D_{x_i}]p_{x_i} \tag{3}$$

Based on Eq. 3, as seen from Fig. 3, the expectation of the solicitation delay at a particular value of *lambda* decreases with the increase in number of nodes having the initial solicitation, N. Also, with the increasing value of N, the rate of change of average delay decreases, meaning with the optimized numbers of the initial solicitors present in the system, an optimistic value of delay can be realized.

3.2   Update Collection Delay

The need for updating a model usually only stays valid for a certain amount of time. Thus, knowledge about how many workers may help the training within a time frame is important. This analysis focuses on the number of holding workers with regards to time. The analysis is based on the assumption that the time is slotted. The duration of the time slot is long enough for establishing a connection and completing the model transmissions. At the same time, the actual time for the training process is not taken into the consideration. We assume that every worker that has a model will create an update.

For a time slot t, the reasons that a worker CV doesn't have an update can either be due to the expiration of the received model at time $t - 1$, or due to the fact that the worker didn't have a model at time $t - 1$ and it doesn't receive a model at time t from any CAV either.

In the analysis, let $p(j, t)$ be the probability that a worker j has an update at time t. And let τ be the probability that the update expires due to aging of the model. Further, suppose $q(j, t)$ be the probability that j didn't receive a model for training at t; and $n(i, j, t)$ be the probability that worker j receives a model from CAV i at time t. Given there are a total of N CAVs, $q(j, t)$ can be expressed in Eq. 4. As such, the problem in question can be described by Eq. 5.

$$q(j, t) = \prod_{k=1}^{N} (1 - n(k, j, t)) \tag{4}$$

$$1 - p(j, t) = \tau p(j, t - 1) + (1 - p(j, t - 1)) q(j, t) \tag{5}$$

Solve Eqs. 4 and 5 and assume t be large enough such that the products approach zero, the limits of $p(j, t)$ $q(j, t)$ and $n(k, j, t)$ become $p(j)$, $q(j)$ and $n(i, j)$ respectively. Thus, we obtain the limit $p(j)$ in Eq. 6:

$$p(j) = \frac{1 - q(j)}{1 - q(j) + \tau} = \frac{1 - \prod_{l=1}^{N}(1 - n(l, k))}{1 - \prod_{l=1}^{N}(1 - n(l, k)) + \tau} \tag{6}$$

The task of Update Collection completes when the CAV encounter any CV that has completed its training. Here, we derive the latency needed for collecting the first update by a CAV. Given the collection process starts after the model distribution, we use the limiting probability that a worker has an update $p(j)$ from 6 to continue our analysis.

To analyze when the first update can be collected by a CAV, we start with capturing the mobility history that a CAV may encounter several non-participating worker CVs before encountering the one with an update, we use an encounter progression matrix. For a CAV y, let F_y be its encounter progression matrix. An element (i,j) in the matrix is the probability $f(i, j)$ that describes the progression of y having encountered CV i, then connecting to CV j. Given there are total M worker CVs, F_y is an $M \times M$ matrix as shown below 7, where $f(k, k) = 1, k = 1, 2, ..., M$.

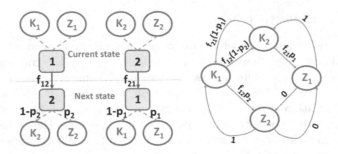

Fig. 4. An example state transition of two nodes for the update collection and the respective Markov Chain

$$F_y = \begin{bmatrix} f(1,1) & f(1,2) & ... & f(1,M) \\ f(2,1) & f(2,2) & ... & f(2,M) \\ & & ... & \\ f(M,1) & f(M,2) & ... & f(M,M) \end{bmatrix} \tag{7}$$

The update collection process can be described similar to worker solicitation Sect. 3.1. A CAV y may encounter multiple CVs without being able to collect any updates until the time of meeting the CV i. Now, during the encounter progression, if the newly connected CV j has an update, we say the progression yielded an update collection for the CAV.

To analyze the encounter progression for y, let's create a Markov Chain where the state space includes every possible state for all the CVs in our analysis. Regarding every possible state for a CV, it can either have the update or not, meaning these two states completely define the possible states for a CV. As such let's create two different sets from every possible states in our analysis. The first set $K = \{k_1, k_2, ..., k_m\}$ contains the states for not having update of every CV, and the second set $Z = \{Z_1, Z_2, ..., Z_m\}$ contains the states for having update of every CV.

With the above definition of every possible states in terms of two sets, let's first define the transition matrix R for the CAV y based on the entries in the matrix. An entry (i, j) in R is the transition probability r_{ij} for transiting from encounter of the CV i to the encounter of the CV j, where the transition probability r_{ij} is expressed in terms of the encounter progression probability $f(i, j)$ and the probability of the CV j for having an update, $p(j)$, as given by Eq. 8. Figure 4 presents an example scenario involving two nodes for the transition. For the two nodes scenario, the CAV y could have been initially in connection with either of the two nodes. Similarly, these two nodes could have been in either of their own two states (having updates or not having updates). Now, if the CAV y moves such that there is the change in the connectivity, it either moves from the connectivity of node 1 to node 2 or from node 2 to node 1. These new nodes could have been in either of their states with the respective probability of the states. Based on this, we construct the Markov Chain. One thing that needs to be noticed in Fig. 4 is that if the node transitions from a state of already having update to a new state without an update, we have the transition probability to be 1 since the CAV already has the required update. Similarly, we have the probability of transition from state of already having update to the new state of already having update, the transition probability is 0, as we do not allow such transitions in our scenario (of first update collection by a CAV).

$$r(i,j) = \begin{cases} f(i,j)(1-p(j)), & \text{if } State(i) \in K, State(j) \in K \\ f(i,j)p(j), & \text{if } State(i) \in K, State(j) \in Z \\ 1, & \text{if } State(i) \in Z, State(j) \in K \\ 0, & \text{otherwise} \end{cases} \tag{8}$$

Based on the definition of the entries, we then construct the entire matrix $\mathbf{R}$. For this, we create a separate $M \times M$ diagonal matrix, $\mathbf{B}$, where each diagonal element is the probability, $p(j)$ for each CV. For example, the diagonal element in third row and third column has the probability of having update for the CV 3. Further, we define $\overline{\mathbf{B}} = I - \mathbf{B}$, where I is the identity matrix. Therefore, using Eqs. 7 and 8, and matrix $\mathbf{B}$, the transition matrix $\mathbf{R}$ is expressed by Eq. 9, where each term is $M \times M$ matrix.

$$R = \begin{bmatrix} \mathbf{F_y}\overline{\mathbf{B}} & \mathbf{F_y}\mathbf{B} \\ \mathbf{0} & \mathbf{1} \end{bmatrix} \tag{9}$$

Thus, based on Eq. 9, we can conclude that the transitions follow the characteristics of a terminating Markov Chain, for which, the upper triangular part $\mathbf{F_y}\overline{\mathbf{B}}$ entirely characterizes the transition matrix. Matrices $\mathbf{0}$ and $\mathbf{1}$ are $M \times M$ matrices with all elements being 0 or 1 respectively. Based on the terminating Markov Chain of the transitions, we next derive the probability of a CAV collecting a new update at a time instance t, $w(i,t)$.

For such, if $B(i,0)$ is the initial connectivity of CAV i, based on the phase type distribution, the probability that an update is collected by an CAV i at time t for the first time, $w(i,t)$ is given by Eq. 10.

$$w(i,t) = B(i,0) \left(\prod_{k=1}^{t-1} F_i\overline{\mathbf{B}} \right) (F_i\mathbf{B}) \tag{10}$$

Thus, as seen from Eq. 10, the latency of the first update collection decreases with the increase in the probability of the CVs having model for training.

4   Performance Evaluation

In this section, we use simulations to compare the performance of NDN based system with the IP based system. The purpose of these comparisons is to see if the name-based routing and the inherent caching of NDN network brings advantage over IP network in terms of wireless channel usage, delay in model dispatch, and the resiliency over mobility. Further, the evaluations will compare more extended NDN based scenarios including pure fog environments and hybrid edge-fog environments. The evaluation will assess whether the former brings further improvements to the latter for the NDN based system.

Therefore, the evaluations involves five different setups, namely, IP-CS1, IP-CS4, NDN-CS1, NDN-CS4, and NDN-AV0.4. IP-CS1 and IP-CS4 are cases of IP-based edge-fog hybrid environment. The two setups of NDN-CS1 and NDN-CS4 are for NDN-based edge-fog hybrid environment. In these settings, CS1 indicates that only one edge server is present in the simulation area, whereas CS4 indicates that four edge servers are in the simulation area, each locates at one of the four midpoints of the four subareas. The last setup NDN-AV0.4 is for the pure fog environment, the proposed system. The CAV presence ratio, which is the ratio of number of CAVs to the total cars in the simulation, is set to 0.4.

In this evaluation, communications mimic the update collection task, where CVs send interests to announce new updates. The CAVs will respond in the pure fog scenario presented in this paper, while the edge servers will respond for the update in the hybrid edge-fog environments.

4.1   Simulation Configuration and Evaluation Metrics

A one square kilometer map of urban San Francisco as shown in Fig. 5 is imported to the traffic simulator, Sumo [19] to generate real-world traces of vehicular mobility in the urban setup. The number of cars in the simulation is varied between 20 and 70 for different rounds of simulations. The mobility traces thus generated are then fed to ndnSIM simulator modified for use in VANETs [12] for the rounds of the network performance measures. The simulation time for all these rounds is set to 100 s so as to minimize the cars reaching the end of the road segments of the map within the simulation time. Similarly, the transmission range of every node is limited to 34 m and thus we use multi-hop communications.

In each round of the simulation, a random subset of cars is selected as the set of CVs that participate in actual training process. To analyze the presence of CAVs for the update collection from the CVs in the proposed system, another random subset of the cars is selected as the set of the CAVs. Every other cars are NDN-enabled for NDN based cases and thus can forward the Interest/Data packets. Similarly, the cars in the IP-based simulation are IP-enabled and can route the IP-packets towards the destination.

The following evaluation metrics are used to evaluate the various setups discussed above.

- **Satisfaction Ratio:** The measure of the satisfaction ratio defines the resiliency of a system to the mobility within the network. For NDN-based systems, we define Satisfaction ratio as the overall number of satisfied Interests per total Interests created during the simulation. Similarly, for IP-based systems, it is the ratio of overall number of packets received to the number of request packets created by the client vehicles.
- **Average Delay:** It is a measure of how quickly a request brings back the data packet. It is defined as the ratio of the sum of all the delays for the

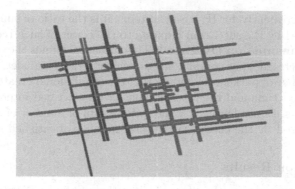

Fig. 5. Simulation map

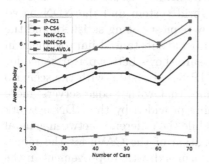

Fig. 6. Average delay in seconds

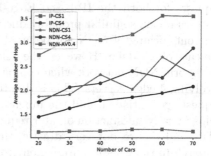

Fig. 7. Average number of hops

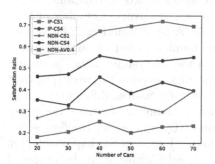

Fig. 8. Satisfaction ratio

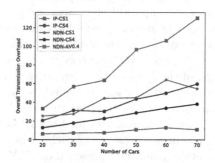

Fig. 9. Overall transmission overhead

satisfied interests to the count of such interests for NDN-based systems. And equivalently, for IP-based systems, it is the ratio of the sum of all the delays for quenched requests to the number of such requests.

– **Average Hop Counts:** Average Hop counts is the average number of hops travelled by the successful requests for the data. It is defined as the ratio of sum of number of hops and the count of satisfied interests for NDN-based systems. Equivalently, for IP-based systems, it is the ratio of sum of number of hops travelled by the successful requests to the count of such request packets.

- **Overall Transmission Overhead:** This measure defines the exploitation of the wireless channel per completion of successful data transfer. It is the ratio of total number of packets (including the retransmissions) created throughout the simulation time and the total number of the satisfied interests for NDN-based systems. Equivalently, it is the ratio of sum of number of all the request packets created by the clients to the total number of satisfied requests.

4.2   Evaluation Results

In this section, we present the discussion on the results of simulation. As seen from Fig. 6, with single Edge Server setup, the average delay for the satisfied requests for both the IP-based Edge-Fog Hybrid system and the NDN based systems remains similar probably due to a few requests being satisfied, and the inherent caching of NDN not being able to provide substantial improvement in the case of the delay. However, the delay measure shows better performance for the hybrid NDN network when compared to IP based system with the scenario involving 4 edge servers. This is due to the fact that with 4 edge servers, more requests get satisfied, and the inherent caching provided by the NDN network helps in early satisfaction of later requests. While the difference between general NDN and IP are not very drastic, the utilization of the CAVs for the model dispatch to the CVs in pure fog environment brings drastic improvement in the delay measures, due to their mobility-assisted closeness to the CVs.

While the average delay of the satisfied requests between NDN and IP systems are comparable for single Edge Server setup, the average number of hops travelled by such requests differ more drastically. As seen from Fig. 7, for various number of cars in the simulation, the average number of hops is almost always lower by 1 for NDN system in comparision to the IP system. This shows that some of the few satisfied requests for the single edge server setup were quenched from the nearby cache provided by the NDN network. Similar differences can be seen for the four server setup as well. The higher number of edge servers provide nearby data source for both IP system and NDN system for the four server setup, but the presence of caching in NDN further improves the hop counts. On the other hand, the presence of CAVs for the model dispatch in the proposed system has substantial improvement in the hop count as well. This is due to the reason that the CAVs become more reliable close-by data dispatch sources and thus the average number of hops always becomes close to 1.

Figures 8 and 9 present the comparison between NDN and IP for Satisfaction Ratio, and Overall Transmission Overhead, respectively. The Satisfaction Ratio for both NDN and IP systems improve with the presence of more sources in 4 Edge Server setups. Similar to the previous metrics, the NDN-based systems have comparatively better Satisfaction Ratios than IP-based systems. Also, the proposed system has the best Satisfaction Ratio measure among all the compared setups. In terms of transmission overhead, NDN-based systems have lower transmission overhead compared to the IP-based systems as seen from Fig. 9.

Among the five compared setups, the proposed system has the best performance in terms of overhead (lowest value) with almost constant overhead for various number of cars in the simulation.

In a nutshell, based on the evaluation results, we see that the hybrid edge-fog based NDN system has better performance compared to the hybrid edge-fog based IP system in terms of every evaluation metrics discussed above. Similarly, the proposed pure fog-based system involving CAVs has the best performance among all the three setups in all the performance metrics.

5 Conclusion

The paper introduces a NDN-based fog computing system built within the IoV designed for federated learning to be used in vehicular environments. The numerical analyses of the system show a promising prospects for fog computing in such environments. At the same time, the simulation based evaluations prove the usefulness of Named Data Networking over traditional IP networks for such systems.

References

1. Ma, Y., Wang, Z., Yang, H., Yang, L.: Artificial intelligence applications in the development of autonomous vehicles: a survey. IEEE/CAA J. Autom. Sin. 7(2), 315–329 (2020)
2. McMahan, H.B., Moore, E., Ramage, D., Hampson, S., et al.: Communication-efficient learning of deep networks from decentralized data (2016). arXiv preprint arXiv:1602.05629
3. Du, Z., Wu, C., Yoshinaga, T., Yau, K.-L.A., Ji, Y., Li, J.: Federated learning for vehicular internet of things: recent advances and open issues. IEEE Open J. Comput. Soc. 1, 45–61 (2020)
4. Lomonaco, V., Maltoni, D.: Core50: a new dataset and benchmark for continuous object recognition (2017). arXiv preprint arXiv:1705.03550
5. Parisi, G.I., Kemker, R., Part, J.L., Kanan, C., Wermter, S.: Continual lifelong learning with neural networks: a review. Neural Netw. 113, 54–71 (2019)
6. Wu, W., He, L., Lin, W., Mao, R., Maple, C., Jarvis, S.A.: SAFA: a semi-asynchronous protocol for fast federated learning with low overhead. IEEE Trans. Comput. 70, 655—668 (2020)
7. Zhou, Z., Liu, P., Feng, J., Zhang, Y., Mumtaz, S., Rodriguez, J.: Computation resource allocation and task assignment optimization in vehicular fog computing: a contract-matching approach. IEEE Trans. Veh. Technol. 68(4), 3113–3125 (2019)
8. Zhu, C., Pastor, G., Xiao, Y., Li, Y., Ylae-Jaeaeski, A.: Fog following me: Latency and quality balanced task allocation in vehicular fog computing. In: 2018 15th Annual IEEE International Conference on Sensing, Communication, and Networking (SECON), pp. 1–9 (2018)
9. Peng, X., Ota, K., Dong, M.: Multiattribute-based double auction toward resource allocation in vehicular fog computing. IEEE Internet of Things J. 7(4), 3094–3103 (2020)

10. Meisel, V.P.M., Zhang, L.: Ad hoc networking via named data. In: Fifth ACM International Workshop on Mobility in the Evolving Internet Architecture, ACM, Chicago, pp. 3–8. ACM (2010)
11. Grassi, G., Pesavento, D., Pau, G., Zhang, L., Fdida, S.: Navigo: interest forwarding by geolocations in vehicular named data networking.' In: IEEE 16th International Symposium on A World of Wireless, Mobile and Multimedia Networks (WoWMoM), pp. 1–10. IEEE (2015)
12. Chowdhury, M., Khan, J.A., Wang, L.: Leveraging content connectivity and location awareness for adaptive forwarding in NDN-based mobile ad hoc networks. In: Proceedings of the 7th ACM Conference on Information-Centric Networking, pp. 59–69 (2020)
13. Grassi, G., et al.: Vanet via named data networking. In: IEEE Conference on Computer Communications Workshops (INFOCOM WKSHPS), 2014, pp. 410–415. IEEE, Toronto (2014)
14. Meng Kuai, X.H., Yu, Q.: Delay-tolerant forwarding strategy for named data networking in vehicular environment. Int. J. Ad Hoc Ubiquit. Comput. $31(1)$, 1 (2019)
15. Kuai, M., Hong, H.: Location-based deferred broadcast for ad-hoc named data networking. Fut. Internet $11(6)$, 139 (2019)
16. Hamza-Cherif, A., Boussetta, K., Diaz, G., Lahfa, F.: Performance evaluation and comparative study of main VDTN routing protocols under small-and large-scale scenarios. Ad Hoc Netw. 81, 122–142 (2018)
17. Shannigrahi, S., Fan, C., Partridge, C.: What's in a name? Naming big science data in named data networking. In: Proceedings of the 7th ACM Conference on Information-Centric Networking, pp. 12–23 (2020)
18. Groenevelt, R., Nain, P., Koole, G.: The message delay in mobile ad hoc networks. Perform. Eval. $62(1-4)$, 210–228 (2005)
19. Lopez, P.A., et al.: Microscopic traffic simulation using sumo. In: 2018 21st International Conference on Intelligent Transportation Systems (ITSC), pp. 2575–2582. IEEE (2018)

Recent Advances in Communications
and Computing

Time-Based Distributed Collaborative Filtering Recommendation Algorithm

Qiao Li[1,2,3], Xiantong Hu[1], Linfei Zhou[1], Xiao Zheng[1,2,3], Wei Zhao[1,3(✉)], Yunquan Gao[1,3], and Xuangou Wu[1,3]

[1] School of Computer Science and Technology, AnHui University of Technology, Maanshan 243032, China
{qiaoli,xzheng,wuxgou}@ahut.edu.cn, zlf0001@mail.ustc.edu.cn, gaoyunquan@bupt.edu.cn
[2] Hefei Comprehensive National Science Center, Institute of Artificial Intelligence, Hefei 230026, China
[3] Anhui Engineering Laboratory for Intelligent Applications and Security of Industrial Internet, AnHui University of Technology, Maanshan 243032, China

Abstract. Recommendation systems based on collaborative filtering are widely used in many fields. Alternating Least Squares (ALS) in the Mlib Library is a distributed and parallel algorithm in Spark framework, which can solve the problems of scalability and speedup in a limited hardware resources of stand-alone systems. However, it does not consider the influence of the factor of time on the recommendation accuracy. Taking restaurant ratings as an example, this month ratings are more reliable than those from last year. Thus, the motivation in our proposal re-scores ratings with different time weights. We improve ALS in its process of data preparation according to requirements on the structure of data input. Consequently, our improvement does not need to modify the main body of ALS. Experimental results validate effectiveness that our proposal outperforms the original ALS in recommendation accuracy.

Keywords: Collaborative filtering · ALS · Time factor · RMSE

1 Introduction

With the development of the Internet, the problem of information overload has become increasingly serious. The emergence of the recommendation system can help people to obtain the interested information [1]. The collaborative filtering algorithm has been widely applied in various recommendation systems.

In recent years, parallel and distributed computing models have been used in recommendation systems [2], which not only speeds up the recommendation process, but also has a good scalability. For example, many researches exploit Hadoop and Spark to improve the parallelism of recommendation system operations [3–6]. These efforts are based on new computing models and platforms,

© ICST Institute for Computer Sciences, Social Informatics and Telecommunications Engineering 2022
Published by Springer Nature Switzerland AG 2022. All Rights Reserved
C. T. Calafate et al. (Eds.): MONAMI 2021, LNICST 418, pp. 245–255, 2022.
https://doi.org/10.1007/978-3-030-94763-7_19

which parallels many classic machine learning algorithms such as apriori, k-means, and so forth. However, the existing research mainly studied the process of matrix decomposition and the iterative phase to improve the algorithm of Alternating Least Square (ALS), from perspective of feature vectors in post-evaluation results. However, the consideration of parallel execution of data pre-processing in the early stage is not enough. Algorithm accuracy, as well as efficiency, can be improved by means of pre-processing data, such as normalization. Thus, this work has the following considerations: We improve the original ALS algorithm within the Spark platform by exploiting influence of the time factor to adjust dataset scores. This process is in the data preparation according to requirements on the structure of data input. Experimental results validate effectiveness of our proposal in terms of the accuracy of Root Mean Square Error (RMSE).

2   Related Work

By exploiting the PySpark framework and Resilient Distributed Datasets (RDD) in Spark, Bhowmick improved existing association rules Apriori algorithm [5]. The datasets with different structures are used to obtain the data analysis experiment results, and the improved method is verified to get a better level of performance. In [6], a parallel computing ALS acceleration algorithm (ALS-NCG) is proposed, in which the performance of running and convergence times is improved. In [7,8], the authors compared advantages and disadvantages in various performance indicators (RMSE, MAE, etc.) during the execution of the collaborative filtering algorithm implemented in Hadoop platform and the Spark platform. It discuss the impact of multiple parameter on recommendation results. And it also emphasized the advantages of memory-based computing frameworks. In [9], users and items are related by the concept of incorporating labels. Then, through the continuous increase of processing nodes, the cold start problem of collaborative filtering is alleviated, and cold start, scalability, throughput and data sparseness in different scenarios are discussed. The literature [10] designed a new loss function by calculating the similarity between users and items, thus improving the accuracy of the evaluation index RMSE. The literatures [9,10] mainly focused on the inherent correlation between users and items, which improves the performance of the entire execution process. Literature [11] propose a hybrid collaborative filtering distributed execution model specifically, it uses the recommended results as input to KMeans clustering algorithm, and verifies scalability, execution time and robustness to demonstrate its effectiveness. Literatures [10,11] considered the optimization of one-step process of parallel execution. Its main point to improve the response time of the recommendation system, and the proposed new model and algorithm also had effects on improving cold start and scalability. In the recommendation system, a very important step is matrix decomposition. A basic version of matrix decomposition has been completed in the Spark framework. Literature [12] designed multiple regular term formulas to derive five different models, considering the prediction of data values in a specific scenario. It analysed missing data under the Spark platform and verified the rationality and effectiveness of the proposed model through analysis of execution time of different sizes of data set and RMSE. Literature [13] describes a new collaborative filtering recommendation algorithm based on probability matrix factorization. Finally, time windiows weighting is integrated into the rating matrix to construct the 3D user-item-time model. The proposed algorithm achieves better overall performance than other algorithms.However, the experimental results in spark parallel framework are not considered in this paper. The above studies [3,4,7,8] mainly focused on the evaluation of performance improvement by using the new framework platform. Both the literature [6] and this paper study ALS algorithms, but we underscore the acceleration and optimization of matrix decomposition. The literature [9–12] mainly focused on step optimization in the matrix decomposition stage, and [10,11] accelerated the system execution by proposing new models and algorithms, such as considering the correlation between users and items. The existing researches mainly focused on the optimization of the matrix decomposition phase of the ALS algorithm. This paper starts from the perspective of the initial stage of data preprocessing. It improves the performance by designing a distributed ALS algorithm based on time factor.

3   Problem Description

3.1   Matrix Factorization

The most common matrix factorization technique is evolved from SVD. Suppose there are m users and n items in total, then the user-item-rating matrix is $P \in \mathbb{P}^{(m \times n)}$, where the rating represents the user's preference for items. This matrix is usually very sparse, most of the scoring elements are missing, and our task is to predict the missing values in it. For each user u set a user vector $x_u \in \mathbb{P}^f$, and each item i set an item vector $y_i \in \mathbb{P}^f$, then the predicted value is expressed as the inner product of the two $\hat{r}_{ui} = x_u^T y_i$. Then the objective function is:

$$L = \min_{x_*, y_*} \sum_{r_{u,i}} (r_{ui} - x_u^T y_i)^2 + \lambda(\sum_u \| x_u \|^2 + \sum_i \| y_i \|^2) \tag{1}$$

SGD is an iterative method (iterative method), while the other method, the protagonist of this article ALS, is a direct method. Since both x_u and y_i in Eq. (1) are unknown, the function is non-convex and it is difficult to optimize directly. However, if all yis are fixed and regarded as constants, then Eq. (1) becomes a least squares problem about x_u, and the analytical solution can be obtained directly. So you can fix y_i to find x_u, and then fix x_u to find y_i. The two alternate continuously, and this process repeats until it converges. Therefore, ALS is called alternate least squares (alternating least squares), which is actually a bit similar to the alternate solution of E step and M step in the EM algorithm.

The following is a detailed derivation of the ALS algorithm flow. The user vector $x_u \in \mathbb{P}^f$ and the item vector $y_i \in \mathbb{P}^f$ have been defined above, then all users can be combined into a matrix $X \in \mathbb{P}^{(m \times f)}$, and all items are combined into a matrix $Y \in \mathbb{P}^{(n \times f)}$, The entire scoring matrix is $P = XY^T \in \mathbb{P}^{(m \times n)}$. Then find the partial derivative of Eq. (1) fixed Y with respect to x_u:

$$\frac{\partial L}{\partial x_u} = -2 \sum_{i \in r_{u*}} (r_{ui} - x_u^T y_i) y_i + 2\lambda x_u = 0 \tag{2}$$

$$x_u = (\sum_{i \in r_{u*}} y_i y_i^T + \lambda I)^{-1} \sum_{i \in r_{u*}} r_{ui} y_i$$
$$= (Y_u^T Y_u + \lambda I)^{-1} Y_u^T P_u \tag{3}$$

Among them, r_{u*} represents all items rated by user u, $Y_u \in \mathbb{P}^{|r_{u*}| \times f}$ represents a matrix of all items rated by user u, and $P_u \in \mathbb{P}^{|r_{u*}|}$ represents a vector of all items rated by user u. In the same way, fix X to obtain the partial derivative of y_i:

$$y_i = (\sum_{u \in r_{*i}} x_u x_u^T + \lambda I)^{-1} \sum_{u \in r_{*i}} r_{ui} x_u$$
$$= (X_i^T X_i + \lambda I)^{-1} X_i^T P_i \tag{4}$$

According to Eq. (1), the partial derivatives of x_u and y_i are obtained, and Eq. (3) and Eq. (4) are obtained. It can be noted that the calculation of each x_u and y_i of Eq. (3) and Eq. (4) are independent, witch can be calculated in parallel to increase the speed.

3.2   System Model

User's scoring behavior on an item in recommendation systems can be expressed as a matrix $P_{(m \times n)}$, indicating scores of n items by m users. $P_{(m \times n)}$ is a sparse matrix with "missing values". One reason in that the labelling process is complex and costly. Model-based collaborative filtering algorithms predict the "missing value" from existing ratings, in a matrix completion process. The ALS algorithm is used to complete $P_{(m \times n)}$ by dimension reduction in training models. $P_{(m \times n)}$ is composed of two low-dimensional matrices $U_{(m \times k)}$ and $V_{(n \times k)}$. The minimum squared error loss function $L(U, V)$ is used to compute U and V while avoiding the overfitting problem.

The original ALS algorithm aims to decompose $P_{(m \times n)}$. Traditional matrix decompositions are difficult to handle huge data given a large size of $P_{(m \times n)}$. It computes $U_{(m \times k)}$ and $V_{(n \times k)}$ in Eq. (5),

$$P_{(m \times n)} \approx U_{(m \times k)} V_{(n \times k)}^T \tag{5}$$

where k is the minimum of m and n, which refers to the correlation dimension. It is also known as "implicit semantic factor".

The objective is to minimize the squared error loss function in Eq. (6),

$$L(U, V) = \sum (r_{u,i} - x_u^T y_i)^2 \tag{6}$$

where $r_{u,i}$ represents the rating of item i by user u, and $x_u^T y_i$ the approximate rating of item i by user u. A regularization term is applied to avoid overfitting in Eq. (7),

$$L(U,V) = \sum (r_{u,i} - x_u^T y_i)^2 + \lambda(\mid x_u \mid^2 + \mid y_i \mid^2) \tag{7}$$

where λ is a regularization coefficient. The specific solution for ALS is similar with the gradient descent method. The calculation process is as follows.

1. Set initial values V and U
2. Find the partial derivative of function $L(U,V)$ for x_u, and let the partial derivative equal to 0 to get:

$$x_u = (V^T V + \lambda I)^{-1} V^T P_u \tag{8}$$

3. Similarly, it is expected to get Eq. (9), where P_u is the p-th row, P_i the ith column of P, and I $k \times k$-dimensional matrix.

$$y_i = (U^T U + \lambda I)^{-1} U^T P_i \tag{9}$$

4. Continue steps 2 and 3 until convergence.

3.3 Time Factor

Our work considers time factor in the training model. In addition, we consider the fact that the latest users have a bigger weight in the evaluation. A weight coefficient in Eq. (10) adjusts user ratings from viewpoint of time drift.

$$\theta = \frac{t_{u,i} - t_{min}^i}{t_{max}^i - t_{min}^i} \tag{10}$$

where $t_{u,i}$ refers to the current time for user u to rate item i, t_{max}^i the last time when all users rate item i, and t_{max}^i the earliest time. The weight increases with the rating timestamp, implying the rating importance. Then we rearrange the rating in Eq. (10) by Eq. (11),

$$R_{u,i} = r_{u,i} \times (1 + \theta) \tag{11}$$

where $r_{u,i}$ the original user rating. Different periods of user ratings are applied in traditional methods. Notice that it ignores influence of weights of different periods on ratings that fluctuate over time. It happens frequently that movies with low ratings at initial releasing periods become classicical along with time. Thus, the time factor should be one of criteria on ratings.

4   Algorithm Implementation

4.1   Algorithm Design

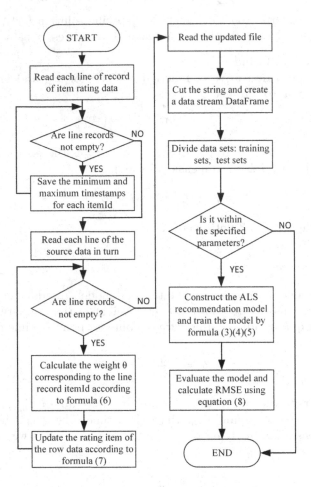

Fig. 1. Algorithm implementation flow chart

Figure 1 shows the process of our algorithm. It includes four components: to pre-process data, to find the minimum and maximum timestamps of all user scores corresponding to each item, to traverse each line of records, and to update scores in the original data by means of Eq. (10) and Eq. (11). These operations can be addressed in the Spark framework. The model is optimized multi-dimensionally with different parameters, and finally the prediction and model evaluation are performed. The specific process and implementation will be described in Algorithm 1.

4.2   Data Processing

The score dataset is processed according to Eq. (10) and Eq. (11). The timestamp in the original dataset is associated with the user's rating. Algorithm 1 shows the data processing.

Algorithm 1: Data Processing

Input: Dataset D
Output: Dataset S considering time weight
1: D = {UserID, ItemId, Rating, TimeStamp}
2: for each line in D:
3:   i ← itemId
4:   if TimeStamp < min_TimeStamp(i):
5:     min_TimeStamp (i) ← TimeStamp;
6:   if TimeStamp > max_TimeStamp (i):
7:     max_TimeStamp (i) ← TimeStamp;
8: end for
9: Obtain max_TimeStamp and mix_TimeStamp according to itemId.
10: for each line in D:
11:    Obtain the TimeStamp field in the raw data
12:    set $t_{(}u, i)$ =TimeStamp.
13:    Set the time weight: $\theta = \frac{t_{u,i}-t^i_{max}}{t^i_{max}-t^i_{min}}$.
14:    Update the original TimeStamp according to the time weight.
15:    Updating TimeStamp: $R_{u,i} = r_{u,i} \times (1 + \theta)$.
16: end for
17: Save $R_{u,i}$.

The input is dataset D to be processed, and the output is the dataset S after the correction of score items according to time weight. Lines from 5–8 obtain the minimum timestamp and the maximum timestamp of each itemId score through circulating each row in dataset D. Lines from 13–16 are to calculate the time weight according to Eq. (10). Line 17 updates scores based on the time weight.

4.3   Recommendation Algorithm

We design a recommendation algorithm to train a model with the goal of the minimum prediction error. We improve the traditional ALS algorithm in Spark in its process of data preparation according to requirements on the structure of data input. Evaluation is performed on the accuracy of RMSE.

In Algorithm 2, the parameter maxIter is the number of iterations at runtime. Each iteration can improve the accuracy of the algorithm. Rank is the number of implicit semantic factors in the model, that is, the number of features. RegParam is a regularization parameter of ALS, indicating the magnitude of λ in Eq. (7).

The algorithm input is the dataset S from Algorithm 1. The output is the prediction error. Lines 1–6 create the data reading specification and the dataset is divided into a training set and a test set. Lines 7 to 11 optimize the ALS model by iterating. Lines 12 to 15 test the training model with the test set and evaluate the model to obtain the error.

Algorithm 2: Recommendation Algorithm

Input: Dataset S obtained in Algorithm 1
Output: Prediction error
1: Get the sc object:spark = SparkSession.builder.
2: Read file = S [userId, itemId, newRating, timestamp]
3: Create a Rating type [Int, Int, Float, Long] and convert each line to Rating.
4: Divide fields according to the Separator
5: Create DataFrame by ratings RDD.
6: Split the DataFrame into training and test.
7: for rank or lambda ∈ [m,n]
9:    for maxIter ∈ [m,n]
10:      Set ALS parameters(rank=rank, maxIter=maxIter,
           regParam=lambda, userCol="userId", itemCol="movieId",
           ratingCol="rating", coldStartStrategy="drop").
11:      Train model by training data.
12:      Predictive model.
13:      Evaluate model and Get the error.
14:      Write the error to text.
15:    end for
16: end for
17: Stop Spark.

---

5   Performance Evaluation

5.1   Datasets and Evaluation Metrics

This experiment is to predict user ratings for each movie. In actual application scenarios, the movie with the highest predicted ratings will be recommended to the user. The experiment uses dataset Movielens with 100,000 and 1 million film records. Each row of dataset records contains four attributes: User ID, Movie ID, User Rating, and Timestamp. We apply the metirc RMSE in Eq. (12) to evaluate our model. It is arithmetic square root of mean square error to measure how much the data changes. Note that prediction accuracy increases inversely with RMSE.

$$RMSE = \sqrt{\frac{\sum_{u,i}(r_{u,i} - p_{u,i})^2}{\mathsf{N}}} \tag{12}$$

where N represents the number of experiment samples, $p_{u,i}$ and $r_{u,i}$ the predicted and observed scores of user u for movie i, respectively.

5.2   Experiment Settings

The purpose of this experiment is to verify the advantages and disadvantages of an improved algorithm considering time factor. The experiment is performed in the PySpark cloud environment which consists of five Alibaba Cloud Server ECSs. One is a master node and the other four are slave nodes.

In collaborative filtering algorithms, the key is to train model parameters accurately. The algorithm has the following parameters: Rank, maxIter, and λ. Rank, the number of implicit semantic factors, has an influence on the fitness of the training model in the test model. MaxIter is the number of iterations. λ is the regularization parameter of ALS. Three parameters are independent variables to observe RMSE.

5.3   Evaluation

Figures 2(a) and (b) are three-dimensional maps of RMSE. X-axis in the figure is the number of the implicit semantic factor Rank from 1 to 10. Y-axis is the number of iterations maxIter from 1 to 10. The Z-axis is RMSE.

The results demonstrate that the improved algorithm has a significant improvement in RMSE. It can be seen that RMSE decreases sharply with Rank. It indicates that the increase of the Rank value results in improvement of performance. RMSE in two algorithms first decreases rapidly, and then becomes stable. Specifically, RMSE fluctuates slightly while Rank changes from 3 to 10, which indicates that Rank should not be too large. In addition, RMSE in Fig. 2(a) is much larger than RMSE in Fig. 2(b) when maxIter is from 1 to 3. This shows that the model is more stable given millions of data.

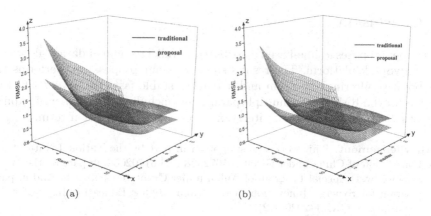

(a)   (b)

Fig. 2. (a) RMSE in 3D map. (b) RMSE given a million-level datase

With 100,000 and a million levels of data, RMSE in the proposed algorithm is smaller than that in the traditional algorithm. It is observed that RMSE tends to converge to a Rank of 10. Therefore, we fix Rank = 10 to observe RMSE by alternating λ and maxIter in Figs. 3(a) and (b).

The X-axis in Figs. 3(a) and (b) are λ in [0.0001, 0.0003, 0.001, 0.003, 0.01, 0.03, 0.1, 0.3, 1, 3]. The Y-axis is the number of iterations maxIter from 1 to 10, and the Z-axis is RMSE. We have the same result that the proposed algorithm is better than the traditional algorithm. In Fig. 3(a), RMSE gradually decreases with λ from 0 to 0.5. When the λ is close to 0.5, the RMSE reaches its lowest value. Afterwards, RMSE increases with λ. In summary, the proposed algorithm considering time factor is more effective than the traditional algorithm from the respect of RMSE.

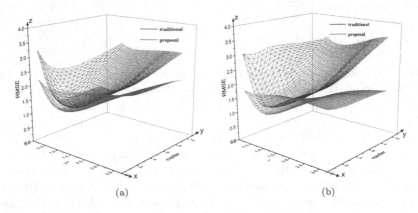

(a)   (b)

Fig. 3. (a) RMSE given a 100000-level datase. (b) RMSE given a million-level dataset

6   Conclusion

This paper proposes a time-based distributed parallel recommendation algorithm in the PySpark platform. The results show that our proposal outperforms the collaborative filtering algorithm and it reaches stable fast. We have verified its effectiveness on RMSE with multiple parameters including the number of implicit semantic factors, the number of iterations, and the regularization term.

Acknowledgement. This work was supported in part by the National Natural Science Foundation of China under Grants 61672038 and 61702006, in part by the Major Technologies R&D Special Program of Anhui under Grant 16030901060. And in part, the Program for Synergy Innovation in the Anhui Higher Education Institutions of China (Grant No. GXXT-2020-012).

References

1. Yang, X., Guo, Y., Liu, Y., Steck, H.: A survey of collaborative filtering based social recommender systems. Comput. Commun. **41**, 1–10 (2014). https://doi.org/10.1016/j.comcom.2013.06.009
2. Karydi, E., Margaritis, K.: Parallel and distributed collaborative filtering: a survey. ACM Comput. Surv. (CSUR) **49**(2), 37 (2016)

3. Gousios, G.: Big data software analytics with apache spark. In: Proceedings of the 40th International Conference on Software Engineering: Companion, pp. 542–543. Association for Computing Machinery, New York (2018)
4. Meng, X., et al.: MLlib: machine learning in apache spark. J. Mach. Learn. Res. **17**(1), 1235–1241 (2016)
5. Gao, F., Bhowmick, C., Liu, J.: Performance analysis using apriori algorithm along with spark and python. In: Proceedings of the 2018 International Conference on Computing and Big Data, pp. 28–31. ACM (2018)
6. Winlaw, M., Hynes, M.B., Caterini, A., De Sterck, H.: Algorithmic acceleration of parallel ALS for collaborative filtering: speeding up distributed big data recommendation in spark. In: 2015 IEEE 21st International Conference on Parallel and Distributed Systems (ICPADS), pp. 682–691. IEEE (2015)
7. Kupisz, B., Unold, O.: Collaborative filtering recommendation algorithm based on hadoop and spark. In: 2015 IEEE International Conference on Industrial Technology (ICIT), pp. 1510–1514. IEEE (2015)
8. Verma, A., Kumar, D.: Evaluating and enhancing efficiency of recommendation system using big data analytics (2017)
9. Panigrahi, S., Lenka, R.K., Stitipragyan, A.: A hybrid distributed collaborative filtering recommender engine using apache spark. Procedia Comput. Sci. **83**, 1000–1006 (2016)
10. Xie, L., Zhou, W., Li, Y.: Application of improved recommendation system based on spark platform in big data analysis. Cybern. Inf. Technol. **16**(6), 245–255 (2016)
11. Lenka, R.K., Barik, R.K., Panigrahi, S., Panda, S.S.: An improved hybrid distributed collaborative filtering model for recommender engine using apache spark. Int. J. Intell. Syst. Appl. **10**(7), 74 (2018)
12. Harper, F.M., Konstan, J.A.: The movielens datasets: history and context. ACM Trans. Interact. Intell. Syst. **5**(4), 19 (2016)
13. Zhang, P., Zhang, Z., Tian, T., Wang, Y.: Collaborative filtering recommendation algorithm integrating time windows and rating predictions. Appl. Intell. **49**(8), 3146–3157 (2019). https://doi.org/10.1007/s10489-019-01443-2

A Novel Visual-Identification Based Forwarding Strategy for Vehicular Named Data Networking

Minh Ngo[✉], Satoshi Ohzahata, Ryo Yamamoto, and Toshihiko Kato

Graduate School of Informatics and Engineering, University of Electro-Communications, Tokyo, Japan

mingus@net.is.uec.ac.jp, ohzahata@uec.ac.jp, {ryo_yamamoto, kato}@is.uec.ac.jp

Abstract. In this paper we propose a robust and lightweight forwarding protocol in Vehicular ad hoc Named Data Networking (V-NDN). The concept of our forwarding protocol is that it adopts a visual-identification based approach where a vehicle would collect its neighbor list by camera to construct a hop-by-hop FIB-based forwarding strategy. Furthermore, due to the Face duplication on wireless environment, we add the visual information to Face to distinguish the incoming and outgoing Face that makes FIB and PIT in our design works more accurate and efficient. The result of performance evaluation focusing on the communication overhead shows that our proposal has better result in network traffic costs overall and also in Interest satisfaction ratio than that of the previous works.

Keywords: NDN for Vehicular Ad-hoc Networks (V-NDN) · Visual identification · Neighbor aware forwarding · FIB based forwarding

1 Introduction

Vehicular Ad Hoc Network (VANET) is a special mobility subclass of Mobile Ad Hoc Network (MANET). In VANETs, the infrastructure-less node moves and exchanges the information like accident, road construction, speed warning, traffic jams to provide safety and convenience to the drivers and passengers. Due to the highly mobile environments, while travelling with high speeds the connection links in VANETs is broken frequently and more challenge to maintain.

Named Data Networking (NDN) has been introduced as a promising technology to deal these problems above [1]. The motivation of NDN is shifting the information objects from host end-points (where) to name of the content (what). NDN uses two types of packets in all communications: Interest and Data. A consumer requesting a content sends an Interest packet containing the content name. A producer providing the corresponding content data returns a Data packet to the consumer. NDN routers transferring the Data packet cache the packet for future redistribution.

Originally, NDN is designed for wired network topology, it progressively be effectively applied to various wireless ad hoc network topology such as VANETs. The purpose of routing in NDN is how to construct Forwarding Information Base (FIB) for

© ICST Institute for Computer Sciences, Social Informatics and Telecommunications Engineering 2022
Published by Springer Nature Switzerland AG 2022. All Rights Reserved
C. T. Calafate et al. (Eds.): MONAMI 2021, LNICST 418, pp. 256–269, 2022.
https://doi.org/10.1007/978-3-030-94763-7_20

name prefixes, which specifies the correspondence between a name prefix and a face (or a neighbor identifier) to the content with this name prefix. However, in the case of wireless ad hoc network, node has only one wireless interface, it means no distinction between incoming and outgoing Face, FIB and PIT table become ineffective. Node have to flood all received Interest that causes broadcast storm. Furthermore, in such dynamic network routing protocol adapted to a highly dynamic environment such as VANETs, the end-to-end routing is costly and inefficiency that leads to almost current works approach to focus on hop-by-hop path and improve the next-hop selection method.

There are several approaches [2–5] has been proposed to solve these problems. N-Spray Wait [2] is a DTN based NDN forwarding by carry and forward Interest. Authors in [3] has a neighbor aware forwarding approach by not maintaining the FIB table and proposed a delay-based broadcast and next-hop selection depend on metrics such as distance, velocity. Besides, ADU [4] or MMM-VNDN [5] attempt to unicast-based by discover network on first phase by broadcasting, recover the function of FIB, PIT table for unicast forwarding by using host ID or MAC address instead of Face. These methods have some limitations, the first neighbor aware approach costs an overhead of control packet, Interest and also Data, the second is the accuracy of FIB based forwarding due to the mobility of nodes.

In this paper, we provide a new visual-identification based forwarding strategy that use neighbor aware approach to maintain FIB table as follows: We take advantage of equipped front rear cameras and propose a real-time next-hop selection based on visual-identification to provide an active neighbor discovery process rather than using control packet or flooding Interest, furthermore we also propose a concept of checking the available of candidate node before transmitting, it prevents a redundant path recovery phase and makes forwarding more flexible with high dynamic network. Our method is adopting two criterions: robust and lightweight. First, the goal of our deign is for supporting the driving assistance service, the Interest be used to request the information of road conditions ahead have to move forward as fast as possible that requires a robust forwarding method. "robust" in our term means despite of network topology changes, once look up the prefix on FIB table, appropriate entry is needed to exist constantly. The second criterion is lightweight, as we all know such kind of information has to updated periodically that causes network overhead, we want to design to minimize the traffic on network, thus possible to concede resources to other important safety information such as accident warning alert service.

The rest of this paper consists of the following sections. Section 2 introduces the related work on V-NDN. Section 3 explains the detailed our new protocol and Sect. 4 shows the performance evaluation focusing on the network overhead. Section 5 concludes this paper.

2 Related Work

2.1 NDN in Nutshell

In NDN the basic operation of a node on NDN is similar to an IP node. Once to request a content, node becomes a Consumer that initially creates an Interest packet including the name prefix of the content. When an intermediate node receives this Interest, the node checks three following tables in order:

- Content store (CS) table: Buffer memory which caches and retrieves contents.
- Forwarding Interest Base (FIB) table: A routing table which stores route of name corresponding to outgoing stream.
- Pending Interest Table (PIT): Not existed in IP based network, PIT stores information about unsatisfied (pending) Interest corresponding to incoming stream.

There will be three cases are considered. If the prefix in the Interest matches with data in CS, this node will become a Producer which return the corresponding content back to Consumer and discard the Interest. If any entry in PIT matches with an Interest, incoming interface (or called Face in NDN) is added into PIT and discard the Interest (same content request has already been forwarded). A NDN node uses information in the FIB table in order to send the Interest toward to Producer. If matched entry was found, Interest will be forwarded based on FIB table and node also records the prefix of Interest and the face which Interest arrives in PIT. If not (no match founded in the FIB table), the Interest will be discarded. Each PIT entry added can be used as the breadcrumb trail to send the data backs to the original Consumer.

2.2 Forwarding Strategies in NDN Based VANETs

The problem of duplicated Face and the mobility of topology that mentioned above is focused as the main challenge of V-NDN currently. A various of forwarding approach has been proposed, there are two approaches common be used are neighbor aware forwarding and FIB based forwarding. For instance, RUFS [6] periodic exchanges the recent satisfied list (RSL) to maintains a neighbor satisfied list (NSL) for the content discovery. Or in N-Spray Wait [2] is a DTN approach by using carry and forward mechanism, when node encounters, it passes the Interest to N nodes and these nodes carry Interest until obtain the Producer. These two methods are neighbor approach that ease the burden of maintaining FIB table by passing the Interest hop-by hop to increase the chance of reaching the Producer.

Reliable Forwarding Strategy (RFS) in [3] is NDN-based version of Greedy Perimeter Stateless Routing (GPSR). RFS has a typical neighbor aware forwarding approach which uses the beacon message to maintain neighbor list periodically. Beacon message contains Node ID, Position, Velocity, etc. On Forwarding Interest, node calculates the best metric neighbor as the next relay node. This hop-by-hop process repeats until Interest arrives to Producer. RFS uses PIT to return Data but do not maintain FIB due to the mobility of wireless network that costs amount of traffic pushed into network.

On the other hand, A Multi-hop and Multipath Routing (MMM-VNDN) [5] is a solution to deal with V-NDN by maintaining FIB and PIT table. MMM-VNDN has two main ideas are replacing Face by MAC address and broadcast-to-unicast switching mechanism. Overall, MMM-VNDN aim to recover V-NDN, makes it work correctly like the theory of NDN which originally supports for Wired Network. The duplicated face problem which mentioned above was solved by using MAC address instead of Face. The rest of MMM-VNDN works like wired-NDN when the Consumer floods the first

Interest to discover content, intermediate nodes update PIT and FIB and forward the Interest until arrives Producer. Data return by PIT and Consumer sends the following Interest with same content in unicast by using FIB table. Although MMM-VNDN is a full-function NDN model, it is not suitable for VANETs, once topology changes, it has to rebuild FIB by returning to flooding Interest phase.

3 Proposal

3.1 Overview

We have adopted the following design principles for our visual-identification based forwarding mechanism.

- To deal the Face problem of NDN on wireless environment and the control packet overhead as descried the above, we introduce a new Node Identifier called Visual Identifier (VI), VI is a result of a beaconless method based on visual recognition by taking the photos of running vehicles, VI helps node of NDN to divide the incoming Face and outgoing Face separately. We also maintain a neighbor table on each node individually that be used for forwarding purpose.
- We keep using FIB, PIT to take advantages of original NDN architecture about scalability problem, cache, content-centric data transmission and mobility. Aim to improve the capability of FIB and PIT, we replace the Face and Requester field by VI of node that help the hop-by-hop forwarding path easy to build and maintain. Through this way, we also eliminate the broadcast-based discovery phase of NDN by detecting a next-hop on the direction along the road via camera to create a new corresponding FIB entry in real-time.
- In path recovery aspect, we design a free-packet method called check before transmit, node uses camera to check the available of next-hop before sending packet, to prevent the broken link that trigger the broadcast mode, we recover that to unicast by replace the non-alive by the new one selected from VI table.

3.2 Visual-Identification and Packet Structures

The concept of visual-identification had implemented in various researches such as to identify and tag the malicious vehicles [15] or be used as a factor of authentication to improve the security issues [7]. Based on these benefits of using visual information, we have an idea to adopt it as metric on Interest forwarding protocol. We assume that all vehicles are equipped with front and rear cameras (drive recorders) which be used to capture the visual identifier of running around vehicles. Visual Identifier (VI) is the core of our design, the concept of VI is using high resolution camera to gather a combination of factors such as licenses plate number, color, brand, car type and others to identify and assign VI to each vehicle, VI is unique and is used as Vehicle Identifier.

On many previous researches, Node ID, MAC address, GPS position are used as Vehicle Identifier, the common disadvantage of all of them are the passive approach. It means the neighbor ID information have to "receive" from the outside passively. For instance, Node ID and Position are included in arrived hello packet or in other solution MAC address is added in Interest and Data packet. Thus, forwarding method based on such kind of Vehicle Identifier have some limitations on delay, packet overhead and accuracy. To encounter the above issues, our proposal focuses on VI as Vehicle Identifier to design a robust neighbor-maintaining method in the active approach. VI is not required any control packet to maintain, fetched via camera quickly and actively, VI also support unicast, multicast forwarding to prevent broadcast storm. Furthermore, VI is line-of-sight method, verify input of camera in real-time that overcoming the previous security issues of digital authentication using control massage.

Table 1 shows the parameters contained in VI table. Although the license number is unique that can become the VI (VI of Car A = 433-234), in some cases license plate number not able to captured (bad weather, obstacle or lack of light, etc.), for that reason we have additional fields such as color, brand, or any other identifies to improve the recognition ability.

The ability of this image processing is varied on specification of cameras on physical layer or the photo analyzing algorithm on application layer, hence we assume that the transmission range of wireless ad hoc network is equal to the range of cameras in our design to make sure line of sight node is always reachable.

Table 1. Visual identifier (VI) table

Visual identifier	License plate number	Color	Brand	Car type	Distance	Others
Car A	433-234	Black	Nissan	Sedan	50	Driver wears hat
Car B	342-567	Red	BMW	SUV	70	

We add three new fields into the Interest and Data packet. The detail of enhanced Interest and Data packet was summarized in Table 2.

Table 2. Parameters in interest and data packet

Interest	Data
Sender-VI	Name
Lifetime	Sender-VI
Nonce	Signature
Name	Data
Receiver-VI	Receiver-VI

- Sender-VI: This field represents the VI of sender (The previous hop-by-hop forwarding sender).
- Receiver-VI: This field represents the VI of next-hop which was selected from VI table.

- Lifetime: Reduced by one before Interest is forwarded to next-hop, Interest is discarded when the lifetime count is equal to zero.

In our design, all the forwarding decision is based on FIB and PIT. An entry is created for an individual name prefix. The addition of VI concept to enhance the original FIB and PIT by switching Face into VI and also able to deal direction of vehicle in the forwarding rather previous works. Tables 3 and 4 show the forwarding parameter is the Node ID (VI) of upstream node in FIB and downstream node in PIT.

Table 3. Enchained forwarding information base (FIB).

Name	Next-hop
Check	Car B

Table 4. Enchained pending interest table (PIT).

Name	Requester
Check	Car A

3.3 Protocol Design

First Phase
Each vehicle takes the photos of running around vehicles and build up VI Table individually. The license number, car type, color, distance etc. are captured to identify the neighbor. To optimize the hop count metric, we decide the farthest in-range vehicle be selected as the candidate node for hop-by-hop forwarding purpose and be explained in the following step.

When a vehicle wants to monitor the road condition ahead for driving assistant service, it is considered as a Consumer and sends Interest. According to the design of NDN, at this point FIB is blank, the initial Interest has to be flooded into network to discover the content, or the Interest can be forwarded in unicast only if the Consumer maintains a neighbor list by beacon message [8]. For this reason, both of them costs in term of traffic overhead, we encounter this limitation by taking advantage of VI idea. Consumer selects the candidate node in VI Table which is closer to the Producer than itself and creates a new FIB entry with VI of next-hop at once. The initial Interest of this time contains Receiver-VI equals to selected next-hop and also Sender-VI equals to Consumer VI.

Once a relay node receives the initial Interest, it normally creates a PIT entry which correspond to the Consumer (extract the Sender-VI field on Interest). After that node selects the candidate node from VI table, create a new FIB entry, replace the current

Sender-VI by its VI and send the Interest in unicast as same as the original Consumer. The Lifetime of the Interest is reduced by one every time the Interest passes a node. This process repeats until the Lifetime equal to 0 or reaches the Producer.

In our scenario, due to the road-event discovering purpose, the Producer is the node that produces a road-event. In case Producer receives the Interest, Producer returns the Data to satisfy received Interest. The Data which also includes Sender-VI and Receiver-VI is sent back to the Consumer through the reverse path of the Interest which is previously maintained by PIT on intermediate nodes.

Second Phase

Node checks FIB entries to make the decision for the second Interest. In case route was found, node sends the Interest that corresponding to FIB entry, otherwise node acts like the first phase to transfer the Interest by VI table. This Interest is relayed until Lifetime becomes zero or arrives the Producers, the Data follows the PIT breadcrumb as mentioned in the first phase.

According to the goal of reducing redundant packet transmission, in the second phase we minimize the path from Consumer to Producer by forwarding the following Interest of same prefix based on FIB instead of using VI table. Selecting next-hop on VI table in this phase will raise the number of routes that points to the Producer and difficult to manage. Alternatively, we use VI concept to support path recovery function be explained in the following section.

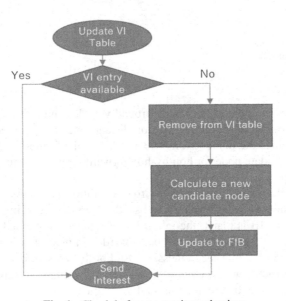

Fig. 1. Check before transmit mechanism

Path Recovery

As described in previous section, the characteristic of visual-identification process is in real-time, VI is captured by vehicle and added into VI table frequently. We have an idea to maintain and recover the route called "check before transmit mechanism", it can be displayed through the flowchart shown in Fig. 1.

Node examines the neighbor and VI table periodically, the VI of vehicle exits in VI table represents to the reachable node in real-time. Due to not using any protocol to populate the prefix, the next-hop of FIB field is updated based on VI Table entries. In our design, the vehicle comes in-sight of camera is considered as the good candidate node. For instance, one previous vehicle is become unable to visual recognize (not able to capture the number-plate or not enough factor to detect VI), it is considered as an unreachable node, node removes it from VI table. Node have to reactive the first phase to recreate a new path by calculating metrics to select a new candidate node, replaces the unreachable next-hop on FIB table by the new one and send the Interest. Comparing with previous researches the check before transmit mechanism reduces the amount of retransmission and route recovery packets.

An Example of Network Discovery in Our Method

From the second phase onwards, the forwarding protocol works based on FIB and PIT in a traditional way of NDN model. Thus, we explain the detail about a communication session between a set of Consumer/Producer in first phase or network discovery phase by the following example.

Figure 2 shows that vehicle A, it looks up entries in FIB table before sending the Interest. In-range of camera, vehicle A captures the number plates and other specifications of running ahead vehicle B and C, and puts B and C into its VI table.

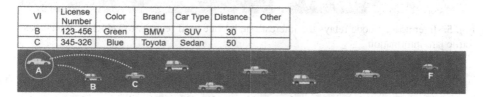

VI	License Number	Color	Brand	Car Type	Distance	Other
B	123-456	Green	BMW	SUV	30	
C	345-326	Blue	Toyota	Sedan	50	

Fig. 2. Vehicle A creates the VI table

In Fig. 3(a), at this time the FIB table of A is empty, A checks the VI Table to select vehicle C which has the best metric as the next-hop (the longest distance). A creates a new FIB entry for prefix "check" with forwarding candidate is vehicle C, puts its VI into Sender-VI and also VI of C into Receiver-VI field, send this Interest to C by unicast to retrieve the content as shown in Fig. 3b.

Figure 4 shows the forwarding when vehicle C receives the Interest, C inspects the CS. Thus, no corresponding data, C creates a new PIT entry respond to A. Similar to the previous implemented process on A, C also selects a next-hop for "check", adds a new FIB entry and send the Interest to D.

The intermediate node repeats this process sequentially to forward the Interest and update PIT simultaneously. Once the Interest reaches to area of vehicle F which has a warning of traffic jam ahead, vehicle F become Producer and terminate the Interest forwarding (Fig. 5).

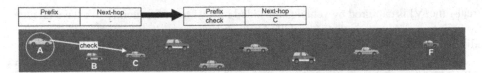

(a)   Vehicle A checks the FIB and create a new entry that points to vehicle C

Name	Sender-VI	Receiver-VI
check	A	C

(b)   Vehicle A edits the Sender-VI and the Receiver-VI to send Interest.

Fig. 3.   Vehicle A sends an initial interest.

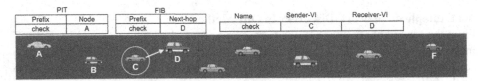

Fig. 4.   Vehicle C repeats the previous process to forward the interest to vehicle D

Fig. 5. Intermediate node relays the interest one by one until reaches to vehicle F which has a traffic jam information.

Figure 6 shows the return way of Data from vehicle F back to vehicle A through the path which is established by each intermedia nodes. F configures an appropriate set of Sender-VI and Receiver-VI and send back the Data to vehicle H. H continues to forward this Data to G and this process repeats until arrives to A.

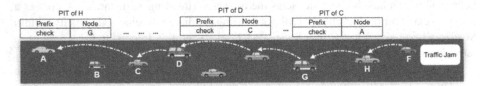

Fig. 6.   Vehicle F return the data back to vehicle A

4   Performance Evaluation

4.1   Scenario Settings and Evaluated Methods

To evaluate the performance of our proposal, we used ndnSIM and SUMO to generate vehicle trace with the following parameters, are shown in Table 5.

Table 5. Simulation parameters

Parameters	Values
Simulation time	200 s
Number of vehicles	30, 40, 50
MAC protocol	802.11a 5 GHz
Transmission range	100 m
Velocity	30–40 km/h

We set up a long road topology has two lanes and one-way traffic. Number of vehicles varying from 30 to 50 in 2500 m area. Vehicles run along the road with minimum gap between car is 30 m and velocity is randomly distributed from 30 to 40 km/h. All the nodes communicate through ad hoc mode 802.11a with 100 m transmission range.

Our scenario is traffic prediction supporting service when a Consumer at the beginning of the road area periodic sends Interest along the road to update the traffic information ahead at 1 packet/second rate. A traffic jam event is occurred at the end of the road, the node in this area become Producer and respond all the satisfied Interest. In addition, during the simulation time we remove one intermediate node for one time to simulate the disconnected network and evaluate the path recovery function on each method.

Due to the goal of our proposal is reducing the redundant traffic, our evaluation focuses on the overhead of control packet, Interest packet transfer and total transmitted packet of relative nodes, we also measure the Interest Satisfaction Ratio (ISR) obtained from the total number of Data returned divided by the total Interest sent of Consumer to evaluate the accuracy of each method.

We evaluate the performance of our proposal compares to GPSR based NDN and MMM-VNDN protocol. The first one is GPSR, a typical IP-based VANETs which uses beacon message to maintain the neighbor list, we use the UdpFace class in ndnSIM to simulate GPSR [9] method under NDN layer, it was detailed explained in our previous research [10].

With MMM-VNDN, we change the default term of Face on ndnSIM to MAC address to identify the node. MAC address of neighbor is tracked in the flood phase and be sent by broadcast to unicast switching in second phase.

In case of our proposal, we assume that the VI table is already built up by captured images taken by camera. Following our design, we imitate a sequence of hop-hop forwarding based on VI table by pre-defining a path from Consumer to Producer. We can use this way to estimate packet overhead in our proposal.

4.2 Simulation Results

Control Packet Overhead: The number of control packets is proportional to the numbers of nodes and times, we can confirm the total beacon *SUM* of *n* nodes in *t* seconds with rate *m* packets/s by following formula:

SUM $= n \times t \times m$.

Figure 7 plots the result of total control packet generated in 200 s simulation time with m $= 1$ then SUM is $n \times 200 \times 1$. Our proposal and MMM-VNDN method use FIB table for decision thus the control packet is zero.

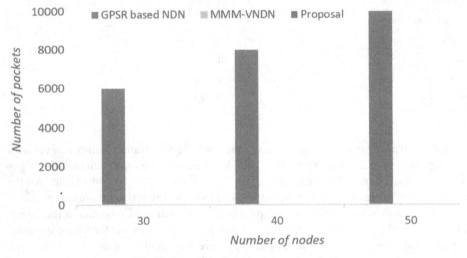

Fig. 7. Number of routing control packets

Interest Overhead: The total Interest includes the content discover Interest, recovery route Interest and retransmit time out Interest. In the same conditions, to prevent the redundant of Interest for the same content, we set Interest rate is 1 packet/s on our simulation. The result on Fig. 8 shows that MMM-VNDN is much higher than the others, the reason is MMM-VNDN has first flooding phase when Interest is rebroadcasted by all the nodes. Moreover, when the path to Producer was broken as explained in setting section above, MMM-VNDN costs retransmit packets and another flooding phase for route recovery.

GPSR based NDN and our proposal show the better result and consistent due to do not have any flooding phase, also in order using beacon and check before transmit mechanism to deal with broken link. We know that such pure FIB based forwarding method like MMM-VNDN suffers when the topology changes.

Total Transmitted Packets: Total transmitted packets are the total number of Interest, control packet and data packet are plotted in Fig. 9. In contrast to the previous good performance in the aspect of Interest overhead, GPSR based NDN generally sent highest traffic into network. The reason is GPSR based NDN method have to trade off a large

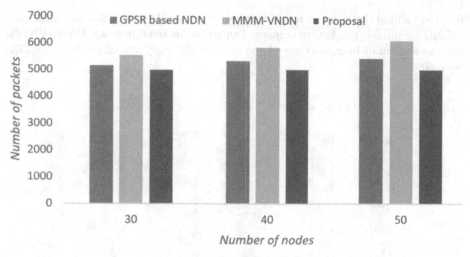

Fig. 8. Number of Interest packets

amount of control packet to keep network link always on (capable of sending an Interest to the next-hop immediately).

Although the number of Data packets increases with the number of Interest and the number of nodes (flooding phase), MMM-VNDN still have better result than GPSR based NDN because this method maintains a FIB table.

We can see that our method transmitted the less traffic to retrieve the content, according to the goal of design, it clearly shows the advantage in packet cost overall.

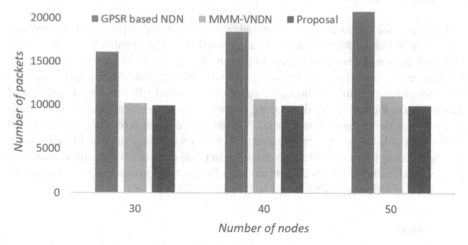

Fig. 9. Total transmitted packets

Interest Satisfaction Ratio (ISR): The result of ISR of three methods are plotted in Fig. 10. Although the GPSR based NDN and our proposal achieve similar values over

90%, our method shows better result with low overhead. This indicates that these two methods are suitable this kind of scenario. Due to the broken link setup, MMM-VNDN suffer an amount of Interest to resend and recover FIB entry that effect the result ISR above 80%.

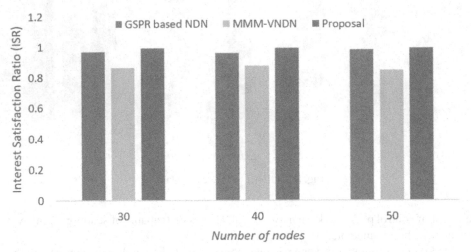

Fig. 10. Interest satisfaction ratio

5   Conclusions

In this paper, we proposed a new visual-identification based approach of Interest forwarding in Vehicular NDN network. Our proposal aimed at maintaining neighbors by taking advantage of front rear camera to capture the specification such as license number plate, color, car type, etc. of running around vehicles, then identify and assign the visual identifier (VI) to each node. We design to construct FIB table by adding visual information as metrics for a FIB selecting process. The visual-identification approach is an active way that reduce control packet into network compares to others beacon based methods. In addition, associating the idea of VI with forwarding based on FIB eliminates the first flooding phase in content discovery or in route recovery. The result showed that the proposed method requires the less amount of packet and in every aspect of overhead good delivery ratio than GPSR based NDN and MMM-VNDN.

References

1. Tariq, A., Rehman, R., Kim, B.: Forwarding strategies in NDN-based wireless networks: a survey. Commun. Surv. Tutor. IEEE **22**(1), 68–95 (2020)
2. Saxena, D., Raychoudhury, V., Becker, C.: Implementation and performance evaluation of name-based forwarding schemes in V-NDN. 18th International Conference on Distributed Computing and Networking, p. 35 (2017)

3. Ahmad, F., Adnane, A.: Design of trust based context aware routing protocol in vehicular networks. In: Proceedings of the 9th IFIP WG 11.11 International Conference on Trust, Hamburg, Germany, May 2015
4. Amadeo, M., Campolo, C., Molinaro, A.: A novel hybrid forwarding strategy for content delivery in wireless information-centric networks. Comput. Commun. **109**, 104–116 (2017)
5. Kalogeiton, E., Kolonko, T., Braun, T.: A multihop and multipath routing protocol using NDN for VANETs. In: 16th Annual Mediterranean Ad Hoc Networking Workshop (Med-Hoc-Net). IEEE (2017)
6. Ahmed, S.H., Bouk, S.H., Kim, D.: RUFS: robust forwarder selection in vehicular content-centric networks. IEEE Commun. Lett. **19**(9), 1616–1619 (2015)
7. Dolev, S., Krzywiecki, L., Panwar, N., Segal, M.: Vehicle authentication via monolithically certified public key and attributes. Wireless Netw. **22**, 879–896 (2016)
8. Angius, F., Pau, G., Gerla, M.: BLOOGO: BLOOm filter based GOssip algorithm for wireless NDN. In: NoM 2012, Proceedings of the 1st ACM workshop on Emerging Name-Oriented Mobile Networking Design - Architecture, Algorithms, and Applications, June 2012
9. Karp, B., Kung, H.T.: GPSR: greedy perimeter stateless routing for wireless networks. In: Proceedings of the International Conference on Mobile Computing and Networking, Mobicom (2000)
10. Ngo, M., Yamamoto, R., Ohzahata, S., Kato, T.: Proposal and performance evaluation of hybrid routing mechanism for NDN ad hoc networks combining proactive and reactive approaches. IEICE Trans. Inf. Syst. **E102.D**, 1784–1796 (2019)
11. Amadeo, M., Campolo, C., Molinaro, A., Ruggeri, G.: Content-centric wireless networking: a survey. Elsevier Comput. Netw. **72**, 1–13 (2014)
12. ndnSIM homepage, https://ndnsim.net/current/
13. Li, X., Wang, S., Wu, W., Chen, X.: Interest tree based Information dissemination via vehicular named data networking. In: 2018 27th International conference on computer communication and networks (ICCCN). pp. 1–9 12. IEEE (2018)
14. Mostafa, A., Hussein, W., El-Seoud, S.: Identification and tagging of malicious vehicles through license plate recognition. In: 2nd International Conference on New Trends in Computing Sciences (ICTCS), Jordan (2019)
15. GPSR on ns-3.22. https://github.com/edlobo127/gpsr-ns-3.22

A Sleep Scheduling Algorithm with Limited Energy Collection in Energy Harvesting Wireless Sensor Networks

Fei Gao, Wuyungerile Li$^{(\boxtimes)}$, Pengyu Li, and Ruihong Wang

Inner Mongolia University, Hohhot, China
gerile@imu.edu.cn

Abstract. Energy harvesting wireless sensor networks (EH-WSNs) have been widely studied. However, in the case of limited illumination time or weak illumination intensity in winter or cloudy days, energy harvested by nodes is also limited, which leads to the corresponding reduction of network lifetime. Therefore, this paper proposes a Sleep scheduling algorithm based on virtual Grid for Limited Energy collection energy harvesting (SGLE), which consists of two parts: (1) A judgment criteria of redundant nodes; The network monitoring region is divided into several small squares of equal area, The network monitoring region is divided into several equal areas, and the covering ratio of the node's sensing region by its neighbor nodes is calculated to determine whether it is redundant or not. (2) A sensor node interacts with its neighbor nodes to decide the sleeping priority; A node exchanges sleep priority information with its neighbor node, so that to decide whether to sleep or not, so as to effectively avoid the occurrence of coverage hole. Simulation results show that, compared with the existing mod-LEACH algorithm, VSGCA algorithm and GAF algorithm, SGLE algorithm has a significant improvement in node survival rate, node mortality rate, network coverage rate and working node ratio under the same conditions.

Keywords: WSN · EH-WSN · Sleep scheduling · Network lifetime

1 Introduction

Wireless sensor network (WSN) is composed of a large number of sensor nodes. Because of its low production cost, less occupied area, good computing and communication capabilities [1], it is widely used in military reconnaissance, smart home [2], oil resource detection [3], smart city [4], and hospital health management [5]. Traditional wireless sensor networks use non renewable resources such as dry batteries to provide power. If the dead nodes in the network reach a certain proportion, the network will not work normally [6]. If the dry battery is replaced manually, it will not only increase the maintenance cost, but also bring hidden danger to the safety of the staff. Therefore, it is very important

© ICST Institute for Computer Sciences, Social Informatics and Telecommunications Engineering 2022
Published by Springer Nature Switzerland AG 2022. All Rights Reserved
C. T. Calafate et al. (Eds.): MONAMI 2021, LNICST 418, pp. 270–281, 2022.
https://doi.org/10.1007/978-3-030-94763-7_21

to reduce the cost of battery maintenance in the later stage of wireless sensor network by using new technology. In order to solve the above problems, energy harvesting wireless sensor network (EH-WSN) has been gradually studied and popularized [7].

EH-WSN uses the energy harvesting equipment carried by the node to harvest the energy in the environment (such as solar energy, wind energy, tidal energy, radio frequency energy, etc.). For EH-WSN with solar charging, in winter or cloudy day, due to the limited illumination time and weak illumination intensity, the energy harvested by the node is also limited. When the harvested energy is lower than the energy consumed by the node or at night, the sensor can only use the limited energy stored in its capacitor to maintain operation. Therefore, how to prolong the lifetime of EH-WSN is an urgent problem under the condition of limited energy harvesting. In order to make rational use of the harvested energy and prolong the network lifetime, this paper proposes a sleep scheduling algorithm based on virtual grid.

The main contributions of our work are as follows:

- The SGLE algorithm puts forward the judgment criterion of redundant nodes. By dividing the network area into grids, it judges whether it is a redundant node according to the ratio of nodes covering the grid.
- We compare the sleep priority of the nodes that meet the sleep conditions with the neighbor nodes to avoid coverage blind areas.
- The SGLE algorithm achieves better performance in terms of node survival rate, node mortality rate, network coverage rate, and working node ratio.

The rest of this paper is organized as follows: In Sect. 2, we give the related work. In Sect. 3, we describe our proposed Sleep scheduling algorithm in EH-WSN and the simulation results are presented in Sect. 4. Finally, Sect. 5 concludes our work.

2   Related Work

At present, the main research purpose of EH-WSN is to effectively manage the energy harvested and consumed by nodes under the premise of ensuring the quality of network service, so as to prolong the life of the network and improve the data transmission rate. Tian He et al. combined the dynamics of energy with the low duty cycle working mode of nodes and proposed a distributed solution [8]. On the basis of ensuring that the fixed E2E (End to End) delay upper bound is not destroyed, this method optimizes energy consumption in order to prolong the network lifetime. S. Peng et al. proposed ENDD (Query Driven Energy Neutral Directed Diffusion) routing protocol [9]. In this protocol, the node decides whether to pass the routing request by its current data harvesting ability; the document also designs an energy evaluation model to improve the reliability and accuracy of the admission control process.

In terms of energy scheduling, L. Sherly Puspha Annabel et al. proposed the asynchronous node wake-up scheduling protocol HMAC [10]. The protocol consists of a wake-up scheduling phase and an energy management phase. In the wake-up scheduling phase, the network first analyzes the number of data packets in the current cache queue, and then adjusts the wake-up mode; In the energy management phase, the data transmission mode of the node is selected according to the QR value generated in the previous, so as to reduce the energy consumption.

In the aspect of node reliability of EH-WSN, Z. A. Eu et al. built an experimental network and verified the reliability of the network [11]. At the same time, Z. A. Eu et al. also proposed a single-hop MAC protocol and probabilistic polling mechanism for data transmission. In this protocol, the node uses its maximum power to send data to other nodes. Because the location of other nodes is uncertain, the packet loss rate of this protocol is relatively high. Zhu J et al. proposed a reliable model of Markov wireless sensor network on the basis of integrating the data acquisition rate between nodes and the connectivity between nodes [12]. Zonouz A et al. established the reliability model of the EH-WSN node and the reliability model of the link on the basis of integrating the number of neighbor nodes, the remaining energy of the node, and environmental interference [13].

When the energy harvested by the EH-WSN is insufficient, the node sleep scheduling method can effectively prolong the lifetime of the network. There are three sleep scheduling algorithms for wireless sensor networks: (1) Sleep scheduling algorithm based on distance clustering [14–17]. In these algorithms, sensor nodes are clustered first. The active nodes in the cluster are responsible for harvesting the information in the sensing region and sending the processed information to the cluster head node; The cluster head node further fuses the received data and sends the data to the aggregation node. The LEACH (low energy adaptive clustering hierarchy) protocol proposed by heinzelman et al. In 2002 is the basis of many sleep scheduling algorithms since then [14]. The protocol runs in rounds, and sets threshold function to conduct cluster head random election. In each round, some nodes in the cluster can enter the dormancy state. After the next round, the cluster head replacement election and cluster division will be carried out. Yong Ding and others proposed a CPA partition algorithm based on grouping principle [15]. CPA algorithm consists of two phases: grouping and scheduling, After the node broadcast. In the process of grouping CPA algorithm, the communication between nodes is considered, so CPA algorithm can ensure the connectivity of the network. Although CPA algorithm effectively guarantees the connectivity of the network, the coverage of the network is not guaranteed, and the blind area may appear.

The second type is sleep scheduling algorithm based on network coverage [18–22]. This kind of algorithm will set a function to calculate the coverage rate of the sensing area of the node, and judge whether the node is redundant by calculating the coverage rate, so that the nodes that meet the conditions enter the sleep state, and the remaining active nodes complete the operation of the whole network. In 1987, Francesca Cuomo et al. Used the method of predicting grid points to judge the redundancy of nodes [18]. The redundancy judgment method proposed in this paper is basically applicable to all kinds of network topologies. The coverage in sensor networks is also discussed. The algorithm only judges the coverage redundancy of nodes in the network based on the location information of nodes, and the accuracy of the results is poor. Suo Longxiang and others proposed VSGCA (a virtual square grid based coverage algorithm of sleeping scheduling for wireless sensor network) [19]. The VSGCA algorithm divides the sensing area of the node first, and calculates the coverage rate of the node by judging the coverage of other nodes. If other nodes can completely cover the sensing area of the node, the node is considered as redundant. The VSGCA algorithm is scheduled according to rounds, and each round is composed of two parts: the sleep node selection stage and the perception stage.

The third type is sleep scheduling algorithm based on network connectivity [18,23,24]. This kind of algorithm is based on the connectivity of the network to determine the dormancy of nodes, and dormant redundant nodes without destroying the network connectivity. Y. Xu et al. proposed the GAF (Geographic adaptive fidelity) algorithm [23]. GAF algorithm is suitable for sensor nodes to deploy more intensive network topology, and needs to know the location information of nodes in advance. Francesca Cuomo et al. proposed SS tree (sense sleep trees) method by using flow model in graph theory and constraint condition method of mathematical programming [18]. In this method, the tree structure is used to schedule the sleeping nodes, and the key is the formation of SS tree. SS tree needs to be recalculated when the network topology changes, which will cause a lot of additional network energy consumption.

Although the sleep scheduling of wireless sensor network guarantees the coverage of the network area to a certain extent, it prolongs the network lifetime. However, the node does not interact with neighbor nodes to determine sleep information before sleep, which may cause network coverage blind spots; the node sleep time is fixed, and different sleep times are not set for nodes with different remaining energy.

3   A Sleep Scheduling Algorithm with Limited Energy Collection

3.1   A Judgment Criteria of Redundant Nodes

In the SGLE algorithm, nodes run in turns, as shown in Fig. 1. Each round includes several stages: neighbor discovery, coverage redundancy judgment, neighbor node information interaction and node sleep.

A) Segmentation Area Range. As described by the basic idea of SGLE algorithm, the whole network monitoring area needs to be divided into 1 m × 1 m square, as shown in Fig. 2.

B) Discover Neighbor Nodes. Sensor nodes broadcast discovery messages to neighbor nodes. If other nodes receive neighbor discovery messages sent by sensor nodes, they send packets to respond to nodes. Nodes determine the location and status of neighbor nodes according to the packets received from other nodes.

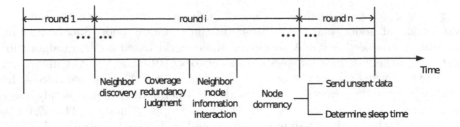

Fig. 1. SGLE algorithm node scheduling.

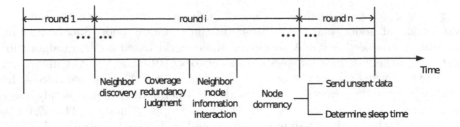

Fig. 2. Region segmentation example.

C) Judgment of Coverage Redundancy. This section describes the method for a node to determine the coverage ratio of its sensing range covered by other sensor nodes, and discusses in detail how to calculate the coverage ratio of sensor nodes covered by other nodes. As shown in Fig. 3, node i determines the number of small squares contained in its sensing area, calculates the number of small squares, and determines the square area set $Q(R_i)$ monitored by target node i. Then the number of small squares contained in other sensor nodes is sensed, and the set $Q(R_{neii})$ of small squares covered by other sensor nodes is determined by comparison. Finally, the coverage of the area monitored by sensor i is obtained by the ratio of the number of elements of set $Q(R_{neii})$ to set $Q(R_i)$. When the coverage of node i is greater than the threshold C_{th}, node i is considered to be a redundant node.

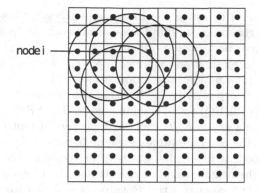

node i

Fig. 3. Example of node sensing range covered by other nodes.

3.2 Sleep Scheduling Method of a Node

In this paper, the network lifetime is divided into several rounds, and the node scheduling is carried out by rounds. This section describes the scheduling mode of nodes in a round.

A) Neighbor Nodes Interact with Each Other. If the node that reaches the dormancy condition after the coverage judgment goes into the sleep state directly, the network may cause the blind area of monitoring due to insufficient coverage. As shown in Fig. 4, node a has released the conditions to enter the dormancy state under the coverage of other nodes, and node b has reached the conditions for entering the sleep state. If node a and b are all dormant, the part covered by node a is not harvested by node b, and the area will become the

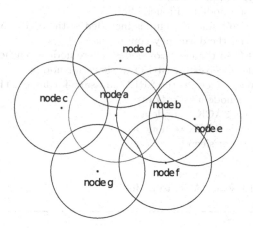

Fig. 4. Example of blind area generated by neighbor nodes without information interaction

"blind area" of monitoring range, it will cause unnecessary losses. Therefore, in order to avoid the generation of blind area of network monitoring, nodes must interact with neighbor nodes before hibernation.

Table 1 shows the method and algorithm for determining whether the node can sleep after the information interaction between the node and the neighbor node to compare the sleep priority. Node a that reaches the sleep condition sends the request message (SREQ) to its neighbor node. The SREQ message includes the P_i value of node a ($P_i = E_i/C_i$, where E_i is the current residual energy of the node, and C_i is the coverage value of the node covered by other nodes). The neighbor node of node a judges its status after receiving the request message sent by node a. If the neighbor node (such as node b) of node a also meets the sleep condition, node b compares the P_i value of node a with its own P_i value. If the P_i value of node b is greater than that of node a, and node a energy is less covered, node a has higher sleep priority, and node b sends a confirmation message (SACK) to node a; Otherwise node b sends a reject message (SCON) to node a. If node a receives a rejection message, node a does not sleep. If the neighbor node of node a fails to meet the sleep condition, it sends confirmation message to node a directly.

Table 1 Pseudo code for neighbor nodes to interact with each other.

Algorithm 1. Pseudo code for neighbor nodes to interact with each other.

1: Definition:
2: SREQ: the request message sent by the node that reaches the sleep condition to the neighbor node
3: SACK: the neighbor node that does not reach the sleep condition or the Pi value is large replies the confirmation message to the sensor node
4: SCON: rejection message from neighbor nodes with smaller PI values to sensor nodes
5: E_i: Residual energy value of nodes
6: C_i: the coverage of a node by its neighbors
7: P_i: The value of E_i/C_i and P_i value is included in the SREQ message
8: when node a reaches the dormancy condition
9: node a sends SREQ to the neighbor nodes where node a reaches coverage
10: the neighbor nodes receives the SREQ message for node a
11: **if** the neighbor nodes receives the SREQ message for node a **then**
12:    **if** node b's P_i ¿ node a's P_i **then**
13:        node b sends SACK to node a
14:    **else** node b sends SCON to node a
15:        node a does not sleep
16:    **end if**
17: **else**
18:    neighbor nodes send SACK to node a
19: **end if**

B) The Node Goes to Sleep. When node a interacts with other nodes, if the SREQ message sent by node a does not receive all SACK message replies, node a will not enter the sleep state; If the SREQ message sent by node a receives all the SACK message replies, node a will enter into the sleep state. The nodes that enter into the sleep state no longer harvest and receive data. Node a checks whether there is any unsent data. If there is any unsent data, node a will send all unsent data first; If node a has no unfinished data, node a enters the sleep state.

4   Simulation Results

4.1   Simulation Parameters

The setting of simulation environment parameters in this paper is shown in Table 1.

Table 1. Simulation experiment parameters.

Parameter name	Parameter value
Network area	$100\,m \times 100\,m$
Base station coordinates	$(50\,m,\ 50\,m)$
Number of nodes	200
Node initial energy	$0.5\,J$
Node communication radius	$10.0\,m$
Packet size	4000 bits
Sending energy consumption	$5 \times 0.001\,J$
Receiving energy consumption	$5 \times 0.001\,J$
Sleep energy consumption	$1 \times 0.000001\,J$
Network coverage threshold C_{th}	95%

4.2   Simulation Results

A) Node Survival Rate. Figure 5 shows the node survival rate comparison of SGLE algorithm, mod-LEACH algorithm, VSGCA algorithm and GAF algorithm. At the same time, under the same conditions, the node survival rate of SGLE algorithm is higher than that of mod-LEACH algorithm, VSGCA algorithm and GAF algorithm. Because SGLE algorithm determines the dormancy time of dormant nodes according to the residual energy of sensor nodes, nodes with less residual energy have longer dormancy time and consume less energy, and the overall energy consumption of the network can be balanced. According to the experimental results, SGLE algorithm can effectively improve the node survival rate under the same conditions.

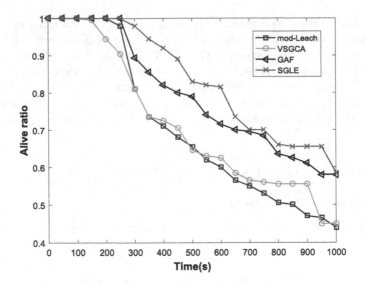

Fig. 5. Example of node sensing range covered by other nodes.

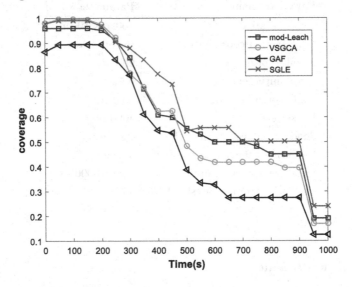

Fig. 6. Example of node sensing range covered by other nodes.

B) Network Coverage. Figure 6 shows the network coverage of SGLE algorithm, mod-LEACH algorithm, VSGCA algorithm and GAF algorithm. Before 200 s, the network coverage rate of VSGCA algorithm is higher than that of the other three algorithms, while the network coverage rate of SGLE algorithm and mod-LEACH algorithm is less different. This is because VSGCA algorithm requires that when the sensing range of nodes reaches the condition of full coverage by neighbor nodes, redundant nodes can enter the sleep state, so VSGCA algorithm has fewer dormant nodes, Its network coverage ratio is relatively large. But in the same period of time, the network coverage of SGLE algorithm and mod-LEACH algorithm is more than 95%, which can basically meet the network service requirements; In the same period of time, the network coverage rate of GAF algorithm is the lowest, which is about 90%, and there may be network coverage blind area.

With the operation of the network, the network coverage rate of SGLE algorithm will be higher than the other three algorithms. This is because SGLE algorithm sets the coverage threshold C_{th}. When the node reaches the coverage threshold, it will judge whether the node enters the sleep state. Moreover, after the node reaches the coverage threshold, the node will interact with the neighbor node to determine the sleep state, It can avoid the blind area caused by several nodes sleeping at the same time, so the network coverage rate of SGLE algorithm is better than other algorithms.

C) **Work Node Ratio.** Figure 7 shows the ratio of working nodes of SGLE algorithm, mod reach algorithm, VSGCA algorithm and GAF algorithm. As shown in Fig. 7, Because the node dormancy mode of GAF algorithm is to divide the network area into virtual square area with equal area according to the communication distance of nodes. One node is selected in each grid for data harvesting and communication, so the number of working nodes in the first 300 s of GAF algorithm is the smallest, but the lower ratio of working nodes in the initial GAF algorithm is at the cost of reducing network coverage. In the initial stage of network operation, the working node of SGLE is significantly lower than that of mod-LEACH algorithm and VSGCA algorithm. At the beginning

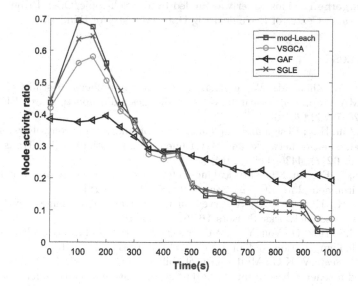

Fig. 7. Example of node sensing range covered by other nodes.

of network operation, the number of working nodes of SGLE is 17% lower than that of mod-LEACH algorithm and 38% lower than that of VSGCA algorithm.

With the operation of the network, the working nodes of SGLE algorithm are lower than those of mod-LEACH algorithm, VSGCA algorithm and GAF algorithm. This is because the nodes in SGLE algorithm can achieve energy load balancing. There are many surviving nodes, and some nodes can meet the operation requirements of the current network. Therefore, SGLE can guarantee the quality of network service and achieve a higher node dormancy ratio, so as to extend the network lifetime.

5   Conclusions

In order to solve the problem of limited energy in wireless sensor networks, researchers apply energy harvesting technology to wireless sensor networks, resulting in a large number of research and application of EH-WSN. However, in the case of limited light time and weak light intensity in winter or cloudy days, the energy that nodes can harvest is limited, or even can not harvest energy. How to extend the lifetime of the network with limited energy harvesting is an important research issue. In order to solve the above problems, this paper proposes a node sleep scheduling algorithm (SGLE) for EH-WSN, which mainly includes two parts: (1). The judgment criterion of redundant nodes; (2). The sensor nodes interact with neighbors before sleeping. Simulation results show that, compared with mod-LEACH algorithm, VSGCA algorithm and GAF algorithm, under the same conditions, SGLE algorithm has significantly improved in node survival rate, node mortality rate, network coverage rate and working node ratio.

Acknowledgement. This paper was funded by the Self-topic/Open Project of Engineering Research Center of Ecological Big Data, Ministry of Education

References

1. Kumar, A., Zhao, M., Wong, K.J., et al.: A comprehensive study of IoT and WSN MAC protocols: research issues, challenges and opportunities. IEEE Access **6**, 76228–76262 (2018)
2. Li, M., Lin, H.J.: Design and implementation of smart home control systems based on wireless sensor networks and power line communications. IEEE Trans. Industr. Electron. **62**(7), 4430–4442 (2014)
3. Galmés, S., Escolar, S.: Analytical model for the duty cycle in solar-based EH-WSN for environmental monitoring. Sensors **18**(8), 2499 (2018)
4. Nellore, K., Hancke, G.P.: A survey on urban traffic management system using wireless sensor networks. Sensors **16**(2), 157 (2016)
5. Jeong, J.S., Han, O., You, Y.Y.: A design characteristics of smart healthcare system as the IoT application. Indian J. Sci. Technol. **9**(37), 52 (2016)
6. Fujii, C., Seah, W.K.G.: Multi-tier probabilistic polling in wireless sensor networks powered by energy harvesting. In: 2011 Seventh International Conference on Intelligent Sensors, Sensor Networks and Information Processing, pp. 383–388. IEEE (2011)

7. Sharma, H., Haque, A., Jaffery, Z.A.: Modeling and optimisation of a solar energy harvesting system for wireless sensor network nodes. J. Sens. Actuator Netw. **7**(3), 40 (2018)

8. Gu, Y., He, T.: Bounding communication delay in energy harvesting sensor networks. In: 2010 IEEE 30th International Conference on Distributed Computing Systems, pp. 837–847. IEEE (2010)

9. Peng, S., Low, C.P.: Energy neutral directed diffusion for energy harvesting wireless sensor networks. Comput. Commun. **63**, 40–52 (2015)

10. Annabel, L.S.P., Murugan, K.: An energy efficient wakeup schedule and power management algorithm for wireless sensor networks. In: 2012 International Conference on Recent Trends in Information Technology, pp. 314–319. IEEE (2012)

11. Eu, Z.A., Tan, H.P., Seah, W.K.G.: Design and performance analysis of MAC schemes for wireless sensor networks powered by ambient energy harvesting. Ad Hoc Netw. **9**(3), 300–323 (2011)

12. Zhu, J., Tang, L., Xi, H., et al.: Reliability analysis of wireless sensor networks using Markovian model. J. Appl. Math. **2012** (2012)

13. Zonouz, A.E., Xing, L., Vokkarane, V.M., et al.: Reliability-oriented single-path routing protocols in wireless sensor networks. IEEE Sens. J. **14**(11), 4059–4068 (2014)

14. Heinzelman, W.B., Chandrakasan, A.P., Balakrishnan, H.: An application-specific protocol architecture for wireless microsensor networks. IEEE Trans. Wireless Commun. **1**(4), 660–670 (2002)

15. Tian, D., Georganas, N.D.: A coverage-preserving node scheduling scheme for large wireless sensor networks. In: Proceedings of the 1st ACM International Workshop on Wireless Sensor Networks and Applications, pp. 32–41 (2002)

16. Ding, Y., Wang, C., Xiao, L.: An adaptive partitioning scheme for sleep scheduling and topology control in wireless sensor networks. IEEE Trans. Parallel Distrib. Syst. **20**(9), 1352–1365 (2008)

17. Deng, J., Han, Y.S., Heinzelman, W.B., et al.: Scheduling sleeping nodes in high density cluster-based sensor networks. Mob. Netw. Appl. **10**(6), 825–835 (2005)

18. Cuomo, F., Abbagnale, A., Cipollone, E.: Cross-layer network formation for energy-efficient IEEE 802.15. 4/ZigBee wireless sensor networks. Ad Hoc Netw. **11**(2), 672–686, (2013)

19. Liu, Y., Suo, L., Sun, D., Wang, A.: A virtul square grid-based coverage algorithm of redundant node for wireless sensor network. J. Netw. Comput. Appl. **36**(2), 101–106 (2013)

20. Kim, E.-J., Kim, M., Youm, S.-K., Choi, S., Kang, C.-H.: Priority-based service differentiation scheme for IEEE 802.15.4 sensor networks. AEUE Int. J. Electron. Commun. **61**(2), 69–81 (2006)

21. Xing, G., Wang, X., Zhang, Y., et al.: Integrated coverage and connectivity configuration for energy conservation in sensor networks. ACM Trans. Sens. Netw. (TOSN) **1**(1), 36–72 (2005)

22. Wu, K., Gao, Y., Li, F., et al.: Lightweight deployment-aware scheduling for wireless sensor networks. Mob. Netw. Appl. **10**(6), 837–852 (2005)

23. Xu, Y., Heidemann, J., Estrin, D.: Geography-informed energy conservation for ad hoc routing. In: Proceedings of the 7th Annual International Conference on Mobile Computing and Networking, pp. 70–84 (2001)

24. Wang, L., Xiao, Y.: A survey of energy-efficient scheduling mechanisms in sensor networks. Mob. Netw. Appl. **11**(5), 723–740 (2006)

NOMA-Based Statistical Signal Transmission for Beyond 5G Communications

Tianheng Xu[1,2], Ning Zhang[3], Ting Zhou[1,2(✉)], Honglin Hu[1], and Xiaoming Tao[4]

[1] Shanghai Advanced Research Institute, Chinese Academy of Sciences, Shanghai, China
{xuth,zhouting,huhl}@sari.ac.cn
[2] Shanghai Frontier Innovation Research Institute, Shanghai, China
[3] Department of Electrical and Computing Engineering, University of Windsor, Windsor, ON, Canada
ning.zhang@uwindsor.ca
[4] Department of Electronic Engineering, Tsinghua University, Beijing, China
taoxm@tsinghua.edu.cn

Abstract. With the rollout of fifth-generation (5G) communications, researches for beyond fifth generation (B5G) communications are being launched globally. In this paper, we explore for possible ways to integrate two promising techniques, including non-orthogonal multiple access (NOMA) and statistical signal transmission (SST), seeking a feasible perspective to promote the development of B5G communications. Specifically, NOMA allows multiple users to occupy the same spectrum resource, which can greatly improve spectrum efficiency. On the other hand, SST utilizes higher-order moments to convey additional data over traditional first-order moment signals, which is capable of supporting inter-system data exchange. To verify the feasibility of combining NOMA and SST, in this paper we outline the transceiver architecture, and conceive the workflow for this promising NOMA-SST system. Considering that NOMA users at a same spectrum resource have intrinsic energy gaps, we further design a dedicated transmission strategy for NOMA-SST technique, aiming at compensating the performance for NOMA users with lower power levels. Numerical results reflect that the proposed technique can achieve satisfactory detection performance, which is promising for applications.

Keywords: NOMA · Beyond 5G · Spectrum efficiency · Statistical signal transmission · Differential window integration

1 Introduction

Wireless communication technologies have experienced incredible growth in the past decades. Now the human society has already initiated a global fifth-generation (5G) communication era [1–5]. Currently, the wireless communication community

© ICST Institute for Computer Sciences, Social Informatics and Telecommunications Engineering 2022
Published by Springer Nature Switzerland AG 2022. All Rights Reserved
C. T. Calafate et al. (Eds.): MONAMI 2021, LNICST 418, pp. 282–298, 2022.
https://doi.org/10.1007/978-3-030-94763-7_22

starts to research the beyond fifth generation (B5G) communication systems [6–8]. B5G is envisioned as a multifarious ecosystem, which contains multi-type subsystems, large amount of different applications and diversified services [9–11]. Accordingly, how to (i) effectively support the accompanying tremendous data in B5G ecosystem [12,13], while (ii) maintaining efficient collaborations among different systems and applications [14–16], becomes a critical challenge.

Non-orthogonal multiple access (NOMA) technique is regarded as an enabling technique for B5G systems [17–19]. Relying on the aid of successive interference cancellation (SIC), NOMA allows multiple users to occupy the same spectrum resource. Lots of studies have proved that NOMA outperforms traditional orthogonal multiple access from multiple aspects, especially in spectrum efficiency [20–22]. On the other hand, statistical signal transmission (SST) is another emerging technique, which can deliver additional data streams over regular signals. The SST data stream is formed in the shape of higher-order moments, it neither affects the transmission performance; nor causes extra spectrum sacrifice from the underlying regular signals (in first-order moment) [23,24]. Moreover, SST is also easy to be implemented and is compatible with common communication systems [25,26]. Therefore, SST can facilitate efficient collaborations among different subsystems and applications for future B5G ecosystem.

Referring to the advantages of the two techniques above, we imagine that if NOMA and SST can be well merged: (i) spectrum efficiency can be doubly refined, thus the huge wireless traffic burden will be alleviated; (ii) efficient collaborations among systems and applications will be facilitated. Accordingly, the union technique of NOMA-SST has the potential to promote a smooth evolution from 5G to B5G. However, existing literature still lacks the answer of whether NOMA and SST can work together. To answer this question, in this paper, we probe for possible ways to combine NOMA and SST. Particularly, the major contributions can be summarized as follows.

- First, we analyze the working principles of both NOMA and SST, then we outline the preliminary transceiver architecture for the union technique of NOMA-SST.
- Second, based on the transceiver architecture, we further conceive the operational workflow for NOMA-SST technique.
- Third, considering that NOMA users at the same spectrum resource have intrinsic energy gaps, we dedicatedly design an enhanced transmission strategy to compensate the weaker users.
- Forth, we provide numerical results and demonstrate that the proposed NOMA-SST technique has satisfactory detection performance.

The reminder of this paper can be organized as follows. First in Sect. 2, we design the transceiver architecture and detection workflow for NOMA-SST technique. The properties of the proposed technique are discussed as well. Then in Sect. 3, we provide the differential window integration strategy to further strengthen the ability of NOMA-SST technique. Section 4 showcases simulation results to verify the performance of the proposed technique. Finally, our work of this paper is concluded in Sect. 5.

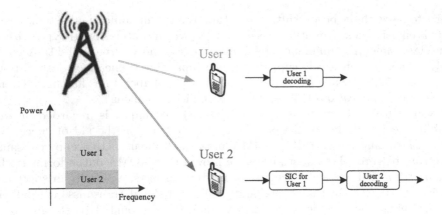

Fig. 1. Downlink NOMA scenario with two users.

2 System Design

NOMA technologies usually exploit power level difference for multiple users to occupy the same spectrum resource [27,28]. Figure 1 illustrates an example of a typical downlink NOMA scenario with two users. The two users are transmitting data on the same spectrum resource. Specifically, User 1 has higher power level than User 2. Since the distinct power level difference, the data of User 1 can be directly detected at the receiver of User 1, while the data of User 2 is regarded as a part of noise. On the other hand, for the receiver of User 2: when receiving the mixed signals, the SIC mechanism first decodes data of User 1; after that, the receiver of User 2 subtracts the content of User 1's data, then successively decodes data of User 2 [29,30].

2.1 Transceiver Architecture Design

Based on the typical NOMA scenario above, we design the transceiver architecture for NOMA-SST, as Fig. 2 shows. At the transmitter, the SST-data of one user (User 1 or User 2), which is performed in the form of high order moment, is embedded into the first order moment of traditional frequency data. Thus, the two kinds of data streams of one user (User 1 or User 2) are combined into the same physical stream. After that, referring to the power level difference, the two users' physical streams further mix together. At last, four paralleled data streams are transmitted at the same band.

Without loss of generality, in this paper we adopt a classical two-antenna transmitting configuration [31]. The detailed operational principle of NOMA-SST can be elaborated as follows. SST signal is produced by a cyclic delay diversity [32,33] based orthogonal frequency division multiplexing (OFDM) system. Before transmitting, the SST data is mapped into a dynamic cyclic delay sequence. Then during the transmission, the first transmitting antenna (antenna-A) sends typical OFDM symbols; at the same time, such symbols are cyclically

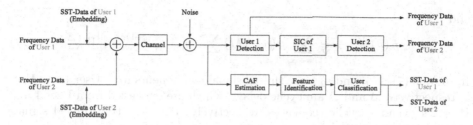

Fig. 2. Transceiver architecture of downlink NOMA-SST technique.

shifted according to the aforementioned dynamic cyclic delay sequence, and sent by the second transmitting antenna (antenna-B). Therefore, SST data is embedded into the frequency data. This implementation does not induce extra bandwidth cost. Particularly, the signal sent by antenna-A can be written as

$$s_A(n) = \sqrt{P_1}s_{1,A}(n) + \sqrt{P_2}s_{2,A}(n), \tag{1}$$

where P_1 and P_2 are transmitting power of User 1 and User 2, respectively. We set User 1 has the higher power level than User 2, thus $P_1 > P_2$. The signal components

$$s_{1,A}(n) = \frac{1}{\sqrt{2N}} \sum_{l=-\infty}^{+\infty} g(n-lM) \sum_{k=0}^{N-1} \alpha_{l,k} W_N^{k[(l+1)M-n]} \tag{2}$$

and

$$s_{2,A}(n) = \frac{1}{\sqrt{2N}} \sum_{l=-\infty}^{+\infty} g(n-lM) \sum_{k=0}^{N-1} \beta_{l,k} W_N^{k[(l+1)M-n]} \tag{3}$$

belong to User 1 and User 2, respectively. In (2) and (3), N is the Fast Fourier Transform size, $M = N+$ cyclic prefix length. $W_N = e^{\frac{-j2\pi}{N}}$, α and β are OFDM data from User 1 and User 2, respectively. l and k denote sequence number of symbol and subcarrier of OFDM signal, respectively. $g(n)$ is the window function, which can be expressed as

$$g(n) = \begin{cases} 1, & n \in [0, M-1], \\ 0, & \text{otherwise.} \end{cases} \tag{4}$$

Antenna-B sends the identical data as that in antenna-A, but the data should be cyclically shifted before transmitting, which can be expressed as

$$s_B(n) = \sqrt{P_1}s_{1,B}(n) + \sqrt{P_2}s_{2,B}(n), \tag{5}$$

with

$$s_{1,B}(n) = \frac{1}{\sqrt{2N}} \sum_{l=-\infty}^{+\infty} g(n-lM) \sum_{k=0}^{N-1} \alpha_{l,k} W_N^{k[(l+1)M-n]} W_N^{k\Delta} \tag{6}$$

and

$$s_{2,B}(n) = \frac{1}{\sqrt{2N}} \sum_{l=-\infty}^{+\infty} g(n - lM) \sum_{k=0}^{N-1} \beta_{l,k} W_N^{k[(l+1)M-n]} W_N^{k\bar{\Delta}}. \tag{7}$$

In (6) and (7), $s_{1,B}$ and $s_{2,B}$ are shifted signal components from User 1 and User 2, respectively. Δ and $\bar{\Delta}$ are cyclic delays, which are extracted from User 1 and User 2's dynamic cyclic sequences, respectively. The final transmitted signals can then be represented as

$$\mathbf{S}(n) = \begin{bmatrix} s_A(n) \\ s_B(n) \end{bmatrix}. \tag{8}$$

2.2   Detection Work Flow Design

In this subsection, we elaborate the detection work flow. The received signal can be written as

$$r(n) = \mathbf{h}\mathbf{S}(n) + v(n), \tag{9}$$

where $v(n)$ denotes the additive white Gaussian noise, $\mathbf{h}$ represents the channel gain, and we have

$$\mathbf{h} = [h_A, h_B]. \tag{10}$$

Referring to Fig. 2, when the receiver gets the signal, the processing modules of frequency domain and SST domain work in parallel. For the frequency domain, it first regards User 2's data as a part of noise, and directly detects User 1's data. After getting User 1's reconstructed data, the SIC process subtracts it from the mixed signal, and then detects User 2's data. Since the NOMA detection process in frequency domain has been well studied in lot of researches, the follow-up details are omitted in this paper.

On the other hand, the SST module works simultaneously in the frequency domain. In particular, it contains three submodules:

- Cyclic autocorrelation function (CAF) estimation;
- Feature identification;
- User classification.

CAF estimation is the first step of SST detection. Notice that manmade signals are mostly cyclostationary random processes [34]. Hence a signal stream' CAF can be represented as waveforms in a three-dimensional coordinate system. Such a coordinate system is usually established by lag parameter, cyclic frequency parameter, and coherence energy value [35,36]. Based on this theory, CAF estimation submodule extracts the peak information of CAF waveforms from the mixed signal. Given L as observation window length of symbol unit, the value of CAF can be estimated as

$$C^{(L)}(b, \tau) = \frac{1}{LM} \sum_{n=0}^{LM-1} r(n)r^*(n + \tau)W_M^{bn}, \tag{11}$$

where $\tau \in [1, M]$ and $b \in [1, M]$ are lag parameter and cyclic frequency parameter, respectively.

After obtaining CAF value, the feature identification submodule exploits a multiple hypothesis test to operate the detection process. Note that cyclic delays have the symmetric property [24], for one user there are $N/2$ distinct SST features in an N-subcarrier system. To avoid conflicts, we set $\Delta \neq \bar{\Delta}$. Hence, for each hypothesis we have

$$H_\Delta : \begin{cases} C^{(L)}(b, \Delta) & = \tilde{C}^{(L)}(b, \Delta) + \varepsilon_r^{(L)}(b, \Delta) \\ C^{(L)}(b, \tau) & = \varepsilon_r^{(L)}(b, \tau) \end{cases} \tag{12}$$

$$\text{for} \quad \tau \in (1, 2, \cdots, N/2), \ \tau \neq \Delta,$$

$$H_{\bar{\Delta}} : \begin{cases} C^{(L)}(b, \bar{\Delta}) & = \tilde{C}^{(L)}(b, \bar{\Delta}) + \varepsilon_r^{(L)}(b, \bar{\Delta}) \\ C^{(L)}(b, \tau) & = \varepsilon_r^{(L)}(b, \tau) \end{cases} \tag{13}$$

$$\text{for} \quad \tau \in (1, 2, \cdots, N/2), \ \tau \neq \bar{\Delta},$$

and

$$H_j : C^{(L)}(b, \tau) = C_v^{(L)}(b, \tau)$$

$$= \frac{1}{LM} \sum_{n=0}^{LM-1} v(n)v^*(n + \tau)W_M^{bn} \tag{14}$$

$$\text{for} \quad \tau \in (1, 2, \cdots, N/2),$$

where $j \in \left(1, 2, \cdots, \frac{N}{2}\right)$ and $j \neq \{\Delta, \bar{\Delta}\}$; $\tilde{C}^{(L)}$, $C_v^{(L)}$ and $\varepsilon_r^{(L)}$ are symbol coherency components, noise coherency components and unrelated coherency components within observation window length L, respectively.

Next, the user classification submodule could extract a local two-dimensional CAF value from the entire three-dimensional coordinate system, and classify the locations of two users' feature peaks. Here we take the CAF value at $b = M$ as an example, and the local feature peaks can then be presented as

$$\Gamma^{(L)}(\tau) = \left| C^{(L)}(M, \tau) \right|. \tag{15}$$

$$\text{for} \quad \tau \in (1, 2, \cdots, N/2)$$

Given available feature location sets as

$$\Omega = \{1, 2, \cdots, N/2\} \tag{16}$$

and

$$\bar{\Omega} = \Omega - \{\Delta\}, \tag{17}$$

respectively. The classification processes for User 1 and User 2 can be performed as

$$\Delta = \arg \max_{\tau \in \Omega} \ \Gamma^{(L)}(\tau) \tag{18}$$

and

$$\bar{\Delta} = \arg \max_{\tau \in \bar{\Omega}} \ \Gamma^{(L)}(\tau), \tag{19}$$

respectively.

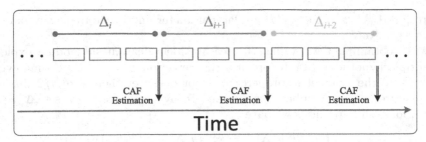

(a) A classical SST scheme.

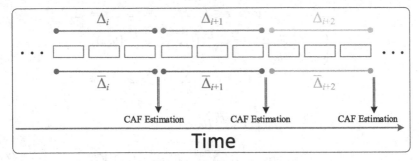

(b) A default NOMA-SST scheme.

Fig. 3. Detection workflow comparison between SST and NOMA-SST schemes. Boxes represent OFDM symbols in time domain, different color coverages indicate different cyclic delay ranges.

To visualize the difference between SST and NOMA-SST, Figs. 3 and 4 exhibit detection workflow comparison and feature comparison between SST and NOMA-SST schemes, respectively. In particular, Fig. 3(a) illustrates a classical SST scheme. In this case, every moment there is always one unique cyclic delay state (i.e. Δ_i series). The detection process is essentially a single-pole feature identification problem, which can be reflected in Fig. 4(a). While in a default NOMA-SST case as Fig. 3(b) shows, multiple cyclic delay states (belonging to different NOMA users) coexist and overlap with each other (i.e. Δ_i series and $\bar{\Delta}_i$ series). The detection process becomes a multi-pole feature identification problem. We can perceive such a phenomenon in Fig. 4(b). Fortunately, although the CAF estimation processes are simultaneously implemented for different NOMA users, their SST features can be easily distinguished owing to the power level gap.

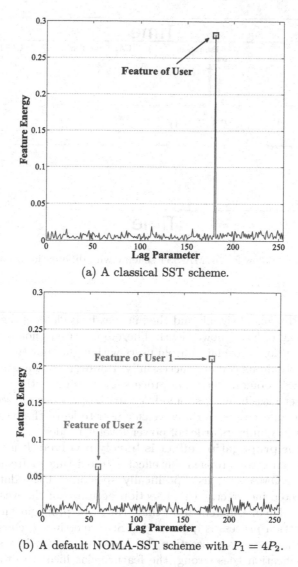

(a) A classical SST scheme.

(b) A default NOMA-SST scheme with $P_1 = 4P_2$.

Fig. 4. Feature comparison between SST and NOMA-SST schemes. This illustration is obtained under a $256 - \Omega$ size SST system with $L = 10$ and SNR $= 10$ dB.

2.3 Properties of NOMA-SST Detection Process

It is noteworthy that NOMA-SST detection process has two major advantages, which are much different from the detection process in frequency domain of pure NOMA systems.

– (i) **No apriori information is required from one user to others.** Note that the SIC procedure subtracts reconstructed content of user with strongest

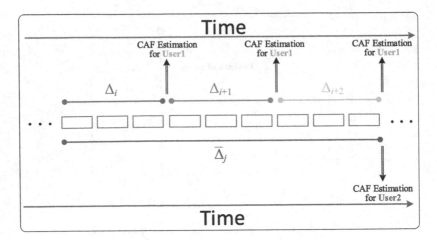

Fig. 5. Detection workflow for NOMA-SST scheme with differential window integration strategy.

power from the mixed signal, and then successively detects the weaker users in a decreasing order of power level. Therefore, a user should at least know the detailed apriori information from users with higher power level than itself, or it cannot obtain its content successfully. However, such a situation is much different in SST domain detection process. According to the workflow (especially the user classification submodule) in the previous subsection, we can find that it is unnecessary for any weaker user to learn the detailed contents of stronger users, only its order of power level is needed.

- (ii) **The error propagation effect is barely involved.** It is widely noticed that there is an error propagation effect [30] existing in frequency domain detection of NOMA systems. Specifically speaking, if the data of stronger users is detected incorrectly, the detection accuracy of the weaker users will be largely hindered. Different from that, the error propagation effect in SST domain detection process is quite slight. Still referring to classification submodule in the previous subsection, we know that even if a stronger user' feature classification goes wrong, the feature classification of a weaker user will hardly be affected. For example, in a $256 - \Omega$ size NOMA-SST system, even if an error detection occurs for the stronger user, the error propagation probability is only 3.9×10^{-3} for the weaker user, which can be neglected in practice.

3   Differential Window Integration Strategy

The previous section has elaborated the operational principle for NOMA-SST technique. However, referring to Fig. 3(b), we notice that the intrinsic power level gaps among NOMA users will inevitably lead to energy gaps among SST

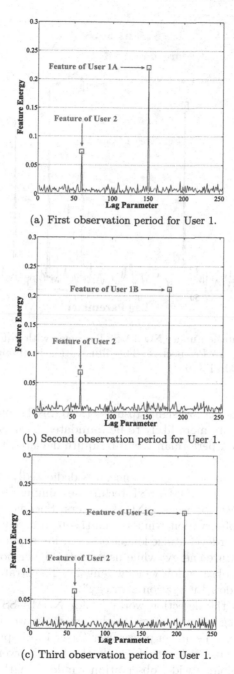

(a) First observation period for User 1.

(b) Second observation period for User 1.

(c) Third observation period for User 1.

Fig. 6. Feature presentation under NOMA-SST scheme with differential window integration strategy: User 1's Perspective. This illustration is obtained under a $256 - \Omega$ size SST system with $P_1 = 4P_2$, $L = 10$ and SNR = 10 dB. Here $\bar{\Delta}_j$ is set as 60 for User 2; Δ_i, Δ_{i+1}, Δ_{i+2} are set as 150, 180 and 210 for User 1, respectively. The differential window configuration is User 1: User 2 = 1:3.

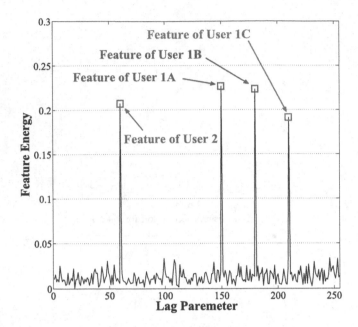

Fig. 7. Feature presentation under NOMA-SST scheme with differential window integration strategy: User 2's Perspective. This illustration is obtained under the exact same situation as that in Fig. 6.

features. Especially under low signal-to-noise ratio (SNR) conditions, the weaker users's SST features are more likely to be inundated by noise. Accordingly, the SST domain detection performance will be quite deviated for different NOMA users.

Confronted with such a circumstance, we dedicatedly design an enhanced transmission strategy for NOMA-SST technique, aiming at compensating SST detection performance for weaker NOMA users. Specifically, the principle is to allocate diverse observation window lengths to different power level users: users with lower power level utilize longer observation window lengths for better accumulations of feature energy; while users with higher power levels retain or decrease the default observation window lengths. The strategy above is named as "Differential Window Integration Strategy".

Figure 5 displays the detection workflow for NOMA-SST scheme with differential window integration strategy. In this example, we use a 3:1 differential window configuration. The higher power user (User 1, occupies Δ_i series) adopts default observation window length L, while the lower power user (User 1, possesses $\bar{\Delta}_j$ series) exploits a wider observation window length $3L$. Since the CAF estimation moments are not synchronized, the detection process here is much different from those of classical SST and default NOMA-SST. Particularly, the feature identification procedure should be divided in two perspective.

Table 1. Simulation parameters.

Parameters	Values
FFT size	128
Cyclic prefix length	32
Channel coding	Convolutional code (5, 7)
Coding rate	1/2
Antenna configuration	2×1
Channel model	Rayleigh fading
Modulation	QPSK
Number of multiplexed NOMA users	2
NOMA mode	Downlink
Proportion of power distribution	Strong user:weak user = 4:1
Default observation window length	10 unit
Differential window configuration	Strong user:weak user = 1:3

- (i) **Perspective of higher power level user.** Figure 6 reveals the feature presentations from User 1's perspective. The three subfigures correspond to the Δ_i, Δ_{i+1} and Δ_{i+2} periods in Fig. 5, respectively. In a User 1's round, it directly calculates the CAF value for past L duration, explores the highest peak from the available feature location range of Ω, and returns the information of the highest peak of Figs. 6(a), 6(b) and 6(c) for Δ_i, Δ_{i+1} and Δ_{i+2}, respectively. The whole identification process above ignores the interference from the weaker power level user since the energy gaps.
- (ii) **Perspective of lower power level user.** Figure 7 shows the feature presentation from User 2's perspective, which corresponds to the $\bar{\Delta}_j$ period in Fig. 5. As we can see in Fig. 7, through the triple-window energy accumulation, User 2's feature energy is comparable to those of User 1's. Direct identification might cause misjudgments. Therefore, the feature identification submodule of User 2's perspective should first collect the identified Δ_i, Δ_{i+1} and Δ_{i+2} from User 1's perspective. Then searches the highest peak from a limit range of $\bar{\Omega} = \Omega - \{\Delta_i, \Delta_{i+1}, \Delta_{i+2}\}$. At last, the peak information is returned to $\bar{\Delta}_j$.

4   Numerical Results

In this section, we evaluate the performance of NOMA-SST technique through numerical analysis. Considering that the frequency domain detection performance of NOMA techniques has been well studied in existing literature, in this section we focus on the SST domain detection performance. The basic simulation parameters are listed in Table 1.

Figure 8 shows the SST domain detection performance of NOMA-SST technique under default mode. It can be observed that the higher power user (User 1,

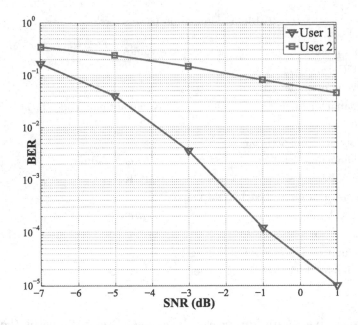

Fig. 8. SST domain detection performance of NOMA-SST under default mode. (Color figure online)

blue curve) achieves an excellent detection performance. It easily gets a bit error rate (BER) of 10^{-5} level after SNR surpasses 0 dB. By contrast, the performance of lower power user (User 2, red curve) is not quite satisfactory. It cannot even reach a 10^{-2} level within the given SNR condition range.

Figure 9 exhibits the detection performance of NOMA-SST technique under differential window integration strategy. Specifically, the differential window configuration is default L for User 1 and triple L for User 2; other system parameters equate to those of Fig. 8. The performances of User 1A, User 1B and User 1C are obtained from anterior, middle and posterior L coverages of User 2's $3L$ observation window, respectively. From the blue, green and purple curves in this figure, we can find two phenomenons: (i) three curves nearly overlap with each other, which reflects that User 1's performance is quite steady under different coverages of User 2's observation window; (ii) User 1's performance in Fig. 9 is very close to that of Fig. 8. This result reveals that differential window integration strategy hardly affects the SST detection performance of higher power user in NOMA system. On the other hand, compared with that in Fig. 8, User 2's performance in Fig. 9 distinctly upgrades by a great order of magnitude: the average gain is about 10 dB throughout the given SNR range of Fig. 8 and Fig. 9, in which the highest gain is 21.7 dB (obtained at SNR = 1 dB). Thus, the effectiveness of differential window integration strategy is verified.

Another interesting phenomenon in Fig. 9 is to find that User 2's performance slightly outperforms those of User 1 at low SNR situations. Note that the differential window configuration is 1:3 for two NOMA users. Theoretically speaking,

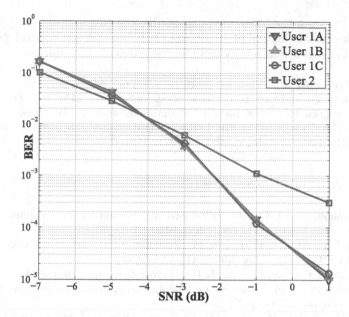

Fig. 9. SST domain detection performance of NOMA-SST under differential window integration strategy. (Color figure online)

such a differential compensation cannot reverse User 2's energy shortage, as the power distribution is 4:1. As such, User 2's performance should be inferior to User 1. Nonetheless, Fig. 9's curve trend at low SNR situations is still reasonable. Because User 2's observation window covers longer time duration than that of User 1. Accordingly, when a sudden adverse channel condition (e.g. deep fading) occurs, User 1's detection performance is easier to be affected; while User 2 has higher possibility to restrain the negative effect, since those sudden adverse channel conditions cannot last long time under power control techniques. Therefore, although the upper bound performance of User 2 is inferior of that of User 1, it is more robust to sudden adverse channel conditions than the latter. This advantage is especially remarkable at low SNR situations.

5   Conclusion

This paper presented a feasible way for integrating NOMA and SST techniques, aiming to seek novel solutions for B5G communications. Specifically, the transceiver architecture, operational workflow and a specialized transmission strategy were successively provided to support the NOMA-SST technique. Numerical results demonstrated that the proposed technique has satisfactory detection performance, which is able to be further enhanced by implementing the add-on differential window integration strategy.

Continuing from the initial research outlined in this paper, future work will be undertaken to further study relationship between user power level gap versus SST detection performance in both uplink and downlink scenarios.

Acknowledgement. The authors' work was supported in part by the Science and Technology Commission Foundation of Shanghai (No. 21511101400), Shanghai Rising-Star Program (No. 21QC1400800), Program of Shanghai Academic/Technology Research Leader (No. 21XD1433700), the National Natural Science Foundation of China (No. 61801460) and the Youth Innovation Promotion Association of CAS.

References

1. Ge, X., Zhou, R., Li, Q.: 5G NFV-based tactile internet for mission-critical IoT services. IEEE Internet Things J. **7**(7), 6150–6163 (2020)
2. Shah, S.A.A., Ahmed, E., Imran, M., Zeadally, S.: 5G for vehicular communications. IEEE Commun. Mag. **56**(1), 111–117 (2018)
3. Xu, T., Zhou, T., Tian, J., Sang, J., Hu, H.: Intelligent spectrum sensing: when reinforcement learning meets automatic repeat sensing in 5G communications. IEEE Wirel. Commun. **27**(1), 46–53 (2020)
4. Aldubaikhy, K., Wu, W., Zhang, N., Cheng, N., Shen, X.: MMWave IEEE 802.11ay for 5G fixed wireless access. IEEE Wirel. Commun. **27**(2), 88–95 (2020)
5. Hassan, N., Yau, K.A., Wu, C.: Edge computing in 5G: a review. IEEE Access **7**, 127276–127289 (2019)
6. Sekander, S., Tabassum, H., Hossain, E.: Multi-tier drone architecture for 5G/B5G cellular networks: challenges, trends, and prospects. IEEE Commun. Mag. **56**(3), 96–103 (2018)
7. Chien, W.-C., Cho, H.-H., Lai, C.-F., Tseng, F.-H., Chao, H.-C.: Intelligent architecture for mobile HetNet in B5G. IEEE Netw. **33**(3), 34–41 (2019)
8. Qi, Q., Chen, X., Lei, L., Zhong, C., Zhang, Z.: Outage-constrained robust design for sustainable B5G cellular Internet of Things. IEEE Trans. Wirel. Commun. **18**(12), 5780–5790 (2019)
9. Zhou, L., Wu, D., Wei, X., Dong, Z.: Seeing isn't believing: QoE evaluation for privacy-aware users. IEEE J. Sel. Areas Commun. **37**(7), 1656–1665 (2019)
10. Jia, R., Chen, X., Qi, Q., Lin, H.: Massive beam-division multiple access for B5G cellular Internet of Things. IEEE Internet Things J. **7**(3), 2386–2396 (2020)
11. Cui, Q., Ni, W., Li, S., Zhao, B., Liu, R.P., Zhang, P.: Learning-assisted clustered access of 5G/B5G networks to unlicensed spectrum. IEEE Wirel. Commun. **27**(1), 31–37 (2020)
12. Vuojala, H., et al.: Spectrum access options for vertical network service providers in 5G. Telecommun. Policy **44**(4), 1–15 (2020)
13. Sakib, S., Tazrin, T., Fouda, M.M., Fadlullah, Z.M., Nasser, N.: An efficient and lightweight predictive channel assignment scheme for multiband B5G-enabled massive IoT: a deep learning approach. IEEE Internet Things J. **8**(7), 5285–5297 (2021)
14. Chen, X., et al.: Age of information aware radio resource management in vehicular networks: a proactive deep reinforcement learning perspective. IEEE Trans. Wirel. Commun. **19**(4), 2268–2281 (2020)
15. Zhou, P., et al.: Edge-facilitated augmented vision in vehicle-to-everything networks. IEEE Trans. Veh. Technol. **69**(10), 12187–12201 (2020)

16. Wang, G., et al.: Coexistence analysis of D2D-unlicensed and Wi-Fi communications. Wirel. Commun. Mob. Comput. **2021**, 1–11 (2021)
17. Zhu, L., Xiao, Z., Xia, X., Wu, D.O.: Millimeter-wave communications with non-orthogonal multiple access for B5G/6G. IEEE Access **7**, 116123–116132 (2019)
18. Li, C., Gao, Z., Xia, J., Deng, D., Fan, L.: Cache-enabled physical-layer secure game against smart UAV-assisted attacks in B5G NOMA networks. EURASIP J. Wirel. Commun. Netw. **2020**(7), 1–9 (2020). https://doi.org/10.1186/s13638-019-1595-x
19. Tusha, A., Dogan, S., Arslan, H.: A hybrid downlink NOMA with OFDM and OFDM-IM for beyond 5G wireless networks. IEEE Sig. Process. Lett. **27**, 491–495 (2020)
20. Zhang, J., Tao, X., Wu, H., Zhang, N., Zhang, X.: Deep reinforcement learning for throughput improvement of the uplink grant-free NOMA system. IEEE Internet Things J. **7**(7), 6369–6379 (2020)
21. Maraqa, O., Rajasekaran, A.S., Al-Ahmadi, S., Yanikomeroglu, H., Sait, S.M.: A survey of rate-optimal power domain NOMA with enabling technologies of future wireless networks. IEEE Commun. Surv. Tutor. **22**(4), 2192–2235 (2020)
22. Wei, F., Zhou, T., Xu, T., Hu, H.: Modeling and analysis on two-way relay networks: a joint mechanism using NOMA and network coding. IEEE Access **7**, 152679–152689 (2019)
23. Napolitano, A.: Cyclostationarity: new trends and applications. Sig. Process. **120**, 385–408 (2016)
24. Wang, X., Zhou, T., Xu, T., Feng, S., Hu, H., Jin, Y.: Fragmental weight-conservation combining scheme for statistical signal transmissions under fast time-varying channels. China Commun. **17**(1), 118–128 (2020)
25. Patra, A.N., Regis, P.A., Sengupta, S.: Distributed allocation and dynamic reassignment of channels in UAV networks for wireless coverage. Pervasive Mob. Comput. **54**, 58–70 (2019)
26. Xu, T., Zhang, M., Hu, H.: Harmonious coexistence of heterogeneous wireless networks in unlicensed bands: solutions from the statistical signal transmission technique. IEEE Veh. Technol. Mag. **14**(2), 61–69 (2019)
27. Chung, K.: NOMA for correlated information sources in 5G systems. IEEE Commun. Lett. **25**(2), 422–426 (2021)
28. Yin, Y., Peng, Y., Liu, M., Yang, J., Gui, G.: Dynamic user grouping-based NOMA over Rayleigh fading channels. IEEE Access **7**, 110964–110971 (2019)
29. Liu, X., Zhai, X.B., Lu, W., Wu, C.: QoS-guarantee resource allocation for multi-beam satellite industrial Internet of Things with NOMA. IEEE Trans. Ind. Inform. **17**(3), 2052–2061 (2021)
30. Zhang, H., Zhang, H., Liu, W., Long, K., Dong, J., Leung, V.C.M.: Energy efficient user clustering, hybrid precoding and power optimization in terahertz MIMO-NOMA systems. IEEE J. Sel. Areas Commun. **38**(9), 2074–2085 (2020)
31. 3rd Generation Partnership Project (3GPP); Technical Specification Group Radio Access Network; Evolved Universal Terrestrial Radio Access (E-UTRA); Physical Channels and Modulation (Release 15), 3GPP TS 36.211 V15.1.0 (2018)
32. Iradukunda, N., Nguyen, H.T., Hwang, W.: On cyclic delay diversity-based single-carrier scheme in spectrum sharing systems. IEEE Commun. Lett. **23**(6), 1069–1072 (2019)
33. Kim, K.J., Liu, H., Wen, M., Orlik, P.V., Poor, H.V.: Secrecy performance analysis of distributed asynchronous cyclic delay diversity-based cooperative single carrier systems. IEEE Trans. Commun. **68**(5), 2680–2694 (2020)

34. Axell, E., Leus, G., Larsson, E.G., Poor, H.V.: Spectrum sensing for cognitive radio: state-of-the-art and recent advances. IEEE Sig. Process. Mag. **29**(3), 101–116 (2012)
35. Sun, H., Yuan, S., Luo, Y.: Cyclic spectral analysis of vibration signals for centrifugal pump fault characterization. IEEE Sens. J. **18**(7), 2925–2933 (2018)
36. Camara, T.V.R.O., Lima, A.D.L., Lima, B.M.M., Fontes, A.I.R., Martins, A.D.M., Silveira, L.F.Q.: Automatic modulation classification architectures based on cyclostationary features in impulsive environments. IEEE Access **7**, 138512–138527 (2019)

Fuzzy MP - A Fuzzy Digital Signature Scheme with Biometrics

Tiong-Sik Ng⬤ and Andrew Beng-Jin Teoh$^{(\boxtimes)}$⬤

School of Electrical and Electronic Engineering,
Yonsei University, Seoul, South Korea
{ngtiongsik,bjteoh}@yonsei.ac.kr

Abstract. The combination of biometrics and cryptography have consistently remained an open problem due to the probabilistic nature of the former and the deterministic nature of the latter. Various fuzzy cryptosystem schemes have arisen in hopes of combining primitives for both disciplines, mostly for practical purposes. In cryptographic primitives, particularly the digital signature, most of the fuzzy signature schemes rely on the fuzzy extractor to generate keys for the algorithm. It is claimed that said schemes can be readily used with biometric inputs due to their fuzzy nature. In our proposed work which we coin the Fuzzy MP scheme, we use an approach different from the fuzzy extractor for a fuzzy signature scheme. The Fuzzy MP selects the keys independently from the biometric input, while the biometric inputs are actively involved in the signature generation. As a proof-of-concept of using biometric inputs, experiments on face biometrics have been conducted. The Fuzzy MP relies on a biometric template protection scheme, and a cryptographic attribute-based credential system based on the monic polynomial for signature generation. The signature and verification processes both are dependent on the pairing protocol of Elliptic Curve Cryptography.

Keywords: Digital signature · Biometrics · Fuzzy cryptography

1 Introduction

Biometrics such as face, fingerprint, and iris, are unique to every individual, such that no two person have exactly the same biometric data [15]. Due to the uniqueness of the biometric data, it can be said that each person is able to claim that their biometric templates truly belongs to them alone, which also signifies a non-repudiation property. However, one major limitation of biometrics is that once if a person's biometric template (a reference stored in the database) is compromised, the replacement is nearly impossible.

Cryptography on the other hand, is targeted towards the protection and security of a deterministic data, *i.e.*, a message. Two de-facto schemes from cryptography are encryption and digital signature, wherein the former's goal is to encrypt a data using a public key to produce a ciphertext [18], such that if an

© ICST Institute for Computer Sciences, Social Informatics and Telecommunications Engineering 2022
Published by Springer Nature Switzerland AG 2022. All Rights Reserved
C. T. Calafate et al. (Eds.): MONAMI 2021, LNICST 418, pp. 299–315, 2022.
https://doi.org/10.1007/978-3-030-94763-7_23

unauthorized party obtains the ciphertext, the said party is not able to obtain the message easily without the secret key (which is only known by the authorized party). As for the latter, the process is reversed, such that a digital signature is generated using a secret key and an input data [10]. The signature can be verified using the public key, which signifies the purpose of a digital signature; a non-repudiatable authentication system, since the public and secret key pairs involved in the signature can only belong to the signer.

It is well known that cryptography and biometrics are not able to integrate well due to the different natures of two fields: the former being exact, while the latter being fuzzy. Researchers have always coveted the idea of integrating biometrics into cryptography, particularly for the purpose of protecting the biometric data, $i.e.$, biometric template protection. However, it is not a simple feat to achieve. Fuzzy inputs to cryptography, especially biometric data, are considered as noise due to its stochasticism, which most cryptographic primitives lack the robustness to handle such data. However, if combined decently, both are able to complement each other to produce an adequate biometric cryptosystem, be it for biometric template protection using cryptography, or for cryptographic applications using biometric inputs.

1.1 Related Works

The usage of biometrics for cryptography, especially for cryptographic key generation is not new, as the proposal of the idea can be dated back up to 1998 [14]. However, the usage of biometrics back then was still rather unstable, considering the high Equal Error Rate (EER). In 2001, a biometric-based digital signature scheme was proposed [8] based on the RSA [18] and DSA [10] algorithm, which demonstrates their algorithm as an extension to the successful iris recognition technology at that time. The signature generation and verification hinges on the usage of the closest number in the template which is relative to the RSA prime $\phi(\mathbb{N})$. However, due to the nature of the RSA and DSA cryptosystem, a large key size is involved during the computation.

In 2005, Sahai and Waters formalized the fuzzy identity-based encryption [19], which gives rise to various fuzzy cryptosystems. This leads to the introduction of the Fuzzy Identity-Based Signature (IBS) by Yang $et\ al.$ in 2008 [26]. The Fuzzy IBS is considered "fuzzy" in the sense that the signature is generated from a private key extracted from a biometric template. This method of extracting a private key from biometric template is similar in spirit to the Fuzzy Extractor [1].

A few years later, Wang and Kim [24] then took upon the liberty to further formalize the security notion of the Fuzzy IBS based on the discrete logarithm (DL) hard problem. This led to a definition of a Fuzzy IBS scheme with provable security [25]. To put it simply, provable security [17] is the linking of a cryptographic scheme to a hard problem (which is considered hard to brute force and is nearly impossible to inverse) via security proofs and mathematical equations, to show that the scheme is secure. The scheme is said to be tightly secure if the probability of breaking the scheme is equals to the probability of solving the hard problem.

Different from the Fuzzy IBS schemes, Takahashi *et al.* introduced the fuzzy signature [22], which is said to be a new notion of digital signatures. The fuzzy signature adopts the generation of a fuzzy signing key instead of a fuzzy verification key. The advantage of Takahashi *et al.*'s scheme is that a helper data (HD) - additional credentials that are involved in biometric authentication, is not required to generate a signature, but the signing is solely dependent on the fuzzy input. The linear sketch was also proposed in their work for error correction purposes, which is necessary at times when biometric templates are involved.

1.2 Motivations

Based on the schemes discussed in Sect. 1.1, it is said that the fuzzy signature schemes proposed so far are able to handle biometric data as input. Such schemes utilize the fuzzy extractor notion [1], such that a cryptographic key is generated from a given biometric input.

Though this notion negates the needs of key and parameter management, it poses the risk of false accepts, where similar biometric templates of different identities are distinguished as the same identity, which in turn leads to the false acceptance of a mismatched template. In addition to that, Error Correction Codes (ECC) are usually employed to mitigate the fuzziness of two biometric instances of the same person, which further increases security issues, wherein the parity storage creates another point of attack for an adversary to obtain the original data [21].

Besides that, the fuzzy signature schemes discussed thus far have not considered biometric template protection notion, where an enrolled biometric input is altered or transformed to "protect" the raw input, such that the protected template can be stored or used instead [15]. This is particularly vital considering that biometric templates cannot be replaced once compromised.

1.3 Our Contribution

In this paper, we propose the Fuzzy MP scheme, where we make use of face biometric as a proof-of-concept for a digital signature scheme. To avoid the storage of the raw templates due to security concerns, biometric template protection scheme is considered. To fulfill this, we apply the Distance Recoverable Encryption (DRE) scheme [12] and the Index-of-Max (IoM) hashing [9]. The DRE serves as a first layer of security by encrypting the face templates, which is followed up by a second layer of protection, which would be the IoM hashing.

Besides protecting the raw face templates (face features) from being revealed, the hashed templates from the IoM hashing are also cancelable, such that the hashed templates can be revoked and renewed if compromised. Due to the performance preserving properties of the DRE and the IoM hashing, there is no glaring degradation in the verification accuracy of the encrypted vectors and the hashed codes respectively. Thus, the usage of the ECC module can be avoided, considering the security risks it poses.

The Fuzzy MP scheme works in a way such that the public and secret keys are selected independently from the biometric data. Instead, we used the face template as part of the digital signature. Though there still lies the issue of key management, our proposed method reduces the possibility of false accepts. Moreover, the biometric templates are protected by the secret key, where an adversary is not able to distinguish between the template and the key. Likewise, the secret key in turn, also protects the biometric templates.

The digital signature algorithm of the Fuzzy MP relies on a modified version of the MoniPoly Attribute-Based Credential (ABC) scheme [23], which is tightly reduced to the $q-$strong co-Diffie-Hellman (co-SDH) hard problem. Given that the scheme is reliant on a credential generation using attributes, we use the biometric data as the attributes to generate the signature. We further provide proof-of-concept experiments on the proposed scheme.

1.4   Organization

This paper is organized as follows. In Sect. 2, we first define the various tools and methods that play a part in constructing our scheme. In Sect. 3, we then define the overview of our scheme, alongside the details in each modules involved. Section 4 then illustrates the experiments and simulation conducted, alongside the security analysis of our scheme. We conclude our findings in Sect. 5.

2   Preliminaries

2.1   Digital Signature Scheme

A digital signature consists of three polynomial-time algorithms: **Key Generation**, **Sign**, and **Verify**. The first two algorithms are probabilistic. The algorithms are described as follows:

1. **Key Generation** $(1^k) \rightarrow (pk, sk)$: A pair of public and secret keys are generated based on the security parameter input 1^k. The public key pk can be transmitted openly, while the secret key sk is kept secret by the user.
2. **Sign** $(m, sk) \rightarrow \sigma$: The user uses the secret key sk to sign on a message m to generate a signature, which is denoted as σ.
3. **Verify** $(m, \sigma, pk) \rightarrow 1/0$: The verifier takes the public key pk and σ as the input to ensure that the signature is genuinely signed by the user. If the signature is authentic, the algorithm returns "1", and "0" otherwise.

2.2   Bilinear Pairing

Let $\mathbb{G}_1$ and $\mathbb{G}_2$ be groups of prime order q based on the curve E over the finite field $\mathbb{F}_p$ where $\mathbb{G}_1 \times \mathbb{G}_2 \to \mathbb{G}_T$. Let g_1 be a generator of $\mathbb{G}_1$ and g_2 be a generator of $\mathbb{G}_2$. Bilinear pairing is a function which maps elements from group $\mathbb{G}_1$ and group $\mathbb{G}_2$ to group $\mathbb{G}_T$, *i.e.*, $e : \mathbb{G}_1 \times \mathbb{G}_2 \to \mathbb{G}_T$. The bilinear pairing function e requires the following properties:

1. Bilinearity: $e(g_1{}^a, g_2{}^b) = e(g_1, g_2)^{ab}$.
2. Non-degeneracy: $e(g_1, g_2) \neq 1$
3. e is efficiently computable, which means there is an algorithm to compute $e(g_1, g_2)$ for any $g_1 \in \mathbb{G}_1$ and $g_2 \in \mathbb{G}_2$.

2.3 $q-$strong co-Diffie-Hellman (co-SDH) Problem

Definition 1. *The $q-$strong co-Diffie-Hellman (co-SDH) Problem [2] is based on the $q-$strong Diffie-Hellman (SDH) Problem [3], with the difference that the co-SDH problem uses the Type-3 pairing [16]. It is said that a polynomial-time algorithm $\mathcal{S}$ ($t_{co-SDH}, \varepsilon_{co-SDH}$)-solves the co-SDH problem for $\mathcal{S}$ running for a time of at most t_{co-SDH} and furthermore:*

$$\left| \Pr[a, b \leftarrow \mathbb{Z}_q^* : \mathcal{S}(g_1, g_1{}^x, ..., g_1{}^{x^q}, g_2, g_2{}^x, ..., g_2{}^{x^q}) = (g^{\frac{1}{x+c}}, c)] \right| \geq \varepsilon_{co-SDH}$$

We assume the co-SDH problem to be $(t_{co-SDH}, \varepsilon_{co-SDH})$-hard in $\mathbb{G}_1$ and $\mathbb{G}_2$ if $\Pr[\mathcal{S}$ solves co-SDH$] \leq \varepsilon_{co-SDH}$ for any $\mathcal{S}$ that runs in time t_{co-SDH}.

2.4   ArcFace Model

The ArcFace model [4] is a face feature extractor based on deep neural networks. To be precise, the ArcFace is a convolutional neural network (CNN) with the ResNet-50 [6] as its backbone architecture. The ArcFace loss function is given as:

$$L = -\frac{1}{N} \sum_{i=1}^{N} \log \frac{e^{s(\cos(\theta_{y_i}+m))}}{e^{s(\cos(\theta_{y_i}+m))} + \sum_{j=1, j \neq y_i}^{n} e^{s \cos \theta_j}}$$

where θ_j represent the angles between the weights and the vectors which are distributed on a hypersphere with radius s, and m represents the margin penalty. The ArcFace model uses face images of size 112×112 as the input, such that a face feature consisting of real values are generated with a dimension of 512 for each image.

2.5   Distance Recoverable Encryption (DRE)

First introduced in [12], the Distance Recoverable Encryption (DRE) preserves the distance between two encrypted vectors without compromising the raw vector (*i.e.*, the raw biometric template). To be specific, with an encryption function E, the encryption of the DRE scheme on two vectors $\vec{\mathcal{X}}$ and $\vec{\mathcal{Y}}$ produces $E(\vec{\mathcal{X}})$ and $E(\vec{\mathcal{Y}})$ such that the distances $\mathrm{Dist}(\vec{\mathcal{X}}, \vec{\mathcal{Y}}) = \mathrm{Dist}(E(\vec{\mathcal{X}}), E(\vec{\mathcal{Y}}))$. The DRE scheme is defined as follows.

Given an orthogonal matrix M where the inverse and transpose of M are equal, such that $M^{-1} \cdot M = M^T \cdot M = I$, where I is the identity matrix. With a user secret key u_{sk}, the encryption is performed by utilizing the following functions:

- Generate a pseudorandom orthogonal matrix $M \in \mathbb{R}^{n \times n}$ from pseudorandom function $\mathrm{PRF}_M(u_{sk})$.
- Generate a pseudorandom vector $\vec{v} \in \mathbb{R}^n$ from pseudorandom function $\mathrm{PRF}_V(u_{sk})$.
- Perform a pseudorandom permutation $\pi(\vec{\mathcal{X}})$ from pseudorandom permutation $\mathrm{PRP}(u_{sk}, \vec{\mathcal{X}})$.

The encryption of the vector is defined as $\vec{c}_{\mathcal{X}} = (\pi(\vec{\mathcal{X}}) + \vec{v})M$.

2.6   Index-of-Max (IoM) Hashing

The Index-of-Max (IoM) hashing [9] is a ranking based hashing proposed as a means of biometrics template protection. The IoM hashing is said to preserve performance in terms of accuracy, where the distance of the "hashed codes" which are generated in integers, are rather similar to the distance of the same raw templates. In short, the IoM hashing is mainly used for the purpose of cancelable biometrics. The IoM hashing scheme, particularly the Gaussian Random Projection (GRP) variant which we will be using, is described as follows.

1. For a feature vector $\mathbf{x} \in \mathbb{R}^d$ and user secret key u_{sk}, set the random seed using u_{sk}, and generate a random Gaussian matrix with $\mathbf{W}$, such that $\mathbf{W} \in \mathbb{R}^{d \times q \times m}$.
2. Multiply $\mathbf{x}$ with $\mathbf{W}$ to obtain $z \in \mathbb{R}^{1 \times q \times m}$.
3. For each z_i such that $i = 1, ..., m$, record the maximum index in the q-th axis to obtain the hash codes $q \in \mathbb{R}^m$.

2.7   MoniPoly Commitment Scheme

The MoniPoly Attribute-Based Credential (ABC) scheme [23] is proposed for the privacy of multiple attributes in mind. In this section, we define the MoniPoly commitment scheme[1], which gives rise to the MoniPoly SDH-CL signature and the MoniPoly ABC scheme, which we will define later on.

---

[1] We did not include the **OpenDifference** and **VerifyDifference** algorithms in this definition, as the **Intersection** algorithms are sufficient for our case.

1. **Setup** $(1^k, n) \rightarrow (pk, sk)$. Construct cyclic groups $\mathbb{G}_1, \mathbb{G}_2, \mathbb{G}_T$ based on prime order p and bilinear pairing $e : \mathbb{G}_1 \times \mathbb{G}_2 \rightarrow \mathbb{G}_T$. Then, select random generators $g_1 \overset{R}{\in} \mathbb{G}_1, g_2 \overset{R}{\in} \mathbb{G}_2$ and generate random number $x \overset{R}{\in} \mathbb{Z}_p^*$. For number of attributes n, compute values $\{a_0, a_1, ..., a_n\} = \{g_1, g_1{}^x, ..., g_1{}^{x^n}\}$ and $\{X_0, X_1, ..., X_n\} = \{g_2, g_2{}^x, ..., g_2{}^{x^n}\}$. The public key and secret key[2] are: $pk = (e, \mathbb{G}_1, \mathbb{G}_2, \mathbb{G}_T, p, \{a_i, X_i\}_{0 \leq i \leq n}), sk = (x)$.

2. **Commit** $(pk, A, o) \rightarrow (C)$. For a set of message $A = \{m_1, ..., m_{n-1}\} \in \mathbb{Z}_p^*$ and a random open value $o \overset{R}{\in} \mathbb{Z}_p^*$, generate a commitment value C. Given $\{m_j\} = \mathsf{MPEncode}^3(A \cup \{o\})$, the value C is given as:

$$C = a_0{}^{(x+o) \prod_{j=1}^{n-1}(x+m_j)} = \prod_{j=0}^{n} a_j{}^{m_j}$$

3. **Open** $(pk, C, A, o) \rightarrow 1/0$. The prover (person who committed earlier) reveals message A' and opening value o'. Compute the value $C' = \prod_{j=0}^{n} a_j{}^{m'_j}$, where $m'_j = \mathsf{MPEncode}(A' \cup \{o'\})$. If the value of $C' = C$, return 1 to accept; else return 0 to reject.

4. **OpenIntersection** $(pk, C, A, o, (A', \ell)) \rightarrow (I, W)/ \perp$. For a threshold ℓ and given $\{w_j\} = \mathsf{MPEncode}((A - I) \cup o)$, return $\perp$ if the ℓ is not met; otherwise return an intersection set $I = A' \cap A$ and witness W if $|A' \cap A| \geq \ell$ holds such that:

$$C = \left(\prod_{j=0}^{n-\ell} a_j{}^{w_j} \right)^{\prod_{m_j \in I} x + m_j}$$

$$= W^{\prod_{m_j \in I} x + m_j}$$

5. **VerifyIntersection** $(pk, C, (I, W), (A', \tilde{\ell})) \rightarrow 1/0$. Given $\{i_j\} = \mathsf{MPEncode}(I)$, $\{m_{1,j}\} = \mathsf{MPEncode}(A')$, and $\{m_{2,j}\} = \mathsf{MPEncode}(A' - I)$, return 1 iff the following check equation as the following is met.

$$e \left(C \prod_{j=0}^{|A'|} a_j{}^{m_{1,j}}, X_0 \right) = e \left(W \prod_{j=0}^{|A'|-\ell} a_j{}^{m_{2,j}}, \prod_{j=0}^{\ell} X_j{}^{i_j} \right)$$

---

[2] sk can be discarded if n is fixed.
[3] MPEncode is the mapping of $\mathbb{Z}_p^n$ to $\mathbb{Z}_p^{n+1}$.

3   Proposed Scheme

3.1   Overview of our Proposed Scheme

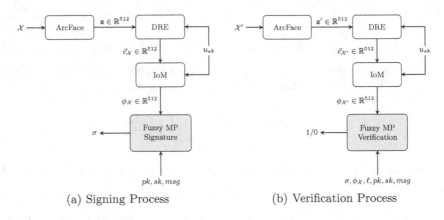

(a) Signing Process   (b) Verification Process

Fig. 1. Overview of fuzzy MP signature scheme

The overview of our scheme is presented in Fig. 1. To begin with the signing process, the raw biometric inputs $\mathcal{X}$ are extracted using the ArcFace, which result in (face) biometric features $\mathbf{z}$ with a dimension of 512. The feature is then encrypted using the DRE to obtain the encrypted vector $\vec{c}_{\mathcal{X}}$, with the help of a (user) secret key u_{sk}. With the same u_{sk}[4], the hash codes of the encrypted vectors $\phi_{\mathcal{X}}$, are generated using the IoM hashing. Given the public and secret keys (pk, sk) with the hashed codes $\phi_{\mathcal{X}}$ as inputs, the digital signature σ is generated.

Similar to the signing process, the verification of the generated digital signature σ is initiated with the feature extraction, encryption, and hashing process. This is used to show that the prover (*i.e.*, the user who wants prove that σ is his signature) is the authentic signer using his biometric template. By the comparison of an honest prover's extracted template $\phi_{\mathcal{X}'}$ with $\phi_{\mathcal{X}}$, the signature will be proven authentic if a certain threshold set by the verifier ℓ is met. We now further elaborate on each modules shown in Fig. 1.

3.2   ArcFace Feature Extractor

For face feature extraction, which is to be used as raw face template after enrollment or as query during signature verification, we used a pretrained ArcFace network. The face images were resized to 112×112 pixels prior to feature extraction. For each of the image, an output face feature vector $\mathbf{z} \in \mathbb{R}^{512}$ is generated.

---

[4] The u_{sk} may be selected by the user, such as a user-specific password to be kept by the user. Though it is shown that the u_{sk} is the same one used for the DRE, the u_{sk} may be a different user secret key too. This will be further elaborated later on.

3.3   Distance Recoverable Encryption (DRE)

Given the output of the ArcFace feature extractor $\mathbf{z} \in \mathbb{R}^{512}$ and a user secret key $u_{sk} \in \mathbb{Z}_q^*$ as inputs, an encrypted feature vector $\vec{c}_{\mathcal{X}} \in \mathbb{R}^{512}$ is generated. As the randomness of the vectors and permutation are greatly affected by the state of randomness, the u_{sk} plays a role as a seed to generate the random vectors and perform the random permutation. With the same u_{sk}, a query biometric template would be permuted and operated on with the same random vectors. Thus, this ensures the distance preservation of the generated vectors.

3.4   Index-of-Max (IoM) Hashing

In consideration that the IoM hashing utilizes the generation of a random Gaussian matrix, the mean and covariance values (μ, σ) are crucial. Apart from that, the randomness of the matrix are also reliant on the random seed, similar to the DRE. Thus, a user specific key can be defined for this purpose. Though it is desirable to use the same u_{sk} as the one in the DRE to avoid key management issues, it is suggested to use a different key instead for better security. Regardless, an appropriate secure key is sufficient to perform the hashing, since the generated hash codes $(\phi_{\mathcal{X}})$ are considered to be cancellable templates.

3.5   Fuzzy MP Signature

The definition of the Fuzzy MP signature scheme is two-fold. The main essence of the signature is based on the MoniPoly variant of the SDH-CL signature [20], where a message is signed on a set of attributes. However, since the MoniPoly SDH-CL is unable to perform verification for fuzzy inputs, we make use of the show proofs defined in the MoniPoly ABC scheme, particularly the ANY/OR proof for the verification.

Apart from handling fuzzy inputs, the verification used for the proposed Fuzzy MP scheme enables the prover (in this case, the signer) to achieve anonymity during the signature verification. To be specific, the intersection of the signing and proving templates are not known to the verifier. A more detailed definition of our scheme is shown in Algorithms 1 and 2, which corresponds to Fig. 1. It is noted that both algorithms demonstrate the honest signature and verification process, where the signer and prover are the same person wherein both templates are within a set threshold ℓ, (i.e., $u_{sk} = u'_{sk}, sk = sk'$, and $(\mathcal{X} \approx \mathcal{X}' || |\mathcal{X} \cap \mathcal{X}'| \geq \ell)$).

It is noted that if a message msg is to be signed, it is appended to $\phi_{\mathcal{X}}$ such that an extra public key value is generated for each element in $\phi_{\mathcal{X}}$, including the message. This msg value corresponds to an extra attribute in the scheme. The same procedure is repeated during the signature verification, where msg is appended to the prover's feature vectors $\phi_{\mathcal{X}'}$.

---

[5] At this point, it can be said that the pairing here is already sufficient to prove the authenticity of the signature, considering that $\phi_{\mathcal{X}}$ is stored. However, an extra pairing process is used during the verification algorithm to prevent replay attacks.

Algorithm 1: Fuzzy MP Signing Algorithm

Input: pk, sk
Output: Signature σ
Data: Signer template $\mathcal{X}$, user secret key u_{sk}
Function ExtractFeatures($\mathcal{X}, u_{sk}$):
| ArcFace($\mathcal{X}$) $\rightarrow \mathbf{z}$
| DRE($\mathbf{z}, u_{sk}$) $\rightarrow \vec{c}_{\mathcal{X}}$
| IoM($\vec{c}_{\mathcal{X}}, u_{sk}$) $\rightarrow \phi_{\mathcal{X}}$
| **return** $\phi_{\mathcal{X}}$

Function KeyGen(1^k):
| $\mathbb{G}_1, \mathbb{G}_2, \mathbb{G}_T$, bilinear pairing $e : \mathbb{G}_1 \times \mathbb{G}_2 \rightarrow \mathbb{G}_T$
| $g_1, b, c \in \mathbb{G}_1,\ g_2 \in \mathbb{G}_2,\ X = g_2{}^{x'},\ x, x', op \overset{R}{\in} \mathbb{Z}_p^*$
| $\{a_0, a_1, ..., a_n\} = \{g_1, g_1{}^x, ..., g_1{}^{x^n}\},\ \{X_0, X_1, ..., X_n\} = \{g_2, g_2{}^x, ..., g_2{}^{x^n}\}$
| $pk = (e, \mathbb{G}_1, \mathbb{G}_2, \mathbb{G}_T, p, b, c, X, \{a_i, X_i\}_{0 \le i \le n}),\ sk = (x, x', op)$
| **return** pk, sk

Function Sign($pk, sk, \phi_{\mathcal{X}}$):
| $s_1, s_2, t \overset{R}{\in} \mathbb{Z}_p^*$, set $\phi_{\mathcal{X}} = (\phi_{\mathcal{X}} \cup \{op\})$
| MPEncode($\phi_{\mathcal{X}}$) $\rightarrow \Phi_{\mathcal{X}} = (\Phi_0, \Phi_1, ..., \Phi_n)$
| $M = \prod_{j=0}^{n} a_j{}^{\Phi_j} b^{s_1},\ s = s_1 + s_2,\ v = (M b^{s_2} c)^{1/(x'+t)}$
| **if** $e(v, X) = e\left(M b^{s_2} c v^{-t}, X_0\right)$ **then**
| | **return**$^5 \sigma = (t, s, v)$
| **end**

---

4 Experiments and Analysis

4.1 Experiment Setup

The implementation and experiments for our scheme are conducted using Python. The main reason for doing so is due to the procedure of extracting face features from the biometric inputs using the ArcFace feature extractor. For the machine, Linux Ubuntu 16.04 is used for the OS, which runs on an NVIDIA RTX 2080 Ti D6 GPU and an Intel i9-9900K CPU with 3.60 GHz and 8 cores. The pre-trained ArcFace feature extractor is applied using TensorFlow v1.14.0 and the GPU.

As for the dataset, we utilize an unconstrained face dataset, namely the Learning From Wild (LFW) [7]. To be precise, we conduct the signing and verification using the standard LFW evaluation protocol which consists of 3000 pairs of matched and non-matched identities each.

Since the signature and verification algorithms of the Fuzzy MP scheme are dependent on bilinear pairing, we make use of the MIRACL [13] library, a pairing-friendly cryptography library, particulary the Python variation. We utilize the

---

Algorithm 2: Fuzzy MP Verification Algorithm

Input: $pk, sk', \phi_{\mathcal{X}}, \sigma$
Output: $1/0$
Data: Prover template $\mathcal{X}'$, user secret key u'_{sk}, threshold ℓ
Function ExtractFeatures$(\mathcal{X}, u'_{sk})$:

> ArcFace$(\mathcal{X}') \rightarrow \mathbf{z}'$
> DRE$(\mathbf{z}', u'_{sk}) \rightarrow \vec{c}_{\mathcal{X}'}$
> IoM$(\vec{c}_{\mathcal{X}'}, u'_{sk}) \rightarrow \phi_{\mathcal{X}'}$
> **return** $\phi_{\mathcal{X}'}$

Function Verify$(pk, sk', \phi_{\mathcal{X}}, \phi_{\mathcal{X}'}, \sigma, \ell)$:

> **Prover:**
> Compute $I = |\phi_{\mathcal{X}'} \cap \phi_{\mathcal{X}}| \geq \ell$, where $\phi_{\mathcal{X}'} = (\phi_{\mathcal{X}'} \cup \{op\})$
> $\{w'_j\}_{0 \leq j \leq n-\ell} = \mathsf{MPEncode}(\phi_{\mathcal{X}} - I), \{m_{2,j}\}_{0 \leq j \leq k-\ell} = \mathsf{MPEncode}(\phi_{\mathcal{X}'} - I)$
> $$W = \left(\prod_{j=0}^{n-\ell} a_j^{w'_j} \right), W' = \left(\prod_{j=0}^{k-\ell} a_j^{m_{2,j}} \right)$$
> **Verifier:**
> $\{m_{1,j}\}_{0 \leq j \leq k} = \mathsf{MPEncode}(\phi_{\mathcal{X}'}), \{\iota_j\}_{0 \leq j \leq \ell} = \mathsf{MPEncode}(I)$
> **if** $e\left(W'W, \prod_{j=0}^{\ell} X_j^{\iota_j} \right) e\left(\prod_{j=0}^{k} a_j^{-m_{1,j}} b^s cv^{-t}, X_0 \right) = e\,(v, X)$ **then**
>> **return** 1
>
> **end**
> **else**
>> **return** 0
>
> **end**

BN-462 elliptic curve for that purpose. The encryption, hashing, and signature/verification are carried out using the CPU. It is noted that the DRE and IoM hashing are also run using the CPU.

For the performance evaluation, we apply the Equal Error Rate (EER) and the Receiver Operating Characteristic (ROC) curve as a performance measurement for the encryption and hashing (*i.e.*, DRE and IoM hashing) procedures. To that end, we employ the cosine distance as a similarity metric. On the other hand, we set the threshold for the signature and verification algorithms using the Hamming distance between the signer and prover's feature vectors in computing the EER for the signature verification.

4.2   Performance Measurement

For the performance comparison described in this section, the following procedure is referred to.

$$\mathrm{ArcFace}(\mathbf{z}) \Rightarrow \mathrm{DRE}(\vec{c}_{\mathcal{X}}) \Rightarrow \mathrm{IoM}(\phi_{\mathcal{X}}) \Rightarrow \text{Fuzzy MP}(\sigma)$$

Parameter Analysis. Table 1 outlines the Equal Error Rate (EER) percentage for different q parameter values. As the face features $\mathbf{z}$ and the encrypted vectors $\vec{c}_\chi$ are not affected by any parameter values, only the results of ϕ_χ and σ are tabulated in Table 1. In consideration that the encrypted vector $\vec{c}_\chi$ has a dimension of 512 due to the ArcFace feature extractor, the parameter m for the IoM hashing is fixed to 512 as well.

Table 1. EER for different q parameters for $m = 512$

EER (%)	q				
	8	16	32	64	128
IoM (ϕ_χ)	**4.23**	5.00	4.57	**4.23**	5.47
Fuzzy MP (σ)	**3.33**	3.50	**3.33**	3.53	3.40

In Table 1, notice that the EER for the Fuzzy MP signature is rather low in comparison to that of the IoM hashing. This is attributed to the usage of Hamming distance, in consideration that the Fuzzy MP signature relies on element-wise comparison between ϕ_χ and $\phi_{\chi'}$ to set the threshold.

Performance of ArcFace, DRE, and IoM Hashing. Figure 2 illustrates the Receiver Operating Characteristic (ROC) curve for the ArcFace, DRE, and IoM hashing feature vectors, particularly for the one where the EER value of ϕ_χ is 4.23. To be precise, the ArcFace curve signifies $\mathbf{z}$, the DRE curve signifies $\vec{c}_\chi$, and the IoM curve signifies ϕ_χ. It is noted that the same u_{sk} is used for performing both the DRE and IoM hashing.

Based on Fig. 2, it can be observed that both the curves for the ArcFace extracted features and the DRE encrypted feature vectors are almost similar. This shows that the DRE is able to preserve the distance performance, which is particularly important in distinguishing genuine and impostor features. As for the IoM hashing, the performance is slightly degraded. The EER based on the curve shown in Fig. 2 is presented in Table 2.

Table 2. EER of feature vectors

Feature	ArcFace	DRE	IoM
EER (%)	3.50	3.10	4.23

Performance of Fuzzy MP Signature. The overall timing to run the algorithms as well as the asymptotic complexity are tabulated in Table 3. For the time taken, an average for a total of 100 rounds of each algorithm are taken for the simulation.

Table 3. Simulation and complexity for fuzzy MP signature

Algorithm	Asymptotic complexity	Time (ms)
Key Gen	$\mathcal{O}(n)$	109,755
Sign	$\mathcal{O}(2n)$	39,777
Verify	$\mathcal{O}(n + 2k)$	28,461

Note: $k = |\phi_{\chi'}| \leq n = |\phi_{\chi}|$

It can be deduced that the values shown in Table 3 is not optimal, as the simulation is carried out using Python. Some possible ways of improving the timing is by implementing a parallelized version of the algorithms, and also by utilizing a GPU for the computations.

4.3 Unlinkability Analysis

In [23], a detailed unlinkability analysis is shown such that the unlinkability of the values in ϕ_{χ} with the generated σ implies the anonymity of ϕ_{χ}. Therefore, we chose not to emphasize further the unlinkability for the Fuzzy MP signature with ϕ_{χ}, since it is already proven.

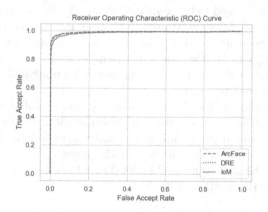

Fig. 2. ROC curve of feature vectors

Instead, in consideration that there is also a lack of unlinkability analysis for the DRE [12], we evaluate the unlinkability of the feature vectors that are generated before the Fuzzy MP signing process. The unlinkability of the feature vectors are equally important to prevent cross-matching attacks, where an adversary is able to obtain the raw templates through compromising the matching scores, taking into account the storage of ϕ_{χ}.

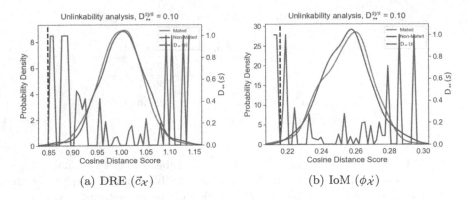

(a) DRE ($\vec{c}_\chi$)   (b) IoM ($\phi_{\dot{\chi}}$)

Fig. 3. Unlinkability analysis

In order to do so, we conduct the evaluation based on the protocol by [5]. The mated sample requires the generation of protected templates with *different seeds* for the *same instances*, while the non-mated sample requires the generation of protected templates with *different seeds* for *different instances*. We carry out the protocol using 10 random seed instances. The results of the unlinkability analysis are disclosed in Fig. 3.

Following the proposed unlinkability protocol [5], the local and global measures are given as $D_{\leftrightarrow}(s) \in [0,1]$ and $D_{\leftrightarrow}^{sys} \in [0,1]$ respectively. For the local measure $D_{\leftrightarrow}(s)$, the score $s = 0$ signifies that an adversary is not able to decide if a protected template is from the same person, and 1 for vice versa. As for the global measure $D_{\leftrightarrow}^{sys}$, the score 0 signifies full unlinkability for the mated subjects, and 1 for vice versa.

In Fig. 3, it is shown that both $\vec{c}_\chi$ and ϕ_χ has a global measure of 0.10, which shows a sufficiently good score of unlinkability. However, there is still room for improvement in the unlinkability analysis, especially for ϕ_χ. One possible improvement is to replace the IoM hashing with the Softmax-Out Transformation Permutation Network (SOTPN) [11], which was dubbed as the neural network version of the URP-IoM [9].

4.4   Security Attacks

In this section, we examine the durability of our scheme in terms of security. We begin by formalizing an adversary $\mathcal{A}$ that intends to attack the scheme from multiple angles. For each of the attacks defined, we first state $\mathcal{A}$'s goals, and how our scheme is able to handle such attacks.

Collision Attack. Also known as the brute force attack in this case, $\mathcal{A}$'s goal in conducting collision attacks is to be able to forge the signature using numerous repetition of biometric templates and user keys, to cause a collision of signature (*i.e.*, a forger) with one of the eventual combinations. However, the likeliness of a collision between (ϕ_X, op) and $(\phi_{X'}, op')$ is unlikely if he does not know the value of op [23]. This means that $\mathcal{A}$ is not able to forge the signature σ using $(\phi_{X'}, op')$ via collision unless he is able to solve the co-SDH hard problem.

False Accept Attack. Also known as the dictionary attack, the false accept attack is similar to the collision attack, however to forge a signature with a predetermined set of "close enough" biometric templates. This leads to a false accept of the said biometric templates. As mentioned in the collision attacks, the signature cannot be forged if $\mathcal{A}$ does not have the value of op, as it is assumed that $\mathcal{A}$ has to solve the co-SDH problem without knowing the value of op.

Replay Attack. It is noted that the first pairing in the signing algorithm to authenticate σ is susceptible to replay attacks during the first verification process. In short, $\mathcal{A}$ is able to forge the σ via replay attacks during the pairing process. This leads to the usage of a user's biometric template for the verification process, as the one in Algorithm 2. With the freshness of $\phi_{X'}$ during each verification process, $\mathcal{A}$ is not able to conduct a replay attack, since the returned values will be different each time.

5 Conclusion

In this paper, we presented a fuzzy digital signature scheme, namely the Fuzzy MP. Though the Fuzzy MP still requires key management, the keys used for our scheme are selected independently from the biometric templates, which reduces the risk of false accepts. Through the experiments and analysis conducted thus far using the LFW face dataset, it can be deduced that the Fuzzy MP is able to achieve a satisfactory performance in terms of the EER, though there is still room for improvement in the timing and complexity to run the algorithm.

Acknowledgements. This work was supported by the National Research Foundation of Korea (NRF) grant funded by the Korea government (MSIP) (NO. NRF-2019R1A2C1003306). The authors would also like to thank Syh-Yuan Tan and Thomas Groß for their helpful advice during the implementation of the MoniPoly scheme.

References

1. Boyen, X.: Reusable cryptographic fuzzy extractors. In: Proceedings of the 11th ACM Conference on Computer and Communications Security, pp. 82–91 (2004)
2. Chatterjee, S., Menezes, A.: On cryptographic protocols employing asymmetric pairings-the role of ψ revisited. Discrete Appl. Math. **159**(13), 1311–1322 (2011)
3. Cheon, J.H.: Security analysis of the strong Diffie-Hellman problem. In: Vaudenay, S. (ed.) EUROCRYPT 2006. LNCS, vol. 4004, pp. 1–11. Springer, Heidelberg (2006). https://doi.org/10.1007/11761679_1

4. Deng, J., Guo, J., Xue, N., Zafeiriou, S.: ArcFace: additive angular margin loss for deep face recognition. In Proceedings of the IEEE/CVF Conference on Computer Vision and Pattern Recognition – CVPR 2019, pp. 4690–4699 (2019)
5. Gomez-Barrero, M., Galbally, J., Rathgeb, C., Busch, C.: General framework to evaluate unlinkability in biometric template protection systems. IEEE Trans. Inf. Forensics Secur. 3(6), 1406–1420 (2018)
6. He, K., Zhang, X., Ren, S., Sun, J.: Deep residual learning for image recognition. In: Proceedings of the IEEE Conference on Computer Vision and Pattern Recognition – CVPR 2016, pp. 770–778 (2016)
7. Huang, G.B., Mattar, M., Berg, T., Learned-Miller, E.: Labeled faces in the wild: a database for studying face recognition in unconstrained environments. In: Workshop on Faces in 'Real-Life' Images: Detection, Alignment, and Recognition (2008)
8. Janbandhu, P.K., Siyal, M.Y.: Novel biometric digital signatures for Internet based applications. Inf. Manage. Comput. Secur. (2001)
9. Jin, Z., Hwang, J.Y., Lai, Y.L., Kim, S., Teoh, A.B.J.: Ranking-based locality sensitive hashing-enabled cancelable biometrics: index-of-max hashing. IEEE Trans. Inf. Forensics Secur. 13(2), 393–407 (2017)
10. Kerry, C.F., Director, C.R.: FIPS PUB 186-4 federal information processing standards publication digital signature standard (DSS). FIPS Publication (2013)
11. Lee, H., Low, C.Y., Teoh, A.B.J.: SoftmaxOut transformation-permutation network for facial template protection. In: 2020 25th International Conference on Pattern Recognition (ICPR), pp. 7558–7565. IEEE (2021)
12. Loh, J.C., et al.: PBio: Enabling Cross-organizational Biometric Authentication Service through Secure Sharing of Biometric Templates. Cryptology ePrint Archive: Report 2020/1381 (2020). ia.cr/2020/1381
13. MIRACL: MIRACL Core (2021). https://github.com/miracl/core/tree/master/python
14. Nichols, R.K.: ICSA Guide to Cryptography. McGraw-Hill Professional, New York (1998)
15. Patel, V.M., Ratha, N.K., Chellappa, R.: Cancelable biometrics: a review. IEEE Sig. Process. Mag. 32(5), 54–65 (2015)
16. Pereira, G.C., Simplício, M.A., Naehrig, M., Barreto, P.S.: A family of implementation-friendly BN elliptic curves. J. Syst. Softw. 84(8), 1319–1326 (2011)
17. Pointcheval, D., Stern, J.: Security proofs for signature schemes. In: Maurer, U. (ed.) EUROCRYPT 1996. LNCS, vol. 1070, pp. 387–398. Springer, Heidelberg (1996). https://doi.org/10.1007/3-540-68339-9_33
18. Rivest, R.L., Shamir, A., Adleman, L.: A method for obtaining digital signatures and public-key cryptosystems. Commun. ACM 21(2), 120–126 (1978)
19. Sahai, A., Waters, B.: Fuzzy identity-based encryption. In: Cramer, R. (ed.) EUROCRYPT 2005. LNCS, vol. 3494, pp. 457–473. Springer, Heidelberg (2005). https://doi.org/10.1007/11426639_27
20. Schäge, S.: Tight proofs for signature schemes without random oracles. In: Paterson, K.G. (ed.) EUROCRYPT 2011. LNCS, vol. 6632, pp. 189–206. Springer, Heidelberg (2011). https://doi.org/10.1007/978-3-642-20465-4_12
21. Stoianov, A.: Security of error correcting code for biometric encryption. In: 2010 Eighth Annual International Conference on Privacy Security and Trust (PST), pp. 231–235 (2010)
22. Takahashi, K., Matsuda, T., Murakami, T., Hanaoka, G., Nishigaki, M.: A signature scheme with a fuzzy private key. In: Malkin, T., Kolesnikov, V., Lewko, A.B., Polychronakis, M. (eds.) ACNS 2015. LNCS, vol. 9092, pp. 105–126. Springer, Cham (2015). https://doi.org/10.1007/978-3-319-28166-7_6

23. Tan, S.-Y., Groß, T.: MoniPoly—an expressive q-SDH-Based anonymous attribute-based credential system. In: Moriai, S., Wang, H. (eds.) ASIACRYPT 2020. LNCS, vol. 12493, pp. 498–526. Springer, Cham (2020). https://doi.org/10.1007/978-3-030-64840-4_17

24. Wang, C.J., Kim, J.H.: Two constructions of fuzzy identity based signature. In: 2009 2nd International Conference on Biomedical Engineering and Informatics, pp. 1–5. IEEE (2009)

25. Wang, C.: A provable secure fuzzy identity based signature scheme. Sci. China Inf. Sci. **55**(9), 2139–2148 (2012)

26. Yang, P., Cao, Z., Dong, X.: Fuzzy Identity Based Signature. IACR Cryptology ePrint Archive (2008)

A Fuzzy Logic Controller for Greenhouse Temperature Regulation System Based on Edge Computing

Yue Ren[1(✉)], Celimuge Wu[1], Tsutomu Yoshinaga[1], and Wugedele Bao[2]

[1] The University of Electro-Communications, Tokyo, Japan
r2031172@edu.cc.uec.ac.jp
[2] Hohhot Minzu College, Hohhot, China

Abstract. Temperature and humidity are important factors affecting the growth of greenhouse crops. Reasonable temperature and humidity control can save energy and increase crop yields. This paper proposes a temperature controller based on fuzzy logic theory and applies it to smart greenhouses through edge computing. Temperature and humidity dynamic model and fuzzy logic controller (FLC) of the greenhouse are simulated by using the Simulink toolbox of MATLAB, and verified by comparison with the proportional integral derivative (PID) controller. The results show that in a multivariate greenhouse system, FLC is more stable than multiple PID controllers in temperature regulation of greenhouse.

Keywords: Edge computing · Fuzzy Logic Controller · PID controller · Simulink · Multivariate system

1 Introduction

Greenhouse environment regulation is an important part of modern agriculture. Constructing a semi-closed microclimate greenhouse environment can provide a controllable growth environment for crops, such as temperature, humidity, and light intensity. In [8,15], the authors show that improving the control performance of greenhouses can save energy while improving the efficiency and quality of crop production. The traditional cloud computing-based smart greenhouse control system collects greenhouse data such as temperature and humidity through sensors and other devices. In this mode, sensors need to upload all data to the cloud platform for analysis and backup, and the cloud platform sends control signaling according to the uploaded data, such as the fan settings. In [18], a cloud computing-based greenhouse is proposed to process data centrally, make data analysis and conduct decision-making. But the cloud based approach increases network latency since the data must be uploaded to the cloud platform and the network in the greenhouse widely use low-bandwidth wireless network

© ICST Institute for Computer Sciences, Social Informatics and Telecommunications Engineering 2022
Published by Springer Nature Switzerland AG 2022. All Rights Reserved
C. T. Calafate et al. (Eds.): MONAMI 2021, LNICST 418, pp. 316–332, 2022.
https://doi.org/10.1007/978-3-030-94763-7_24

such as Zigbee. In [7, 14], deploying edge computing in the greenhouse, data can be processed and uploaded to the cloud platform in real-time at edge devices. The users can view and monitor the greenhouse environment status in real-time. The edge computing-based smart greenhouse can realize real-time data processing, reduce network delays and improve data processing efficiency.

In addition, since the greenhouse system is a nonlinear, hysteresis, and multivariable strong-coupling system, the control system deployed at the edge can accurately control environmental variables such as temperature and humidity. The PID control system is a commonly used temperature and humidity control system at present, but due to the strong coupling of the internal environmental variables of the greenhouse system, the PID control system is often difficult to complete the accurate control of the temperature. Therefore, a control system based on FLC that does not need to establish an accurate mathematical model can apply expert experience and play a very important role in a greenhouse control system. FLC has proven to be a successful control approach to many complex nonlinear systems or even nonanalytic systems. It has been suggested as an alternative approach to conventional control techniques in many cases [9].

In this paper, we propose a fuzzy logic based temperature controller for smart greenhouses based on edge computing. The controller can be installed at edge devices, to control the sunshade system, ventilation-wet curtain system, and heating system. We implement a smart greenhouse system by installing the controller on Pi devices where data collection and processing are conducted by Raspberry Pi with multiple sensors at the edge. Raspberry Pi devices upload data to Thingsboard IoT platform for data monitoring and analysis in real-time. We also use Simulink to construct a dynamic greenhouse model of temperature and humidity, and compare the performance of PID controller and FLC in this model.

2   System Structure

As shown in Fig. 1, this system consists of four layers: perception layer, device layer, network layer, and platform & application layer.

Perception Layer. The perception layer is mainly composed of temperature and humidity sensors, light sensors, flame sensors, buzzers, fans, wet curtains, and so on. Considering the factors such as anti-interference, reliability, stability, economy, the sensor uses air temperature and humidity sensor DHT11, light sensor BH1750, flame sensor YG1006. These devices are connected to the Raspberry Pi through the breadboard. The Raspberry Pi periodically collects the data from the sensors and directly controls devices such as fans based on these data. The hardware design diagram of the perception layer device connected to the Raspberry Pi is shown in Fig. 2.

Device Layer. The device layer is composed of multiple Raspberry Pis. The location of each Raspberry Pi can be planned according to the actual spatial structure of the greenhouse to achieve full coverage by deploying Raspberry Pis.

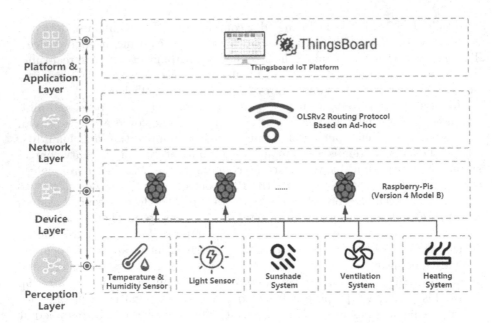

Fig. 1. Smart greenhouse system architecture.

Network Layer. The Raspberry Pi and the platform are interconnected through the ad-hoc network that configured the Optimized Link State Routing Protocol version 2 (OLSRv2) routing protocol. As shown in Fig. 3, each Raspberry Pi will find the shortest path to access the platform according to the OLSRv2 routing table. When a certain Raspberry Pi fails, the OLSRv2 will convergence and switch to another path.

Platform & Application Layer. The platform & application layer is implemented based on the Thingsboard that is an open-source IoT platform. Thingsboard can implement device registration, management, and data receiving and sending by Message Queuing Telemetry Transport (MQTT) protocol, and can configure dashboards for users.

3   Dynamic Modelling and Simulation of Greenhouse

Temperature and humidity are important environmental factors in the greenhouse. On the one hand, they are affected by environmental factors such as outdoor temperature, solar radiation, and on the other hand, they are affected by environmental control facilities such as ventilation systems in the greenhouse. Therefore, on the basis of analyzing the influence of indoor and outdoor factors on the temperature and humidity in the greenhouse, combined with the influence of sunshade system, ventilation-wet curtain system, and heating system on temperature and humidity, this paper proposes a modified dynamic greenhouse

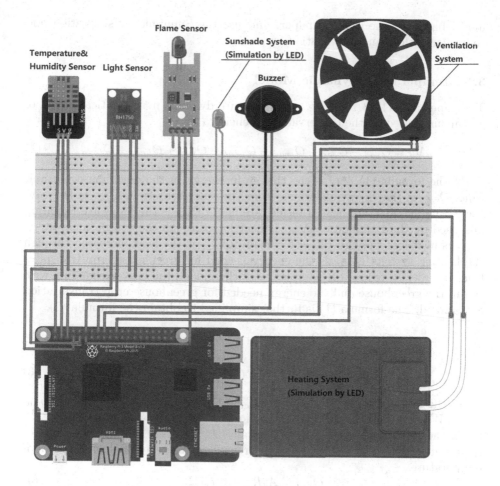

Fig. 2. Hardware design.

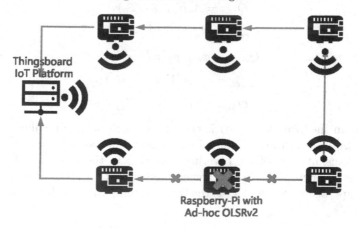

Fig. 3. OLSRv2.

model based on the existing paper, and use the Simulink for simulation and controller performance verification.

3.1   Temperature Dynamic Model

The paper [3,5,11,13,17] gives a temperature dynamic mathematical model of greenhouse based on the conservation of energy (1).

$$\Delta Q = Q_{rad} - Q_{cac} - Q_{crad} - Q_{vent} - Q_{wet} + Q_{heat} + Q_{tran} \tag{1}$$

In the formula (1), ΔQ is the change in energy in the greenhouse per unit time, Q_{rad} is the energy-absorbing from the solar radiation, Q_{cac} is the convection and conduction heat transfer rate, and Q_{crad} is the longwave radiation absorbed by the greenhouse, Q_{vent} is heat loss through the ventilation system, Q_{wet} is heat loss through the wet curtain, Q_{heat} is the heat increased through the heating system, Q_{tran} is the energy needed for greenhouse crop transpiration. In order to reduce the complexity of the model, the heat exchanging with soil in the greenhouse and the energy needed for greenhouse crop transpiration are ignored. The formula (1) is further simplified to obtain the formula (2).

$$\Delta Q = Q_{rad} - Q_{cac} - Q_{crad} - Q_{vent} - Q_{wet} + Q_{heat} \tag{2}$$

$$\Delta Q = V\rho C_p \frac{\mathrm{d}T_i}{\mathrm{d}t} \tag{3}$$

In the formula (2) (3), the unit of Q_{rad}, Q_{cac}, Q_{crad}, Q_{vent}, Q_{wet} and Q_{heat} are all $W \cdot m^{-2}$. V is the volume of greenhouse m^3, ρ is the air density $(kg \cdot m^{-3})$, C_p is the specific heat capacity of the air $(J \cdot kg^{-1} \cdot m^{-3})$, T_i is the indoor temperature (K), and t is time (s), $\frac{\mathrm{d}T_i}{\mathrm{d}t}$ represents the rate of change of indoor temperature.

$$Q_{rad} = A_s I_r \tau + 0.7 A_s I_r \tag{4}$$

$$Q_{cac} = A_s K_g (T_i - T_o) \tag{5}$$

$$Q_{crad} = A_g \varepsilon_{12} \sigma (T_i^4 - T_o^4)) \tag{6}$$

$$Q_{vent} = \phi_{vent} \rho C_p (T_i - T_o) \tag{7}$$

$$Q_{wet} = \phi_{wet} \rho W (H_a - H_b) \tag{8}$$

$$Q_{heat} = A_p h_p (T_p - T_i) \tag{9}$$

Where, in the formula (4), A_s is the surface area of the greenhouse covering material (m^2), I_r is the radiation flux density outdoor $(W \cdot m^{-2})$, and τ is the light transmittance of the covering material. In the formula (5), K_g is the greenhouse cover material heat transfer coefficient $(W \cdot m^{-2} \cdot K^{-1})$, T_i is the indoor temperature (K), and T_o is the outdoor temperature (K). In the formula

(6), ε_{12} is the surface emissivity, and σ is the Stefan-Boltzman constant ($W \cdot m^{-2} \cdot K^{(4)}$). In the formula (7), ϕ_{vent} is the ventilation volume of the ventilation system ($m^3 \cdot s^{-1}$). In the formula (8), ϕ_{wet} is the ventilation rate of the wet curtain ($m^3 \cdot s^{-1}$), W is the latent heat of evaporation, T_{avg} is the average of indoor temperature, H_a is the humidity before the wet curtain (%), and H_b is the humidity after the wet curtain (%). In the formula (7), A_p is the surface area of the heating system (m^2), h_p is the heat transfer coefficient of the heating system, and T_p is the heating system temperature (K).

3.2 Humidity Dynamic Model

The paper [2,12,19] gives a humidity dynamic mathematical model of greenhouse based on the water vapor in greenhouse (10).

$$\Delta E = E_{tran} + E_{wet} - E_{vent} - E_{cond} \tag{10}$$

In the formula (10), E_{tran} is the sum of water vapor generated by crop transpiration and soil surface water evaporation, E_{wet} is the water vapor generated by the wet curtain, E_{vent} is the water vapor lost by the ventilation system, and E_{cond} is the water vapor lost by condensation on the greenhouse surface. In order to reduce the complexity of the model, as a result of the simulation time is not long, E_{tran} and E_{cond} can be ignored. The formula (10) is further simplified to obtain the formula (11).

$$\Delta E = E_{wet} - E_{vent} \tag{11}$$

$$\Delta E = h \frac{dH_i}{dt} \tag{12}$$

In the formula (11) (12), the unit of E_{wet} and E_{vent} are both, h is the average height of the greenhouse, H_i is the indoor humidity (%), t is the time (s), $\frac{dH_i}{dt}$ is the rate of change of the indoor humidity.

$$E_{wet} = \frac{\phi_{wet}\rho}{A_g} \tag{13}$$

$$E_{vent} = \frac{\phi_{vent}(H_i - H_o)}{d_s} \tag{14}$$

Where, A_g is the surface area of the greenhouse ground (m^2), H_i is the indoor humidity (%), H_o is the outdoor humidity (%), and d_s is the density of water ($kg \cdot m^{-3}$).

3.3 Simulation of Greenhouse Dynamic Temperature and Humidity Model

The greenhouse model in this paper is based on the Venlo modern greenhouse, and the greenhouse covering material is glass. Assuming that the greenhouse is equipped with a sunshade system that can cover half of the greenhouse surface, a ventilation system composed of a fan of $5\,m^3 \cdot s^{-1}$, and a steam heating system with a surface area of $80\,m^2$. The value of each parameter is shown in the Table 1.

Table 1. Parameters of greenhouse environment

Parameter	Symbol	Value
Volume of greenhouse	$\rho/kg \cdot m^{-3}$	1.2
Heat capacity of air	$C_p/J \cdot kg^{-1} \cdot m^{-3}$	1006
Radiation flux density outdoor	I_r	0.89
Covering film light transmittance	τ	0.89
Covering film heat transfer coefficient	$K_g/W \cdot m^{-2} \cdot K^{-1}$	$1.86(T_i - T_o)^{0.33}$
Surface emissivity coefficients	ε_{12}	$(\varepsilon_1^{-1} + \varepsilon_1^{-1} - 1)^{-1}$
Air emissivity coefficients	ε_1	0.9
Cladding material emissivity coefficients	ε_2	0.9
Latent heat of evaporation	W	$2501 - 2.36T_{avg}$
Heating system heat transfer coefficient	h_p	$1.95(T_p - T_i)^{0.33}$
Stefan-Boltzman constant	σ	5.67×10^{-8}
Density of water	$d_s/kg \cdot m^{-3}$	997

The greenhouse is in a closed or semi-closed state for a long time, and the indoor temperature and humidity are affected by various indoor and outdoor environmental factors. Therefore, the dynamic model of the greenhouse is a multivariable, non-linear system, and the relationship between various variables and parameters is complicated. Using the Simulink, the formula (2) (11) is divided into several subsystems in a modular way, and then the various subsystems are combined to obtain a simulation diagram of the temperature and humidity dynamic model of the greenhouse, as shown in Fig. 4.

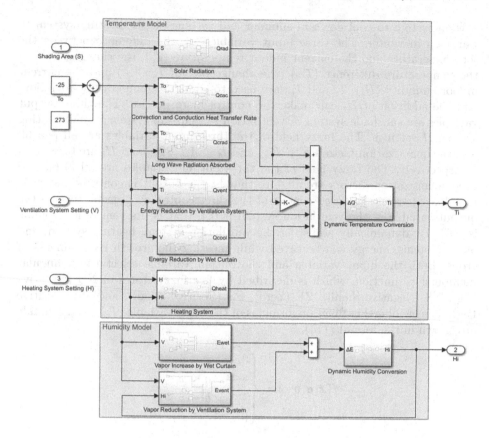

Fig. 4. Greenhouse model.

4 Fuzzy Logic Controller Design

Fuzzy Logic Controller (FLC) is based on the way of thinking of people in a dynamic environment. It abstracts the operator's experience into a series of conditional sentences and completes process control with the help of a computer. For greenhouses with nonlinear and hysteresis, as a result of FLC has less dependence on the accuracy of the greenhouse mathematical model and has good robustness, FLC is very suitable for the environmental controller of the greenhouse. Due to the greenhouse complex dynamics of the envelopment physics, the fuzzy control represents a useful tool to be applied to this type of processes [15].

This paper focuses on the temperature control of the greenhouse and chooses an optimal FLC with three inputs and three outputs.

4.1 Fuzzification

This paper chooses to control the temperature in the greenhouse. The main control methods include turning on the sunshade system and ventilation-wet curtain system to cool down in summer and turning on the heating system to warm up in winter. The three input variables are the difference between the set temperature and the current indoor temperature (T_e), the changing rate of the temperature difference (T_{ec}) (the change rate of T_e: $\frac{dT_e}{dt}$) and the current indoor humidity (H_i). T_e and T_{ec} are used to eliminate temperature deviation, and the addition of H_i can make the control more precise. The three output variables are sunshade system S, ventilation-wet curtain system V, and heating system H settings. The fuzzy field of the three input variables are all $[-6\ 6]$, and the quantization factors K_{e1}, K_{e2} and K_{e3} of T_e, T_{ec} and H_i are 6, 10, and 6 respectively. The fuzzy field of the three output variables are all $[0\ 6]$, and their quantization factors are all $1/6$, that is, the output is controlled at $[0\ 1]$ to achieve percentage-based control of the three controlled objects, such as the output variable of the ventilation system is 0.4, that is, its ventilation volume is 40%. By dynamically adjusting the ventilation system, heating system, and other systems, energy can be saved while meeting the growth requirements of crops. Both the input variable and the output variable select the triangular membership function, which is described by five fuzzy states of NB (Negative Big), NS (Negative Small), ZE (Zero), PS (Positive Small), and PB (Positive Big). The membership function formulas of the input variable (T_e) as an example are shown in the formula (15).

$$f(x, a, b, c) = \begin{cases} 0 & x \le a \\ \frac{x-a}{b-a} & a \le x \le b \\ \frac{c-x}{c-b} & b \le x \le c \\ 0 & c \le x \end{cases} \tag{15}$$

Where, taking variable T_e as an example, the membership functions of NB, NS, ZE, PS, and PB are respectively $f(x, -6, -6, -3)$, $f(x, -6, -3, 0)$, $f(x, -3, 0, 3)$, $f(x, 0, 3, 6)$ and $f(x, 3, 6, 6)$. The membership functions of T_{ec} and H_i are consistent with T_e. The membership function image of the input variable T_e as an example is shown in Fig. 5.

It has been pointed out that the manual tuning process of production rules and membership functions is extremely time-consuming in the development of fuzzy control system [4]. So now there is a lot of work to add neural networks to FLC, and neural networks are used for automatic configuration of membership functions, etc., which can reduce workload and increase the accuracy of FLC.

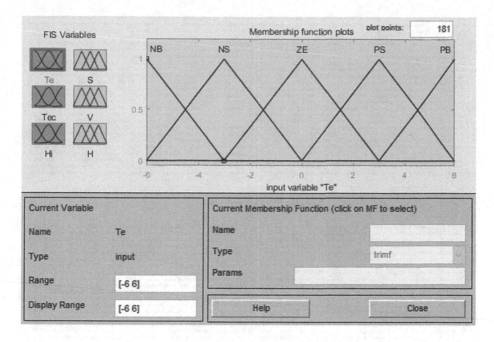

Fig. 5. Membership function.

4.2 Fuzzy Rule Base

According to the expert experience and existing papers [1, 6, 16], the following empirical rule base for environmental temperature control based on IF-THEN is obtained. When in summer, the heating system is closed:

- 1. IF T_e is PB, THEN S is NB, AND V is PB.
- 2. IF T_e is PS, AND T_{ec} is Negative, THEN S is NS, AND V are PS.
- 3. IF H_i is PB, THEN V needs to reduced one level.

When in winter, the wet curtain is closed and the ventilation system is in a low gear state:

- 1. IF T_e is NB, THEN S and H are NB.
- 2. IF T_e is NS, AND T_{ec} is Positive, THEN S and H are NS.
- 3. IF H_i is PB, THEN V needs to increased one level.

According to the above rules, T_e and T_{ec} can be used to eliminate the temperature difference, and the current humidity H_i can make the system controlling more precise. According to the above rules, establish a fuzzy control rule table of that three output variables, as shown in Fig. 6, 7 and 8.

1. If (temp is NB) and (tempt is NB) and (humidity is NB) then (sun is PB)(vent is NB)(heat is PB) (1)
2. If (temp is NB) and (tempt is NB) and (humidity is NS) then (sun is PB)(vent is NB)(heat is PB) (1)
3. If (temp is NB) and (tempt is NB) and (humidity is ZE) then (sun is PB)(vent is NB)(heat is PB) (1)
4. If (temp is NB) and (tempt is NB) and (humidity is PS) then (sun is PB)(vent is NB)(heat is PB) (1)
5. If (temp is NB) and (tempt is NB) and (humidity is PB) then (sun is PB)(vent is NS)(heat is PB) (1)
6. If (temp is NB) and (tempt is NS) and (humidity is NB) then (sun is PB)(vent is NB)(heat is PB) (1)
7. If (temp is NB) and (tempt is NS) and (humidity is NS) then (sun is PB)(vent is NB)(heat is PB) (1)
8. If (temp is NB) and (tempt is NS) and (humidity is ZE) then (sun is PB)(vent is NB)(heat is PB) (1)
9. If (temp is NB) and (tempt is NS) and (humidity is PS) then (sun is PB)(vent is NB)(heat is PB) (1)
10. If (temp is NB) and (tempt is NS) and (humidity is PB) then (sun is PB)(vent is NS)(heat is PB) (1)
11. If (temp is NB) and (tempt is ZE) and (humidity is NB) then (sun is PB)(vent is NB)(heat is PB) (1)
12. If (temp is NB) and (tempt is ZE) and (humidity is NS) then (sun is PB)(vent is NB)(heat is PB) (1)
13. If (temp is NB) and (tempt is ZE) and (humidity is ZE) then (sun is PB)(vent is NB)(heat is PB) (1)
14. If (temp is NB) and (tempt is ZE) and (humidity is PS) then (sun is PB)(vent is NB)(heat is PB) (1)
15. If (temp is NB) and (tempt is ZE) and (humidity is PB) then (sun is PB)(vent is NS)(heat is PB) (1)
16. If (temp is NB) and (tempt is PS) and (humidity is NB) then (sun is PB)(vent is NB)(heat is PB) (1)
17. If (temp is NB) and (tempt is PS) and (humidity is NS) then (sun is PB)(vent is NB)(heat is PB) (1)
18. If (temp is NB) and (tempt is PS) and (humidity is ZE) then (sun is PB)(vent is NB)(heat is PB) (1)
19. If (temp is NB) and (tempt is PS) and (humidity is PS) then (sun is PB)(vent is NB)(heat is PB) (1)
20. If (temp is NB) and (tempt is PS) and (humidity is PB) then (sun is PB)(vent is NS)(heat is PB) (1)
21. If (temp is NB) and (tempt is PB) and (humidity is NB) then (sun is PS)(vent is NB)(heat is PB) (1)
22. If (temp is NB) and (tempt is PB) and (humidity is NS) then (sun is PS)(vent is NB)(heat is PB) (1)
23. If (temp is NB) and (tempt is PB) and (humidity is ZE) then (sun is PS)(vent is NB)(heat is PB) (1)
24. If (temp is NB) and (tempt is PB) and (humidity is PS) then (sun is PS)(vent is NB)(heat is PB) (1)
25. If (temp is NB) and (tempt is PB) and (humidity is PB) then (sun is PS)(vent is ZE)(heat is PB) (1)

26. If (temp is NS) and (tempt is NB) and (humidity is NB) then (sun is PB)(vent is NB)(heat is PB) (1)
27. If (temp is NS) and (tempt is NB) and (humidity is NS) then (sun is PB)(vent is NB)(heat is PB) (1)
28. If (temp is NS) and (tempt is NB) and (humidity is ZE) then (sun is PB)(vent is NB)(heat is PB) (1)
29. If (temp is NS) and (tempt is NB) and (humidity is PS) then (sun is PB)(vent is NB)(heat is PB) (1)
30. If (temp is NS) and (tempt is NB) and (humidity is PB) then (sun is PB)(vent is NS)(heat is PB) (1)
31. If (temp is NS) and (tempt is NS) and (humidity is NB) then (sun is PB)(vent is NB)(heat is PB) (1)
32. If (temp is NS) and (tempt is NS) and (humidity is NS) then (sun is PB)(vent is NB)(heat is PB) (1)
33. If (temp is NS) and (tempt is NS) and (humidity is ZE) then (sun is PB)(vent is NB)(heat is PB) (1)
34. If (temp is NS) and (tempt is NS) and (humidity is PS) then (sun is PB)(vent is NB)(heat is PB) (1)
35. If (temp is NS) and (tempt is NS) and (humidity is PB) then (sun is PB)(vent is NS)(heat is PB) (1)
36. If (temp is NS) and (tempt is ZE) and (humidity is NB) then (sun is PB)(vent is NB)(heat is PB) (1)
37. If (temp is NS) and (tempt is ZE) and (humidity is NS) then (sun is PB)(vent is NB)(heat is PB) (1)
38. If (temp is NS) and (tempt is ZE) and (humidity is ZE) then (sun is PB)(vent is NB)(heat is PB) (1)
39. If (temp is NS) and (tempt is ZE) and (humidity is PS) then (sun is PB)(vent is NS)(heat is PB) (1)
40. If (temp is NS) and (tempt is ZE) and (humidity is PB) then (sun is PB)(vent is NS)(heat is PB) (1)
41. If (temp is NS) and (tempt is PS) and (humidity is NB) then (sun is PS)(vent is NS)(heat is PS) (1)
42. If (temp is NS) and (tempt is PS) and (humidity is NS) then (sun is PS)(vent is NS)(heat is PS) (1)
43. If (temp is NS) and (tempt is PS) and (humidity is ZE) then (sun is PS)(vent is NS)(heat is PS) (1)
44. If (temp is NS) and (tempt is PS) and (humidity is PS) then (sun is PS)(vent is NS)(heat is PS) (1)
45. If (temp is NS) and (tempt is PS) and (humidity is PB) then (sun is PS)(vent is ZE)(heat is PS) (1)
46. If (temp is NS) and (tempt is PB) and (humidity is NB) then (sun is PS)(vent is NS)(heat is PS) (1)
47. If (temp is NS) and (tempt is PB) and (humidity is NS) then (sun is PS)(vent is NS)(heat is PS) (1)
48. If (temp is NS) and (tempt is PB) and (humidity is ZE) then (sun is PS)(vent is NS)(heat is PS) (1)
49. If (temp is NS) and (tempt is PB) and (humidity is PS) then (sun is PS)(vent is NS)(heat is PS) (1)
50. If (temp is NS) and (tempt is PB) and (humidity is PB) then (sun is PS)(vent is ZE)(heat is PS) (1)

Fig. 6. Fuzzy rule base 1.

51. If (temp is ZE) and (tempt is NB) and (humidity is NB) then (sun is PS)(vent is NS)(heat is PS) (1)
52. If (temp is ZE) and (tempt is NB) and (humidity is NS) then (sun is PS)(vent is NS)(heat is PS) (1)
53. If (temp is ZE) and (tempt is NB) and (humidity is ZE) then (sun is PS)(vent is NS)(heat is PS) (1)
54. If (temp is ZE) and (tempt is NB) and (humidity is PS) then (sun is PS)(vent is NS)(heat is PS) (1)
55. If (temp is ZE) and (tempt is NB) and (humidity is PB) then (sun is PS)(vent is ZE)(heat is PS) (1)
56. If (temp is ZE) and (tempt is NS) and (humidity is NB) then (sun is PS)(vent is NS)(heat is PS) (1)
57. If (temp is ZE) and (tempt is NS) and (humidity is NS) then (sun is PS)(vent is NS)(heat is PS) (1)
58. If (temp is ZE) and (tempt is NS) and (humidity is ZE) then (sun is PS)(vent is NS)(heat is PS) (1)
59. If (temp is ZE) and (tempt is NS) and (humidity is PS) then (sun is PS)(vent is NS)(heat is PS) (1)
60. If (temp is ZE) and (tempt is NS) and (humidity is PB) then (sun is PS)(vent is ZE)(heat is PS) (1)
61. If (temp is ZE) and (tempt is ZE) and (humidity is NB) then (sun is ZE)(vent is ZE)(heat is ZE) (1)
62. If (temp is ZE) and (tempt is ZE) and (humidity is NS) then (sun is ZE)(vent is ZE)(heat is ZE) (1)
63. If (temp is ZE) and (tempt is ZE) and (humidity is ZE) then (sun is ZE)(vent is ZE)(heat is ZE) (1)
64. If (temp is ZE) and (tempt is ZE) and (humidity is PS) then (sun is ZE)(vent is ZE)(heat is ZE) (1)
65. If (temp is ZE) and (tempt is ZE) and (humidity is PB) then (sun is ZE)(vent is PS)(heat is ZE) (1)
66. If (temp is ZE) and (tempt is PS) and (humidity is NB) then (sun is ZE)(vent is ZE)(heat is ZE) (1)
67. If (temp is ZE) and (tempt is PS) and (humidity is NS) then (sun is ZE)(vent is ZE)(heat is ZE) (1)
68. If (temp is ZE) and (tempt is PS) and (humidity is ZE) then (sun is ZE)(vent is ZE)(heat is ZE) (1)
69. If (temp is ZE) and (tempt is PS) and (humidity is PS) then (sun is ZE)(vent is ZE)(heat is ZE) (1)
70. If (temp is ZE) and (tempt is PS) and (humidity is PB) then (sun is ZE)(vent is PS)(heat is ZE) (1)
71. If (temp is ZE) and (tempt is PB) and (humidity is NB) then (sun is NS)(vent is PS)(heat is NS) (1)
72. If (temp is ZE) and (tempt is PB) and (humidity is NS) then (sun is NS)(vent is PS)(heat is NS) (1)
73. If (temp is ZE) and (tempt is PB) and (humidity is ZE) then (sun is NS)(vent is PS)(heat is NS) (1)
74. If (temp is ZE) and (tempt is PB) and (humidity is PS) then (sun is NS)(vent is PS)(heat is NS) (1)
75. If (temp is ZE) and (tempt is PB) and (humidity is PB) then (sun is NS)(vent is PB)(heat is NS) (1)

76. If (temp is PS) and (tempt is NB) and (humidity is NB) then (sun is ZE)(vent is ZE)(heat is ZE) (1)
77. If (temp is PS) and (tempt is NB) and (humidity is NS) then (sun is ZE)(vent is ZE)(heat is ZE) (1)
78. If (temp is PS) and (tempt is NB) and (humidity is ZE) then (sun is ZE)(vent is ZE)(heat is ZE) (1)
79. If (temp is PS) and (tempt is NB) and (humidity is PS) then (sun is ZE)(vent is ZE)(heat is ZE) (1)
80. If (temp is PS) and (tempt is NB) and (humidity is PB) then (sun is ZE)(vent is NS)(heat is ZE) (1)
81. If (temp is PS) and (tempt is NS) and (humidity is NB) then (sun is ZE)(vent is ZE)(heat is ZE) (1)
82. If (temp is PS) and (tempt is NS) and (humidity is NS) then (sun is ZE)(vent is ZE)(heat is ZE) (1)
83. If (temp is PS) and (tempt is NS) and (humidity is ZE) then (sun is ZE)(vent is ZE)(heat is ZE) (1)
84. If (temp is PS) and (tempt is NS) and (humidity is PS) then (sun is ZE)(vent is ZE)(heat is ZE) (1)
85. If (temp is PS) and (tempt is NS) and (humidity is PB) then (sun is ZE)(vent is NS)(heat is ZE) (1)
86. If (temp is PS) and (tempt is ZE) and (humidity is NB) then (sun is NS)(vent is PS)(heat is NS) (1)
87. If (temp is PS) and (tempt is ZE) and (humidity is NS) then (sun is NS)(vent is PS)(heat is NS) (1)
88. If (temp is PS) and (tempt is ZE) and (humidity is ZE) then (sun is NS)(vent is PS)(heat is NS) (1)
89. If (temp is PS) and (tempt is ZE) and (humidity is PS) then (sun is NS)(vent is PS)(heat is NS) (1)
90. If (temp is PS) and (tempt is ZE) and (humidity is PB) then (sun is NS)(vent is ZE)(heat is NS) (1)
91. If (temp is PS) and (tempt is PS) and (humidity is NB) then (sun is NS)(vent is PS)(heat is NS) (1)
92. If (temp is PS) and (tempt is PS) and (humidity is NS) then (sun is NS)(vent is PS)(heat is NS) (1)
93. If (temp is PS) and (tempt is PS) and (humidity is ZE) then (sun is NS)(vent is PS)(heat is NS) (1)
94. If (temp is PS) and (tempt is PS) and (humidity is PS) then (sun is NS)(vent is PS)(heat is NS) (1)
95. If (temp is PS) and (tempt is PS) and (humidity is PB) then (sun is NS)(vent is PS)(heat is NS) (1)
96. If (temp is PS) and (tempt is PB) and (humidity is NB) then (sun is NS)(vent is PS)(heat is NS) (1)
97. If (temp is PS) and (tempt is PB) and (humidity is NS) then (sun is NS)(vent is PS)(heat is NS) (1)
98. If (temp is PS) and (tempt is PB) and (humidity is ZE) then (sun is NS)(vent is PS)(heat is NS) (1)
99. If (temp is PS) and (tempt is PB) and (humidity is PS) then (sun is NS)(vent is PS)(heat is NS) (1)
100. If (temp is PS) and (tempt is PB) and (humidity is PB) then (sun is NS)(vent is ZE)(heat is NS) (1)

Fig. 7. Fuzzy rule base 2.

4.3 Defuzzification

This FLC adopts the minimum method to implement the AND operator, adopts the maximum method to implement the OR operator, adopts the Mamdani fuzzy inference method, and adopts the Center of Gravity (COG) method as the defuzzification method.

4.4 Fuzzy Logic Controller Simulation

Based on the above theory, use the Simulink toolbox to establish a fuzzy controller as shown in the Fig. 9.

5 Edge Computing on Greenhouse System

Finally, install the program for reading and uploading sensor data and FLC simulated by Simulink according to the previous paper on the Raspberry-Pis (version 4 model B) to realize the control of fans and other devices at the edge. This FLC is built by Skfuzzy in the Python library and installed on the Raspberry Pi. It can effectively maintain suitable temperature and humidity and

101. If (temp is PB) and (tempt is NB) and (humidity is NB) then (sun is NS)(vent is PS)(heat is NS) (1)
102. If (temp is PB) and (tempt is NB) and (humidity is NS) then (sun is NS)(vent is PS)(heat is NS) (1)
103. If (temp is PB) and (tempt is NB) and (humidity is ZE) then (sun is NS)(vent is PS)(heat is NS) (1)
104. If (temp is PB) and (tempt is NB) and (humidity is PS) then (sun is NS)(vent is PS)(heat is NS) (1)
105. If (temp is PB) and (tempt is NB) and (humidity is PB) then (sun is NS)(vent is ZE)(heat is NS) (1)
106. If (temp is PB) and (tempt is NS) and (humidity is NB) then (sun is NB)(vent is PB)(heat is NB) (1)
107. If (temp is PB) and (tempt is NS) and (humidity is NS) then (sun is NB)(vent is PB)(heat is NB) (1)
108. If (temp is PB) and (tempt is NS) and (humidity is ZE) then (sun is NB)(vent is PB)(heat is NB) (1)
109. If (temp is PB) and (tempt is NS) and (humidity is PS) then (sun is NB)(vent is PB)(heat is NB) (1)
110. If (temp is PB) and (tempt is NS) and (humidity is PB) then (sun is NB)(vent is PS)(heat is NB) (1)
111. If (temp is PB) and (tempt is ZE) and (humidity is NB) then (sun is NB)(vent is PB)(heat is NB) (1)
112. If (temp is PB) and (tempt is ZE) and (humidity is NS) then (sun is NB)(vent is PB)(heat is NB) (1)
113. If (temp is PB) and (tempt is ZE) and (humidity is ZE) then (sun is NB)(vent is PB)(heat is NB) (1)
114. If (temp is PB) and (tempt is ZE) and (humidity is PS) then (sun is NB)(vent is PB)(heat is NB) (1)
115. If (temp is PB) and (tempt is ZE) and (humidity is PB) then (sun is NB)(vent is PS)(heat is NB) (1)
116. If (temp is PB) and (tempt is PS) and (humidity is NB) then (sun is NB)(vent is PB)(heat is NB) (1)
117. If (temp is PB) and (tempt is PS) and (humidity is NS) then (sun is NB)(vent is PB)(heat is NB) (1)
118. If (temp is PB) and (tempt is PS) and (humidity is ZE) then (sun is NB)(vent is PB)(heat is NB) (1)
119. If (temp is PB) and (tempt is PS) and (humidity is PS) then (sun is NB)(vent is PB)(heat is NB) (1)
120. If (temp is PB) and (tempt is PS) and (humidity is PB) then (sun is NB)(vent is PS)(heat is NB) (1)
121. If (temp is PB) and (tempt is PB) and (humidity is NB) then (sun is NB)(vent is PB)(heat is NB) (1)
122. If (temp is PB) and (tempt is PB) and (humidity is NS) then (sun is NB)(vent is PB)(heat is NB) (1)
123. If (temp is PB) and (tempt is PB) and (humidity is ZE) then (sun is NB)(vent is PB)(heat is NB) (1)
124. If (temp is PB) and (tempt is PB) and (humidity is PS) then (sun is NB)(vent is PB)(heat is NB) (1)
125. If (temp is PB) and (tempt is PB) and (humidity is PB) then (sun is NB)(vent is PS)(heat is NB) (1)

Fig. 8. Fuzzy rule base 3.

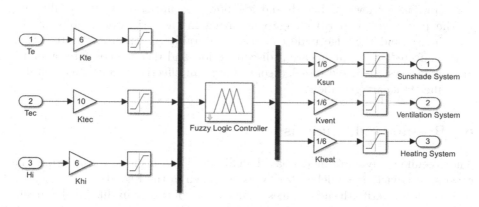

Fig. 9. Fuzzy logic controller.

other greenhouse environment factors. The Raspberry-Pi will directly make policy decisions based on the sensor data, and upload the sensor data and decision data to the IoT platform in real-time, as shown in the Fig. 10, users can view the environmental status and settings of controlled devices of the greenhouse in real-time.

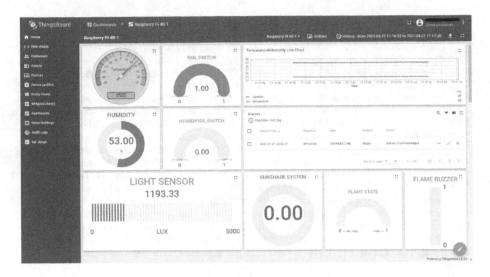

Fig. 10. Thingsboard dashboard.

The edge computing on greenhouse system integrates computing, storage, and network functions into edge devices such as Raspberry-Pi. It is actually a distributed deployment form that can effectively reduce network latency and is very suitable for low-bandwidth and low-power scenarios such as greenhouses. In the paper [10], deploying edge computing in the irrigation system of the greenhouse, and the edge node can realize a stable AI irrigation system that is not affected by communication disconnection and delay. Therefore, a smart greenhouse system based on edge computing can effectively construct a stable and efficient smart greenhouse.

6   Results and Analysis

The greenhouse dynamic model based on Simulink has been established, and the greenhouse dynamic model with FLC is as shown in the Fig. 11.

In order to verify the advantages of fuzzy control theory in this MIMO greenhouse system, as shown in the Fig. 11, PID control is introduced into the greenhouse dynamic model for comparison. Since there are three control variables: sunshade system, ventilation system, and heating system, three PID controllers are established to control these three systems respectively. The values of K_p, K_i, and K_d of the three PID controllers are adjusted separately based on the control variable method, as shown in the Table 2.

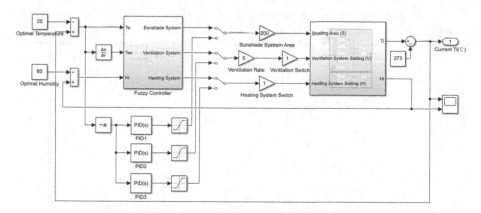

Fig. 11. Greenhouse dynamic model With FLC and PID controller.

Table 2. An example table of the current state

	K_p	K_i	K_d
Sunshade system	0.1	0.00000001	0
Ventilation system	−0.007	0.0000087	0.0000017
Heating system	0.008	0.00002	0.000004

Simulating the greenhouse state in summer and winter respectively, and the simulation time is two hours. As a result of the outdoor temperature does not change much within two hours, the outdoor temperature in summer and winter are set to fixed values of 30 °C and −25 °C, respectively. In summer, the temperature images of FLC and PID controller are shown in the Fig. 12.

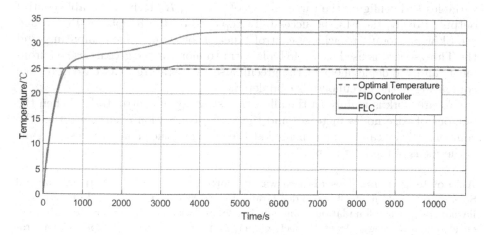

Fig. 12. FLC and PID controller in summer.

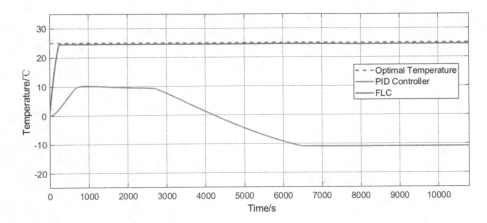

Fig. 13. FLC and PID controller in winter.

In winter, the temperature images of FLC and PID controller are shown in the Fig. 13.

7 Conclusion and Future Work

Since the greenhouse is a non-linear, hysteresis, and multi-variable coupling system, it is difficult to directly control environmental factors such as temperature and humidity. This paper proposes a FLC for smart greenhouse. We deploy FLC and PID controllers in the greenhouse separately, combine three input variables (T_e, T_{ec}, H_i), and compare the performance of these two controllers in different seasons. The results show that in a greenhouse system with multiple inputs and multiple outputs, FLC is more stable for temperature control, and the PID controller needs to completely decouple the relationship between environmental variables and configure the three factors of K_p, K_i, K_d to have a stable control output. Finally, the FLC is successfully deployed on the Raspberry-Pi through the Skfuzzy module to achieve control function based on edge computing, and the Thingsboard is used as the IoT platform to monitor the greenhouse environment, and the deployment of the greenhouse temperature FLC based on edge computing in the greenhouse is completed.

Future work is mainly on the allocation strategy of control tasks. When the number of edge nodes increases and the traffic congestion occurs, whether the control strategy can be implemented at the edge and the cloud at the same time is the focus of the next step.

Acknowledgement. This research was supported in part by the National Natural Science Foundation of China under Grant No. 62062031, in part by Inner Mongolia natural science foundation grant number 2019MS06035, and Inner Mongolia Science and Technology Major Project, China, in part by ROIS NII Open Collaborative Research 21S0601, and in part by JSPS KAKENHI grant numbers 18KK0279, 19H04093, 20H00592, and 21H03424, and in part by G-7 Scholarship Foundation.

References

1. Alaviyan, Y., Aghaseyedabdollah, M., Sadafi, M., Yazdizade, A.: Design and manufacture of a smart greenhouse with supervisory control of environmental parameters using fuzzy inference controller. In: 2020 6th Iranian Conference on Signal Processing and Intelligent Systems (ICSPIS), pp. 1–6 (2020). https://doi.org/10.1109/ICSPIS51611.2020.9349619
2. Azaza, M., Echaieb, K., Tadeo, F., Fabrizio, E., Iqbal, A., Mami, A.: Fuzzy decoupling control of greenhouse climate. Arab. J. Sci. Eng. **40**(9), 2805–2812 (2015). https://doi.org/10.1007/s13369-015-1719-5
3. Ben Ali, R., Aridhi, E., Mami, A.: Dynamic model of an agricultural greenhouse using matlab-simulink environment. In: 2015 16th International Conference on Sciences and Techniques of Automatic Control and Computer Engineering (STA), pp. 346–350 (2015). https://doi.org/10.1109/STA.2015.7505185
4. Castañeda-Miranda, R., Ventura-Ramos, E., del Rocío Peniche-Vera, R., Herrera-Ruiz, G.: Fuzzy greenhouse climate control system based on a field programmable gate array. Biosyst. Eng. **94**(2), 165–177 (2006). https://doi.org/10.1016/j.biosystemseng.2006.02.012. https://www.sciencedirect.com/science/article/pii/S1537511006000729
5. Chen, L., Zhang, H., Du, S.: Greenhouse temperature control system based on fuzzy theory. In: 2013 Third International Conference on Instrumentation, Measurement, Computer, Communication and Control, pp. 1673–1677 (2013). https://doi.org/10.1109/IMCCC.2013.370
6. Chen, L., Zhang, B., Yao, F., Cui, L.: Modeling and simulation of a solar greenhouse with natural ventilation based on error optimization using fuzzy controller. In: 2016 35th Chinese Control Conference (CCC), pp. 2097–2102 (2016). https://doi.org/10.1109/ChiCC.2016.7553676
7. Chen, X., Wang, X., Shen, H.: Design of greenhouse environment monitoring system based on NB-IoT and edge computing. In: 2021 IEEE 5th Advanced Information Technology, Electronic and Automation Control Conference (IAEAC), vol. 5, pp. 1319–1324 (2021). https://doi.org/10.1109/IAEAC50856.2021.9390671
8. El Ghoumari, M., Tantau, H.J., Serrano, J.: Non-linear constrained MPC: real-time implementation of greenhouse air temperature control. Comput. Electron. Agric. **49**(3), 345–356 (2005). https://doi.org/10.1016/j.compag.2005.08.005. https://www.sciencedirect.com/science/article/pii/S016816990500133X. Modelling and control in agricultural processes
9. Feng, G.: A survey on analysis and design of model-based fuzzy control systems. IEEE Trans. Fuzzy Syst. **14**(5), 676–697 (2006). https://doi.org/10.1109/TFUZZ.2006.883415
10. Kawai, T., Mineno, H.: Evaluation environment using edge computing for artificial intelligence-based irrigation system. In: 2020 16th International Conference on Mobility, Sensing and Networking (MSN), pp. 214–219 (2020). https://doi.org/10.1109/MSN50589.2020.00046
11. Kimball, B.: Simulation of the energy balance of a greenhouse. Agric. Meteorol. **11**, 243–260 (1973). https://doi.org/10.1016/0002-1571(73)90067-8. https://www.sciencedirect.com/science/article/pii/0002157173900678
12. Liu, R., Li, M., Guzmán, J., Rodríguez, F.: A fast and practical one-dimensional transient model for greenhouse temperature and humidity. Comput. Electron. Agric. **186**, 106186 (2021). https://doi.org/10.1016/j.compag.2021.106186. https://www.sciencedirect.com/science/article/pii/S0168169921002039

13. Ma, D., Carpenter, N., Maki, H., Rehman, T.U., Tuinstra, M.R., Jin, J.: Greenhouse environment modeling and simulation for microclimate control. Comput. Electron. Agric. **162**, 134–142 (2019). https://doi.org/10.1016/j.compag.2019.04.013. https://www.sciencedirect.com/science/article/pii/S0168169918316090
14. O'Grady, M., Langton, D., O'Hare, G.: Edge computing: a tractable model for smart agriculture? Artif. Intell. Agric. **3**, 42–51 (2019). https://doi.org/10.1016/j.aiia.2019.12.001.   https://www.sciencedirect.com/science/article/pii/S2589721719300339
15. Revathi, S., Sivakumaran, N.: Fuzzy based temperature control of greenhouse. IFAC-PapersOnLine **49**(1), 549–554 (2016). https://doi.org/10.1016/j.ifacol.2016.03.112.   https://www.sciencedirect.com/science/article/pii/S2405896316301124. 4th IFAC Conference on Advances in Control and Optimization of Dynamical Systems ACODS 2016
16. Robles Algarín, C., Callejas Cabarcas, J., Polo Llanos, A.: Low-cost fuzzy logic control for greenhouse environments with web monitoring. Electronics **6**(4) (2017). https://doi.org/10.3390/electronics6040071. https://www.mdpi.com/2079-9292/6/4/71
17. Taki, M., Rohani, A., Rahmati-Joneidabad, M.: Solar thermal simulation and applications in greenhouse. Inf. Process. Agric. **5**(1), 83–113 (2018). https://doi.org/10.1016/j.inpa.2017.10.003. https://www.sciencedirect.com/science/article/pii/S2214317317300628
18. Wenshun, C., Shuo, C., Lizhe, Y., Jiancheng, S.: Design and implementation of sunlight greenhouse service platform based on IoT and cloud computing. In: Proceedings of 2013 2nd International Conference on Measurement, Information and Control, vol. 01, pp. 141–144 (2013). https://doi.org/10.1109/MIC.2013.6757934
19. Xiu-hua, W., Lei, Z.: Simulation on temperature and humidity nonlinear controller of greenhouses. In: 2011 Fourth International Conference on Intelligent Computation Technology and Automation, vol. 1, pp. 500–503 (2011). https://doi.org/10.1109/ICICTA.2011.138

Workshop: The New Era of Computer Network by using Machine Learning

Moving Object Recognition for Airport Ground Surveillance Network

Zhizhuo Zhang, Xiang Zhang$^{(\boxtimes)}$, Donghang Chen, and Haifei Yu

Yangtze Delta Region Institute (Quzhou), University of Electronic Science
and Technology of China, Quzhou 324000, Zhejiang, China
{zhangzhizhuo,chendh,yuhaifei}@std.uestc.edu.cn,
uestchero@uestc.edu.cn

Abstract. In this paper we first introduce an airport ground surveillance network, which is composed of data acquisition terminal based on multiple cameras, data transmission based on high-speed optical fiber, and processing terminal including some airport intelligent applications, e.g. intrusion warning and conflict prediction. Next we present a moving object recognition algorithm named AMORnet which is the basis of the intelligent applications in this surveillance network. Unlike the traditional object detection which cannot distinguish static and moving objects and moving object detection requiring accurate silhouette segmentation, the AMORnet only locate moving object and much faster than the time-consuming segmentation. To achieve this purpose, firstly we estimate the scene background through a motion estimation network, compared to the commonly used temporal histogram based approach, our background estimation method can better cope with infrequent aircraft movements in airports. Secondly, we use feature pyramids to perform regression and classification at multiple levels of feature abstractions. In this way, only moving objects are correctly recognized. Finally, experiments are conducted on an airport ground surveillance benchmark to verify the effectiveness of the proposed AMORnet.

Keywords: Airport ground surveillance · Moving object recognition

1 Introduction

In recent years, the number of passengers carried by civil aviation in the world has continued to increase, the airport structure has become increasingly complex. The difficulty of visual monitoring of ground moving objects in the field by administrators has gradually increased. The safety hazards of manual command and management have become more obvious. To satisfy the need for automated scene surveillance, the airport surveillance network that cover the entire airport field area are used in modern airport.

This work was supported by the Project of Quzhou Municipal Government (2020D011), and National Science Foundation of China (U1733111, U19A2052).

© ICST Institute for Computer Sciences, Social Informatics and Telecommunications Engineering 2022
Published by Springer Nature Switzerland AG 2022. All Rights Reserved
C. T. Calafate et al. (Eds.): MONAMI 2021, LNICST 418, pp. 335–343, 2022.
https://doi.org/10.1007/978-3-030-94763-7_25

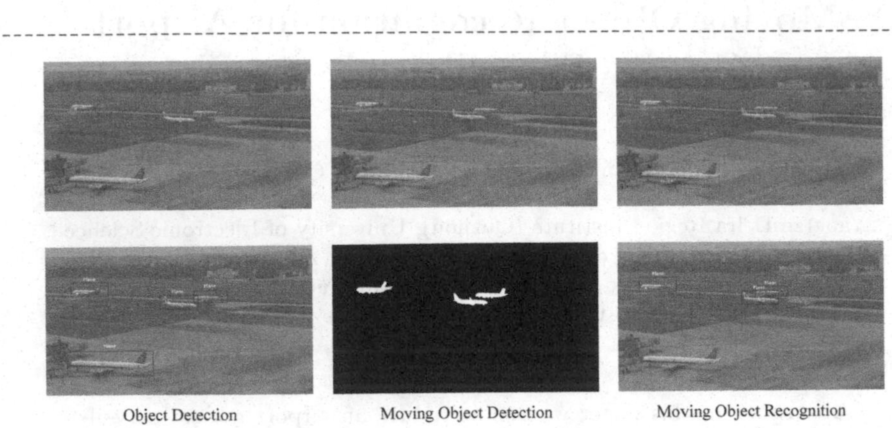

Fig. 1. Difference between the three tasks: object detection, moving object detection, moving object recognition.

The Airport ground surveillance network has access to a large amount of real-time video information, on which we can develop intelligent applications such as intrusion warning, conflict prediction, etc. Moving object detection and object detection are the foundation of many video based intelligent applications, but are subject to some limitations when applied in airport ground surveillance networks. Moving object detection aims to present and label foreground objects that undergo spatial position changes in the image sequence or video. Moving object detection algorithm use few input video frames to estimate an initially clean background image, and then the pixel-wise segmentation is carried out between estimated background and input video frames. Traditional approaches are unsupervised and have poor performance because of lighting and shadows in the airport ground [1–4]. The supervised moving object detection algorithm s based on convolutional neural networks (CNNs) [5–8] has good accuracy in AGVS benchmark [9], but the algorithms cannot distinguish the class of the target and are time-consuming. In addition, the objective of object detection is to find objects with different geometries as well as to assign an accurate label to each detected object. Object detection algorithms can be divided into two approaches: two-stage [10–12] and one-stage [13–15], and it is often believed that the former works slower, but the detection accuracy is higher. However, existing object detection algorithms cannot distinguish static and moving objects, which are not intuitive enough in the airport ground surveillance network.

Based on moving object detection and object detection, we further implement moving object recognition. The difference between object detection, moving object detection and moving object recognition is given in Fig. 1. Compared to the first two methods, the moving object recognition localization and classification of moving objects which are more suitable for the development of intelligent applications for airport ground surveillance networks. The rest of the paper is organized as follows: the airport ground surveillance network is briefly

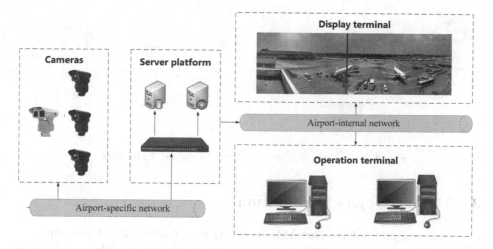

Fig. 2. Structure of airport ground surveillance network.

described in Sect. 2. Section 3 presents the details of the proposed moving object recognition algorithm. Experimental results are given in Sect. 4, followed by the conclusion in Sect. 5.

2   The Airport Ground Surveillance Network

The airport ground surveillance network is shown in Fig. 2. It consists of four parts: video surveillance front-end, server platform, display terminal, and operation terminal. The video surveillance front-end consists of multiple fixed cameras and pan-tilt cameras, which is because the airport field is very wide and needs to overlap multiple cameras field of view to realize the video surveillance of the whole airport, the format of the captured video is transmitted to the server platform in the form of H264 through the airport-specific network, the server platform will stitch and store the video according to the geometric relationship of the cameras, and transmit it to the display terminal and the operation terminal through the airport-internal network. The display terminal can display the real-time airport scenes processed by the operator terminal.

The proposed moving object recognition algorithm can be applied at the operation terminal, as shown in Fig. 2, where the display terminal shows the result of the algorithm proposed in this paper, the aircraft on the right side of the screen has just entered the ground without stopping, while the aircraft on the left side has stayed for some time, and the algorithm is able to detect the moving object separately. Based on the moving object detection algorithm, we can also develop higher-level applications. For example, we automatically send conflict prediction to staff when objects are too close to each other; we can also train classes of objects that may have trespassing, such as private cars, drones, etc., and automatic alarm when the target is in view. We also present the initial implementation of conflict prediction in the next session d.

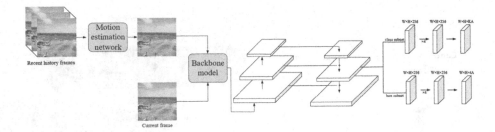

Fig. 3. Schematic illustration of the proposed AMORnet.

3   Moving Object Recognition

Our proposed method is called AMORnet (Airport moving object recognition). We propose a motion estimation network based on the moving object detection method, and a regression and classification block based on the object detection method, which together form AMORnet. The whole AMORnet is shown in Fig. 3, and we will discuss the functions of each module in the following subsections.

3.1   Motion Estimation Network

We use the method of moving object detection to realize the estimation of motion. And the key to this is how to get a clean and accurate background image. Recently, temporal histogram based approach for background estimation which is proposed [16]. At each pixel location, temporal histogram is obtained using Eqs. (1) and (2).

$$Hist_{(m,n)}(l) = \sum_{t=1}^{N} f(I(m,n,t),l); l \in [0,255] \tag{1}$$

$$f(x,y) = \begin{cases} 1 & x = y \\ 0 & else \end{cases} \tag{2}$$

From estimated pixel-level temporal histogram, accurate background pixel intensity at particular location (m, n) is obtained using Eq. (3).

$$BG_n(m,n) = \arg\max_l (Hist_{(m,n)}(l)); l \in [0,255] \tag{3}$$

where, argmax(.) is maximum value of the histogram bin index. The estimated background results of pixel-level temporal histogram based approach are illustrated in Fig. 5(b). However, Due to the slow speed of the moving objects in the airport scene and the frequent motion and stillness of the objects. Temporal histogram based approach can't yield good results. On this basis, we propose motion estimation network based on Convolutional Neural Network, the network structure is shown in Fig. 4. The background is learned through a sequence

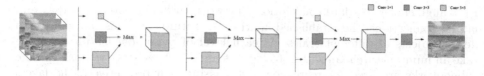

Fig. 4. Structure of motion estimation network, where each convolutional layer is followed by Relu as the activation function

of multi-scale receptive feature blocks using recent temporal history. Each stage captures the maximum response from multiple receptive fields of size 1×1, 3×3 and 5×5. This allows us to obtain background statistical information while still ensuring the adaptability of the network to different changing scenarios. The visualization results of the proposed motion estimation network are shown in Fig. 5.

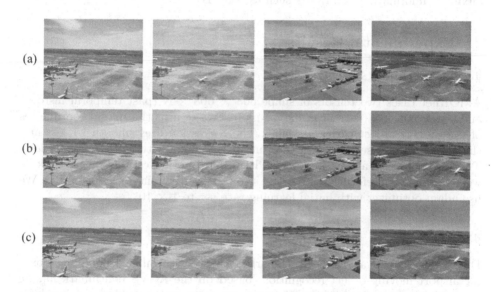

Fig. 5. Comparison of proposed motion estimation network with temporal histogram based approach: (a) Current frame (b) Temporal histogram based approach (c) Motion estimation network

3.2   Regression and Classification Blocks

Regression and classification blocks are composed of a backbone network and two task-specific subnetworks, as shown in Fig. 3. The backbone is responsible for computing a convolutional feature map over the entire input images. We adopt the Feature Pyramid Network (FPN) from [16] as the backbone network.

FPN augments a standard convolutional network with a top-down pathway and lateral connections, the established multi-scale feature pyramids can be used to detect objects of different scales. At each level of pyramidal feature map, we take an input feature map with 256 channels and set 9 anchors, two task-specific subnetworks are used for regression and classification respectively, the layers follow similar configurations as in [15].

3.3   Conflict Prediction

We set when there are two bounding box between the IOU threshold of 0.7 or more will automatically send a conflict prediction to the relevant staff, the diagrammatic sketch is shown in Fig. 6, 16th. But due to the filming perspective, there may be a crisscross on the video between aircraft that are far away from each other, and the implemented algorithm is not completely accurate, there are often false alarms, so to achieve accurate conflict prediction also need to add auxiliary information of airports such as ADS-B.

4   Experimental Results

4.1   Experiment Settings

AMORnet takes two tensors of shape $608 \times 608 \times N$ (past temporal history) and $608 \times 608 \times 3$ (current frame) as input and returns the spatial coordinates of the moving object with class label. The regression uses smooth L1 loss and the classification use focal loss, the sum of which constitutes the training loss. The loss gradients are backpropagated through motion estimation network as well. Training is performed with batch size = 1 over Nvidia RTX 2060 GPU. We use adam optimizer with initial learning rate set to 1×10^{-5}.

4.2   Dataset

Due to the lack of available benchmark datasets with labeled bounding boxes for airport moving object recognition, based on the AGVS benchmark [9], we manually annotated 20 of the 25 segments. The first 10 videos are used for training and the last 10 videos are used for testing.

T

16

19

20

Fig. 6. Qualitative results of our method for 16th,19th and 20th from AGVS benchmark.

4.3   Evaluation Metrics

Since the experimental results are similar to those of objection detection, we use mAP, which is commonly used for object detection, as the evaluation metrics. The mAP is used to measure the average of the Precision at different Recall. A predicted object instance is predicted to be True Positives if the predicted object instance has at least 50% crosslinking with the corresponding ground truth object instance.

Table 1. Algorithm performance under different input past temporal history frames

Depth\mAP	14	16	19	20	Overall
20	56.5	73.5	67.9	82.4	70.0
30	59.2	76.2	**73.7**	82.2	72.8
50	**61.2**	76.3	71.4	**83.2**	**73.0**
70	51.0	**76.9**	69.9	82.9	70.1

4.4   Qualitative Analysis

The detection results of our method on the AGVS dataset are shown in Table 1, which we can conclude that the best result is when the number of historical

Fig. 7. Comparison of proposed method with Faster RCNN: (a) Current frame (b) Faster RCNN (c) AMORnet

frames input by Motion estimation network is 50. Among them, the 16th video has the process of moving the aircraft from motion to static, the 19th video has occlusion between the aircrafts, and the 20th video the aircraft is incomplete in the image. The algorithm in these three video detection results are shown in Fig. 6, and the comparison result with the Faster RCNN [12] detection results is shown in Fig. 7, from the figure it can be seen that our method can not only distinguish between stationary and moving objects in all these scenes, but also fully detect occluded or defective objects.

5   Conclusion

An airport ground surveillance network was introduced in this paper. It consists of four parts: video surveillance front-end, server platform, display terminal, and operation terminal. The proposed moving object recognition algorithm based on object detection and moving object detection can be applied to the airport ground surveillance network. The proposed method AMORnet first obtains a relatively accurate background through the motion estimation network, and then implements the moving object detection through the classification and regression network. Experimental results on the AGVS benchmark demonstrated the effectiveness of the proposed method.

References

1. Stauffer, C., Grimson, E.: Adaptive background mixture models for real-time tracking. In: IEEE Conference on Computer Vision and Pattern Recognition, October 1999
2. Kim, K., Chalidabhongse, T., Harwood, D., Davis, L.: Background modeling and subtraction by codebook construction. In: IEEE International Conference on Image Processing, October 2004
3. Zivkovic, Z.: Efficient adaptive density estimation per image pixel for the task of background subtraction. Pattern Recogn. Lett. **27**(7), 773–780 (2006)
4. Barnich, O., Droogenbroeck, M.V.: ViBe: a powerful random technique to estimate the background in video sequences. In: International Conference on Acoustics, Speech, and Signal Processing, April 2009
5. Lim, L., Keles, H.: Foreground segmentation using a triplet convolutional neural network for multiscale feature encoding. Pattern Recogn. Lett. **112**, 256–262 (2018)
6. Liao, J., Guo, G., Yan, Y., Wang, H.: Multiscale cascaded scene-specific convolutional neural networks for background subtraction. In: Hong, R., Cheng, W.-H., Yamasaki, T., Wang, M., Ngo, C.-W. (eds.) PCM 2018. LNCS, vol. 11164, pp. 524–533. Springer, Cham (2018). https://doi.org/10.1007/978-3-030-00776-8_48
7. Tezcan, M.O., Ishwar, P., Konrad, J.: BSUV-Net: a fully-convolutional neural network for background subtraction of unseen videos. In: IEEE Winter Conference on Applications of Computer Vision, March 2020
8. Bakkay, M., Rashwan, H., Salmane, H., Khoudour, L., Puig, D., Ruichek, Y.: BSCGAN: deep background subtraction with conditional generative adversarial networks. In: IEEE International Conference on Image Processing, October 2018
9. www.agvs-caac.com
10. Uijlings, J.R., van de Sande, K.E., Gevers, T., Smeulders, A.W.: Selective search for object recognition. Int. J. Comput. Vis. **4**(2), 154–171 (2013)
11. Girshick, R., Donahue, J., Darrell, T., Malik, J.: Rich feature hierarchies for accurate object detection and semantic segmentation. In: IEEE Conference on Computer Vision and Pattern Recognition, June 2014
12. Ren, S., He, K., Girshick, R., Sun, J.: Faster R-CNN: towards real-time object detection with region proposal networks. IEEE Trans. Pattern Anal. Mach. Intell. **39**(6), 1137–1149 (2017)
13. Redmon, J., Divvala, S., Girshick, R., Farhadi, A.: You only look once: unified, real-time object detection. In: IEEE Conference on Computer Vision and Pattern Recognition, June 2016
14. Liu, W., et al.: SSD: single shot multibox detector. In: Leibe, B., Matas, J., Sebe, N., Welling, M. (eds.) ECCV 2016. LNCS, vol. 9905, pp. 21–37. Springer, Cham (2016). https://doi.org/10.1007/978-3-319-46448-0_2
15. Lin, T.Y., Goyal, P., Girshick, R., He, K., Dollár, P.: Focal loss for dense object detection. IEEE Trans. Pattern Anal. Mach. Intell. **42**(2), 318–327 (2017)
16. Lin, T.Y., Dollar, P., Girshick, R., He, K., Hariharan, B., Belongie, S.: Feature pyramid networks for object detection. In: IEEE Conference on Computer Vision and Pattern Recognition, July 2017

IOT Based Sensor Monitoring System for Smart Complex and Shopping Malls

Vipul Narayan[✉] and A. K. Daniel

Department of Computer Science and Engineering, Madan Mohan Malaviya University, Gorakhpur, U.P., India
vipulupsainian2470@gmail.com

Abstract. Wireless Sensor Network (WSN) plays a significant role in smart offices/workplaces and academic research nowadays. Due to the vast range of technologies research is being conducted in the domain such as environmental monitoring, human safety, military operations, intelligent remote monitoring, shopping malls, smart complex, healthcare etc. Clustering is a technique through which the efficiency of network is enhanced. Two Stage Energy Efficient Routing Protocol (TS-EERP) is proposed, which divides the network into different levels. Increasing the number of Cluster Head (CH) nodes at various levels improves the Residual Energy (RE) of cluster nodes/nodes. The aim of the paper is to develop an efficient CH selection mechanism based on maximum RE of Sensor Node (SN) and minimum Base Station (BS) distance. The proposed protocol works in two steps as follows: The data is collected from smart offices in the first step and from residential buildings in the next step. The collected data is aggregated by the Cluster head(s) and transmit to the BS in the Internet of Things (IoT) based network. The simulation performance of the proposed protocol improves the lifetime of the network compared to the SEP protocol.

Keywords: Cluster head selection · IoT · Lifetime · Residual Energy · Sensor Network

1 Introduction

The future internet aim is to integrate a wide range of wireless and wired technology together for smart living. In [1] author discussed IoT consists of a large network to links a wide range of objects and entities. The sensor nodes are used for continuously monitoring of objects in the network. The WSN plays a significant role in various places as military and non-military domains, climate forecasting, environmental monitoring, smart buildings, shopping malls, smart offices, smart cities and military surveillance etc. In the current decade sensors with essential characteristics like smaller size, cheaper cost and intelligent processing system made this easily possible. In [2] author discussed around 5 billion smart devices are connected together in the future days. According to the survey, around 30 billion objects will be connected to IoT devices by 2022. This gives up several opportunities for IoT research in a variety of disciplines. The SN performs the data collection task and transmits to CH node. The aggregation of data is performed by CH node and transmit it to BS shows in Fig. 1.

© ICST Institute for Computer Sciences, Social Informatics and Telecommunications Engineering 2022
Published by Springer Nature Switzerland AG 2022. All Rights Reserved
C. T. Calafate et al. (Eds.): MONAMI 2021, LNICST 418, pp. 344–354, 2022.
https://doi.org/10.1007/978-3-030-94763-7_26

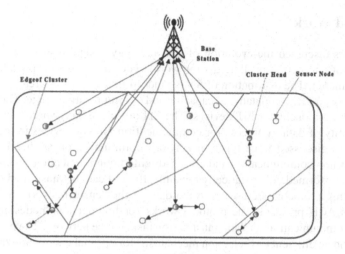

Fig. 1. Architecture of WSN.

The wireless interface characteristic of the sensor allows them to connect and establish a wireless network. In [3] author discussed the architecture of WSN is influenced by important factors as cost, hardware and limited battery power. The homogeneous and heterogeneous nodes are used in the network. Sensor node battery replacement is a difficult task in the network. The various node deployment techniques are used to cover the monitoring area by using optimum SN in the network. In [4] authors discussed deterministic and random node deployment schemes. The nodes have limited battery power for performing tasks in the network. The various energy optimization techniques are used to enhanced node residual energy and improved network performance.

The network lifetime is improved by using clustering techniques. The number of SN are grouped to form clusters in the network. The single node in an individual cluster serves as a CH, while the remaining SN acts as a cluster member of the network. The aggregation of data is performed by CH nodes and transmits to BS. In [5] authors discussed hybrid routing techniques to solve the issues in the IoT based network. The normal node sent data to BS directly while the advanced node through the clustering process and enhanced network performance. The proposed Two Stage Energy Efficient Routing Protocol for IoT based WSN. The network area is partitioned into regions and sub regions. The RE of Cluster nodes/nodes is improved by increasing Cluster Head (CH) nodes at various levels in the network. The TS-EERP protocol performed its operation in two steps: In the first step, it collects the data from the smart offices and in the second step collects data from the residential buildings.

The research article is structured as follows: Sect. 2 elaborates the previous research work. Two Stage Energy Efficient Routing Protocol is discussed in Sect. 3. Simulation results are discussed in Sect. 4 and Conclusion and Future directions in the last section.

2 Related Work

In [6] authors discussed the evolution of IoT and play a significant role to boost up the demand of internet users all across the world. The IoT makes people's lives easier and works smarter. The distribution of SN is random in the network area. The SN have limited battery power, computational capacity, and communication range. The SN is one of the major components of IoT devices. The SN are placed anywhere and consist of a large quantity of data to process for communication among devices in the network. In [7] authors discussed three types of network communication as direct communication, multi-hop communication and cluster-oriented communication. The Clustering technique is performed either statically/dynamically and data is transmitted to BS. The various routing protocols are used to route data in the sensor network. In [8] author discussed LEACH protocol. The protocol works for homogenous nodes and follows single-hop communication for data transmission tasks in the network. The protocol uses clustering and an efficient CH selection mechanism for optimal energy utilization in the network.

The IoT plays a vital for connecting smart devices to cloud infrastructure. To improve the efficiency of IoT-based applications, several routing protocols are introduced. The data transmission tasks consume more energy in the network therefore to develop a routing protocol for the WSN is an important task. The integration of WSN with IoT devices plays an important role in every aspect of life. In [9] authors investigated a good solution for data collection and processing tasks in the smart complexes/buildings for the IoT based wireless network. The solution is modeled for IoT devices and simulated in the Cooja simulator. The proposed solution performed efficient utilization of energy in the IoT based smart building and complexes. In [10] author survey the IoT based building management system for optimum use of resources and efficient energy management systems for smart complex/malls. The edge computing is also widely used to minimize the energy issues in the IoT based network and improve network performance. In [11] author discussed selection of CH plays an important role in the clustering algorithm. The CH node is responsible for the data fusion process and data processing task in the network. The energy consumption is more in the network when the BS is situated outside the network. The replacement of dead CH nodes consumes more energy in the network and the performance of network is degraded.

In [12] author discussed LEACH centralized with chain protocol. The protocol used a centralized clustering technique to minimize delay in the network and enhanced network performance compared to the LEACH protocol.

In [13] author discussed the working principle of the Centralized LEACH protocol. The steady phase of the protocol is different compared to LEACH protocol. The SN is equipped with a global positioning system for tracking objects in the network. The CH election is based on a threshold value and keeps a record of the previously selected CH. The protocol improves the performance of the system and enhanced network lifetime. In [14] authors discussed Multi-hop LEACH (MH-LEACH) protocol for data transmission to BS. The data is collected by the SN and forwarded to the respective zonal CH. The CH-to-CH communication in the zonal region which enhanced RE of CH node and improves performance of the system. In [15] author discussed Advance Zonal Rectangular LEACH (ARZ-LEACH) protocol. The network area is categorized into advanced clusters, rectangular clusters and zonal clusters to maintain the load inside the network and enhanced network lifetime. In [16] introduced SEP protocol which uses Normal nodes (NN) and Advanced nodes (AN). The weighted probability is used for CH selection in the protocol. The protocol improves stability and improves network performance.

In [17] author introduced Enhanced Stable Election Protocol. The protocol uses three-level architecture and intermediate SN. The AN have more energy than NN in the network. The heterogeneity level is improved by adding one more layer and improves network performance.

In [18] author proposed multi-hop routing with stable election (MR-SEP) protocol. The MR-SEP protocol divides the network into multiple cluster levels. The minimum BS distance is used as a criterion for CH selection and requests member SN to join the CH. The top layer CH works as super CH for lower layer and increase the network performance.

In [19] introduced HEED protocol and CH is selected based on RE of node and proximity principal. The protocol minimizes network overhead and enhances the network life span. In [20] introduced Energy Efficient Density Control (EEDCA) method in which the CH selection criteria are based on node position and RE of SN. The EEDCA protocol maintains a table of its neighboring SN and transmits data to BS.

The TS-EERP protocol uses the following performance metrics:

(i)   Stability Period: The time span in which all the SN cover the region of interest until dead of first SN in the network.
(ii) Network lifetime: The time period in which all nodes cover the region of interest until the death of all SN.
(iii) Throughput: The packets successfully transmitted to BS.

3   Proposed Two Stage Energy Efficient Routing Protocol (TS-EERP)

The proposed TS-EERP protocol divides the network into multiple regions and sub regions. The CH is selected by using SN maximum node RE and minimum BS distance. The random number is chosen and compares to a threshold value. If the selected number is less to the threshold value the SN acts as a CH in the network, while the other node acts as a CM in the network. The CH-to-CH communication takes place in the network which enhanced the RE of SN and the lifetime of the network.

The proposed protocol works in two stages: In the first step data is collected from smart offices in one cluster and in the second step data is collected from residential buildings. The collected data is aggregated by CH nodes and transmitted to BS in the IoT-based network (Figs. 2 and 3).

The automation of smart homes and offices is widely used in corporate offices, shopping malls, shopping complexes, etc. in various places nowadays. The goal of the automation process is to integrate new technology with IoT devices for easy control in smart home appliances such as fans, lights, refrigerators, television, electric induction,

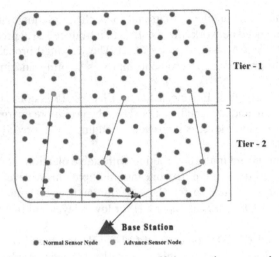

Fig. 2. The two-stage energy efficient routing protocol.

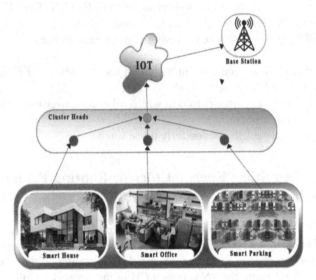

Fig. 3. IoT applications.

smart doors, smart windows, gas detections, light monitoring, and air conditioners. The automation process saves power consumption and improves the standard of living.

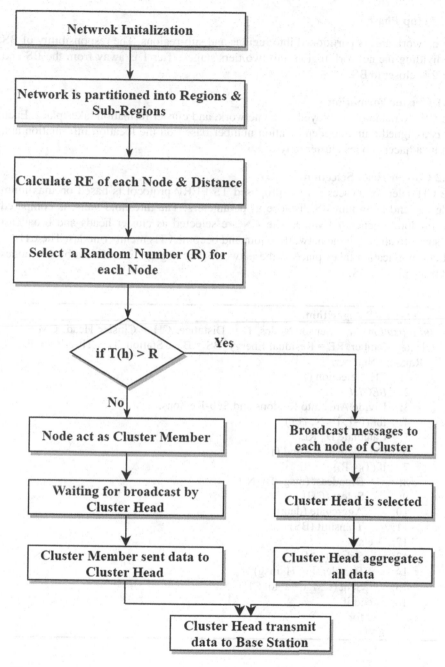

The working of the proposed Two Stage Energy Efficient Routing Protocol as follows:

3.1 Setup Phase

The network area is partitioned into regions and sub-regions. The responsibility of BS for dividing the network region into two tiers/stages. Tier 1 is away from the BS and Tier 2 is closer to BS.

3.1.1 Cluster Formation

The SN are randomly deployed in the network, and cluster formation takes place. Each SN is assigned a unique identification number based on the location information and join its adjacent nodes cluster only.

3.1.2 Cluster Head Selection

The CH selection process in the proposed TS-EERP protocol is based on maximum node RE and minimum BS distance as parameters. The threshold value is compared to a randomly generated value. The AN are selected as cluster heads and broadcast messages to all NN in the network to join and become CHs member nodes. The CH-to-CH communication takes place in the network. The aggregation of data by CH nodes and transmit it to BS.

TS-EERP Algorithm

Initialization: N = Sensor Nodes, D = Distance, CH = Cluster Head, CM = Cluster Member, RE = Residual Energy, BS = Base Station, T_h = Threshold, R = Random Number.

```
 1:  CH_Selection ()
 2:  BEGIN
 3:  Divide Area into Regions and Sub-Regions.
 4:  for (i=1; i ≤ N; i++)
 5:  Calculate Di, REi
 6:  Calculate Ri = Rand ()
 7:  if (Th> Ri)
 8:      Broadcast (msg_To_Ni)
 9:      Select (CH)
10:      Aggregate (data)
11:      Transmit (BS)
12:  else
13:      Select (CM)
14:      Broadcast (CH_msg)
15:      Sent (CM_data_to_CH)
16:  end if
17: end for
18: END
```

3.2 Steady State Phase

The Time Division Multiple Access slots for each node for communication purposes. The SN use predetermined allocated TDMA slot to communicate with their corresponding cluster leaders and the rest of SN is kept in the sleep state during the unallocated time.

4 Simulation Results and Validation

Matlab software is used for simulation purposes. The software provides a good framework for data virtualization, algorithms and simulating various parameters. The heterogeneous nodes are used for the simulation purpose in terms of alive nodes, cluster head per round and no. of packet successfully transmitted to BS. The two-tier architecture for the data transmission in the network. The CH-to-CH communications take place in the network and data is transmitted to BS.

Network Designing Assumptions and Key Parameters. The 150 nodes are randomly deployed in the (150,150) m^2 area for simulation purposes. The nodes are placed static after random distribution in the network. The simulation is performed for 6000 rounds of packet transmission. The position of BS is somewhere outside the area of the network. The CH selection probability and advanced nodes are 10% in the network.

The following assumptions for the proposed protocol.

1. The nodes distributed are random and static in nature.
2. The heterogeneous nodes are used for designing the protocol.
3. The node battery power is limited and BS supplies power continuously.
4. The collision and noise factors are ignored in the system.
5. The advanced node worked as CH in the network and transmitted the packet to BS (Table 1).

Table 1. Key parameters.

Parameters	Values
Number of SN	100
Network area	(150,150) m^2
Free model ($E fs$)	10 pJ//bit//m^2
Multipath model (E_{amp})	0.0013 pJ/bit/m^4
Initial level battery (E_0)	0.5 J
Electronic circuitry (E_{RX})	50 nJ//bit
Data aggregation (E_{DA})	10 nJ/bit

The simulation result shows SEP protocol first packet drop at 1199 rounds and proposed protocol at 2999 rounds. The lifetime of the SEP protocol is 4049 rounds and the proposed TS-EERP is 5059 rounds show is Fig. 4.

The CH selection plays an important role to improve the energy efficiency of the WSN. The number of SN to become CH in the TS-EERP protocol is greater initially and remains same for some time as compared with SEP protocol. The simulation performance

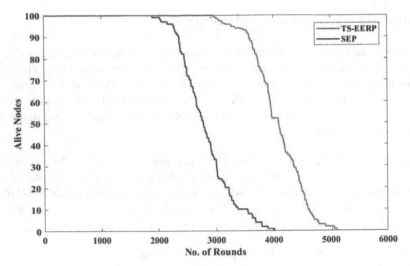

Fig. 4. Alive node number.

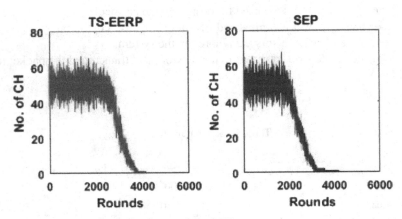

Fig. 5. Number of CH per round.

of the TS-EERP protocol shows improvement in stability number of CH per round and enhanced network lifetime compared to the SEP protocol show in Fig. 5.

The TS-EERP protocol successfully transmits 2.1×10^4 packets to BS whereas SEP transmits 1.5×10^4 packets to BS. The TS-EERP protocol shows enhancement in packet transmission to BS compared to SEP show in Fig. 6.

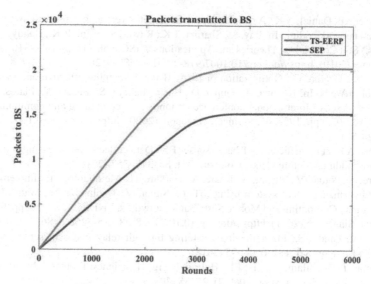

Fig. 6. Packet successfully transmitted to BS.

5 Conclusion and Research Directions

The proposed protocol increases the number of cluster head nodes at different levels to enhance node residual energy and the performance of the system. The data is collected from the smart offices in the first cluster, and for residential buildings in the second cluster and transmitted to BS. The simulation performance of the proposed protocol show enhancement in network lifetime compared to the SEP protocol. The three-level hierarchical network architecture will be developed in the future for an efficient CH selection process for large network area to increase network lifetime.

References

1. Chauhan, J., Goswami, P.: An integrated metaheuristic technique-based energy aware clustering protocol for Internet of Things based smart classroom. Mod. Phys. Lett. B **34**(22), 2050360 (2020)
2. Paunikar, V.L., et al.: A user authentication scheme of Iot devices using blockchain-enabled fog nodes. Int. J. All Res. Writ. **1**(11), 19–22 (2020)
3. Narayan, V., Daniel, A.K.: Multi-tier cluster based smart farming using wireless sensor network. In: 2020 5th International Conference on Computing, Communication and Security (ICCCS). IEEE (2020)
4. Narayan, V., Daniel, A.K.: A novel approach for cluster head selection using trust function in WSN. Scalable Comput. Pract. Exp. **22**(1), 1–13 (2021)
5. Chaturvedi, P., Daniel, A.K.: A hybrid scheduling protocol for target coverage based on trust evaluation for wireless sensor networks. In: IAENG Int. J. Comput. Sci. **44**(1) (2017)
6. Atzori, L., Iera, A., Morabito, G.: Understanding the Internet of Things: definition, potentials, and societal role of a fast-evolving paradigm. Ad Hoc Netw. **56**, 122–140 (2017)

7. Chaturvedi, P., Daniel, A.K.: A novel approach for target coverage in wireless sensor networks based on network coding. In: Ray, K., Sharma, T.K., Rawat, S., Saini, R.K., Bandyopadhyay, A. (eds.) Soft Computing: Theories and Applications. AISC, vol. 742, pp. 303–310. Springer, Singapore (2019). https://doi.org/10.1007/978-981-13-0589-4_28

8. Bhagat, A., Geetha, G.: Optimization of LEACH for developing effective energy-efficient protocol in WSN. In: Khanna, A., Gupta, D., Bhattacharyya, S., Snasel, V., Platos, J., Hassanien, A.E. (eds.) International conference on innovative computing and communications. AISC, vol. 1059, pp. 195–206. Springer, Singapore (2020). https://doi.org/10.1007/978-981-15-0324-5_17

9. Plageras, A.P., et al.: Efficient IoT-based sensor BIG Data collection–processing and analysis in smart buildings. Future Gener. Comput. Syst. **82**, 349–357 (2018)

10. Harkare, A., Potdar, V., Mishra, A., Kekre, A., Harkare, H.: Methodology for implementation of building management system using IoT. In: Suma, V., Bouhmala, N., Wang, H. (eds.) Evolutionary Computing and Mobile Sustainable Networks. LNDECT, vol. 53, pp. 939–948. Springer, Singapore (2021). https://doi.org/10.1007/978-981-15-5258-8_86

11. Chugh, A., Panda, S.: Strengthening clustering through relay nodes in sensor networks. Procedia Comput. Sci. **132**, 689–695 (2018)

12. Boubiche, D.E., Bilami, A.: HEEP (Hybrid Energy Efficiency Protocol) based on chain clustering. Int. J. Sensor Netw. **10**(1–2), 25–35 (2011)

13. Kumar, S.A., Ilango, P., Dinesh, G.H.: A modified LEACH protocol for increasing lifetime of the wireless sensor network. Cybern. Inf. Technol. **16**(3), 154–164 (2016)

14. Neto, J.H.B., et al.: MH-LEACH: a distributed algorithm for multi-hop communication in wireless sensor networks. In: ICN 2014, pp. 55–61 (2014)

15. Khan, M.K., et al.: Hierarchical routing protocols for wireless sensor networks: functional and performance analysis. J. Sens. (2021)

16. Smaragdakis, G., Matta, I., Bestavros, A.: SEP: a stable election protocol for clustered heterogeneous wireless sensor networks. In: Second International Workshop on Sensor and Actor Network Protocols and Applications (SANPA 2004), vol. 3 (2004)

17. Islam, M.M., Matin, M.A., Mondol, T.K.: Extended Stable Election Protocol (SEP) for three-level hierarchical clustered heterogeneous WSN, pp. 43–43 (2012)

18. Kaur, H., Sharma, H., Manu, G.: Multi-hop Routing SEP (MR-SEP) for clustering in wireless sensor network. Int. J. Eng. Technol. Manage. Appl. Sci. **2**(3), 54–65 (2014)

19. Yang, M., Yang, D., Huang, C.: An improved HEED clustering algorithm for wireless sensor network. J. Chongqing Univ. **35**(8), 101–106 (2012). Chongqing Daxue Xuebao (Ziran Kexue Ban)

20. Meddah, M., Haddad, R., Ezzedine, T.: An energy-efficient and density control clustering algorithm for wireless sensor network. In: 2017 13th International Wireless Communications and Mobile Computing Conference (IWCMC). IEEE (2017)

Author Index

Banno, Ryohei   218
Bao, Wugedele   73, 316

Cao, Yangjie   39, 100, 182
Cao, Yuanlong   194
Chen, Donghang   335
Chen, Xianfu   138
Cheng, Hong   39

Daniel, A. K.   344
Du, Jianbo   127
Duan, Pengsong   115, 167, 182

Feng, Jie   127

Gao, Fei   270
Gao, Yunquan   245

Hong, Xiaoyan   227
Hu, Honglin   3, 282
Hu, Xiantong   245

Ji, Yusheng   152
Jiao, Chenfei   115, 167, 182
Jin, Yan   25

Kato, Toshihiko   256
Katto, Jiro   17
Kong, Jinsheng   167, 182

Lai, Hongyang   73
Li, Chen   167
Li, Jingxin   182
Li, Jinhao   73
Li, Junfeng   100
Li, Peng   60
Li, Pengyu   270
Li, Qiao   245
Li, Qiyue   39
Li, Wuyungerile   270
Lin, Wen   89
Liu, Lei   127

Liu, Qinghua   194
Liu, Tao   60
Liu, Zhi   39, 100
Luo, Haibo   89

Narayan, Vipul   344
Ng, Tiong Sik   299
Ngo, Minh   256
Nguyen, Quang Ngoc   17

Ohzahata, Satoshi   256
Ouyang, Yuling   25

Pei, Qingqi   127

Qi, Wei   138

Ren, Yue   316
Ruan, Zhiqiang   89

Shao, Xun   152, 194
Song, Hang   17
Subedi, Pawan   227
Sun, Wei   39

Tang, Haochen   39
Tao, Xiaoming   282
Teoh, Andrew Beng-Jin   299

Wang, Chao   115
Wang, Hao   194
Wang, Kaijie   201
Wang, Ruihong   270
Wei, Bo   17
Wu, Celimuge   73, 138, 316
Wu, Jingyi   201
Wu, Lingxin   89
Wu, Qi   100
Wu, Xuangou   245

Xiao, Lianghui   89
Xiao, Ming   127
Xiao, Qiqi   138
Xu, Guiying   3
Xu, Tianheng   201, 282

Yamamoto, Ryo 256
Yang, Beichen 227
Yang, Wei 194
Yang, Yangzhao 39
Yang, Zhuocheng 73
Ye, Biao 115
Yin, Caiyuan 25
Yin, Rui 138
Yoshinaga, Tsutomu 316
Yoshizawa, Toshinori 218
Yu, Haifei 335
Yuan, Jiantao 138

Zhang, Bo 100
Zhang, Cheng 60

Zhang, Haonan 152
Zhang, Heli 152
Zhang, Ning 282
Zhang, Weixing 115
Zhang, Wenjing 127
Zhang, Wenning 167
Zhang, Xiang 335
Zhang, Zhiming 194
Zhang, Zhizhuo 335
Zhao, Wei 245
Zhao, Xi 3
Zheng, Xiao 245
Zhou, Linfei 245
Zhou, Ting 25, 201, 282

Printed in the United States
by Baker & Taylor Publisher Services

Printed in the United States
by Baker & Taylor Publisher Services